TAKING RIGHTS SERIOUSLY

Taking Rights Seriously

RONALD DWORKIN

Harvard University Press
Cambridge, Massachusetts
1978

Copyright © 1977, 1978 by Ronald Dworkin
All rights reserved
Fifth printing, 1978
Library of Congress Catalog Card Number 76–53134
ISBN 0–674–86710–6 (cloth)
ISBN 0–674–86711–4 (paper)

Printed in the United States of America

Contents

Introduction

The chapters of this book were written separately during a period of great political controversy about what law is and who must obey it and when. During the same period the political attitude called 'liberalism', once the posture of almost all politicians, seemed to lose a great deal of its appeal. The middle-aged blamed liberalism for permissiveness and the young blamed it for rigidity, economic injustice and the war in Vietnam. Uncertainty about law reflected uncertainty about a conventional political attitude.

The various chapters define and defend a liberal theory of law. They are nevertheless sharply critical of another theory that is widely thought to be a liberal theory. This theory has been so popular and influencial that I shall call it the ruling theory of law. The ruling theory has two parts, and insists on their independence. The first is a theory about what law is; in less dramatic language it is a theory about the necessary and sufficient conditions for the truth of a proposition of law. This is the theory of legal positivism, which holds that the truth of legal propositions consists in facts about the rules that have been adopted by specific social institutions, and in nothing else. The second is a theory about what the law ought to be, and how the familiar legal institutions ought to behave. This is the theory of utilitarianism, which holds that law and its institutions should serve the general welfare, and nothing else. Both parts of the ruling theory derive from the philosophy of Jeremy Bentham.

The critical portions of these essays criticize both parts of the theory, and also criticize the assumption that they are independent of one another. The constructive portions emphasize an idea that is also part of the liberal tradition, but that has no place in either legal positivism or utilitarianism. This is the old idea of individual human rights. Bentham called that idea 'nonsense on stilts'.

A general theory of law must be normative as well as conceptual. Its normative part must treat a variety of topics indicated by the following catalogue. It must have a theory of legislation, of adjudication, and of compliance; these three theories look at the normative questions of law from the standpoints of a lawmaker, a judge, and an ordinary citizen. The theory of legislation must contain a theory of legitimacy, which describes the circumstances under which a particular person or group is entitled to make law, and a theory of legislative justice, which describes the law they are entitled or obliged to make. The theory of adjudication must also be complex: it must contain a theory of controversy, which sets out standards that judges should use to decide hard cases at law, and a theory of jurisdiction, which explains why and when judges, rather than other groups or institutions, should make the decisions required by the theory of controversy. The theory of compliance must contrast and discuss two roles. It must contain a theory of deference, which discusses the nature and limits of the citizen's duty to obey the law in different forms of state, and under different circumstances, and a theory of enforcement, which identifies the goals of enforcement and punishment, and describes how officials should respond to different categories of crime or fault.

A general theory of law will comprehend subjects that do not fall within any of these categories, and a topic that falls within one may fall within others as well. The politically sensitive issue of constitutionalism is, for example, an issue in the theory of legitimacy. Why should the elected representatives of the majority ever be disabled from enacting law that seems to them fair and efficient? But a related question is also an issue in the conceptual part of a legal theory. Can the most fundamental principles of the constitution, which define who is competent to make law and how, themselves be considered as part of the law? That conceptual question plainly bears on other questions of legitimacy and jurisdiction. If the political principles embedded in the constitution are law, then the title of judges to decide what the constitution requires is, at least *prima facie*, confirmed; if these principles are law in spite of the fact that they are not the product of deliberate social or political decision, then the fact that law can be, in that sense, natural argues for the constraint on majority power that a constitution imposes. Both the conceptual question and the questions of jurisdiction and legitimacy bear in obvious ways on the theory of compliance; they bear, for example, on the issue of whether a dissident can plausibly or even coherently say that his idea of what the fundamental law of the constitution requires may be superior to that of the legislature and the judges.

The interdependencies of the various parts of a general theory of law are therefore complex. In the same way, moreover, a general theory of law will have many connections with other departments of philosophy. The normative theory will be embedded in a more general political and moral philosophy which may in turn depend upon philosophical theories about human nature or the objectivity of morality. The conceptual part will draw upon the philosophy of language and therefore upon logic and metaphysics. The issue of what propositions of law mean, and whether they are always true or false, for example, establishes immediate connections with very difficult and controverted questions in philosophical logic. A general theory of law must therefore constantly take up one or another disputed position on problems of philosophy that are not distinctly legal.

3.

Bentham was the last philosopher in the Anglo-American stream to offer a theory of law that is general in the way just described. One may find in his work a conceptual part and a normative part of a general theory of law, and one may find, within the latter, distinct theories of legitimacy, legislative justice, jurisdiction and controversy, all suitably related under a political and moral theory of utilitarianism and a more general metaphysical theory of empiricism. Each component of this general theory has been developed and refined, by different academic lawyers, but the ruling theory of law, in both British and American law schools, remains a Benthamite theory.

The conceptual part of his theory – legal positivism – has been much improved. The most powerful contemporary version of positivism is that proposed by H. L. A. Hart, and it is Hart's version which is criticized in this book. The normative part of Bentham's theory has been much refined through the use of economic analysis in legal theory. Economic analysis provides standards for identifying and measuring the welfare of the individuals who make up a community (though the nature of these standards is much in dispute) and holds that the normative questions of a theory of legitimacy, legislative justice, jurisdiction and controversy, as well as deference and enforcement, must all be answered by supposing that legal institutions compose a system whose overall goal is the promotion of the highest average welfare among these individuals. This general normative theory emphasizes what earlier versions of utilitarianism often neglected: that this overall goal might be advanced more securely by assigning different types of questions to different institutions according to some theory of institutional competence, rather than by supposing that all institutions are equally able to calculate the impact on overall welfare of any particular political decision.[1]

Since legal positivism and economic utilitarianism are complex doctrines, the ruling theory of law has many antagonists many of which are equally antagonistic to each other. The ruling theory is opposed, for

---

[1] See, for example, the influential teaching materials by H. M. Hart and A. Sachs, *The Legal Process* (mimeographed materials published by the Harvard Law School).

example, by various forms of collectivism. Legal positivism assumes that law is made by explicit social practice or institutional decision; it rejects the more romantic and obscure idea that legislation can be the product of an implicit general or corporate will. Economic utilitarianism is also (though only to a degree) individualistic. It sets as a standard of justice in legislation, the goal of overall or average welfare, but it defines overall welfare as a function of the welfare of distinct individuals, and steadily opposes the idea that a community has, as a distinct entity, some independent interest or entitlement.

The ruling theory is also criticized because it is rationalistic. It teaches, in its conceptual part, that law is the product of deliberate and purposeful decision by men and women planning, through such decisions, to change the community through general obedience to the rules their decisions create. It commends, in its normative part, decisions based on such plans, and it therefore supposes that men and women in political office can have the skill, knowledge and virtue to make such decisions effectively under conditions of considerable uncertainty in highly complex communities.

Some of those who criticize the individualism and rationalism of the ruling theory represent what is often called, in political discussions, the 'left'. They believe that the formalism of legal positivism forces courts to substitute a thin sense of procedural justice, which serves conservative social policies, for a richer substantive justice that would undermine these policies. They believe that economic utilitarianism is unjust in its consequences, because it perpetuates poverty as a means to efficiency, and deficient in its theory of human nature, because it sees individuals as self-interested atoms of society, rather than as inherently social beings whose sense of community is an essential part of their sense of self.

Many other critics of the ruling theory, on the other hand, are associated with the political right.[1] They follow the curious philosophy of Edmund Burke, who has become newly popular in American political theory, and believe that the true law of the community is not simply the deliberate decisions that legal positivism takes to be exclusive, but also the diffuse customary morality that exercises a great influence on these decisions. They believe that economic utilitarianism, which insists that deliberate decisions contrary to conventional morality can improve the community's welfare, is hopelessly optimistic. They argue, with Burke, that the rules best suited to promote the welfare of a community will emerge only from experience of that community, so that more trust must be put in established social culture than in the social engineering of utilitarians who suppose that they know better than history.

---

[1] See, for example, Hayek, *Law, Liberty and Legislation*.

Neither of these very different critiques of the ruling theory challenges one specific feature of that theory I mentioned, however. Neither argues that the ruling theory is defective because it rejects the idea that individuals can have rights against the state that are prior to the rights created by explicit legislation. On the contrary, opposition from the left and the right is united in condemning the ruling theory for its excessive concern, as they take it to be, with the fate of individuals as individuals. The idea of individual rights, in the strong sense in which that idea is defended in this book, is for them simply an exaggerated case of the disease from which the ruling theory already suffers.

4.

That idea has, of course, been advanced by many different philosophers in many different forms, but the ruling theory rejects the idea in any form. Legal positivism rejects the idea that legal rights can pre-exist any form of legislation; it rejects the idea, that is, that individuals or groups can have rights in adjudication other than the rights explicitly provided in the collection of explicit rules that compose the whole of a community's law. Economic utilitarianism rejects the idea that political rights can pre-exist legal rights; that is, that citizens can justifiably protest a legislative decision on any ground except that the decision does not in fact serve the general welfare.

Much of the ruling theory's opposition to natural rights is the consequence of an idea Bentham promoted: that natural rights can have no place in a respectably empirical metaphysics. Liberals are suspicious of ontological luxury. They believe that it is a cardinal weakness in various forms of collectivism that these rely on ghostly entities like collective wills or national spirits, and they are therefore hostile to any theory of natural rights that seems to rely on equally suspicious entities. But the idea of individual rights that these essays defend does not presuppose any ghostly forms; that idea is, in fact, of no different metaphysical character from the main ideas of the ruling theory itself. It is, in fact, parasitic on the dominant idea of utilitarianism, which is the idea of a collective goal of the community as a whole.

Individual rights are political trumps held by individuals. Individuals have rights when, for some reason, a collective goal is not a sufficient justification for denying them what they wish, as individuals, to have or to do, or not a sufficient justification for imposing some loss or injury upon them. That characterization of a right is, of course, formal in the sense that it does not indicate what rights people have or guarantee, indeed, that they have any. But it does not suppose that rights have some special metaphysical character, and the theory defended in these essays therefore departs from older theories of rights that do rely on that supposition.

The theory requires a vocabulary for making distinctions among the different types of rights individuals have. A vocabulary is proposed in Chapter 4. The most important of the distinctions made there is the distinction between two forms of political rights: background rights, which are rights that hold in an abstract way against decisions taken by the community or the society as a whole, and more specific institutional rights that hold against a decision made by a specific institution. Legal rights may then be identified as a distinct species of a political right, that is, an institutional right to the decision of a court in its adjudicative function.

Legal positivism, in this vocabulary, is the theory that individuals have legal rights only insofar as these have been created by explicit political decisions or explicit social practice. That theory is criticised in Chapters 2 and 3 as an inadequate conceptual theory of law. Chapter 4 suggests an alternative conceptual theory which shows how individuals may have legal rights other than those created by explicit decision or practice; that is, that they may have rights to specific adjudicative decisions even in hard cases when no explicit decision or practice requires a decision either way.

The argument of Chapter 4 provides a bridge between the conceptual and the normative parts of the alternate theory. It provides a normative theory of adjudication, which emphasizes the distinction between arguments of principle and policy, and defends the claim that judicial decisions based on arguments of principle are compatable with democratic principles. Chapter 5 applies that normative theory of adjudication to the central and politically important cases of constitutional adjudication. It uses the theory to criticize the debate between what is called judicial activism and restraint in constitutional law, and defends the propriety of judicial review limited to arguments of principle, even in politically controversial cases.

Chapter 6 discusses the foundation of a theory of legislative rights. It argues, through an analysis of John Rawls's powerful and influential theory of justice, that our intuitions about justice presuppose not only that people have rights but that one right among these is fundamental and even axiomatic. This most fundamental of rights is a distinct conception of the right to equality, which I call the right to equal concern and respect.

Chapters 7 and 8 defend a normative theory of compliance. Chapter 7 considers cases in which an individual's legislative, though not necessarily his legal, rights are in dispute. It does not argue for any particular set of individual rights, but only for certain consequences of conceding that individuals have some legislative rights distinct from and prior to their legal rights. This theory of compliance does not, therefore, rest on any presumptions about the character of the background and legislative rights people actually have; it does not presuppose even the abstract conclusion of Chapter 6. It therefore fulfills an important requirement of any political theory that gives a prominent place to rights: it provides a theory of compliance under conditions of uncertainty and controversy about what rights people actually have.

Chapter 8 extends the analysis to cases of uncertainty and controversy about legal rights. It takes up two important and often neglected questions of a theory of compliance: What are the background rights and responsibilities of a citizen when his constitutional rights are uncertain, but he genuinely believes that the government has no legal right to compel him to do what he believes is wrong? What are the responsibilities of officials who believe that he is wrong but sincere in his opinion of what the law is?

Chapter 9 returns to the right to concern and respect described in Chapter 6. It shows how that conception of equality may be used to interpret the famous Equal Protection Clause of the Fourteenth Amendment to the United States Constitution, and how, used in that way, the conception confirms our intuitions about racial discrimination and supports the politically controversial practice called reverse discrimination.

Chapters 10, 11 and 12 consider the competing claims of a different right that has also been considered by many political philosophers to be the most fundamental of political rights; this is the so-called right to liberty, which is often thought not only to be a rival to the right to equality, but to be, in at least some cases, inconsistent with that right. Chapter 12 argues that there is no right to liberty as such; indeed that the idea of such a right is itself a confusion. It does not reject the idea that individuals have rights to certain distinct liberties, like the right to personal moral decisions discussed in Chapter 10, or the right to the liberties described in the Constitutional Bill of Rights. On the contrary, Chapter 12 argues that these conventional rights are derivative, not from a more abstract general right to liberty as such, but from the right to equality itself. The essays therefore contradict the popular and dangerous idea that individualism is the enemy of equality. That idea is the common mistake of libertarians who hate equality and egalitarians who hate liberty; each attacks his own ideal under its other name.

5.

The essays provide the main structure for a distinct theory of law. But though they were all written in pursuit of that theory, they were written separately and therefore contain, as a group, overlappings and differences in emphasis and detail. They do not anticipate all the objections that will be made to what is said, nor do they say all that I should like to say about many of the topics they consider.

It is no part of my theory, for example, that any mechanical procedure exists for demonstrating what political rights, either background or legal, a particular individual has. On the contrary, the essays emphasize that there are hard cases, both in politics and at law, in which reasonable lawyers will disagree about rights, and neither will have available any argument that must necessarily convince the other. It may be objected that in such circumstances it is nonsense to suppose that any rights exist at all. This objection presupposes a general philosophical theory according to which no proposition can be true unless some procedure exists, at least in principle, for demonstrating its truth in such a way that any rational person must concede that it is true. Chapter 13 argues that we have no reason to accept that general philosophical position and good reason to reject it, particularly insofar as it applies to arguments about rights.[1]

Someone might wish to object, however, that in any case, as a practical matter, there can be no point in making or arguing about claims of right unless these can be demonstrated to be true or false. That objection is misguided. We could not understand the important ideas of sincerity in political argument, or of responsibility in political decision, if that were so; nor, indeed, could we comprehend the commonplace practice, in which we all engage, of arguing about rights in hard cases. It is important, however, that a political theory recognize that many claims of right, including some very important claims, are not demonstrable, and therefore provide principles to govern official decision when rights are controversial. The theory of compliance developed in Chapters 7 and 8, as I have said, provides such principles.

Chapter 12 offers an argument in favor of recognizing certain specific background and institutional rights. It might be wise to repeat here what I say there, which is that neither the rights there described, nor the method used to argue for these rights, is meant to be exclusive of other rights or of other methods of argument. The general theory of rights allows that there may be different sorts of argument, each sufficient to establish some reason why a collective goal that normally provides a justification for a political decision does not justify a particular disadvantage to some individual.

The book nevertheless suggests one favored form of argument for

---

[1] See also 'No Right Answer', in *Law, Morality and Society: Essays in Honour of H. L. A. Hart*, London 1977.

political rights, which is the derivation of particular rights from the abstract right to concern and respect taken to be fundamental and axiomatic. Chapter 6 shows how a familiar argument for economic rights on behalf of the worst-off group can be traced to that abstract right, and Chapters 9 and 12 show how a different argument might generate the familiar civil rights from the same source. Chapter 12 suggests, moreover, that the right to concern and respect is fundamental among rights in a different way, because it shows how the idea of a collective goal may itself be derived from that fundamental right. If so, then concern and respect is a right so fundamental that it is not captured by the general characterization of rights as trumps over collective goals, except as a limiting case, because it is the source both of the general authority of collective goals and of the special limitations on their authority that justify more particular rights.

That promise of unity in political theory is indistinct in these essays, however. It must be defended, if at all, elsewhere. In particular it must be shown how the same conception of equal concern that justifies the trade-offs characteristic of economic collective goals also justifies exemption, in the form of economic rights, for those who suffer most from those trade-offs. Some conception of levels of need is needed here, so that it can be shown that while equal concern justifies trade-offs within needs of a given level of urgency, it does not permit sacrifices in needs at a more urgent level even for the sake of the fuller satisfaction of more needs that are less urgent.

I

Jurisprudence

When lawyers argue cases, or advise clients, or draft laws to meet specific social goals, they face problems that are technical, in the sense that there is general agreement within the profession as to what sort of argument or evidence is relevant. But sometimes lawyers must deal with problems that are not technical in this sense, and there is no general agreement on how to proceed. One example is the ethical problem that is presented when a lawyer asks, not whether a particular law is effective, but whether it is fair. Another example is the conceptual puzzles that arise when lawyers try to describe the law in concepts that are unclear. A lawyer may want to say, for instance, that the law of torts holds men liable only for damage caused by their faults. Another lawyer may challenge this statement, and the issue between them may be a disagreement not about fact or doctrine, but about what fault means. Or two lawyers may disagree whether the Supreme Court, in the 1954 segregation case, was following established principles or making new law; and the issue between them may turn on what principles are and what it means to apply them. It is unclear how conceptual issues like these are to be resolved; certainly they lie beyond the ordinary techniques of the practicing lawyers.

Lawyers call these recalcitrant questions 'jurisprudential', and they disagree, as one would expect, on whether it is important to resolve them. Law schools generally provide special courses, called 'Jurisprudence' or 'Legal Theory' or something of the sort, devoted to their study, but since the distinguishing mark of these issues is just that there is no agreement on what sort of issues they are, and what techniques of study they require, these courses vary widely in the methods they use. The method chosen, moreover, influences the choice of the particular issues selected for study, though this choice is also affected by intellectual fashion and public affairs. Just now, for example, the question of whether men have a moral obligation to obey the law figures prominently in jurisprudence courses throughout the country; but two decades ago almost no one mentioned that issue.

Until recently the dominant approach to jurisprudence in England and America was what one might call a professional approach. The lawyers who taught jurisprudence recognized that jurisprudential questions, like those I have listed, were troublesome just because they were not amenable to ordinary legal techniques; but they proposed nevertheless to meet this difficulty by picking out those aspects of the questions that could be treated with these techniques while ignoring the rest. When lawyers deal with the technical questions I mentioned, they use a combination of three particular skills. Lawyers are trained to analyze statutes and judicial opinions to extract legal doctrine from these official sources. They are trained to analyze complex factual situations in order to summarize the essential facts accurately. And they are trained to think in tactical terms, to design statutes and legal institutions that will bring about particular social changes decided upon in advance. The professional approach to jurisprudence tried to reformulate jurisprudential issues so that one or more of these skills could be brought to bear. This approach produced only the illusion of progress, and left the genuinely important issues of principle in the law untouched.

To sustain this serious charge I must describe where jurisprudence stood at mid-century. In England the subject was taught out of standard textbooks like *Salmond on Jurisprudence* and *Paton on Jurisprudence*. Most of these texts were devoted to what they called analytical jurisprudence, which they carefully distinguished from 'ethical jurisprudence' or the study of what the law ought to be. By analytical jurisprudence they meant the careful elaboration of the meaning of certain terms (like 'fault', 'possession', 'ownership', 'negligence', and 'law') that are fundamental to law in the sense that they appear not just in one or another branch but throughout the range of legal doctrine. These concepts, like those I mentioned earlier, are troublesome because lawyers use them even though they do not understand exactly what they mean.

But the English texts attacked these concepts, not by elucidating their meaning in ordinary speech, but rather by using conventional doctrinal methods to demonstrate their specifically *legal* meaning as revealed in cases and statutes. They studied the opinions of judges and legal experts and extracted from them summaries of the various legal rules and doctrines in which these troublesome concepts appeared, but they did little to connect these rules with the various non-legal judgments about fault, possession, etc., that the layman makes.

If we ask *why* lawyers argue about these concepts, however, we can see why this emphasis on doctrine appears irrelevant. A lawyer worries about the concept of fault, not because he is unaware of how the courts have used the term, or what the rules for determining legal fault are, but because he uses the non-legal concept of fault to justify or criticize the law. He believes – as a matter of habit or conviction – that it is morally wrong to punish someone for something not his fault; he wants to know whether the law offends this moral principle in holding an employer liable for what his employee does, or in holding a negligent driver liable for the death of a man he ran down if the injury was slight but the victim was a haemophiliac. He knows these facts of legal doctrine very well, but he is unclear whether the facts clash with the principle. Is harm a man's fault if it is committed by someone under his charge, or if it results from his act because of circumstances he could not possibly foresee? These questions call for an analysis of the moral concept of fault, not the legal concept that the lawyer already understands; but it is just the moral use of the concept that the doctrinal approach of English jurisprudence ignored.

The record of American jurisprudence is more complex. It devoted itself largely to one issue that English theory had, in comparison, neglected: How do courts decide difficult or controversial lawsuits? Our courts had played a larger role than the English courts in reshaping nineteenth-century law to the needs of industrialization, and our constitution made legal issues out of problems that in England were political only. In England, for example, the issue of whether minimum wage legislation is fair was a political issue, but in America it was a constitutional, that is, judicial, issue as well. American lawyers were therefore pressed harder to furnish an accurate description of what the courts were doing, and to justify this if they could; the call was most urgent when the courts appeared to be making new and politically controversial law instead of simply applying old law as orthodox legal theory required.

Early in this century, John Chipman Gray and, later, Oliver Wendell Holmes published skeptical accounts of the judicial process, debunking the orthodox doctrine that judges merely apply existing rules. This skeptical approach broadened, in the 1920s and '30s, into the powerful intellectual movement called 'legal realism'. Its leaders (Jerome Frank, Karl Llewelyn, Wesley Sturges, and Morris and Felix Cohen, among others) argued that orthodox theory had gone wrong because it had taken a doctrinal approach to jurisprudence, attempting to describe what judges do by concentrating on the rules they mention in their decision. This is an error, the realists argued, because judges actually decide cases according to their own poltical or moral tastes, and then choose an appropriate legal rule as a rationalization. The realists asked for a 'scientific' approach that would fix on what judges do, rather than what they say, and the actual impact their decisions have on the larger community.

The main line of American jurisprudence followed this call for realism, and avoided the doctrinal approach of the English texts. It emphasized the two other professional skills – the lawyer's skills at marshalling facts and at designing tactics for social change. We can trace the later impact of realism more clearly if we distinguish these two techniques. The emphasis on facts developed into what Roscoe Pound of Harvard called sociological jurisprudence; he meant the careful study of legal institutions as social processes, which treats a judge, for example, not as an oracle of doctrine, but as a man responding to various sorts of social and personal stimuli. Some lawyers, like Jerome Frank and Pound himself, attempted to carry out this sort of study, but they discovered that lawyers do not have the training or statistical equipment necessary to describe complex institutions in other than an introspective and limited way. Sociological jurisprudence therefore became the province of sociologists.

The emphasis on tactics had a more lasting effect within the law schools. Scholars like Myres McDougal and Harold Lasswell at Yale, and Lon L. Fuller, Henry Hart, and Albert Sachs at Harvard, though different from one another, all insisted on the importance of regarding the law as an instrument for moving society toward certain large goals, and they tried to settle questions about the legal process instrumentally, by asking which solutions best advanced these goals.

But this emphasis on fact and strategy ended by distorting jurisprudential issues in much the same way as the English doctrinal approach distorted them, that is, by eliminating just those issues of moral principle that form their core. This failure emerges if we consider in greater detail the central problem that the sociologists and instrumentalists discussed: Do judges always follow rules, even in difficult and controversial cases, or do they sometimes make up new rules and apply them retroactively?

Lawyers have argued this issue for decades, not because they are ignorant of the sorts of decisions judges make or the reasons they give, but because they are unclear what the concept of following rules really means. In easy cases (when a man is charged with violating a statute that forbids driving over sixty miles an hour, for example) it seems right to say that the judge is simply applying a prior rule to a new case. But can we say this when the Supreme Court overturns precedent and orders the schools desegregated, or outlaws procedures that for decades the police have been using and the courts condoning? In these dramatic cases the Court gives reasons – it does not cite statutes, but it does appeal to principles of justice and policy. Does that mean that the Court is following rules after all, although of a more general and abstract quality? If so, where do these abstract rules come from, and what makes them valid? Or does it mean that the Court is deciding the case in accordance with its own moral and political beliefs?

The lawyers and laymen who ask these questions are not worrying aimlessly or out of idle curiosity; they know that judges wield great political power, and they are concerned with whether that power is justified, in general or in particular cases. They are not necessarily persuaded that judges who make up new rules are acting improperly. But they want to know how far the justification for judicial power available in easy cases – that the judge is applying standards already established – extends to hard ones, and therefore how much, and what sort of, supplementary justification these hard cases require.

The question of justification has important ramifications, because it affects not only how far judicial authority extends, but the extent of an individual's political and moral obligation to obey judge-made law. It also affects the grounds on which a controversial opinion may be challenged. If it makes sense to say that a judge should follow existing standards in hard cases, then it makes sense for a conscientious objector to argue that the judge has made a mistake in the law when he holds the draft constitutional. But if judges can only make new law in hard cases, that claim is nonsense. So though the question of whether judges follow rules may sound linguistic, it reveals concerns that are in the last degree practical.

I have spelled out these implications to show that here, as in the case of the concept of fault, there are issues of moral principle that lie beneath an apparently linguistic problem. Critics of law accept, again either by habit or through conviction, the principle that a judicial decision is fairer if it represents the application of established standards rather than the imposition of new ones. But they are unclear what counts as applying established standards, and they express this uncertainty by asking whether judges are really following rules, in some sense at least, even in novel cases. Jurisprudence should respond to this concern by exploring the nature of moral argument, trying to clarify the principle of fairness which the critics have in mind to see whether judicial practice does, in fact, satisfy that principle.

But American jurisprudence made no such attempt. The sociologists, for their part, refused to talk about following rules, on the ground that that concept was too vague to be studied in experimental or quantitative ways. The very fact that men are unable to agree on what following a rule means, they pointed out, disqualifies that concept for science; if each investigator were to use his own sense of the term, there would be no objective data and no joint progress. So sociologists like Glendon Schubert, C. Herman Pritchett, and Stuart Nagel substituted questions that seemed related and more precise : Do judges from particular economic or social backgrounds, or from particular sorts of legal practice, or with particular political affiliations, or particular value schemes, tend to decide in favor of corporate defendants? Do the judges in the Supreme Court form parties that stick together when cases involving race, or labor unions, or antitrust are decided? These empirical questions seemed relevant, because if social background or prior allegiance determines a judge's decision, this suggests that he is not following rules.

But in fact this information, though interesting and useful for other purposes, throws little light on the issues of principle that inspired the original question. Lawyers need no evidence to show that judges disagree, and that their decisions often reflect their background and temperament. They are puzzled, however, as to whether this means only that the judges differ on the nature and point of fundamental legal principles, or whether it demonstrates that there are no such principles. If it means the former, then this argues that judges are trying to follow rules, as they see them, and that people who disagree with their decisions may still be right on the law; if it means the latter then this argument, as I said, is absurd. The lawyers are also uncertain whether the fact of divergence, on either account, is to be regretted, or accepted as inevitable, or applauded as dynamic, and how all this connects with the crucial issues of political obligation and law enforcement that lawyers face. The sociological approach, in reframing the question, eliminated just those aspects that bear on all these issues.

The instrumental branch of post-realism also reframed the question, though in a different way. Henry Hart and Sachs, in their brilliant materials on the legal process, suggested that conceptual questions about rules could be bypassed by putting the issue this way: How should judges reach their decisions in order best to advance the goals of the legal process? But their hope that this would avoid the puzzles about rules was vain, because it proved impossible to state the goals of the legal process without those problems appearing at a later stage. If we state the goal of the process in some vacuous way (by saying that the law should do justice, or advance the just state) then the question is inescapable whether, as many suppose, justice requires decisions according to prior rules; and this question, in turn, requires an analysis of what it is to follow a rule. If we attempt to state some more particular or precise goal (that the legal process should increase the gross national product, for example) then the exercise loses its point, because there is no warrant for assuming that any such particular goal is the proper exclusive concern of law.

We may argue (as some writers did) that the law will be economically more efficient if judges are allowed to take the economic impact of their decision into account; but this will not answer the question of whether it is fair for them to do so, or whether we can regard economic standards as part of existing law, or whether decisions based on economic impact carry more or less moral weight for that reason. Suppose that a judge is persuaded, for example, that the automobile industry will prosper if he repeals an old rule and invents a new one for its benefit, and that the general economy will benefit if the automobile industry does. Is this a good reason for changing the rule? We cannot decide this sort of question by analysis that simply relates means to ends.

So the various branches of the professional approach to jurisprudence failed for the same underlying reason. They ignored the crucial fact that jurisprudential issues are at their core issues of moral principle, not legal fact or strategy. They buried these issues by insisting on a conventional legal approach. But if jurisprudence is to succeed, it must expose these issues and attack them as issues of moral theory.

This simple fact explains Professor H. L. A. Hart's importance and success. Hart is a moral philosopher; he has an instinct for issues of principle, and a marvelous lucidity in setting them out. In his first book, *The Concept of Law*, for example, he raised the issue of whether judges follow rules in a way that made plain the connection between this problem and the moral issue of when it is proper for one man to charge another with an obligation. He offered an analysis of the rules that our community follows, as a matter of convention, in making and criticizing arguments about moral obligation, and argued that judges follow much the same rules in reasoning about legal obligation. In another book, *Causation in the Law*, Hart and a co-author, A. M. Honore, discussed the conceptual puzzles about fault, which I mentioned earlier, but unlike Hart's predecessors, they undertook to explain the ordinary as well as the strictly legal meanings of that concept. Like Hart's colleagues in the Oxford school of philosophy, particularly J. L. Austin, they used the study of ordinary language to show the ways in which members of the community habitually ascribe fault and responsibility to one another; and they then used these conventional judgments to explain, for example, the legal rule that holds a man fully liable if he injures a haemophiliac.

They pointed out that ordinary language draws a distinction between unusual circumstances existing at the time a man acts and unlikely coincidences that arise afterward. It distinguishes, for example, the case in which the careless driver slightly injures a man who dies because he is haemophiliac from the case in which a careless driver slightly injures a man who dies of blood poisoning through a doctor's negligence. Most people would say that in the first case the careless driver caused the death and that it was his fault; but they would not say this in the second case. This distinction, in turn, reflects a popular conception of causation : the ordinary man distinguishes a causally effective act as an act that operates upon a stage already set; contemporaneous circumstances, like the blood disease, are part of the stage setting and not competing causes. But later events, like a doctor's negligence, are interventions that break the causal chain. So, the legal rule is comprehensible as an extension of popular theories of morality and cause.

But Hart has not been content simply to explain the law by showing how it incorporates the ordinary man's moral judgments. He views this sort of analysis as a necessary preliminary to a critical evaluation both of the law and of the popular morality on which it rests. Until we are clear what moral practice or judgment the law reflects, we cannot criticize it intelligently; but once we are clear about this it remains to ask whether this practice or judgment is sensible, or sound, or consistent with the other principles the law claims to serve.

Hart's more recent book, *Punishment and Responsibility*, is an excellent example of this process of criticism. The book reprints a series of his essays on jurisprudential issues in criminal law; most of these essays treat the problem of whether a man should be excused from liability for a criminal act because of his mental state. Should he be excused (or should his penalty be reduced) if his act was an accident, or if he acted negligently rather than deliberately, or if he was mentally ill? The law generally grants an excuse, or at least mitigates punishment, in such cases, but some contemporary critics argue that this policy is wrong.

If the criminal law aimed at vengeance and retribution, they say, the point of these mental defences would be obvious, for there is no satisfaction to be gained from taking revenge on someone who acted by mistake or was insane. But if the law's goals are only to prevent further harm by the criminal, and deter others by his example, the defenses seem counterproductive. We could prevent harm more by jailing the accident-prone driver than by jailing the man who murders his father for an inheritance; and we would increase the deterrent power of the law if we accepted no excuses whatever, and did not encourage potential criminals to hope that they could fake an insanity plea if caught. So the critics argue that the law should sharply limit these defenses, on the ground that the defenses increase the expense of trials and legal education, that they are abused, and that their purpose in an enlightened criminal system seems obscure.

Hart disagrees. He begins his response by reminding us that it is wrong to assume that the criminal law (or any other branch of the law) has a set of goals that are overriding, in the sense that every feature of the law must be tailored to these goals. The criminal law aims at preventing crime, to be sure, but it must pursue this aim subject to principles that may limit its efficiency in reaching them; it would be wrong to punish an innocent man as a hostage even if to do so would in fact reduce crime. We must understand the mental defenses in that light, so the fact that they may interfere with crime prevention is not a conclusive argument. But this point is only negative, and leaves open the question whether the mental defenses are in fact justified, or ought to be changed. Hart attacks this issue in the manner I described; he begins by asking whether the mental defenses reflect any moral tradition, or any general aim or policy, of the community.

He considers first the suggestion of some criminal lawyers, like Professor Jerome Hall, that the point of the mental defense is to insure that the law punishes as criminals only men who are morally blameworthy on conventional standards. This attractive notion has initial plausibility. In ordinary life we do not blame someone who has done harm if he acted unintentionally or inadvertently (unless, perhaps, he was also careless); nor do we do so if we believe that he is suffering from a serious mental disorder. It is therefore plausible to suppose that judges and legislators would carry these attitudes into the criminal law, in the form of a doctrine that men should not be punished under these conditions, even though it would be more efficient to do so.

Hart rejects this theory, however, on the ground that there are many crimes – for example, the failure to abide by the English rail transport regulations – which are not in themselves morally blameworthy. The existence of such crimes, he argues, shows that the law has no general purpose to condemn only blameworthy acts, and so proves this could not be the point of the mental defenses.

But Hart is wrong to dismiss the blameworthiness theory in this way; he is confusing, I think, two grounds on which a violation of law might be morally wrong. It might be wrong to break a law because the act the law condemns (killing, for example) is wrong in itself. Or it might be wrong, even though the act condemned is not wrong in itself, just because the law forbids it, and railroad legislation may be a case in point. Perhaps it is doubtful whether it is wise or fair for England to nationalize the railroads; it might still be true that once the law is passed everyone has a moral obligation to obey it.

Of course, it does not follow that a man is morally to blame every time he does what the law prohibits. He might not be blameworthy because the law is so unfair or unjust that the normal moral obligation to obey the law was lapsed, an argument that was made by some conscientious objectors to the draft. (It is arguable that the point of the due process and other clauses of the United States Constitution is to guard against a man's being punished in that case.) Or he may not be blameworthy because his act was committed by accident, or inadvertently, or because he had a mental disease and so was not responsible for his conduct. Professor Hall's argument, which Hart rejects too quickly, is that the point of the mental defenses is to guard against punishing a man in this case.

Even if Hall is right, however, the critical questions remain, because we must ask whether our conventional attitudes about blame and punishment are really relevant to the law. Those who doubt the value of the mental defenses argue that since the goal of the criminal law is to reform and deter, and not to punish, these conventions are irrelevant, and the mental defenses should be abandoned. They drive this point home by proposing to drop the word 'punishment', and speak of 'treatment' instead. If a man has committed a crime, they argue, then how society should treat him – whether he should be confined, or hospitalized, or released – should depend on which course would best prevent a repetition. It confuses the issue, on this account, as to whether he was morally blameworthy in doing what he did, because treatment might be unnecessary even if he was, and advisable even if he was not. We must ask whether the mental defenses serve any purpose that is relevant to this revised notion of the criminal law.

In one of the early essays, 'Legal Responsibility and Excuses', reprinted in the recent book, Hart offers this suggestion. The mental defenses increase each man's control over his own fate, by reducing the number of occasions on which the law will interfere with his freedom in a way he could not have predicted from his own deliberate acts. If the defenses were repealed, we would all have to live with the fact that some accident or piece of inadvertence would send us to jail, or involve us in a lengthy, expensive, and degrading trial. By virtue of the defenses, we can count on the fact that in general we will be prosecuted only for acts done with the awareness that prosecution might follow, which has the incidental benefit that those who are punished have had at least the satisfaction of taking and carrying out a decision to break the law.

But this is a weak argument, if it is addressed entirely to the increased personal security that the mental defenses afford, because this increased security is minimal. After all, the community has accepted a great many decisions that make life much more perilous, such as the decision to foster competition in commerce, to permit automobiles, and to wage war. These decisions vastly increase the likelihood that particular men will suffer harm which they could not foresee and which does not flow from their deliberate acts; but society still accepts these decisions, and runs these risks, for the sake of some goal of efficiency or profit or national policy. If, as Hart is willing to suppose, eliminating the mental defenses would increase the efficiency of the criminal law in preventing crime, then this would add to the ordinary citizen's personal safety and control over his own fate in a measure that would presumably outweigh the increased risk of his being subject to liability for an accident.

Hart is more successful, I think, when he provides a different and more general justification for the mental defenses in a later essay, 'Punishment and the Elimination of Responsibility': 'Human society is a society of persons; and persons do not view themselves or each other merely as so many bodies moving in ways which are sometimes harmful and have to be prevented or altered. Instead persons interpret each other's movements as manifestations of intentions . . . .' Elsewhere, and in the same vein, he says that the law would treat people as means rather than ends if it abandoned these defenses.

These statements unite the legal doctrines with a wide range of moral traditions. The principle they urge is that the government must treat its citizens with the respect and dignity that adult members of the community claim from each other. The government may restrain a man for his own or the general good, but it may do so only on the basis of his behavior, and it must strive to judge his behavior from the same standpoint as he judges himself, that is, from the standpoint of his intentions, motives, and capacities. Men generally feel that they have chosen to act as they have, but they do not feel this to be so in particular circumstances of accident, compulsion, duress, or disease. And each of us makes this distinction not only for himself but in judging how to respond to others he regards with any respect. Even a dog, Holmes said, knows the difference between being kicked and being tripped over.

The criminal law might be more efficient if it disregarded this troublesome distinction, and jailed men or forced them to accept treatment whenever this seemed likely to decrease future crime. But that, as Hart's principle suggests, would cross the line that separates treating someone else as a fellow human being from treating him as a resource for the benefit of others, and there can be no more profound insult, under the conventions and practices of our community, than that. The insult is as great whether the process is called one of punishment or treatment. It is true that we sometimes restrain and give treatment to a man just because we believe that he does not have control over his conduct. We do this under civil commitment statutes and typically, after a man is acquitted of a serious crime on grounds of insanity. But we ought to recognize the compromise with principle that this policy involves; and should treat a man against his will only when the danger he presents is vivid, not whenever we calculate that it would probably reduce crime if we did.

Of course this line of argument raises more questions than it settles. Some philosophers think, on the basis of contemporary physiology and psychology, that this phenomenological distinction between choice and compulsion makes no sense. They believe that all human behavior is determined by factors beyond individual control, so that the feelings of free choice we often have are just illusions. But the scientific evidence for this is far from conclusive, and even those who think it weighty must decide how the law should respond until the case is proved (if it ever is or can be). If we accepted the view that all behavior is determined, for example, would it follow that we should abandon entirely the idea that human beings have rights that their government is morally bound to respect? If we chose not to go so far, either because the scientific evidence is inconclusive, or because we are reluctant to abandon the notion of rights in any event, would it not be inconsistent to abandon the mental defenses in the name of science? If, on the other hand, we retain these defenses, and accept as their basis the phenomenological distinction between choosing or not choosing to do something, as this argument suggests, how should that guide our approach to troublesome cases, like that of the psychopath? Is the psychopath in control of himself, according to conventional standards of behavior, or is his case a half-way house, which explains our confusion? There is no space here to pursue these issues (some of which Hart discusses), and I mention them only to show that the approach to jurisprudence that emphasizes principle cannot stop at simply showing the links between legal and social practice, but must continue to examine and criticize social practice against independent standards of consistency and sense.

The mental defenses are not the only controversial aspects of the rules of criminal procedure – regarding interrogation, confessions, and preventive detention, for example – that protect the alleged criminal at some cost to police efficiency. It might be useful to point out the value of a more philosophic approach to these issues than academic lawyers have yet provided. So far the liberal position has been presented chiefly in instrumental terms. The liberal argues that the proper goals of the criminal law include the protection of individual freedom as well as the prevention of crime, and that the procedural safeguards strike a balance between these two goals. But this way of putting the point suggests that a balance between the two goals is in order; it encourages others to ask why the majority of law-abiding citizens should not strike the balance further on the side of its own protection.

The liberal is placed in a difficult position by that question. He might reply that he, personally, values the liberty of others more than his own increased security, but he would have to admit that this is a minority position. He might argue that the majority would itself be better off in the long run by promoting freedom at the cost of a little security, but this argument, though popular with liberals, is plainly wrong. The criminal law presents more of a threat to the black narcotics addict than to the middle-class white, and there is little reason to suppose that interrogating the former without counsel, or locking him up pending trial, will even in the long run affect the latter's liberty.

Here again Hart's general approach is helpful. The liberal position should be argued, it would suggest, by emphasizing moral principles that act as constraints on the law rather than citing the law's conflicting goals. It should fix on legal doctrines that are embedded in our traditions (like the doctrines that no man may be forced to condemn himself, and that a man is presumed innocent until proved guilty) to support the claim that society has no right to interrogate a man without a lawyer, and that an accused suspect is entitled to be free before his trial, whether the majority benefits or not. Of course there may be conflicts between these principles and practical needs, but these are not occasions for fair compromise, but rather, if the principles must be dishonored, for shame and regret.

Those who take a different view, and want to increase police efficiency, accept the doctrines I mentioned, such as the privilege against self-incrimination, but deny that they guarantee the particular rights the liberals claim. They would argue that this privilege, for example, protects a man from being tortured to extract a confession, but does not entitle him to withdraw a voluntary confession just because it was given without reflection. So the controversy must be pressed in philosophical terms: does the use of unadvised confessions, or preventive detention, contradict the moral principles underlying the established doctrines? I think they do, but it remains for jurisprudence to construct the bridges between legal and moral theory that support that claim.

Perhaps the principle Hart cited, that the government must show the minimum of respect even to accused criminals and treat them as humans rather than as opportunities, will help establish that a contradiction exists. This principle, for example, informs the doctrine that a man is innocent until proved guilty, and helps to explain why it seems wrong to imprison a man awaiting trial on the basis of a prediction that he might commit further crimes if released on bail. For any such prediction, if it is sound, must be based on the view that an individual is a member of a class having particular features, which class is more likely than others to commit crime. The prediction, that is, must be actuarial, like the prediction an insurance company makes about the likelihood of teenagers to have automobile accidents. But it is unjust to put someone in jail on the basis of a judgment about a class, however accurate, because that denies his claim to equal respect as an individual.

2

The Model of Rules I

I. EMBARRASSING QUESTIONS

Lawyers lean heavily on the connected concepts of legal right and legal obligation. We say that someone has a legal right or duty, and we take that statement as a sound basis for making claims and demands, and for criticizing the acts of public officials. But our understanding of these concepts is remarkably fragile, and we fall into trouble when we try to say what legal rights and obligations are. We say glibly that whether someone has a legal obligation is determined by applying 'the law' to the particular facts of his case, but this is not a helpful answer, because we have the same difficulties with the concept of law.

We are used to summing up our troubles in the classic questions of jurisprudence: What is 'the law'? When two sides disagree, as often happens, about a proposition 'of law', what are they disagreeing about, and how shall we decide which side is right? Why do we call what 'the law' says a matter of legal 'obligation'? Is 'obligation' here just a term of art, meaning only what the law says? Or does legal obligation have something to do with moral obligation? Can we say that we have, in principle at least, the same reasons for meeting our legal obligations that we have for meeting our moral obligations?

These are not puzzles for the cupboard, to be taken down on rainy days for fun. They are sources of continuing embarrassment, and they nag at our attention. They embarrass us in dealing with particular problems that we must solve, one way or another. Suppose a novel right-of-privacy case comes to court, and there is no statute or precedent claimed by the plaintiff. What role in the court's decision should be played by the fact that most people in the community think that private individuals are 'morally' entitled to that particular privacy? Supposing the Supreme Court orders some prisoner freed because the police used procedures that the Court now says are constitutionally forbidden, although the Court's earlier decisions upheld these procedures. Must the Court, to be consistent, free all other prisoners previously convicted through these same procedures?[1] Conceptual puzzles about 'the law' and 'legal obligation'

[1] See *Linkletter v. Walker*, 381 U.S. 618 (1965).

become acute when a court is confronted with a problem like this.

These eruptions signal a chronic disease. Day in and day out we send people to jail, or take money away from them, or make them do things they do not want to do, under coercion of force, and we justify all of this by speaking of such persons as having broken the law or having failed to meet their legal obligations, or having interfered with other people's legal rights. Even in clear cases (a bank robber or a wilful breach of contract), when we are confident that someone had a legal obligation and broke it, we are not able to give a satisfactory account of what that means, or why that entitles the state to punish or coerce him. We may feel confident that what we are doing is proper, but until we can identify the principles we are following we cannot be sure that they are sufficient, or whether we are applying them consistently. In less clear cases, when the issue of whether an obligation has been broken is for some reason controversial, the pitch of these nagging questions rises, and our responsibility to find answers deepens.

Certain lawyers (we may call them 'nominalists') urge that we solve these problems by ignoring them. In their view the concepts of 'legal obligation' and 'the law' are myths, invented and sustained by lawyers for a dismal mix of conscious and subconscious motives. The puzzles we find in these concepts are merely symptoms that they are myths. They are unsolvable because unreal, and our concern with them is just one feature of our enslavement. We would do better to flush away the puzzles and the concepts altogether, and pursue our important social objectives without this excess baggage.

This is a tempting suggestion, but it has fatal drawbacks. Before we can decide that our concepts of law and of legal obligation are myths, we must decide what they are. We must be able to state, at least roughly, what it is we all believe that is wrong. But the nerve of our problem is that we have great difficulty in doing just that. Indeed, when we ask what law is and what legal obligations are, we are asking for a theory of how we use those concepts and of the conceptual commitments our use entails. We cannot conclude, before we have such a general theory, that our practices are stupid or superstitious.

Of course, the nominalists think they know how the rest of us use these concepts. They think that when we speak of 'the law' we mean a set of timeless rules stocked in some conceptual warehouse awaiting discovery by judges, and that when we speak of legal obligation we mean the invisible chains these mysterious rules somehow drape around us. The theory that there are such rules and chains they call 'mechanical jurisprudence', and they are right in ridiculing its practitioners. Their difficulty, however, lies in finding practitioners to ridicule. So far they have had little luck in caging and exhibiting mechanical jurisprudents (all specimens captured – even Blackstone and Joseph Beale – have had to be released after careful reading of their texts).

In any event, it is clear that most lawyers have nothing like this in mind when they speak of the law and of legal obligation. A superficial examination of our practices is enough to show this for we speak of laws changing and evolving, and of legal obligation sometimes being problematical. In these and other ways we show that we are not addicted to mechanical jurisprudence.

Nevertheless, we do use the concepts of law and legal obligation, and we do suppose that society's warrant to punish and coerce is written in that currency. It may be that when the details of this practice are laid bare, the concepts we do use will be shown to be as silly and as thick with illusion as those the nominalists invented. If so, then we shall have to find other ways to describe what we do, and either provide other justifications or change our practices. But until we have discovered this and made these adjustments, we cannot accept the nominalists' premature invitation to turn our backs on the problems our present concepts provide.

Of course the suggestion that we stop talking about 'the law' and 'legal obligation' is mostly bluff. These concepts are too deeply cemented into the structure of our political practices – they cannot be given up like cigarettes or hats. Some of the nominalists have half-admitted this and said that the myths they condemn should be thought of as Platonic myths and retained to seduce the masses into order. This is perhaps not so cynical a suggestion as it seems; perhaps it is a covert hedging of a dubious bet.

If we boil away the bluff, the nominalist attack reduces to an attack on mechanical jurisprudence. Through the lines of the attack, and in spite of the heroic calls for the death of law, the nominalists themselves have offered an analysis of how the terms 'law' and 'legal obligation' should be used which is not very different from that of more classical philosophers. Nominalists present their analysis as a model of how legal institutions (particularly courts) 'really operate'. But their model differs mainly in emphasis from the theory first made popular by the nineteenth century philosopher John Austin, and now accepted in one form or another by most working and academic lawyers who hold views on jurisprudence. I shall call this theory, with some historical looseness, 'legal positivism'. I want to examine the soundness of legal positivism, particularly in the powerful form that Professor H. L. A. Hart has given to it. I choose to focus on his position, not only because of its clarity and elegance, but because here, as almost everywhere else in legal philosophy, constructive thought must start with a consideration of his views.

2. POSITIVISM

Positivism has a few central and organizing propositions as its skeleton, and though not every philosopher who is called a positivist would subscribe to these in the way I present them, they do define the general position I want to examine. These key tenets may be stated as follows :

(a) The law of a community is a set of special rules used by the community directly or indirectly for the purpose of determining which behavior will be punished or coerced by the public power. These special rules can be identified and distinguished by specific criteria, by tests having to do not with their content but with their *pedigree* or the manner in which they were adopted or developed. These tests of pedigree can be used to distinguish valid legal rules from spurious legal rules (rules which lawyers and litigants wrongly argue are rules of law) and also from other sorts of social rules (generally lumped together as 'moral rules') that the community follows but does not enforce through public power.

(b) The set of these valid legal rules is exhaustive of 'the law', so that if someone's case is not clearly covered by such a rule (because there is none that seems appropriate, or those that seem appropriate are vague, or for some other reason) then that case cannot be decided by 'applying the law.' It must be decided by some official, like a judge, 'exercising his discretion,' which means reaching beyond the law for some other sort of standard to guide him in manufacturing a fresh legal rule or supplementing an old one.

(c) To say that someone has a 'legal obligation' is to say that his case falls under a valid legal rule that requires him to do or to forbear from doing something. (To say he has a legal right, or has a legal power of some sort, or a legal privilege or immunity, is to assert, in a shorthand way, that others have actual or hypothetical legal obligations to act or not to act in certain ways touching him.) In the absence of such a valid legal rule there is no legal obligation; it follows that when the judge decides an issue by exercising his discretion, he is not enforcing a legal right as to that issue.

This is only the skeleton of positivism. The flesh is arranged differently by different positivists, and some even tinker with the bones. Different versions differ chiefly in their description of the fundamental test of pedigree a rule must meet to count as a rule of law.

Austin, for example, framed his version of the fundamental test as a series of interlocking definitions and distinctions.[1] He defined having an obligation as lying under a rule, a rule as a general command, and a command as an expression of desire that others behave in a particular way, backed by the power and will to enforce that expression in the event of disobedience. He distinguished classes of rules (legal, moral or religious) according to which person or group is the author of the general command the rule represents. In each political community, he thought, one will find a sovereign – a person or a determinate group whom the rest obey habitually, but who is not in the habit of obeying anyone else. The legal rules of a community are the general commands its sovereign has deployed. Austin's definition of legal obligation followed from this definition of law. One has a legal obligation, he thought, if one is among the addressees of some general order of the sovereign, and is in danger of suffering a sanction unless he obeys that order.

Of course, the sovereign cannot provide for all contingencies through any scheme of orders, and some of his orders will inevitably be vague or have furry edges. Therefore (according to Austin) the sovereign grants those who enforce the law (judges) discretion to make fresh orders when novel or troublesome cases are presented. The judges then make new rules or adapt old rules, and the sovereign either overturns their creations or tacitly confirms them by failing to do so.

Austin's model is quite beautiful in its simplicity. It asserts the first tenet of positivism, that the law is a set of rules specially selected to govern public order, and offers a simple factual test – what has the sovereign commanded? – as the sole criterion for identifying those special rules. In time, however, those who studied and tried to apply Austin's model found it too simple. Many objections were raised, among which were two that seemed fundamental. First, Austin's key assumption that in each community a determinate group or institution can be found, which is in ultimate control of all other groups, seemed not to hold in a complex society. Political control in a modern nation is pluralistic and shifting, a matter of more or less, of compromise and cooperation and alliance, so that it is often impossible to say that any person or group has that dramatic control necessary to qualify as an Austinian sovereign. One wants to say, in the United States for example, that the 'people' are sovereign. But this means almost nothing, and in itself provides no test for determining what the 'people' have commanded, or distinguishing their legal from their social or moral commands.

Second, critics began to realize that Austin's analysis fails entirely to account for, even to recognize, certain striking facts about the attitudes

[1] J. Austin, *The Province of Jurisprudence Determined* (1832).

we take toward 'the law.' We make an important distinction between law and even the general orders of a gangster. We feel that the law's strictures – and its sanctions – are different in that they are obligatory in a way that the outlaw's commands are not. Austin's analysis has no place for any such distinction, because it defines an obligation as subjection to the threat of force, and so founds the authority of law entirely on the sovereign's ability and will to harm those who disobey. Perhaps the distinction we make is illusory – perhaps our feelings of some special authority attaching to the law is based on religious hangover or another sort of mass self-deception. But Austin does not demonstrate this, and we are entitled to insist that an analysis of our concept of law either acknowledge and explain our attitudes, or show why they are mistaken.

H. L. A. Hart's version of positivism is more complex than Austin's, in two ways. First, he recognizes, as Austin did not, that rules are of different logical kinds. (Hart distinguishes two kinds, which he calls 'primary' and 'secondary' rules). Second, he rejects Austin's theory that a rule is a kind of command, and substitutes a more elaborate general analysis of what rules are. We must pause over each of these points, and then note how they merge in Hart's concept of law.

Hart's distinction between primary and secondary rules is of great importance.[1] Primary rules are those that grant rights or impose obligations upon members of the community. The rules of the criminal law that forbid us to rob, murder or drive too fast are good examples of primary rules. Secondary rules are those that stipulate how, and by whom, such primary rules may be formed, recognized, modified or extinguished. The rules that stipulate how Congress is composed, and how it enacts legislation, are examples of secondary rules. Rules about forming contracts and executing wills are also secondary rules because they stipulate how very particular rules governing particular legal obligations (*i.e.*, the terms of a contract or the provisions of a will) come into existence and are changed.

His general analysis of rules is also of great importance.[2] Austin had said that every rule is a general command, and that a person is obligated under a rule if he is liable to be hurt should he disobey it. Hart points out that this obliterates the distinction between being *obliged* to do something and being *obligated* to do it. If one is bound by a rule he is obligated, not merely obliged, to do what it provides, and therefore being bound by a rule must be different from being subject to an injury if one disobeys an order. A rule differs from an order, among other ways, by being *normative*, by setting a standard of behavior that has a call on

[1] See H. L. A. Hart, *The Concept of Law*, 89-96 (1961).
[2] *Id.* at 79-88.

its subject beyond the threat that may enforce it. A rule can never be binding just because some person with physical power wants it to be so. He must have *authority* to issue the rule or it is no rule, and such authority can only come from another rule which is already binding on those to whom he speaks. That is the difference between a valid law and the orders of a gunman.

So Hart offers a general theory of rules that does not make their authority depend upon the physical power of their authors. If we examine the way different rules come into being, he tells us, and attend to the distinction between primary and secondary rules, we see that there are two possible sources of a rule's authority :[1]

(a) A rule may become binding upon a group of people because that group through its practices *accepts* the rule as a standard for its conduct. It is not enough that the group simply conforms to a pattern of behavior : even though most Englishmen may go to the movies on Saturday evening, they have not accepted a rule requiring that they do so. A practice constitutes the acceptance of a rule only when those who follow the practice regard the rule as binding, and recognize the rule as a reason or justification for their own behavior and as a reason for criticizing the behavior of others who do not obey it.

(b) A rule may also become binding in quite a different way, namely by being enacted in conformity with some *secondary* rule that stipulates that rules so enacted shall be binding. If the constitution of a club stipulates, for example, that by-laws may be adopted by a majority of the members, then particular by-laws so voted are binding upon all the members, not because of any practice of acceptance of these particular by-laws, but because the constitution says so. We use the concept of *validity* in this connection : rules binding because they have been created in a manner stipulated by some secondary rule are called 'valid' rules.

Thus we can record Hart's fundamental distinction this way : a rule may be binding (a) because it is accepted or (b) because it is valid.

Hart's concept of law is a construction of these various distinctions.[2] Primitive communities have only primary rules, and these are binding entirely because of practices of acceptance. Such communities cannot be said to have 'law,' because there is no way to distinguish a set of legal rules from amongst other social rules, as the first tenet of positivism

---

[1] *Id.* at 97-107.
[2] *Id. passim*, particularly ch. 6.

requires. But when a particular community has developed a fundamental secondary rule that stipulates how legal rules are to be identified, the idea of a distinct set of legal rules, and thus of law, is born.

Hart calls such a fundamental secondary rule a 'rule of recognition'. The rule of recognition of a given community may be relatively simple ('What the king enacts is law') or it may be very complex (the United States Constitution, with all its difficulties of interpretation, may be considered a single rule of recognition). The demonstration that a particular rule is valid may therefore require tracing a complicated chain of validity back from that particular rule ultimately to the fundamental rule. Thus a parking ordinance of the city of New Haven is valid because it is adopted by a city council, pursuant to the procedures and within the competence specified by the municipal law adopted by the state of Connecticut, in conformity with the procedures and within the competence specified by the constitution of the state of Connecticut, which was in turn adopted consistently with the requirements of the United States Constitution.

Of course, a rule of recognition cannot itself be valid, because by hypothesis it is ultimate, and so cannot meet tests stipulated by a more fundamental rule. The rule of recognition is the sole rule in a legal system whose binding force depends upon its acceptance. If we wish to know what rule of recognition a particular community has adopted or follows, we must observe how its citizens, and particularly its officials, behave. We must observe what ultimate arguments they accept as showing the validity of a particular rule, and what ultimate arguments they use to criticize other officials or institutions. We can apply no mechanical test, but there is no danger of our confusing the rule of recognition of a community with its rules of morality. The rule of recognition is identified by the fact that its province is the operation of the governmental apparatus of legislatures, courts, agencies, policemen, and the rest.

In this way Hart rescues the fundamentals of positivism from Austin's mistakes. Hart agrees with Austin that valid rules of law may be created through the acts of officials and public institutions. But Austin thought that the authority of these institutions lay only in their monopoly of power. Hart finds their authority in the background of constitutional standards against which they act, constitutional standards that have been accepted, in the form of a fundamental rule of recognition, by the community which they govern. This background legitimates the decisions of government and gives them the cast and call of obligation that the naked commands of Austin's sovereign lacked. Hart's theory differs from Austin's also, in recognizing that different communities use different ultimate tests of law, and that some allow other means of creating law than the deliberate act of a legislative institution. Hart mentions 'long customary practice' and 'the relation [of a rule] to judicial decisions' as other criteria that are often used, though generally along with and subordinate to the test of legislation.

So Hart's version of positivism is more complex than Austin's, and his test for valid rules of law is more sophisticated. In one respect, however, the two models are very similar. Hart, like Austin, recognizes that legal rules have furry edges (he speaks of them as having 'open texture') and, again like Austin, he accounts for troublesome cases by saying that judges have and exercise discretion to decide these cases by fresh legislation.[1] (I shall later try to show why one who thinks of law as a special set of rules is almost inevitably drawn to account for difficult cases in terms of someone's exercise of discretion.)

3. RULES, PRINCIPLES, AND POLICIES

I want to make a general attack on positivism, and I shall use H. L. A. Hart's version as a target, when a particular target is needed. My strategy will be organized around the fact that when lawyers reason or dispute about legal rights and obligations, particularly in those hard cases when our problems with these concepts seem most acute, they make use of standards that do not function as rules, but operate differently as principles, policies, and other sorts of standards. Positivism, I shall argue, is a model of and for a system of rules, and its central notion of a single fundamental test for law forces us to miss the important roles of these standards that are not rules.

I just spoke of 'principles, policies, and other sorts of standards'. Most often I shall use the term 'principle' generically, to refer to the whole set of these standards other than rules; occasionally, however, I shall be more precise, and distinguish between principles and policies. Although nothing in the present argument will turn on the distinction, I should state how I draw it. I call a 'policy' that kind of standard that sets out a goal to be reached, generally an improvement in some economic, political, or social feature of the community (though some goals are negative, in that they stipulate that some present feature is to be protected from adverse change). I call a 'principle' a standard that is to be observed, not because it will advance or secure an economic, political, or social situation deemed desirable, but because it is a requirement of justice or fairness or some other dimension of morality. Thus the standard that automobile accidents are to be decreased is a policy, and the standard that no man may profit by his own wrong a principle. The distinction can be collapsed by construing a principle as stating a social goal (*i.e.*, the goal of a

[1] *Id.* ch. 7.

society in which no man profits by his own wrong), or by construing a policy as stating a principle (*i.e.*, the principle that the goal the policy embraces is a worthy one) or by adopting the utilitarian thesis that principles of justice are disguised statements of goals (securing the greatest happiness of the greatest number). In some contexts the distinction has uses which are lost if it is thus collapsed.[1]

My immediate purpose, however, is to distinguish principles in the generic sense from rules, and I shall start by collecting some examples of the former. The examples I offer are chosen haphazardly; almost any case in a law school casebook would provide examples that would serve as well. In 1889 a New York court, in the famous case of *Riggs v. Palmer*,[2] had to decide whether an heir named in the will of his grandfather could inherit under that will, even though he had murdered his grandfather to do so. The court began its reasoning with this admission : 'It is quite true that statutes regulating the making, proof and effect of wills, and the devolution of property, if literally construed, and if their force and effect can in no way and under no circumstances be controlled or modified, give this property to the murderer.'[3] But the court continued to note that 'all laws as well as all contracts may be controlled in their operation and effect by general, fundamental maxims of the common law. No one shall be permitted to profit by his own fraud, or to take advantage of his own wrong, or to found any claim upon his own iniquity, or to acquire property by his own crime.'[4] The murderer did not receive his inheritance.

In 1960, a New Jersey court was faced, in *Henningsen v. Bloomfield Motors, Inc.*[5] with the important question of whether (or how much) an automobile manufacturer may limit his liability in case the automobile is defective. Henningsen had bought a car, and signed a contract which said that the manufacturer's liability for defects was limited to 'making good' defective parts – 'this warranty being expressly in lieu of all other warranties, obligations or liabilities.' Henningsen argued that, at least in the circumstances of his case, the manufacturer ought not to be protected by this limitation, and ought to be liable for the medical and other expenses of persons injured in a crash. He was not able to point to any statute, or to any established rule of law, that prevented the manufacturer from standing on the contract. The court nevertheless agreed with Henningsen. At various points in the court's argument the

---

[1] See Chapter 4. See also Dworkin, 'Wasserstrom: The Judicial Decision', 75 *Ethics* 47 (1964), reprinted as 'Does Law Have a Function?', 74 *Yale Law Journal* 640 (1965).

[2] 115 N.Y. 506, 22 N.E. 188 (1889).

[3] *Id.* at 509, 22 N.E. at 189.

[4] *Id.* at 511, 22 N.E. at 190.

[5] 32 N.J. 358, 161 A.2d 69 (1960).

following appeals to standards are made: (a) '[W]e must keep in mind the general principle that, in the absence of fraud, one who does not choose to read a contract before signing it cannot later relieve himself of its burdens.'[1] (b) 'In applying that principle, the basic tenet of freedom of competent parties to contract is a factor of importance.'[2] (c) 'Freedom of contract is not such an immutable doctrine as to admit of no qualification in the area in which we are concerned.'[3] (d) 'In a society such as ours, where the automobile is a common and necessary adjunct of daily life, and where its use is so fraught with danger to the driver, passengers and the public, the manufacturer is under a special obligation in connection with the construction, promotion and sale of his cars. Consequently, the courts must examine purchase agreements closely to see if consumer and public interests are treated fairly.'[4] (e) ' "[I]s there any principle which is more familiar or more firmly embedded in the history of Anglo-American law than the basic doctrine that the courts will not permit themselves to be used as instruments of inequity and injustice?" '[5] (f) ' "More specifically the courts generally refuse to lend themselves to the enforcement of a 'bargain' in which one party has unjustly taken advantage of the economic necessities of other . . . ." '[6]

The standards set out in these quotations are not the sort we think of as legal rules. They seem very different from propositions like 'The maximum legal speed on the turnpike is sixty miles an hour' or 'A will is invalid unless signed by three witnesses'. They are different because they are legal principles rather than legal rules.

The difference between legal principles and legal rules is a logical distinction. Both sets of standards point to particular decisions about legal obligation in particular circumstances, but they differ in the character of the direction they give. Rules are applicable in an all-or-nothing fashion. If the facts a rule stipulates are given, then either the rule is valid, in which case the answer it supplies must be accepted, or it is not, in which case it contributes nothing to the decision.

This all-or-nothing is seen most plainly if we look at the way rules operate, not in law, but in some enterprise they dominate – a game, for example. In baseball a rule provides that if the batter has had three strikes, he is out. An official cannot consistently acknowledge that this is an accurate statement of a baseball rule, and decide that a batter who has had three strikes is not out. Of course, a rule may have exceptions

---

[1] *Id.* at 386, 161 A.2d at 84.

[2] *Id.*

[3] *Id.* at 388, 161 A.2d at 86.

[4] *Id.* at 387, 161 A.2d at 85.

[5] *Id.* at 389, 161 A.2d at 86 (quoting Frankfurter, J., in *United States v. Bethlehem Steel*, 315 U.S. 289, 326 [1942]).

[6] *Id.*

(the batter who has taken three strikes is not out if the catcher drops the third strike). However, an accurate statement of the rule would take this exception into account, and any that did not would be incomplete. If the list of exceptions is very large, it would be too clumsy to repeat them each time the rule is cited; there is, however, no reason in theory why they could not all be added on, and the more that are, the more accurate is the statement of the rule.

If we take baseball rules as a model, we find that rules of law, like the rule that a will is invalid unless signed by three witnesses, fit the model well. If the requirement of three witnesses is a valid legal rule, then it cannot be that a will has been signed by only two witnesses and is valid. The rule might have exceptions, but if it does then it is inaccurate and incomplete to state the rule so simply, without enumerating the exceptions. In theory, at least, the exceptions could all be listed, and the more of them that are, the more complete is the statement of the rule.

But this is not the way the sample principles in the quotations operate. Even those which look most like rules do not set out legal consequences that follow automatically when the conditions provided are met. We say that our law respects the principle that no man may profit from his own wrong, but we do not mean that the law never permits a man to profit from wrongs he commits. In fact, people often profit, perfectly legally, from their legal wrongs. The most notorious case is adverse possession – if I trespass on your land long enough, some day I will gain a right to cross your land whenever I please. There are many less dramatic examples. If a man leaves one job, breaking a contract, to take a much higher paying job, he may have to pay damages to his first employer, but he is usually entitled to keep his new salary. If a man jumps bail and crosses state lines to make a brilliant investment in another state, he may be sent back to jail, but he will keep his profits.

We do not treat these – and countless other counter-instances that can easily be imagined – as showing that the principle about profiting from one's wrongs is not a principle of our legal system, or that it is incomplete and needs qualifying exceptions. We do not treat counter-instances as exceptions (at least not exceptions in the way in which a catcher's dropping the third strike is an exception) because we could not hope to capture these counter-instances simply by a more extended statement of the principle. They are not, even in theory, subject to enumeration, because we would have to include not only these cases (like adverse possession) in which some institution has already provided that profit can be gained through a wrong, but also those numberless imaginary cases in which we know in advance that the principle would not hold. Listing some of these might sharpen our sense of the principle's weight (I shall mention that dimension in a moment), but it would not make for a more accurate or complete statement of the principle.

A principle like 'No man may profit from his own wrong' does not even purport to set out conditions that make its application necessary. Rather, it states a reason that argues in one direction, but does not necessitate a particular decision. If a man has or is about to receive something, as a direct result of something illegal he did to get it, then that is a reason which the law will take into account in deciding whether he should keep it. There may be other principles or policies arguing in the other direction – a policy of securing title, for example, or a principle limiting punishment to what the legislature has stipulated. If so, our principle may not prevail, but that does not mean that it is not a principle of our legal system, because in the next case, when these contravening considerations are absent or less weighty, the principle may be decisive. All that is meant, when we say that a particular principle is a principle of our law, is that the principle is one which officials must take into account, if it is relevant, as a consideration inclining in one direction or another.

The logical distinction between rules and principles appears more clearly when we consider principles that do not even look like rules. Consider the proposition, set out under '(d)' in the excerpts from the *Henningsen* opinion, that 'the manufacturer is under a special obligation in connection with the construction, promotion and sale of his cars'. This does not even purport to define the specific duties such a special obligation entails, or to tell us what rights automobile consumers acquire as a result. It merely states – and this is an essential link in the *Henningsen* argument – that automobile manufacturers must be held to higher standards than other manufacturers, and are less entitled to rely on the competing principle of freedom of contract. It does not mean that they may never rely on that principle, or that courts may rewrite automobile purchase contracts at will; it means only that if a particular clause seems unfair or burdensome, courts have less reason to enforce the clause than if it were for the purchase of neckties. The 'special obligation' counts in favor, but does not in itself necessitate, a decision refusing to enforce the terms of an automobile purchase contract.

This first difference between rules and principles entails another. Principles have a dimension that rules do not – the dimension of weight or importance. When principles intersect (the policy of protecting automobile consumers intersecting with principles of freedom of contract, for example), one who must resolve the conflict has to take into account the relative weight of each. This cannot be, of course, an exact measurement, and the judgment that a particular principle or policy is more important than another will often be a controversial one. Nevertheless, it is an integral part of the concept of a principle that it has this dimension, that it makes sense to ask how important or how weighty it is.

Rules do not have this dimension. We can speak of rules as being *functionally* important or unimportant (the baseball rule that three strikes are out is more important than the rule that runners may advance on a balk, because the game would be much more changed with the first rule altered than the second). In this sense, one legal rule may be more important than another because it has a greater or more important role in regulating behavior. But we cannot say that one rule is more important than another within the system of rules, so that when two rules conflict one supersedes the other by virtue of its greater weight.

If two rules conflict, one of them cannot be a valid rule. The decision as to which is valid, and which must be abandoned or recast, must be made by appealing to considerations beyond the rules themselves. A legal system might regulate such conflicts by other rules, which prefer the rule enacted by the higher authority, or the rule enacted later, or the more specific rule, or something of that sort. A legal system may also prefer the rule supported by the more important principles. (Our own legal system uses both of these techniques.)

It is not always clear from the form of a standard whether it is a rule or a principle. 'A will is invalid unless signed by three witnesses' is not very different in form from 'A man may not profit from his own wrong', but one who knows something of American law knows that he must take the first as stating a rule and the second as stating a principle. In many cases the distinction is difficult to make – it may not have been settled how the standard should operate, and this issue may itself be a focus of controversy. The first amendment to the United States Constitution contains the provision that Congress shall not abridge freedom of speech. Is this a rule, so that if a particular law does abridge freedom of speech, it follows that it is unconstitutional? Those who claim that the first amendment is 'an absolute' say that it must be taken in this way, that is, as a rule. Or does it merely state a principle, so that when an abridgement of speech is discovered, it is unconstitutional unless the context presents some other policy or principle which in the circumstances is weighty enough to permit the abridgement? That is the position of those who argue for what is called the 'clear and present danger' test or some other form of 'balancing'.

Sometimes a rule and a principle can play much the same role, and the difference between them is almost a matter of form alone. The first section of the Sherman Act states that every contract in restraint of trade shall be void. The Supreme Court had to make the decision whether this provision should be treated as a rule in its own terms (striking down every contract 'which restrains trade', which almost any contract does) or as a principle, providing a reason for striking down a contract in the absence of effective contrary policies. The Court construed the provision as a rule, but treated that rule as containing the word 'unreasonable', and as prohibiting only 'unreasonable' restraints of trade.[1] This allowed the provision to function logically as a rule (whenever a court finds that the restraint is 'unreasonable' it is bound to hold the contract invalid) and substantially as a principle (a court must take into account a variety of other principles and policies in determining whether a particular restraint in particular economic circumstances is 'unreasonable').

Words like 'reasonable', 'negligent', 'unjust', and 'significant' often perform just this function. Each of these terms makes the application of the rule which contains it depend to some extent upon principles or policies lying beyond the rule, and in this way makes that rule itself more like a principle. But they do not quite turn the rule into a principle, because even the least confining of these terms restricts the *kind* of other principles and policies on which the rule depends. If we are bound by a rule that says that 'unreasonable' contracts are void, or that grossly 'unfair' contracts will not be enforced, much more judgment is required than if the quoted terms were omitted. But suppose a case in which some consideration of policy or principle suggests that a contract should be enforced even though its restraint is not reasonable, or even though it is grossly unfair. Enforcing these contracts would be forbidden by our rules, and thus permitted only if these rules were abandoned or modified. If we were dealing, however, not with a rule but with a policy against enforcing unreasonable contracts, or a principle that unfair contracts ought not to be enforced, the contracts could be enforced without alteration of the law.

4. PRINCIPLES AND THE CONCEPT OF LAW

Once we identify legal principles as separate sorts of standards, different from legal rules, we are suddenly aware of them all around us. Law teachers teach them, lawbooks cite them, legal historians celebrate them. But they seem most energetically at work, carrying most weight, in difficult lawsuits like *Riggs* and *Henningsen*. In cases like these, principles play an essential part in arguments supporting judgments about particular legal rights and obligations. After the case is decided, we may say that the case stands for a particular rule (e.g., the rule that one who murders is not eligible to take under the will of his victim). But the rule does not exist before the case is decided; the court cites principles as its justification for adopting and applying a new rule. In *Riggs*, the court

[1] *Standard Oil v. United States*, 221 U.S. 1, 60 (1911); *United States v. American Tobacco Co.*, 221 U.S. 106, 180 (1911).

cited the principle that no man may profit from his own wrong as a background standard against which to read the statute of wills and in this way justified a new interpretation of that statute. In *Henningsen*, the court cited a variety of intersecting principles and policies as authority for a new rule respecting manufacturers' liability for automobile defects.

An analysis of the concept of legal obligation must therefore account for the important role of principles in reaching particular decisions of law. There are two very different tacks we might take:

(a) We might treat legal principles the way we treat legal rules and say that some principles are binding as law and must be taken into account by judges and lawyers who make decisions of legal obligation. If we took this tack, we should say that in the United States, at least, the 'law' includes principles as well as rules.

(b) We might, on the other hand, deny that principles can be binding the way some rules are. We would say, instead, that in cases like *Riggs* or *Henningsen* the judge reaches beyond the rules that he is bound to apply (reaches, that is, beyond the 'law') for extra-legal principles he is free to follow if he wishes.

One might think that there is not much difference between these two lines of attack, that it is only a verbal question of how one wants to use the word 'law'. But that is a mistake, because the choice between these two accounts has the greatest consequences for an analysis of legal obligation. It is a choice between two *concepts* of a legal principle, a choice we can clarify by comparing it to a choice we might make between two concepts of a legal rule. We sometimes say of someone that he 'makes it a rule' to do something, when we mean that he has chosen to follow a certain practice. We might say that someone has made it a rule, for example, to run a mile before breakfast because he-wants to be healthy and believes in a regimen. We do not mean, when we say this, that he is *bound* by the rule that he must run a mile before breakfast, or even that he regards it as binding upon him. Accepting a rule as binding is something different from making it a rule to do something. If we use Hart's example again, there is a difference between saying that Englishmen make it a rule to see a movie once a week, and saying that the English have a rule that one must see a movie once a week. The second implies that if an Englishman does not follow the rule, he is subject to criticism or censure, but the first does not. The first does not exclude the possibility of a *sort* of criticism – we can say that one who does not see movies is neglecting his education – but we do not suggest that he is doing something wrong *just* in not following the rule.[1]

If we think of the judges of a community as a group, we could describe the rules of law they follow in these two different ways. We could say, for instance, that in a certain state the judges make it a rule not to enforce wills unless there are three witnesses. This would not imply that the rare judge who enforces such a will is doing anything wrong just for that reason. On the other hand we can say that in that state a rule of law requires judges not to enforce such wills; this does imply that a judge who enforces them is doing something wrong. Hart, Austin and other positivists, of course, would insist on this latter account of legal rules; they would not at all be satisfied with the 'make it a rule' account. It is not a verbal question of which account is right. It is a question of which describes the social situation more accurately. Other important issues turn on which description we accept. If judges simply 'make it a rule' not to enforce certain contracts, for example, then we cannot say, before the decision, that anyone is 'entitled' to that result, and that proposition cannot enter into any justification we might offer for the decision.

The two lines of attack on principles parallel these two accounts of rules. The first tack treats principles as binding upon judges, so that they are wrong not to apply the principles when they are pertinent. The second tack treats principles as summaries of what most judges 'make it a principle' to do when forced to go beyond the standards that bind them. The choice between these approaches will affect, perhaps even determine, the answer we can give to the question whether the judge in a hard case like *Riggs* or *Henningsen* is attempting to enforce pre-existing legal rights and obligations. If we take the first tack, we are still free to argue that because such judges are applying binding legal standards they are enforcing legal rights and obligations. But if we take the second, we are out of court on that issue, and we must acknowledge that the murderer's family in *Riggs* and the manufacturer in *Henningsen* were deprived of their property by an act of judicial discretion applied *ex post facto*. This may not shock many readers – the notion of judicial discretion has percolated through the legal community – but it does illustrate one of the most nettlesome of the puzzles that drive philosophers to worry about legal obligation. If taking property away in cases like these cannot be justified by appealing to an established obligation, another justification must be found, and nothing satisfactory has yet been supplied.

In my skeleton diagram of positivism, previously set out, I listed the doctrine of judicial discretion as the second tenet. Positivists hold that

---

[1] The distinction is in substance the same as that made by Rawls, 'Two Concepts of Rules', 64 *Philosophical Review* 3 (1955).

when a case is not covered by a clear rule, a judge must exercise his discretion to decide that case by what amounts to a fresh piece of legislation. There may be an important connection between this doctrine and the question of which of the two approaches to legal principles we must take. We shall therefore want to ask whether the doctrine is correct, and whether it implies the second approach, as it seems on its face to do. En route to these issues, however, we shall have to polish our understanding of the concept of discretion. I shall try to show how certain confusions about that concept and in particular a failure to discriminate different senses in which it is used, account for the popularity of the doctrine of discretion. I shall argue that in the sense in which the doctrine does have a bearing on our treatment of principles, it is entirely unsupported by the arguments the positivists use to defend it.

5. DISCRETION

The concept of discretion was lifted by the positivists from ordinary language, and to understand it we must put it back in *habitat* for a moment. What does it mean, in ordinary life, to say that someone 'has discretion?' The first thing to notice is that the concept is out of place in all but very special contexts. For example, you would not say that I either do or do not have discretion to choose a house for my family. It is not true that I have 'no discretion' in making that choice, and yet it would be almost equally misleading to say that I do have discretion. The concept of discretion is at home in only one sort of context; when someone is in general charged with making decisions subject to standards set by a particular authority. It makes sense to speak of the discretion of a sergeant who is subject to orders of superiors, or the discretion of a sports official or contest judge who is governed by a rule book or the terms of the contest. Discretion, like the hole in a doughnut, does not exist except as an area left open by a surrounding belt of restriction. It is therefore a relative concept. It always makes sense to ask, 'Discretion under which standards?' or 'Discretion as to which authority?' Generally the context will make the answer to this plain, but in some cases the official may have discretion from one stand-point though not from another.

Like almost all terms, the precise meaning of 'discretion' is affected by features of the context. The term is always colored by the background of understood information against which it is used. Although the shadings are many, it will be helpful for us to recognize some gross distinctions.

Sometimes we use 'discretion' in a weak sense, simply to say that for some reason the standards an official must apply cannot be applied mechanically but demand the use of judgment. We use this weak sense when the context does not already make that clear, when the background our audience assumes does not contain that piece of information. Thus we might say, 'The sergeant's orders left him a great deal of discretion', to those who do not know what the sergeant's orders were or who do not know something that made those orders vague or hard to carry out. It would make perfect sense to add, by way of amplification, that the lieutenant had ordered the sergeant to take his five most experienced men on patrol but that it was hard to determine which were the most experienced.

Sometimes we use the term in a different weak sense, to say only that some official has final authority to make a decision and cannot be reviewed and reversed by any other official. We speak this way when the official is part of a hierarchy of officials structured so that some have higher authority but in which the patterns of authority are different for different classes of decision. Thus we might say that in baseball certain decisions, like the decision whether the ball or the runner reached second base first, are left to the discretion of the second base umpire, if we mean that on this issue the head umpire has no power to substitute his own judgment if he disagrees.

I call both of these senses weak to distinguish them from a stronger sense. We use 'discretion' sometimes not merely to say that an official must use judgment in applying the standards set him by authority, or that no one will review that exercise of judgment, but to say that on some issue he is simply not bound by standards set by the authority in question. In this sense we say that a sergeant has discretion who has been told to pick any five men for patrol he chooses or that a judge in a dog show has discretion to judge airedales before boxers if the rules do not stipulate an order of events. We use this sense not to comment on the vagueness or difficulty of the standards, or on who has the final word in applying them, but on their range and the decisions they purport to control. If the sergeant is told to take the five most experienced men, he does not have discretion in this strong sense because that order purports to govern his decision. The boxing referee who must decide which fighter has been the more aggressive does not have discretion, in the strong sense, for the same reason.[1]

If anyone said that the sergeant or the referee had discretion in these cases, we should have to understand him, if the context permitted, as using the term in one of the weak senses. Suppose, for example, the

---

[1] I have not spoken of that jurisprudential favorite, 'limited' discretion, because that concept presents no special difficulties if we remember the relativity of discretion. Suppose the sergeant is told to choose from 'amongst' experienced men, or to 'take experience into account'. We might say either that he has (limited) discretion in picking his patrol, or (full) discretion to either pick amongst experienced men or decide what else to take into account.

lieutenant ordered the sergeant to select the five men he deemed most experienced, and then added that the sergeant had discretion to choose them. Or the rules provided that the referee should award the round to the more aggressive fighter, with discretion in selecting him. We should have to understand these statements in the second weak sense, as speaking to the question of review of the decision. The first weak sense – that the decisions take judgment – would be otiose, and the third, strong sense is excluded by the statements themselves.

We must avoid one tempting confusion. The strong sense of discretion is not tantamount to license, and does not exclude criticism. Almost any situation in which a person acts (including those in which there is no question of decision under special authority, and so no question of discretion) makes relevant certain standards of rationality, fairness, and effectiveness. We criticize each other's acts in terms of these standards, and there is no reason not to do so when the acts are within the center rather than beyond the perimeter of the doughnut of special authority. So we can say that the sergeant who was given discretion (in the strong sense) to pick a patrol did so stupidly or maliciously or carelessly, or that the judge who had discretion in the order of viewing dogs made a mistake because he took boxers first although there were only three airedales and many more boxers. An official's discretion means not that he is free to decide without recourse to standards of sense and fairness, but only that his decision is not controlled by a standard furnished by the particular authority we have in mind when we raise the question of discretion. Of course this latter sort of freedom is important; that is why we have the strong sense of discretion. Someone who has discretion in this third sense can be criticized, but not for being disobedient, as in the case of the soldier. He can be said to have made a mistake, but not to have deprived a participant of a decision to which he was entitled, as in the case of a sports official or contest judge.

We may now return, with these observations in hand, to the positivists' doctrine of judicial discretion. That doctrine argues that if a case is not controlled by an established rule, the judge must decide it by exercising discretion. We want to examine this doctrine and to test its bearing on our treatment of principles; but first we must ask in which sense of discretion we are to understand it.

Some nominalists argue that judges always have discretion, even when a clear rule is in point, because judges are ultimately the final arbiters of the law. This doctrine of discretion uses the second weak sense of that term, because it makes the point that no higher authority reviews the decisions of the highest court. It therefore has no bearing on the issue of how we account for principles, any more than it bears on how we account for rules.

The positivists do not mean their doctrine this way, because they say that a judge has no discretion when a clear and established rule is available. If we attend to the positivists' arguments for the doctrine we may suspect that they use discretion in the first weak sense to mean only that judges must sometimes exercise judgment in applying legal standards. Their arguments call attention to the fact that some rules of law are vague (Professor Hart, for example, says that all rules of law have 'open texture'), and that some cases arise (like *Henningsen*) in which no established rule seems to be suitable. They emphasize that judges must sometimes agonize over points of law, and that two equally trained and intelligent judges will often disagree.

These points are easily made; they are commonplace to anyone who has any familiarity with law. Indeed, that is the difficulty with assuming that positivists mean to use 'discretion' in this weak sense. The proposition that when no clear rule is available discretion in the sense of judgment must be used is a tautology. It has no bearing, moreover, on the problem of how to account for legal principles. It is perfectly consistent to say that the judge in *Riggs*, for example, had to use judgment, and that he was bound to follow the principle that no man may profit from his own wrong. The positivists speak as if their doctrine of judicial discretion is an insight rather than a tautology, and as if it does have a bearing on the treatment of principles. Hart, for example, says that when the judge's discretion is in play, we can no longer speak of his being bound by standards, but must speak rather of what standards he 'characteristically uses'.[1] Hart thinks that when judges have discretion, the principles they cite must be treated on our second approach, as what courts 'make it a principle' to do.

It therefore seems that positivists, at least sometimes, take their doctrine in the third, strong sense of discretion. In that sense it does bear on the treatment of principles; indeed, in that sense it is nothing less than a restatement of our second approach. It is the same thing to say that when a judge runs out of rules he has discretion, in the sense that he is not bound by any standards from the authority of law, as to say that the legal standards judges cite other than rules are not binding on them.

So we must examine the doctrine of judicial discretion in the strong sense. (I shall henceforth use the term 'discretion' in that sense.) Do the principles judges cited in cases like *Riggs* or *Henningsen* control their decisions, as the sergeant's orders to take the most experienced men or the referee's duty to choose the more aggressive fighter control the decisions of these officials? What arguments could a positivist supply to show that they do not?

[1] H. L. A. Hart, *The Concept of Law*, 144 (1961).

(1) A positivist might argue that principles cannot be binding or obligatory. That would be a mistake. It is always a question, of course, whether any particular principle is *in fact* binding upon some legal official. But there is nothing in the logical character of a principle that renders it incapable of binding him. Suppose that the judge in *Henningsen* had failed to take any account of the principle that automobile manufacturers have a special obligation to their consumers, or the principle that the courts seek to protect those whose bargaining position is weak, but had simply decided for the defendant by citing the principle of freedom of contract without more. His critics would not have been content to point out that he had not taken account of considerations that other judges have been attending to for some time. Most would have said that it was his duty to take the measure of these principles and that the plaintiff was entitled to have him do so. We mean no more, when we say that a *rule* is binding upon a judge, than that he must follow it if it applies, and that if he does not he will on that account have made a mistake.

It will not do to say that in a case like *Henningsen* the court is only 'morally' obligated to take particular principles into account, or that it is 'institutionally' obligated, or obligated as a matter of judicial 'craft', or something of that sort. The question will still remain why this type of obligation (whatever we call it) is different from the obligation that rules impose upon judges, and why it entitles us to say that principles and policies are not part of the law but are merely extra-legal standards 'courts characteristically use'.

(2) A positivist might argue that even though some principles are binding, in the sense that the judge must take them into account, they cannot determine a particular result. This is a harder argument to assess because it is not clear what it means for a standard to 'determine' a result. Perhaps it means that the standard *dictates* the result whenever it applies so that nothing else counts. If so, then it is certainly true that the individual principles do not determine results, but that is only another way of saying that principles are not rules. Only rules dictate results, come what may. When a contrary result has been reached, the rule has been abandoned or changed. Principles do not work that way; they incline a decision one way, though not conclusively, and they survive intact when they do not prevail. This seems no reason for concluding that judges who must reckon with principles have discretion because a set of principles *can* dictate a result. If a judge believes that principles he is bound to recognize point in one direction and that principles pointing in the other direction, if any, are not of equal weight, then he must decide accordingly, just as he must follow what he believes

to be a binding rule. He may, of course, be wrong in his assessment of the principles, but he may also be wrong in his judgment that the rule is binding. The sergeant and the referee, we might add, are often in the same boat. No one factor dictates which soldiers are the most experienced or which fighter the more aggressive. These officials must make judgments of the relative weights of these various factors; they do not on that account have discretion.

(3) A positivist might argue that principles cannot count as law because their authority, and even more so their weight, are congenitally *controversial*. It is true that generally we cannot *demonstrate* the authority or weight of a particular principle as we can sometimes demonstrate the validity of a rule by locating it in an act of Congress or in the opinion of an authoritative court. Instead, we make a case for a principle, and for its weight, by appealing to an amalgam of practice and other principles in which the implications of legislative and judicial history figure along with appeals to community practices and understandings. There is no litmus paper for testing the soundness of such a case – it is a matter of judgment, and reasonable men may disagree. But again this does not distinguish the judge from other officials who do not have discretion. The sergeant has no litmus paper for experience, the referee none for aggressiveness. Neither of these has discretion, because he is bound to reach an understanding, controversial or not, of what his orders or the rules require, and to act on that understanding. That is the judge's duty as well.

Of course, if the positivists are right in another of their doctrines – the theory that in each legal system there is an ultimate *test* for binding law like Professor Hart's rule of recognition – it follows that principles are not binding law. But the incompatibility of principles with the positivists' theory can hardly be taken as an argument that principles must be treated any particular way. That begs the question; we are interested in the status of principles because we want to evaluate the positivists' model. The positivist cannot defend his theory of a rule of recognition by fiat; if principles are not amenable to a test he must show some other reason why they cannot count as law. Since principles seem to play a role in arguments about legal obligation (witness, again, *Riggs* and *Henningsen*), a model that provides for that role has some initial advantage over one that excludes it, and the latter cannot properly be inveighed in its own support.

These are the most obvious of the arguments a positivist might use for the doctrine of discretion in the strong sense, and for the second approach to principles. I shall mention one strong counter-argument against that doctrine and in favor of the first approach. Unless at least some principles are acknowledged to be binding upon judges, requiring them as a set to reach particular decisions, then no rules, or very few rules, can be said to be binding upon them either.

In most American jurisdictions, and now in England also, the higher courts not infrequently reject established rules. Common law rules – those developed by earlier court decisions – are sometimes overruled directly, and sometimes radically altered by further development. Statutory rules are subjected to interpretation and reinterpretation, sometimes even when the result is not to carry out what is called the 'legislative intent.'[1] If courts had discretion to change established rules, then these rules would of course not be binding upon them, and so would not be law on the positivists' model. The positivist must therefore argue that there are standards, themselves binding upon judges, that determine when a judge may overrule or alter an established rule, and when he may not.

When, then, is a judge permitted to change an existing rule of law? Principles figure in the answer in two ways. First, it is necessary, though not sufficient, that the judge find that the change would advance some principle, which principle thus justifies the change. In *Riggs* the change (a new interpretation of the statute of wills) was justified by the principle that no man should profit from his own wrong; in *Henningsen* the previously recognized rules about automobile manufacturers' liability were altered on the basis of the principles I quoted from the opinion of the court.

But not any principle will do to justify a change, or no rule would ever be safe. There must be some principles that count and others that do not, and there must be some principles that count for more than others. It could not depend on the judge's own preferences amongst a sea of respectable extra-legal standards, any one in principle eligible, because if that were the case we could not say that any rules were binding. We could always imagine a judge whose preferences amongst extra-legal standards were such as would justify a shift or radical reinterpretation of even the most entrenched rule.

Second, any judge who proposes to change existing doctrine must take account of some important standards that argue against departures from established doctrine, and these standards are also for the most part principles. They include the doctrine of 'legislative supremacy', a set of principles that require the courts to pay a qualified deference to the acts of the legislature. They also include the doctrine of precedent, another set of principles reflecting the equities and efficiencies of consistency. The doctrines of legislative supremacy and precedent incline

---

[1] See Wellington and Albert, 'Statutory Interpretation and the Political Process: A Comment on Sinclair v. Atkinson', 72 *Yale L. J.* 1547 (1963).

toward the *status quo*, each within its sphere, but they do not command it. Judges are not free, however, to pick and choose amongst the principles and policies that make up these doctrines – if they were, again, no rule could be said to be binding.

Consider, therefore, what someone implies who says that a particular rule is binding. He may imply that the rule is affirmatively supported by principles the court is not free to disregard, and which are collectively more weighty than other principles that argue for a change. If not, he implies that any change would be condemned by a combination of conservative principles of legislative supremacy and precedent that the court is not free to ignore. Very often, he will imply both, for the conservative principles, being principles and not rules, are usually not powerful enough to save a common law rule or an aging statute that is entirely unsupported by substantive principles the court is bound to respect. Either of these implications, of course, treats a body of principles and policies as law in the sense that rules are; it treats them as standards binding upon the officials of a community, controlling their decisions of legal right and obligation.

We are left with this issue. If the positivists' theory of judicial discretion is either trivial because it uses 'discretion' in a weak sense, or unsupported because the various arguments we can supply in its defense fall short, why have so many careful and intelligent lawyers embraced it? We can have no confidence in our treatment of that theory unless we can deal with that question. It is not enough to note (although perhaps it contributes to the explanation) that 'discretion' has different senses that may be confused. We do not confuse these senses when we are not thinking about law.

Part of the explanation, at least, lies in a lawyer's natural tendency to associate laws and rules, and to think of 'the law' as a collection or system of rules. Roscoe Pound, who diagnosed this tendency long ago, though that English speaking lawyers were tricked into it by the fact that English uses the same word, changing only the article, for 'a law' and 'the law'.[1] (Other languages, on the contrary, use two words: 'loi' and 'droit', for example, and 'Gesetz' and 'Recht'.) This may have had its effect, with the English speaking positivists, because the expression 'a law' certainly does suggest a rule. But the principal reason for associating law with rules runs deeper, and lies, I think, in the fact that legal education has for a long time consisted of teaching and examining those established rules that form the cutting edge of law.

In any event, if a lawyer thinks of law as a system of rules, and yet recognizes, as he must, that judges change old rules and introduce new

[1] R. Pound, *An Introduction to the Philosophy of Law* 56 (rev. ed. 1954).

ones, he will come naturally to the theory of judicial discretion in the strong sense. In those other systems of rules with which he has experience (like games), the rules are the only special authority that govern official decisions, so that if an umpire could change a rule, he would have discretion as to the subject matter of that rule. Any principles umpires might mention when changing the rules would represent only their 'characteristic' preferences. Positivists treat law like baseball revised in this way.

There is another, more subtle consequence of this initial assumption that law is a system of rules. When the positivists do attend to principles and policies, they treat them as rules *manquées*. They assume that *if* they are standards of law they must be rules, and so they read them as standards that are trying to be rules. When a positivist hears someone argue that legal principles are part of the law, he understands this to be an argument for what he calls the 'higher law' theory, that these principles are the rules of a law about the law.[1] He refutes this theory by pointing out that these 'rules' are sometimes followed and sometimes not, that for every 'rule' like 'no man shall profit from his own wrong' there is another competing 'rule' like 'the law favors security of title', and that there is no way to test the validity of 'rules' like these. He concludes that these principles and policies are not valid rules of a law above the law, which is true, because they are not rules at all. He also concludes that they are extra-legal standards which each judge selects according to his own lights in the exercise of his discretion, which is false. It is as if a zoologist had proved that fish are not mammals, and then concluded that they are really only plants.

6. THE RULE OF RECOGNITION

This discussion was provoked by our two competing accounts of legal principles. We have been exploring the second account, which the positivists seem to adopt through their doctrine of judicial discretion, and we have discovered grave difficulties. It is time to return to the fork in the road. What if we adopt the first approach? What would the consequences of this be for the skeletal structure of positivism? Of course we should have to drop the second tenet, the doctrine of judicial discretion (or, in the alternative, to make plain that the doctrine is to be read merely to say that judges must often exercise judgment). Would we also have to abandon or modify the first tenet, the proposition that law is distinguished by tests of the sort that can be set out in a master rule like Professor Hart's rule of recognition? If principles of the *Riggs* and

[1] See, e.g., Dickinson, 'The Law Behind Law (pts. 1 & 2)', 29, *Columbia Law Review* 112, 254 (1929).

Henningsen sort are to count as law, and we are nevertheless to preserve the notion of a master rule for law, then we must be able to deploy some test that all (and only) the principles that do count as law meet. Let us begin with the test Hart suggests for identifying valid *rules* of law, to see whether these can be made to work for principles as well.

Most rules of law, according to Hart, are valid because some competent institution enacted them. Some were created by a legislature, in the form of statutory enactments. Others were created by judges who formulated them to decide particular cases, and thus established them as precedents for the future. But this test of pedigree will not work for the *Riggs* and *Henningsen* principles. The origin of these as legal principles lies not in a particular decision of some legislature or court, but in a sense of appropriateness developed in the profession and the public over time. Their continued power depends upon this sense of appropriateness being sustained. If it no longer seemed unfair to allow people to profit by their wrongs, or fair to place special burdens upon oligopolies that manufacture potentially dangerous machines, these principles would no longer play much of a role in new cases, even if they had never been overruled or repealed. (Indeed, it hardly makes sense to speak of principles like these as being 'overruled' or 'repealed'. When they decline they are eroded, not torpedoed.)

True, if we were challenged to back up our claim that some principle is a principle of law, we would mention any prior cases in which that principle was cited, or figured in the argument. We would also mention any statute that seemed to exemplify that principle (even better if the principle was cited in the preamble of the statute, or in the committee reports or other legislative documents that accompanied it). Unless we could find some such institutional support, we would probably fail to make out our case, and the more support we found, the more weight we could claim for the principle.

Yet we could not devise any formula for testing how much and what kind of institutional support is necessary to make a principle a legal principle, still less to fix its weight at a particular order of magnitude. We argue for a particular principle by grappling with a whole set of shifting, developing and interacting standards (themselves principles rather than rules) about institutional responsibility, statutory interpretation, the persuasive force of various sorts of precedent, the relation of all these to contemporary moral practices, and hosts of other such standards. We could not bolt all of these together into a single 'rule', even a complex one, and if we could the result would bear little relation to Hart's picture of a rule of recognition, which is the picture of a fairly stable master rule specifying 'some feature or features possession of which by a suggested rule is taken as a conclusive affirmative indication that it is a rule. . ."[1]

Moreover, the techniques we apply in arguing for another principle do not stand (as Hart's rule of recognition is designed to) on an entirely different level from the principles they support. Hart's sharp distinction between acceptance and validity does not hold. If we are arguing for the principle that a man should not profit from his own wrong, we could cite the acts of courts and legislatures that exemplify it, but this speaks as much to the principle's acceptance as its validity. (It seems odd to speak of a principle as being valid at all, perhaps because validity is an all-or-nothing concept, appropriate for rules, but inconsistent with a principle's dimension of weight.) If we are asked (as we might well be) to defend the particular doctrine of precedent, or the particular technique of statutory interpretation, that we used in this argument, we should certainly cite the practice of others in using that doctrine or technique. But we should also cite other general principles that we believe support that practice, and this introduces a note of validity into the chord of acceptance. We might argue, for example, that the use we make of earlier cases and statutes is supported by a particular analysis of the point of the practice of legislation or the doctrine of precedent, or by the principles of democratic theory, or by a particular position on the proper division of authority between national and local institutions, or something else of that sort. Nor is this path of support a one-way street leading to some ultimate principle resting on acceptance alone. Our principles of legislation, precedent, democracy, or federalism might be challenged too; and if they were we should argue for them, not only in terms of practice, but in terms of each other and in terms of the implications of trends of judicial and legislative decisions, even though this last would involve appealing to those same doctrines of interpretation we justified through the principles we are now trying to support. At this level of abstraction, in other words, principles rather hang together than link together.

So even though principles draw support from the official acts of legal institutions, they do not have a simple or direct enough connection with these acts to frame that connection in terms of criteria specified by some ultimate master rule of recognition. Is there any other route by which principles might be brought under such a rule?

Hart does say that a master rule might designate as law not only rules enacted by particular legal institutions, but rules established by *custom* as well. He has in mind a problem that bothered other positivists, including Austin. Many of our most ancient legal rules were never

[1] H. L. A. Hart, *The Concept of Law* 92 (1961).

explicitly created by a legislature or a court. When they made their first appearance in legal opinions and texts, they were treated as already being part of the law because they represented the customary practice of the community, or some specialized part of it, like the business community. (The examples ordinarily given are rules of mercantile practice, like the rules governing what rights arise under a standard form of commercial paper.)[1] Since Austin thought that all law was the command of a determinate sovereign, he held that these customary practices were not law until the courts (as agents of the sovereign) recognized them, and that the courts were indulging in a fiction in pretending otherwise. But that seemed arbitrary. If everyone thought custom might in itself be law, the fact that Austin's theory said otherwise was not persuasive.

Hart reversed Austin on this point. The master rule, he says, might stipulate that some custom counts as law even before the courts recognize it. But he does not face the difficulty this raises for his general theory because he does not attempt to set out the criteria a master rule might use for this purpose. It cannot use, as its only criterion, the provision that the community regard the practice as *morally* binding, for this would not distinguish legal customary rules from moral customary rules, and of course not all of the community's long-standing customary moral obligations are enforced at law. If, on the other hand, the test is whether the community regards the customary practice as *legally* binding, the whole point of the master rule is undercut, at least for this class of legal rules. The master rule, says Hart, marks the transformation from a primitive society to one with law, because it provides a test for determining social rules of law other than by measuring their acceptance. But if the master rule says merely that whatever other rules the community accepts as legally binding are legally binding, then it provides no such test at all, beyond the test we should use were there no master rule. The master rule becomes (for these cases) a non-rule of recognition; we might as well say that every primitive society has a secondary rule of recognition, namely the rule that whatever is accepted as binding is binding. Hart himself, in discussing international law, ridicules the idea that such a rule could be a rule of recognition, by describing the proposed rule as 'an empty repetition of the mere fact that the society concerned . . . observes certain standards of conduct as obligatory rules'.[2]

---

[1] See Note, 'Custom and Trade Usage: Its Application to Commercial Dealings and the Common Law', 55 *Columbia Law Review* 1192 (1955), and materials cited therein at 1193 n.l. As that note makes plain, the actual practices of courts in recognizing trade customs follow the pattern of applying a set of general principles and policies rather than a test that could be captured as part of a rule of recognition.

[2] H. L. Hart, *The Concept of Law* 230 (1961). A master rule might specify some particular feature of a custom that is independent of the community's attitude; it

Hart's treatment of custom amounts, indeed, to a confession that there are at least some rules of law that are not binding because they are valid under standards laid down by a master rule but are binding – like the master rule – because they are accepted as binding by the community. This chips at the neat pyramidal architecture we admired in Hart's theory : we can no longer say that only the master rule is binding because of its acceptance, all other rules being valid under its terms.

This is perhaps only a chip, because the customary rules Hart has in mind are no longer a very significant part of the law. But it does suggest that Hart would be reluctant to widen the damage by bringing under the head of 'custom' all those crucial principles and policies we have been discussing. If he were to call these part of the law and yet admit that the only test of their force lies in the degree to which they are accepted as law by the community or some part thereof, he would very sharply reduce that area of the law over which his master rule held any dominion. It is not just that all the principles and policies would escape its sway, though that would be bad enough. Once these principles and policies are accepted as law, and thus as standards judges must follow in determining legal obligations, it would follow that *rules* like those announced for the first time in *Riggs* and *Henningsen* owe their force at least in part to the authority of principles and policies, and so not entirely to the master rule of recognition.

So we cannot adapt Hart's version of positivism by modifying his rule of recognition to embrace principles. No tests of pedigree, relating principles to acts of legislation, can be formulated, nor can his concept of customary law, itself an exception to the first tenet of positivism, be made to serve without abandoning that tenet altogether. One more possibility must be considered, however. If no rule of recognition can provide a test for identifying principles, why not say that principles are ultimate, and *form* the rule of recognition of our law? The answer to the general question 'What is valid law in an American jurisdiction?' would then require us to state all the principles (as well as ultimate constitutional rules) in force in that jurisdiction at the time, together with appropriate assignments of weight. A positivist might then regard the complete set of these standards as the rule of recognition of the jurisdiction. This

might provide, for example, that all customs of very great age, or all customs having to do with negotiable instruments count as law. I can think of no such features that in fact distinguish the customs that have been recognized as law in England or America, however. Some customs that are not legally enforceable are older than some that are, some practices relating to commercial paper are enforced and others not, and so forth. In any event, even if a distinguishing feature were found that identified all rules of law established by custom, it would remain unlikely that such a feature could be found for principles which vary widely in their subject matter and pedigree and some of which are of very recent origin.

solution has the attraction of paradox, but of course it is an unconditional surrender. If we simply designate our rule of recognition by the phrase 'the complete set of principles in force', we achieve only the tautology that law is law. If, instead, we tried actually to list all the principles in force we would fail. They are controversial, their weight is all important, they are numberless, and they shift and change so fast that the start of our list would be obsolete before we reached the middle. Even if we succeeded, we would not have a key for law because there would be nothing left for our key to unlock.

I conclude that if we treat principles as law we must reject the positivists' first tenet, that the law of a community is distinguished from other social standards by some test in the form of a master rule. We have already decided that we must then abandon the second tenet – the doctrine of judicial discretion – or clarify it into triviality. What of the third tenet, the positivists' theory of legal obligation?

This theory holds that a legal obligation exists when (and only when) an established rule of law imposes such an obligation. It follows from this that in a hard case – when no such established rule can be found – there is no legal obligation until the judge creates a new rule for the future. The judge may apply that new rule to the parties in the case, but this is *ex post facto* legislation, not the enforcement of an existing obligation.

The positivists' doctrine of discretion (in the strong sense) required this view of legal obligation, because if a judge has discretion there can be no legal right or obligation – no entitlement – that he must enforce. Once we abandon that doctrine, however, and treat principles as law, we raise the possibility that a legal obligation might be imposed by a constellation of principles as well as by an established rule. We might want to say that a legal obligation exists whenever the case supporting such an obligation, in terms of binding legal principles of different sorts, is stronger than the case against it.

Of course, many questions would have to be answered before we could accept that view of legal obligation. If there is no rule of recognition, no test for law in that sense, how do we decide which principles are to count, and how much, in making such a case? How do we decide whether one case is better than another? If legal obligation rests on an undemonstrable judgment of that sort, how can it provide a justification for a judicial decision that one party had a legal obligation? Does this view of obligation square with the way lawyers, judges and laymen speak, and is it consistent with our attitudes about moral obligation? Does this analysis help us to deal with the classical jurisprudential puzzles about the nature of law?

These questions must be faced, but even the questions promise more than positivism provides. Positivism, on its own thesis, stops short of just those puzzling, hard cases that send us to look for theories of law. When we read these cases, the positivist remits us to a doctrine of discretion that leads nowhere and tells nothing. His picture of law as a system of rules has exercised a tenacious hold on our imagination, perhaps through its very simplicity. If we shake ourselves loose from this model of rules, we may be able to build a model truer to the complexity and sophistication of our own practices.

3

The Model of Rules II

In Chapter 2 I argued that the central propositions of the legal theory I called positivism were in error and must be abandoned.[1] In particular, I argued that it is wrong to suppose, as that theory does, that in every legal system there will be some commonly recognized fundamental test for determining which standards count as law and which do not. I said that no such fundamental test can be found in complicated legal systems, like those in force in the United States and Great Britain, and that in these countries no ultimate distinction can be made between legal and moral standards, as positivism insists.

I might summarize the argument I made in this way. I said that the thesis that there exists some commonly recognized test for law is plausible if we look only at simple legal rules of the sort that appear in statutes or are set out in bold type in textbooks. But lawyers and judges, in arguing and deciding lawsuits, appeal not only to such black-letter rules, but also to other sorts of standards that I called legal principles, like, for example, the principle that no man may profit from his own wrong. This fact faces the positivist with the following difficult choice. He might try to show that judges, when they appeal to principles of this sort, are not appealing to legal standards, but only exercising their discretion. Or he might try to show that, contrary to my doubts, some commonly-recognized test always does identify the principles judges count as law, and distinguishes them from the principles they do not. I argued that neither strategy could succeed.

A number of lawyers have been kind enough to reply to my argument; an article by Dr. Raz is a distinguished example.[2] The chief points

[1] See p. 16 ff.

[2] Raz, 'Legal Principles and the Limits of Law', 81 *Yale L. J.* 823 (1972). See also G. Carrio, *Legal Principles and Legal Positivism* (1971); Christie, 'The Model of Principles', 1968, *Duke L. J.* 649; Gross, 'Jurisprudence', 1968/69 *Annual Survey of Am. L.* 575; Probert, 'The Right Way', *Human Rights* 163 (E. Pollack ed. 1971); Sartorius, 'Social Policy and Judicial Legislation', 8 *Am. Phil. Q.* 151 (1971); Tapper, 'A Note on Principles', 1971 *Modern L. Rev.* 628. For an earlier article, *see* Mac-Callum, 'Dworkin on Judicial Discretion', 60 *J. Phil.* 638 (1963). I do not attempt to reply to or even mention all the points and questions presented in these articles. I have selected for discussion those points made most often, or found most persuasive by students.

made against my argument seem to be these. (i) It is not clear, it is said, that my thesis really involves anything more than an amendment to the positivist's doctrine. If one reads carefully the work of Professor H. L. A. Hart, whose work I took to be the clearest example of a positivist theory, one will see that his theory is able to include my conclusions with only minor amendment.[1] (ii) It is said that my own arguments are inconsistent in this way: my argument against the theory of discretion supposes that in fact some principles do and some principles do not count as law, but if this is so then there must be a test for law of just the sort that I deny.[2] (iii) The arguments I make, moreover, suggest the form of this ultimate test. I said that judges identify principles at least in part by reference to the role that these principles have played in previous legal argument, and this kind of test, which I described as a test of 'institutional structure',[3] can supply the ultimate test for principles that I say cannot be found. (iv) My argument that judges do not have discretion in the matter of principles ignores the fact that judges may sometimes be *forced* to exercise discretion by virtue of the fact that it is not plain which principles count and for how much.[4] (v) The distinction between rules and principles, on which my argument seems to depend, is in fact untenable.[5]

There is a further objection, which might be made, but which I shall not try to answer. I have no answer to the argument that the term 'law' can be used in such a way as to make the positivist's thesis true by stipulation. It can be used, that is, in such a way that the speaker recognizes as 'legal' standards only those standards judges and lawyers cite which are in fact identified by some commonly-recognized test. No doubt 'law' can be used in that way, and perhaps some lawyers do so. But I was concerned with what I took to be an argument about the concept of law now in general employment, which is, I take it, the concept of the standards that provide for the rights and duties that a government has a duty to recognize and enforce, at least in principle, through the familiar institutions of courts and police. My point was that positivism, with its doctrine of a fundamental and commonly-recognized test for law, mistakes part of the domain of that concept for the whole.

Before I turn to the specific objections I listed, however, I want to consider one very general objection that I did not list, but which I believe, for reasons that will be clear, underlines several of those I did. This general objection depends on a thesis that Hart defended in *The*

---

[1] See, e.g., Carrio at 22.
[2] Sartorius at 155.
[3] *Id.* at 156.
[4] Raz at 843 ff., Carrio at 27; Christie at 669; MacCallum *loc. cit.*
[5] Raz at 834-54, Christie at 656 ff.

Concept of Law,[1] a thesis which belongs to moral as well as to legal philosophy. It argues, in its strongest form, that no rights or duties of any sort can exist except by virtue of a uniform social practice of recognizing these rights and duties. If that is so, and if law is, as I suppose, a matter of rights and duties and not simply of the discretion of officials, then there must be a commonly recognized test for law in the form of a uniform social practice, and my argument must be wrong.

In the first section of this essay I shall elaborate this powerful thesis, with special reference to the duty of judges to apply particular standards as law. I shall then argue that the thesis must be rejected. In the remaining sections I shall, on some occasions, recast my original arguments to show why they depend on rejecting it.

I. SOCIAL RULES

I shall begin by noticing an important distinction between two of the several types of concepts we use when we discuss our own or other people's behavior. Sometimes we say that on the whole, all things considered, one 'ought' or 'ought not' to do something. On other occasions we say that someone has an 'obligation' or a 'duty' to do something, or 'no right' to do it. These are different sorts of judgments: it is one thing, for example, simply to say that someone ought to give to a particular charity and quite another to say that he has a duty to do so, and one thing to say simply that he ought not to drink alcohol or smoke marijuana and quite another to say that he has no right to do so. It is easy to think of cases in which we should be prepared to make the first of each of these claims, but not the second.

Moreover, something might well turn, in particular cases, on which claim we did feel was justified. Judgments of duty are commonly much stronger than judgments simply about what one ought to do. We can demand compliance with an obligation or a duty, and sometimes propose a sanction for non-compliance, but neither demands nor sanctions are appropriate when it is merely a question of what one ought, on the whole, to do. The question of when claims of obligation or duty are appropriate, as distinct from such general claims about conduct, is therefore an important question of moral philosophy, though it is a relatively neglected one.

The law does not simply state what private citizens ought or ought not to do; it provides what they have a duty to do or no right to do. It does not, moreover, simply advise judges and other officials about the decisions they ought to reach; it provides that they have a duty to

---

[1] H. L. A. Hart, *The Concept of Law* 79-88 (1961).

recognize and enforce certain standards. It may be that in some cases a judge has no duty to decide either way; in this sort of case we must be content to speak of what he ought to do. This, I take it, is what is meant when we say that in such a case the judge has 'discretion'. But every legal philosopher, with the exception of the most extreme of the American legal realists, has supposed that in at least some cases the judge has a duty to decide in a particular way, for the express reason that the law requires that decision.

But it is a formidable problem for legal theory to explain why judges have such a duty. Suppose, for example, that a statute provides that in the event of intestacy a man's property descends to his next of kin. Lawyers will say that a judge has a duty to order property distributed in accordance with that statute. But what imposes that duty on the judge? We may want to say that judges are 'bound' by a general rule to the effect that they must do what the legislature says, but it is unclear where that rule comes from. We cannot say that the legislature is itself the source of the rule that judges must do what the legislature says, because that explanation presupposes the rule we are trying to justify. Perhaps we can discover a basic legal document, like a constitution, that says either explicitly or implicitly that the judges must follow the legislature. But what imposes a duty on judges to follow the constitution? We cannot say the constitution imposes that duty without begging the question in the same way.

If we were content to say merely that judges *ought* to follow the legislature, or the constitution, then the difficulty would not be so serious. We might provide any number of reasons for this limited claim; for example, that everyone would be better off in the long run, on balance, if judges behaved in this way. But this sort of reason is unpersuasive if we want to claim, as our concept of law seems to assume, that judges have a *duty* to follow the legislature or the constitution. We must then try to find, not just reasons why judges should do so, but grounds for asserting that duty, and this requires that we face the issue of moral philosophy I just named. Under what circumstances do duties and obligations arise?

Hart's answer may be summarized in this way.[1] Duties exist when social rules exist providing for such duties. Such social rules exist when the practice-conditions for such rules are met. These practice-conditions are met when the members of a community behave in a certain way; this behavior *constitutes* a social rule, and imposes a duty. Suppose that

---

[1] Hart's analysis, *loc. cit.*, is of the concept of 'obligation'. I use the word 'duty' here as well because it is more usual to speak of the judge's duty than of his obligation to impose the law, and because Hart means his analysis to apply to both terms; indeed he uses them almost interchangeably in *The Concept of Law*. See *id.* at 27, 238.

a group of churchgoers follows this practice: (a) each man removes his hat before entering church, (b) when a man is asked why he does so, he refers to 'the rule' that requires him to do so, and (c) when someone forgets to remove his hat before entering church, he is criticized and perhaps even punished by the others.[1] In those circumstances, according to Hart, practice-conditions for a duty-imposing rule are met. The community 'has' a social rule to the effect that men must not wear hats in church, and that social rule imposes a duty not to wear hats in church. That rule takes the issue of hat-wearing in church out of the general run of issues which men may debate in terms of what they ought to do, by creating a duty. The existence of the social rule, and therefore the existence of the duty, is simply a matter of fact.

Hart then applies this analysis to the issue of judicial duty. He believes that in each legal system the practice-conditions are met, by the behavior of judges, for a social rule that imposes a duty to identify and apply certain standards as law. If, in a particular community, these officials (a) regularly apply the rules laid down by the legislature in reaching their decisions, (b) justify this practice by appeal to 'the rule' that judges must follow the legislature, and (c) censure any official who does not follow the rule, then, on Hart's theory, this community can be said to have a social rule that judges must follow the legislature. If so, then judges in that community have a duty to do so. If we now ask why judges have a duty to follow social rules, after the fashion of our earlier quibbles, Hart will say that we have missed the point. It belongs to the concept of a duty, on his account, that duties are created by social rules of the sort he describes.

But Hart's theory, as so far presented, is open to an objection that might be put in the following way. When a sociologist says that a particular community 'has' or 'follows' a particular rule, like the no-hat-in-church rule, he means only to describe the behavior of that community in a certain respect. He means only to say that members of that community suppose that they have a particular duty, and not that he agrees. But when a member of the community himself appeals to a rule, for the purpose of criticizing his own or someone else's behavior, then he means not simply to describe the behavior of other people but to evaluate it. He means not simply that others believe that they have a certain duty, but that they *do* have that duty. We must therefore recognize a distinction between two sorts of statements each of which uses the concept of a rule. The sociologist, we might say, is asserting a *social* rule, but the

---

[1] Hart uses this example for a different purpose. See Hart, *op. cit.*, at 121. I have drafted the example so that the social rule here in play would be an obligation (or duty) imposing rule, e.g., by providing that the social pressures for conformity are severe.

churchgoer is asserting a *normative* rule. We might say that the sociologist's assertion of a social rule is true (or warranted) if a certain factual state of affairs occurs, that is, if the community behaves in the way Hart describes in his example. But we should want to say that the churchgoer's assertion of a normative rule is true (or warranted) only if a certain normative state of affairs exists, that is, only if individuals in fact do have the duty that they suppose they have in Hart's example. The judge trying a lawsuit is in the position of the churchgoer, not the sociologist. He does not mean to state, as a cold fact, simply that most judges believe that they have a duty to follow what the legislature has said; he means that they do in fact have such a duty and he cites that duty, not others' beliefs, as the justification for his own decision. If so, then the social rule cannot, without more, be the source of the duty he believes he has.

Hart anticipates this objection with an argument that forms the heart of his theory. He recognizes the distinction I have drawn between assertions of a 'social rule' and assertions of a 'normative rule', though he does not use these terms. However, he denies, at least as to the cases he discusses, that these two sorts of assertions can be said to assert two different sorts of rules. Instead, he asks us to distinguish between the *existence* of a rule and its *acceptance* by individual members of the community in question. When the sociologist asserts the existence of a social rule he merely asserts its existence: he says only that the practice-conditions for that rule have been met. When the churchgoer asserts its existence he also claims that these practice-conditions are met, but *in addition* he displays his *acceptance* of the rule as a standard for guiding his own conduct and for judging the conduct of others. He both identifies a social practice and indicates his disposition to conform his behavior to it. Nevertheless, insofar as each refers to a rule, it is the same rule, that is, the rule that is constituted by the social practice in question.

The difference between a statement of a social rule and a statement of a normative rule, then, is not a difference in the type of rule each asserts, but rather a difference in the attitude each displays towards the social rule it does assert. When a judge appeals to the rule that whatever the legislature enacts is law, he is taking an internal point of view towards a social rule; what he says is true because a social practice to that effect exists, but he goes beyond simply saying that this is so. He signals his disposition to regard the social practice as a justification for his conforming to it.

So Hart advances both a general theory about the concept of obligation and duty, and a specific application of that theory to the duty of judges to enforce the law. For the balance of this initial section, I shall be concerned to criticize the general theory, which I shall call the social rule theory, and I shall distinguish strong and weaker versions of that theory. On the strong version, whenever anyone asserts a duty he must be understood as presupposing the existence of a social rule and signifying his acceptance of the practice the rule describes. So if I say that men have a duty not to lie, I must mean at least that a social rule exists to that effect, and unless it does my statement must be false. On a weaker version, it is simply *sometimes* the case that someone who asserts a duty should be understood as presupposing a social rule that provides for that duty. For example, it might be the case that a churchgoer who says that men must not wear hats in church must be understood in that way, but it would not follow that the man who asserts a duty not to lie must be understood in the same way. He might be asserting a duty that does not in fact depend upon the existence of a social rule.

Hart does not make entirely plain, in the relevant pages of *The Concept of Law*, which version he means to adopt, though much of what he says suggests the strong version. But the application of his general theory to the problem of judicial duty will, of course, depend upon which version of the social rule theory he means to make out. If the strong version is right, then judges who speak about a fundamental duty to treat what the legislature says as law, for example, must presuppose a social rule to that effect. But if some weaker version of the social rule theory holds, then it simply might be the case that this is so, and further argument would be needed to show that it is.

The strong version of the theory cannot be correct if it proposes to explain all cases in which people appeal to duties, or even to all cases in which they appeal to rules as the source of duties. The theory must concede that there are some assertions of a normative rule that cannot be explained as an appeal to a social rule, for the reason that no corresponding social rule exists. A vegetarian might say, for example, that we have no right to kill animals for food because of the fundamental moral rule that it is always wrong to take life in any form or under any circumstance. Obviously no social rule exists to that effect: the vegetarian will acknowledge that very few men now recognize any such rule or any such duty and indeed that is his complaint.

However, the theory might argue that this use of the concepts of rule and duty designates a special case, and belongs in fact to a distinct kind of moral practice that is parasitic upon the standard practice the theory is designed to explain. The vegetarian must be understood, on this account, really to be saying not that men and women presently have a duty not to take life, but rather that since there are very strong grounds for saying that one *ought* not to take life, a social rule to that effect *ought to* exist. His appeal to 'the rule' might suggest that some such rule already does exist, but this suggestion is a sort of figure of speech, an attempt on his part to capture the imperative force of social rules, and extend that force to his own very different sort of claim.

But this defense misunderstands the vegetarian's claim. He wants to say, not simply that it is desirable that society rearrange its institutions so that no man ever has the right to take life, but that in fact, as things stand, no one ever does have that right. Indeed, he will want to urge the existence of a moral duty to respect life as a reason why society should have a social rule to that effect. The strong version of the social rule theory does not permit him to make that argument. So that theory can accommodate his statements only by insisting that he say something that he does not want to say.

If the social rule theory is to be plausible, therefore, it must be weakened at least to this extent. It must purport to offer an explanation of what is meant by a claim to duty (or an assertion of a normative rule of duty) only in one sort of case, namely, when the community is by-and-large agreed that some such duty does exist. The theory would not apply in the case of the vegetarian, but it would apply in the case of the churchgoer. This weakening would not much affect the application of the theory to the problem of judicial duty, because judges do in fact seem to follow much the same rules in deciding what to recognize as the law they are bound to enforce.

But the theory is not plausible even in this weakened form. It fails to notice the important distinction between two kinds of social morality, which might be called *concurrent* and *conventional* morality. A community displays a concurrent morality when its members are agreed in asserting the same, or much the same, normative rule, but they do not count the fact of that agreement as an essential part of their grounds for asserting that rule. It displays a conventional morality when they do. If the churchgoers believe that each man has a duty to take off his hat in church, but would not have such a duty but for some social practice to that general effect, then this is a case of conventional morality. If they also believe that each man has a duty not to lie, and would have this duty even if most other men did, then this would be a case of concurrent morality.

The social rule theory must be weakened so as to apply only to cases of conventional morality. In cases of concurrent morality, like the lying case, the practice-conditions Hart describes would be met. People would on the whole not lie, they would cite 'the rule' that lying is wrong as a justification of this behavior, and they would condemn those who did lie. A social rule would be constituted by this behavior, on Hart's theory, and a sociologist would be justified in saying that the community 'had a rule' against lying. But it would distort the claim that members of the community made, when they spoke of a duty not to lie, to suppose them to be *appealing* to that social rule, or to suppose that they count its existence necessary to their claim. On the contrary, since this is a case of concurrent morality, the fact is that they do not. So the social rule theory must be confined to conventional morality.

This further weakening of the theory might well reduce its impact on the problem of judicial duty. It may be that at least some part of what judges believe they must do represents concurrent rather than conventional morality. Many judges, for example, may believe that they have a duty to enforce decision of a democratically elected legislature on the grounds of political principles which they accept as having independent merit, and not simply because other judges and officials accept them as well. On the other hand, it is at least plausible to suppose that this is not so, and that at least the bulk of judges in typical legal systems would count some general judicial practice as an essential part of the case for any claim about their judicial duties.

However, the social rule theory is not even an adequate account of conventional morality. It is not adequate because it cannot explain the fact that even when people count a social practice as a necessary part of the grounds for asserting some duty, they may still disagree about the scope of that duty. Suppose, for example, that the members of the community which 'has the rule' that men must not wear hats in church are in fact divided on the question of whether 'that' rule applies to the case of male babies wearing bonnets. Each side believes that its view of the duties of the babies or their parents is the sounder, but neither view can be pictured as based on a social rule, because there is no social rule on the issue at all.

Hart's description of the practice-conditions for social rules is explicit on this point: a rule is constituted by the conforming behavior of the bulk of a population. No doubt he would count, as conforming behavior, behavior that everyone agrees would be required in a particular case even though the case has not arisen. So the social rule would 'cover' the case of a red-headed man, even if the community did not happen to include one as yet. But if half the churchgoers claim that babies are required to take off their bonnets and the other half denies any such requirement, what social rule does this behavior constitute? We cannot say either that it constitutes a social rule that babies must take off their bonnets, or a social rule that provides that they do not have that duty.

We might be tempted to say that the social rule about men wearing hats in church is 'uncertain' as to the issue of babies. But this involves confusion of just the sort that the social rule theory is meant to avoid. We cannot say that the social rule is uncertain when all the relevant facts about social behavior are known, as they are in this case, because that would violate the thesis that social rules are constituted by behavior.

A social rule about wearing hats in church might be said to be uncertain when the facts about what people did and thought had not yet been gathered, or, perhaps, if the question of babies had not yet arisen, so that it was unclear whether the bulk of the community would be of one mind or not. But nothing like this kind of uncertainty is present here; the case has arisen and we know that members of the community do not agree. So we must say, in this kind of case, not that the social rule about wearing hats in church is uncertain, but rather that the only social rule that the behavior of the community constitutes is the rule that prohibits grown men from wearing hats in church. The existence of that rule is certain, and it is equally certain that no social rule exists on the issue of babies at all.

But all this seems nearly fatal to the social rule theory, for this reason : when people assert normative rules, even in cases of conventional morality, they typically assert rules that differ in scope or in detail, or, in any event, that would differ if each person articulated his rule in further detail. But two people whose rules differ, or would differ if elaborated, cannot be appealing to the same social rule, and at least one of them cannot be appealing to any social rule at all. This is so even though they agree in most cases that do or might arise when the rules they each endorse are in play. So the social rule theory must be weakened to an unacceptable form if it is to survive at all. It must be held to apply only in cases, like some games, when it is accepted by the participants that if a duty is controversial it is no duty at all. It would not then apply to judicial duties.

The theory may try to avoid that conclusion in a variety of ways. It might argue, first, that when someone appeals to a rule, in a controversial case, what he says must be understood as having two parts : first, it identifies the social rule that does represent agreement within the community (that grown men must not wear hats in church) and then it urges that this rule *ought* to be extended to cover more controversial cases (babies in church). The theory might, in other words, take the same line towards all controversial appeals to rules as I said it might in the case of the vegetarian. But the objection I made in discussing the vegetarian's case could then be made, with much greater effect, as a general critique of the theory as a whole. People, at least people who live outside philosophy texts, appeal to moral standards largely in controversial circumstances. When they do, they want to say not that the standard ought to apply to the case in hand, whatever that would mean, but that the standard does apply; not that people ought to have the duties and responsibilities that the standard prescribed, but that they do have them. The theory could hardly argue that all these claims are special or parasitic employments of the concept of duty; if it did, it would limit its own application to the trivial.

The theory might be defended, alternatively, in a very different way : by changing the concept of a social rule that it employs. It might do this by fixing on the fact that, at least in the case of conventional morality, certain verbal formulations of a rule often become standard, like the form, 'men must take off their hats in church.' On the revised concept, a social rule exists when a community accepts a particular verbal formulation of its duties, and uses that formulation as a guide to conduct and criticism; the rule can then be said to be 'uncertain' to the degree that the community disagrees about the proper application of some one or more terms in the standard formulation, provided that it is agreed that the controversial cases must be decided on the basis of one or another interpretation of these terms. The revision would provide an answer to the argument I made. The churchgoers do accept one single social rule about their hat-wearing responsibilities, namely the rule that men must not wear hats in church. But that rule is uncertain, because there is disagreement whether 'men' includes male babies, or whether 'hats' includes bonnets.

But this revision of the concept places much too much weight upon the accident of whether members of the community in question are able to, or do in fact, locate their disagreements about duties as disagreements in the interpretation of some key word in a particular verbal formulation that has become popular. The churchgoers are able to put their disagreement in this form, but it does not follow that they all will. The verbal formulation of the rule might have been different without the underlying social facts having been different, as if people were in the habit of saying that only women may cover their heads in church; in that case the disagreement would have to be framed, not as a disagreement over whether 'women' includes 'male babies' but whether the popular version was a correct statement of the right normative rule.

Moreover, the theory would lose most of its original explanatory power if it were revised in this way. As originally presented it captured, though it misrepresented, an important fact, which is that social practice plays a central role in justifying at least some of our normative claims about individual responsibility or duty. But it is facts of consistent practice that count, not accidents of verbal behavior. Our moral practices are not exercises in statutory interpretation.

Finally, the social rule theory might retain Hart's original definition of a social rule, as a description of uniform practice, but retreat in a different way and cut its losses. It might give up the claim that social rules ever set the *limit* of a man's duties, but keep the idea that they set their *threshold*. The function of social rules in morality might then be said to be this : social rules distinguish what is settled by way of duties, not simply in the factual sense that they describe an area of consensus, but in the conceptual sense that when such consensus exists, it is undeniable that members of that community have at least the duties it embraces, though they may, and perhaps may properly, refuse to honor these duties. But the social rule does not settle that individuals have no rights or duties beyond its terms even in the area of conventional morality; the fact that the social rule does not extend to some case, like the case of babies in church, means rather that someone asserting a duty in that case must rely on arguments that go beyond a simple appeal to practice.

If the social rule theory is revised in this way it no longer supports Hart's thesis of a social rule of recognition in the way that the original theory I described does. If judges may have a duty to decide a case in a particular way, in spite of the fact that no social rule imposes that duty, then Hart's claim that social practice accounts for all judicial duty is lost. I should like to point out, however, the weakness that remains in even this revised form of the social rule theory. It does not conform with our moral practice to say even that a social rule stipulates the minimum level of rights and duties. It is generally recognized, even as a feature of conventional morality, that practices that are pointless, or inconsistent in principle with other requirements of morality, do not impose duties, though of course, when a social rule exists, only a small minority will think that this provision in fact applies. When a social rule existed, for example, that men extend certain formal courtesies to women, most people said that women had a right to them; but someone of either sex who thought these courtesies an insult would not agree.

This fact about conventional morality, which the social rule theory ignores, is of great importance because it points toward a better understanding of the connection between social practice and normative judgments than that theory provides. It is true that normative judgments often assume a social practice as an essential part of the case for that judgment; this is the hallmark, as I said, of conventional morality. But the social rule theory misconceives the connection. It believes that the social practice *constitutes* a rule which the normative judgment accepts; in fact the social practice helps to *justify* a rule which the normative judgment states. The fact that a practice of removing hats in church exists justifies asserting a normative rule to that effect – not because the practice constitutes a rule which the normative judgment describes and endorses, but because the practice creates ways of giving offense and gives rise to expectations of the sort that are good grounds for asserting a duty to take off one's hat in church or for asserting a normative rule that one must.

The social rule theory fails because it insists that a practice must somehow have the same *content* as the rule that individuals assert in its name. But if we suppose simply that a practice may justify a rule, then while the rule so justified may have the same content as the practice, it may not; it may fall short of, or go beyond it. If we look at the relationship between social practice and normative claims in this way, then we can account, smoothly, for what the social rule theory labors to explain. If someone finds a social practice pointless, or silly, or insulting, he may believe that it does not even in principle justify asserting any duties or normative rules of conduct, and in that case he will say, not that it imposes a duty upon him which he rejects, but that, in spite of what others think, it imposes no duty at all.

If a community has a particular practice, moreover, like the no-hat-in-church practice, then it will be likely, rather than surprising, that members will assert different normative rules, each allegedly justified by that practice. They will disagree about whether babies must wear bonnets because they will differ about whether, all things considered, the fact of the practice justifies asserting that duty. Some may think that it does because they think that the practice as a whole establishes a form of insult or disrespect that can be committed vicariously by an infant's parents. Others may disagree, for a variety of reasons. It is true that they will frame their dispute, even in this trivial case, as a dispute over what 'the rule' about hats in church requires. But the reference is not to the rule that is constituted by common behavior, that is, a social rule, but the rule that is justified by common behavior, that is, a normative rule. They dispute precisely about what *that* rule is.

It may be that judicial duty is a case of conventional morality. It does not follow that some social rule states the limit, or even the threshold, of judicial duty. When judges cite the rule that they must follow the legislature, for example, they may be appealing to a normative rule that some social practice justifies, and they may disagree about the precise content of that normative rule in a way that does not represent merely a disagreement about the facts of other judges' behavior. The positivist may be right, but he must make out his case without the short-cut that the social rule theory tries to provide.

2. DO I REALLY DISAGREE WITH HART?

It has been suggested that my disagreement with positivism, at least in the form presented by Hart, is not really so broad as I have claimed. Perhaps I have shown that a sensible account of law would have a place for principles as well as rules. But nothing in Hart's theory seems to deny this. It is true that he speaks only about rules, but he does not define 'rule' in the limited way in which I define that term in Chapter 2, and he might therefore be understood, when he speaks of rules, to include principles as well as rules in a narrow sense. Perhaps I have shown that any fundamental test for law, if it is to include principles as well as rules of law, must be more complex than the examples Hart offers as specimens of a rule of recognition. But Hart says that the rule of recognition may be complex; that it may be composed, indeed, of several criteria arranged in a hierarchy. His simple examples – like the rule that what the Queen in Parliament enacts is law – are intended to be merely examples.

Where then does the disagreement lie? It is true that Chapter 2 appears to deny Hart's thesis, that every legal system has a fundamental test for law in the form of a rule of recognition. But, as Professor Sartorius points out, I cannot really mean that a legal system can exist which has no fundamental test for identifying rules and principles of law.[1] It was part of my argument that some principles must be considered as law, and therefore figure in judicial argument, while others may not. But if that is true, then there must be some sort of test that can be used to distinguish the two. So my statement that no such fundamental rule exists must be understood as meaning merely that the fundamental test must be too complex to state in a simple rule. But since Hart never argued that the fundamental rule must be a simple one, this point of difference is limited.

So runs the first of the objections I want to consider. When I wrote Chapter 2 I thought that the positivist's thesis, that a fundamental test for law exists in every legal system, was sufficiently clear as to need very little elaboration. I thought that any ambiguities could be resolved by taking Professor Hart's careful formulation of that thesis as an example. The objection I have just described convinces me that I was wrong in this, and I shall now try to repair the damage by stating more clearly what I take the positivists' claim to be, and how that claim differs from claims that I myself would want to make.

I shall start by setting out three different theses, each of which has something to do with the idea of a fundamental test for law. In describing these different theses, I shall make use of the distinction I made in the last section, the distinction between describing social behavior through the concept of a social rule, on the one hand, and asserting a normative position through the concept of a normative rule, on the other. (i) The first thesis holds that, in every nation which has a developed legal system, some *social* rule or set of social rules exists within the community of its judges and legal officials, which rules settle

---

[1] Sartorius, *op. cit.* at 155.

the limits of the judge's duty to recognize any other rule or principle as law. The thesis would hold for England, for example, if English judges as a group recognized a duty to take into account, when determining legal rights and obligations, only rules or principles enacted by Parliament, or laid down in judicial decisions, or established by long standing custom, and recognized, as a group, that they had no duty to take into account anything else. Hart advances this first thesis; in fact, his theory that a social rule of recognition exists in every legal system may be regarded as one of the most important contributions he has made to the positivist tradition. (ii) The second thesis holds that in every legal system some particular *normative* rule or principle, or complex set of these, is the proper standard for judges to use in identifying more particular rules or principles of law. Someone who accepts this second thesis might believe, for example, that in England judges have a duty to recognize only statutes, precedents and clear customs as law, whether or not they actually reach their decisions in that fashion. (iii) The third thesis holds that in each legal system most of the judges accept *some* normative rule or theory governing their duty to count other standards as legal standards. This thesis argues that if one studies the patterns of decisions of the various English judges, for example, one would find that each judge, more or less consciously, follows a particular rule designating certain exclusive sources of law, or a more complex theory stipulating how law is to be found. It would not follow from this thesis, though it might also be true, that the bulk of the English judges follow the *same* rule or theory; if they did, then the first thesis would also be true of England, at least, but not otherwise.

The disagreement between Hart and myself is about the first of these three theses. He proposes that thesis, and I deny it. The issue is important; upon it hinges the orthodox idea that legal standards can be distinguished in principle and as a group from moral or political standards. If the first thesis is right, then in every legal system some commonly-accepted test does exist for law, in the shape of a social rule, and this is enough to distinguish legal from moral rules and principles. But if the first thesis is false, then no such test exists.

It is not enough that some version of the second or third thesis might be sound. Suppose that I myself accept a normative theory of law of the sort contemplated by the second thesis. My theory, if it is not shared by everyone else, will include controversial provisions; it might include, for example, a controversial theory of precedent that argues that courts must give more weight to recent than to out-of-date precedents. I would then be required to support the claim that my view of precedent correctly states a judge's duty, and I could do so only by deploying a further theory about the point or value of the institution of precedent. My case for this further theory would no doubt depend on controversial principles of political morality, principles, for example, about the proper place of a judiciary in a democracy. It is just this sort of dependence that positivism is most concerned to deny.

The distinctions I have drawn between these three different theses show why Sartorius's objection misses the point. He thinks that if I say that judges have a duty to use some principles but not others, or to assign a given weight to one principle but not a greater weight, it follows that I myself am committed to the idea that there is a fundamental test for law. It does follow that I am committed to some version of the second thesis, that is, that I myself think that a persuasive case can be made in support of one theory rather than some other about how judges must decide hard cases. But it does not follow that I must accept the first thesis, that some social rule exists among judges that settles that issue. That is Hart's thesis, but it is not, nor need it be, mine.

However, one feature of Hart's theory suggests that I attribute to him too rigid a theory. He is careful to say that a social rule of recognition might be uncertain in some cases, so that it does not settle every issue that might arise about what counts as law.[1] It is enough, for such a rule to exist, that it settles most such issues. He gives this example. There is no doubt, he says, that it is at least part of the rule of recognition of England that whatever Parliament enacts is law. It is nevertheless uncertain whether Parliament now has the power to bind future Parliaments, as it might try to do if, for example, it adopted a particular rule of law, and then entrenched both that rule and the entrenching provision by providing that neither could be repealed except by a two-thirds majority. If this happened, judges might well be divided as to the legal consequences of an attempt by a future Parliament to repeal these rules by a simple majority. If judges were so divided, this would show that the rule of recognition is uncertain on this point, and the issue could only then be settled, and the rule of recognition clarified, if some court made the decision one way or the other, and turned out to have the political power to make its decision stick.

So Hart, it might seem, is not committed to the notion that in every legal system some social rule exists that settles all issues of which standards count as law. It is enough to establish the first thesis, he might say, that a social rule is treated as *governing* all decisions of law, even though it is not so precise that what it requires is never open to dispute. He might then add that when judges are in fact divided (as they would be about entrenchment, or, to continue my own example, about the force

[1] Hart, *op. cit.* at 144.

to be given to older precedents) they reveal an area of uncertainty within a social rule that is for the most part certain.

But Hart's qualification, that the rule of recognition may be uncertain at particular points, does not simply add flexibility and sophistication to his theory. On the contrary, it undermines it, for reasons I tried to make plain in the last section. It simply does not fit the concept of a social rule, as Hart uses that concept, to say that a social rule may be uncertain in the sense that Hart now has in mind. If judges are in fact divided about what they must do if a subsequent Parliament tries to repeal an entrenched rule, then it is not uncertain whether any social rule governs that decision; on the contrary, it is certain that none does. The example simply shows that the statement, that in England a social rule exists among judges to the effect that whatever Parliament enacts is law, is strictly speaking inaccurate, though it might be accurate enough for most purposes.

A careful statement of the position, using the concept of a social rule, would have to be made along these lines. A social rule exists among judges to the effect that whatever Parliament enacts, short of a law purporting to bind future Parliaments, is law. No social rule exists on the issue of whether Parliament can bind future Parliaments; on this issue judges are divided. Some think that it can, and that they therefore have a duty not to recognize any purported repeal of an entrenched rule as law. Others think that it cannot and that they therefore have a duty to recognize repealing legislation as law. (This simple formulation ignores the more complex positions that different judges might in fact take.)

But, of course, putting the matter that way offers a counter-example to the claim of the first thesis, that some social rule always exists that stipulates necessary and sufficient conditions for what judges must recognize as law. If such disagreements among judges were limited only to extraordinary and rare cases, like entrenchment clauses, then such counter-examples would be few, and offer no real impediment to the claim. But if, as I suppose, disagreements among judges of this sort are very frequent, and indeed can be found whenever appellate tribunals attempt to decide difficult or controversial cases, then the general weakness this argument discloses is fatal.

It might now be said that I take too literally Hart's statement that the rule of recognition is a social rule constituted by the common behavior of the members of a particular community, like judges and other officials. He might want to revise that strict concept in the manner I suggested in the last section, to say that a rule of recognition exists as a social rule when judges accept a particular verbal formulation of their duty, like the verbal formulation, 'Whatever Parliament enacts is law'. If so, then

Hart may say that a social rule of recognition exists, but is nevertheless uncertain, when members of the community disagree about the proper application of that verbal formulation to particular cases. So the rule of recognition, that whatever Parliament does is law, exists as a social fact, but it is uncertain to the degree that judges disagree over particular cases like the case of entrenched statutes.

But this revision of the concept, as I said earlier, places too much weight upon accidents of language and history. The present example confirms this. It may be conventional to say that whatever Parliament enacts is law. But it is hardly possible to frame the disagreement about entrenched statutes as a disagreement about the proper interpretation of terms within that conventional formulation. No one would say that the controversy was over the meaning of 'whatever' or what force should be given to the term 'enacts'. Nor can many of the more pedestrian and numerous controversies I had in mind, like disagreement about the weight to be given to older precedents, be described as disagreements about the meaning of terms within some settled verbal formula.

Someone might take a different objection to my argument. He would remind me of the distinction I made on the last section, between statements about what judges ought to do and statements about what they have a duty to do. The first thesis does not claim that a social rule always exists that decides what judges *ought* to do in controversial cases like the entrenchment case. It claims only that a social rule stipulates what judges are *required* to do in such cases; the limit, that is, of their duties. If judges do disagree about whether to enforce a statute purporting to repeal an entrenched rule, the very fact of this disagreement, according to this objection, would show that judges have no duty either way. The matter would then be one that is left to their discretion, until some court, by the force of its decision one way or the other, encourages other judges to accept that decision as creating a duty.

If this were so, then the first thesis would be immune from the argument I made. But why should we suppose that it is so? The objection depends upon an assumption of moral philosophy. It assumes that duties cannot be controversial in principle. It assumes that if it is not plain what a judge's duty is, and not agreed what further evidence would decide the question, then he cannot have any duty, and we must only speak about what he ought to do. But that assumption is at least questionable. It does not square with the way we use the concept of duty in moral argument. The vegetarian need not accept that our duties are limited to what are uncontroversially or demonstrably our duties. It does not even square with how lawyers treat the issue of judicial duty. In the entrenchment clause dispute, for example, the one proposition that is common ground amongst the disputants is that the matter is not one in which judges are free to exercise discretion. Those who think that Parliament does have power to bind its successors believe that judges have no right to recognize a subsequent attempt at repeal. Those who believe that Parliament does not have this power believe that judges have a duty to recognize the subsequent repealer. It is true that some judges might be uncertain. But they are uncertain about their duties, not certain that they have none. Of course, if the strong version of the social rule theory were right, the assumption I described would be sound. But since that theory is false, some other support for the assumption must be found, and none, I think, can.

I hope that no one will want to say that in this sort of case judges are disagreeing about their political or moral duty as judges, but not about their legal duty. The only ground for this distinction is one which, in this context, plainly begs the question. The first thesis I distinguished is designed to explain the distinction the positivist draws between legal and other sorts of duties, and so it cannot assume that distinction. Hart himself says that the fundamental rule of recognition is a legal rule only in the sense in which the standard metre bar in Paris is one metre long;[1] if judges have a duty to enforce entrenchment clauses, that must be a legal duty in just that sense. But the question of terminology is beside the point. If judges may have a duty to apply some rule or principle in their determination of what the law requires, in spite of the fact that no social rule provides for that duty, then the first thesis is wrong, however that duty is described.

3. DOES 'INSTITUTIONAL SUPPORT' CONSTITUTE A RULE OF RECOGNITION?

In Chapter 2 I said that principles, like the principle that no man may profit from his own wrong, could not be captured by any simple rule of recognition, like the rule that what Parliament enacts is law. The positivist, I said, has this choice. He might argue that these principles are not part of the law, because the judge has no duty, but only a discretion, to take them into account. Or he might concede that they are law, and show how a more complicated social rule of recognition might be constructed that does capture such principles. Of course, the positivist might combine these strategies: he might argue that a more complex rule of recognition would capture some of the principles that judges cite, and then argue that judges have no duty to enforce any principles but these.

Dr Raz wishes to combine both strategies in that way. His principal

[1] Hart at 106.

reliance is on the argument, which I shall consider in the next section, that judges have a discretion, but no duty, to employ certain principles. But he believes that judges do have a duty to take into account at least some principles, and that these can be brought under something like a social rule of recognition, through the notion of what he calls a 'judicial custom'.[1] Suppose a particular principle is in fact cited by many judges over a period of time as a principle that must be taken into account. Then that very practice, he points out, would constitute a distinct social rule which would then stand, along with rules of recognition of the conventional sort that Hart had in mind, within a cluster of social rules that together provide a test for law.

But, for two reasons, this concept of judicial custom cannot carry the argument very far. First, the great bulk of the principles and policies judges cite are controversial, at least as to weight; the weight of the principle that no man may profit from his own wrong, for example, was sufficiently controversial to provoke a dissent in *Riggs v. Palmer*.[2] Second, a great many appeals to principle are appeals to principles that have not been the subject of any established judicial practice at all; this is true of several of the examples I gave from the decision in the *Henningsen* case, which included principles that had not in fact been formulated before, in anything like the same fashion, like the principle that automobile manufacturers have a special responsibility to the public.

So Raz's notion of judicial custom would not distinguish many of the principles that judges treat as principles they must take into account. We shall therefore have to consider very seriously his argument that judges in fact have no duty to give effect to principles that are not the subject of such a judicial custom. But first I want to consider a different and more complex idea of how the notion of a social rule of recognition can be adapted to capture principles as well as rules.

Professor Sartorius agrees with me in rejecting the idea that when judges appeal to principles in hard cases they do so in the exercise of some discretion.[3] If he wishes to embrace the first thesis I distinguished, therefore, he must describe a form of social rule that does in fact capture or at least provide for all these principles. This he attempts to do, and he proposes to use my own arguments against me. He admits that the development of a fundamental test for law would be extremely laborious, but he believes that it is in principle possible. He believes, further, that the nerve of any such ultimate test would lie in the concept of 'institutional support' that I developed in Chapter 2. He quotes the following passage from that chapter as authority for his own position:

[1] Raz at 852. Carrio at 25 uses the same term and concept.
[2] 115 N.Y. 506, 22 N.E. 188 (1889).
[3] Sartorius at 155.

[I]f we were challenged to back up our claim that some principle is a principle of law, we would mention any prior cases in which that principle was cited, or figured in the argument. We would also mention any statute that seemed to exemplify that principle (even better if the principle were cited in the preamble of the statute, or in the committee reports or other legislative documents that accompanied it). Unless we could find some such institutional support, we would probably fail to make out our case, and the more support we found the more weight we could claim for the principle.[1]

Of course Professor Sartorius would want to develop this doctrine of institutional support in much more detail than that. I myself should elaborate it in the following way,[2] and his article suggests that he might accept this elaboration. Suppose we were to gather together all the rules that are plainly valid rules of law in, for example, a particular American state, and add to these all the explicit rules about institutional competence that we relied upon in saying that the first set of rules were indeed valid rules of that jurisdiction. We would now have an imposing set of legal materials. We might then ask what set of principles taken together would be necessary to *justify* the adoption of the explicit rules of law and institutional rules we had listed. Suppose that each judge and lawyer of that state were to develop a 'theory of law' which described that set of principles and assigned relative weights to each (I ignore the fact that the labor of a lifetime would not be enough for a beginning). Each of them might then argue that his set of principles must count as principles of the legal system in question.

We might formulate the test for law that this story suggests in this way : a principle is a principle of law if it figures in the soundest theory of law that can be provided as a justification for the explicit substantive and institutional rules of the jurisdiction in question. Sartorius says, apparently with this sort of test in mind, that '[a]lthough perhaps it is a good way from Hart's version of positivism it is in accord with the fundamental positivist tenet as described by Dworkin, *viz.* that "the law of a community . . . can be identified and distinguished by specific criteria, by tests having to do not with . . . content but with . . . pedigree . . . " '.[3]

But some clarification is now needed. Sartorius could not mean that any particular lawyer's theory of law provides a *social* rule of recognition.

---

[1] *Id.* at 156, my Chapter 2 at 48.

[2] This elaboration is only a summary of the long argument of Chapter 4.

[3] Sartorius at 156, quoting my Chapter 2 at 17.

If I had developed a theory of law for a particular jurisdiction I might well hold that theory as a normative theory of judicial duty, in the spirit of the *second* thesis I distinguished. If most judges in the jurisdiction each had such a theory, then the *third* thesis would hold, for that jurisdiction. But each judge's theory would be more or less different from that of the next judge. Some of the principles he advanced would be different, and some of those that are the same would differ in weight. These differences insure that no one lawyer's theory can itself be taken as a complex social rule of the sort required by the *first* thesis.

So Sartorius must say, not that any particular lawyer's theory of law supplies a social rule of recognition, but rather that the test of institutional support *itself* is such a social rule. He might say, that is, that the social rule of recognition is just the rule that a principle must be applied as law if it is part of the soundest theory of law, and must be applied with the weight it is given by that theory. On this view, the different theories of law different lawyers would offer are simply different theories about how that social rule should be applied to particular cases.

But I do not see how one can put the matter that way, and still retain the idea that the test of institutional support provides 'specific criteria' of 'pedigree' rather than 'content'. The concept of a theory of law, in the way I described it, does not suppose that principles and policies explain the settled rules in the way in which a legal historian might explain them, by identifying the motives of those who adopted these rules, or by calling attention to the pressure groups which influenced their enactments. If a theory of law is to provide a basis for judicial duty, then the principles it sets out must try to *justify* the settled rules by identifying the political or moral concerns and traditions of the community which, in the opinion of the lawyer whose theory it is, do in fact support the rules. This process of justification must carry the lawyer very deep into political and moral theory, and well past the point where it would be accurate to say that any 'test' of 'pedigree' exists for deciding which of two different justifications of our political institutions is superior.

The simple example I gave earlier illustrates the point. If I disagree with another lawyer about the relative force to be given to older precedents, I will urge a theory of law that takes a view of the point of precedent that supports my case. I might say that the doctrine of precedent serves equality of treatment before the law, and that simplicity of treatment becomes less important and even perverse as the time elapsed between the two occasions increases. He might reply that the point of precedent is not so much equality as predictability of decision, which is best served by ignoring distinctions of age between precedents. Each of us will point to features of adjudication that support one view against the other. If one of us could find none, then, as I said in the quoted passage, his case would be weak. But the choice between our views will not depend only on the number of features each can find. It will depend as well on the moral case I can make for the duty of equal treatment that my argument presupposes, because the thesis that this duty justifies precedent assumes that the duty exists.

I do not mean to say that no basis can be found for choosing one theory of law over another. On the contrary, since I reject the doctrine of discretion described in the next section, I assume that persuasive arguments *can* be made to distinguish one theory as superior to another. But these arguments must include arguments on issues of normative political theory, like the nature of society's duty of equality, that go beyond the positivist's conception of the limits of the considerations relevant to deciding what the law is. The test of institutional support provides no mechanical or historical or morally neutral basis for establishing one theory of law as the soundest. Indeed, it does not allow even a single lawyer to distinguish a set of legal principles from his broader moral or political principles. His theory of law will usually include almost the full set of political and moral principles to which he subscribes; indeed it is hard to think of a single principle of social or political morality that has currency in his community and that he personally accepts, except those excluded by constitutional considerations, that would not find some place and have some weight in the elaborate scheme of justification required to justify the body of laws. So the positivist will accept the test of institutional settlement as filling the role of his ultimate test for law only at the cost of abandoning the rest of his script.

If that is so, then the consequences for legal theory are considerable. Jurisprudence poses the question: what is law? Most legal philosophers have tried to answer this question by distinguishing the *standards* that properly figure in arguments on behalf of legal rights and duties. But if no such exclusive list of standards can be made, then some other way of distinguishing legal rights and duties from other sorts of rights and duties must be found.

4. DO JUDGES HAVE TO HAVE DISCRETION?

I must now discuss, once again, the second of the two strategies for positivism that I distinguished at the beginning of the last section. This is the argument that when judges disagree about matters of principle they disagree not about what the law requires but about how their discretion should be exercised. They disagree, that is, not about where their duty to decide lies, but about how they ought to decide, all things considered, given that they have no duty to decide either way.

I tried to explain, in my original article, that this argument in fact depends upon a kind of ambiguity in the concept of discretion. We use that concept, in discussions about duty, in three different ways. First, we say that a man has discretion if his duty is defined by standards that reasonable men can interpret in different ways, as a sergeant has discretion if he is told to take the five most experienced men on patrol. Second, we say that a man has discretion if his decision is final, in the sense that no higher authority may review and set aside that decision, as when the decision whether a player is offside is left to the discretion of the linesman. Third, we say that a man has discretion when some set of standards which impose duties upon him do not in fact purport to impose any duty as to a particular decision, as when a clause in a lease gives the tenant the option in his discretion to renew.

It is plain that if no social rule unambiguously requires a particular legal decision, and the profession is split on what decision is in fact required, then judges will have discretion in the first of these senses, because they will have to exercise initiative and judgment beyond the application of a settled rule. It is also plain, if these judges form the highest court of appeal, that they will have discretion in the second sense. But, unless we accept the strongest form of the social rule theory, that duties and responsibilities can be generated only by social rules, it does not follow that these judges have discretion in the third sense. A judge may have discretion in both the first and second senses, and nevertheless properly regard his decision as raising an issue of what his duty as a judge is, an issue which he must decide by reflecting on what is required of him by the varying considerations that he believes are pertinent. If so, then this judge does not have discretion in the third sense, which is the sense a positivist needs to establish if he is to show that judicial duty is defined exclusively by an ultimate social rule or set of social rules.

Raz was not persuaded by my argument.[1] He repeats the distinction that I drew among these three senses of discretion, but having repeated that distinction he ignores it. He apparently thinks that I meant to argue as follows. (i) Judges have no discretion with respect to a decision when they all agree that a particular set of principles is decisive. (ii) That is sometimes the case even when no rule of law settles the case. (iii) Therefore it is never the case that judges have discretion when no rule settles the case.

That is a fallacious argument; fortunately it is not mine. Judges are

---

[1] Raz at 843 ff. See MacCallum, *loc. cit.*

sometimes united on a set of principles. But even when they are divided on principles they sometimes treat the issue as one of judicial responsibility, that is, as one that raises the question of what, as judges, they have a duty to do. In such a case they have discretion in the first sense I distinguished, but that is irrelevant. They nevertheless do not believe they have discretion in the third sense, which is the sense that counts.

Why should Raz ignore the distinctions I drew? He supposes that there are features of any legal system that have this consequence: If judges have discretion in the first sense, because no social rule directly or indirectly dictates the result they must reach, then they must also have discretion in the third sense, so that their decision cannot be a matter of judicial duty. Judges may be mistaken in this: they may inappropriately use the language of duty. But we must not, as Raz says, perpetuate mistakes just because they are popular. Still, it is necessary to show that they are mistakes, and Raz does not. What arguments might he make?

Raz's inclination, to convert discretion in the first into discretion in the third sense, is extraordinarily common among legal philosophers.[1] We must try to diagnose its source. When a judge faces a difficult decision he must suppose, before beginning his research, that there are in principle these three possibilities. The set of standards that he must take into account, taken together, require him to decide for the plaintiff, or require him to decide for the defendant, or require neither decision but permit either one. He must also recognize that he might be to some degree uncertain which of these three possibilities in fact holds; in that case he must decide on the basis of the case that seems to him the strongest. But that uncertainty might apply just as much to the third possibility as to the other two; the law might grant him a discretion, in the third sense, to reach either decision, but whether it does is a matter of what the legal materials, taken together, come to, and one may be as uncertain whether the materials justify *that* conclusion as either of the other two.

Raz apparently thinks that if it is uncertain whether the first or the second possibility is realized, then it follows that the third is. He thinks, that is, that if a judge is uncertain whether to decide for the plaintiff or defendant it follows that he should be certain that he has discretion to decide for either. I can think of only two arguments to support that extraordinary conclusion.

The first depends on the assumption of moral philosophy I described earlier, that duties cannot be controversial in principle. Raz makes that assumption, because he argues from the fact that judges may disagree

[1] It is displayed in all the articles referred to in note 6.

about principles, and particularly about their weight, to the conclusion that judges must have discretion in the sense I deny. That is a non sequitur unless something like that assumption holds, but we have no reason to suppose that it does, as I said, once we reject the strong version of the social rule theory.

The second argument relies on a different assumption, namely that every legal system contains a rule of decision which provides affirmatively that judges have discretion in hard cases. Some legal systems may employ such a rule. But the English and American systems do not. They contain no such explicit rule, nor as Raz agrees, does judicial behavior show that any such rule is recognized implicitly.

On the contrary, for us the proposition that judges have discretion in the third sense on some issue or other is a proposition that must be established affirmatively, on the balance of argument, and not simply by default. Sometimes judges do reach that conclusion; for example, when passing sentences under criminal statutes that provide a maximum and minimum penalty, or when framing equitable relief under a general equity jurisdiction. In such cases judges believe that no one has a right to any particular decision; they identify their task as selecting the decision that is best on the whole, all things considered, and here they talk not about what they must do but about what they should do. In most hard cases, however, judges take the different posture I described. They frame their disagreement as a disagreement about what standards they are forbidden or obliged to take into account, or what relative weights they are obliged to attribute to these, on the basis of arguments like the arguments I described in the last section illustrating the theory of institutional support. In such cases, some judges argue for the first possibility I mentioned, others for the second and others are undecided; but all exclude the third. There is plainly not even the beginnings of a social rule that converts the discretion that requires judgment into the discretion that excludes duty.

5. ARE RULES REALLY DIFFERENT FROM PRINCIPLES?

In Chapter 2 I distinguished rules from principles by distinguishing the different force that the two types of standards have in argument. My purpose was twofold: first, to call attention to a distinction which I thought was of importance in understanding how lawyers reason, and second, to call attention to the fact that some of the standards to which judges and lawyers appeal pose special problems for positivism, because these standards cannot be captured under a fundamental test for law like Hart's rule of recognition. These two purposes were distinct; even if the particular logical distinction that I claim between rules and principles can be shown to be spurious, it might still be that standards like those I mentioned, however identified, and whether or not classified as rules, cannot be captured by any such test. If I do not succeed in establishing my distinction between rules and principles, therefore, it by no means follows that the general argument I make against legal positivism is undermined.

Nevertheless, I do continue to think that the distinction that I drew between rules and principles is both genuine and important, and I should want to defend it. I do not mean, of course, that it is wrong to draw other sorts of distinctions among types of legal standards, or even that it is wrong or confusing to use the terms 'rule' and 'principle' to make these distinctions rather than the one I drew.

Raz's chief objection to my distinction might be put this way.[1] I argued that principles, like those I mentioned, conflict and interact with one another, so that each principle that is relevant to a particular legal problem provides a reason arguing in favor of, but does not stipulate, a particular solution. The man who must decide the problem is therefore required to assess all of the competing and conflicting principles that bear upon it, and to make a resolution of these principles rather than identifying one among others as 'valid'. Raz wishes to argue that it is not simply principles that properly conflict with one another in this way, but rules as well, and he believes that this fact undermines the distinction that I have drawn. He offers examples from both moral and legal argument. I shall consider each set of examples in turn.

Raz has it in mind that a man might accept, as moral rules for the guidance of his conduct, both the rule that one must never tell a lie and the rule that one must always keep his promises. He points out that on particular occasions these two rules might conflict, and require the man who accepts them both to choose between them on the basis of which under the circumstances has the greater weight, or importance, or on some other basis. He concludes that moral rules follow the logic that I described for principles, that is, that they point in one direction though they are not necessarily decisive of any moral issue.

But, in the first place, though it is possible that a man might accept moral rules for the guidance of his conduct in the way this argument assumes, it is far from the case that most men who take morality seriously do anything of the sort. For most people moral argument or decision is a matter of giving reasons for or against the morality of a certain course of conduct, rather than appealing to rules set down in advance whether by social or individual decision. It is true that a moral man may find himself in difficulty when he must choose between telling a lie or break-

---

[1] It is developed in Raz at 829 ff.

ing a promise, but it does not follow that he has accepted rules which come into conflict over the issue. He might simply have recognized that telling lies and breaking promises are both in principle wrong.

Of course we might describe his predicament by saying that he was forced to choose between two moral standards, even if he would not put the matter that way himself. But in that case, if we use the distinction I made, we should say that he was forced to resolve competing principles, not rules, because that would be the more accurate way of describing his situation. He recognizes that no moral consideration is by itself of overwhelming and overriding effect, and that any reason that counts against an act may in some circumstances have to yield to a competing consideration. Any philosopher or sociologist who wants to report his moral practices in terms of a code of standards must therefore say that for him morality is a matter of principle and not of rule.

But it is possible that some man might accept a moral rule for the guidance of his conduct in the way that Raz supposes. He might say, for example, that he has undertaken a personal commitment never to tell a lie. If he can accept one flat moral rule in this way, then he can accept others, and these may conflict in the way the example supposes. It would then be wrong to say, using my distinction, that this man has simply accepted a set of principles which might in principle conflict, because that wrongly describes his attitudes towards the several commitments he believes he has made. He believes he is committed to his different standards as rules, that is, as propositions which demand a particular course of conduct in the circumstances they name.

But I did not deny, in my original article, that conflicts in rules might exist. I said that in our legal system such conflicts would be occasions of emergency, occasions requiring a decision that would alter the set of standards in some dramatic way. Indeed this description fits the present non-legal example as well. Our moral hero, if he understands at all the concepts he has been using, cannot continue to say, after he has resolved his conflict, that he has been following both of his standards as flat rules. If he still wishes to present his morality as a consistent code, he may amend one or both of them to provide for the conflict, or he may revise his attitude towards one or both so as to convert them from rules into principles. He may do neither, but rather, when a conflict appears, announce himself to be in a state of moral dilemma, and do nothing, or flip a coin or decide in some other irrational way that the legal system does not permit. In any case, the distinction between rules and principles that I drew, so far from being called into question by the behavior of this unusual man, is in fact needed to explain it.

Raz takes his other examples from law. He calls our attention, for example, to rules of criminal law like the rule that prohibits an assault; this rule, he says, is in conflict with another rule which permits assault in self defense. Here, he concludes, we have two legal rules, both of them plainly valid, which are in conflict with one another. He believes that in particular cases, when these two rules do conflict, as they will when someone commits an assault in self defense, it is necessary for the judge to weigh the rules and decide to apply the more important, which will always be the rule that permits an assault in self defense. He offers this as an example of two rules which conflict acceptably, and with no sense of emergency, in the way that I said rules do not.

But this example surely rests on a bizarre notion of what a conflict is. If a criminal code contains a general rule to the effect that no one shall be criminally liable for an act committed in self defense, then that rule does not conflict with particular rules defining particular crimes, even if these particular rules make no mention of self defense. The general rule about self defense must be read to mean that notwithstanding the particular rules of criminal law, no act shall be a crime if committed in self defense. Indeed, rules providing general defenses are often drafted in just this way, but even when they are not, they are understood in that way. But a rule that provides an exception to another rule is not in conflict with that other rule, at least not in the sense that if a man accused of assault has proved a case of self-defense, the judge is then faced with two rules pulling in opposite directions, which he has somehow to weigh against one another in reaching his decision. The two rules taken together determine the result in a manner which does not require the judge to choose between them, or to determine their relative importance.

Why should Raz suppose that two rules are in conflict even when one has plainly the force of an exception to the other? The answer lies, I think, in what he says about the individuation of laws.[1] He supposes that I would want to answer his point, that the rule prohibiting assault conflicts with the rule permitting assault in self defense, by arguing that these two rules are really part of the same rule. He says that I could do that only at the price of accepting an unacceptable theory about the individuation of laws, and, anticipating such a mistake on my part, he says that I pay insufficient attention to the general problem of the individuation of laws. In this he is too generous for it would be more accurate to say that I pay no attention to that problem at all. I did not in fact rely upon the argument that a rule and its exception really count as one rule, but neither would I be disposed to argue that they must be in reality two rules.

---

[1] Raz at 825 ff.

Raz is of two minds about his theory of individuation of laws. Sometimes he treats a theory of individuation as a strategy of exposition, that is to say, a theory about the most illuminating way in which the legal system of a nation may be described. Plainly, the author of a textbook on criminal law, for example, needs a strategy of exposition. He needs to distinguish the doctrine of *mens rea* from the doctrine of necessity and to distinguish both of these general doctrines from the more particular rules which they cut across as qualifications and exemptions. But of course, though some strategies of exposition might be perverse or misguided, because they describe the law in an unmanageable or unassimilable form, a great many different strategies might be more or less equally competent.

At other times, however, Raz seems to think that the problem of individuation of laws has to do, not with any strategy of explaining what the law is to students or lawyers, but with the more philosophical question of what law is. He says that it is a problem about the formal structure of the law, which is of importance to the legal philosopher, and not to the author of a text. He poses the central problem in this way: 'What is to count as one complete law?', and he adopts Bentham's elaboration of this question. 'What is a law? What the part of a law? The subject of these questions, it is to be observed, is the *logical*, the *ideal*, the *intellectual* whole, not the *physical* one . . .'[1]

This sort of question carries us very far away from techniques of legal exposition: it carries us to the point at which, as Dr. Raz insists, theories of law may rise or fall depending upon the right answer to the question, 'What is to count as one complete law?'[2] That seems to me much too far. Suppose that you have read a long book about geology, and I ask you to tell me what information it contains. You will do so in a series of propositions of fact. But now suppose I ask you first how many propositions of fact the book contains, and what theory you used in counting them. You would think me mad, not simply because the question is preposterously difficult, as if I had asked you how many separate grains of sand there were in a particular beach, or because it requires a difficult conceptual discrimination, as if I had asked you how many human beings there were in a group that included a woman in early pregnancy. You would think me mad because I had asked entirely the wrong sort of question about the material at hand. The book contains a great deal of information; propositions are ways of presenting that information, but the number of propositions used will depend on considerations independent of the content of the information,

---

[1] Raz at 825.
[2] Raz at 825, 827-8.

such as, for example, whether one uses the general term 'rocks' or the names of particular sorts of rocks.

In the same way, lawyers use rules and principles to report legal information, and it is wrong to suppose that any particular statement of these is canonical. This is true even of what we call statutory rules, because it is a commonplace that lawyers will often misrepresent the rules that a statute enacted if they simply repeat the language that the statute used. Two lawyers might summarize the effect of a particular statute using different words, and one might use more rules than another; they might still both be saying the same thing.

My point was not that 'the law' contains a fixed number of standards, some of which are rules and others principles. Indeed, I want to oppose the idea that 'the law' is a fixed set of standards of any sort. My point was rather that an accurate summary of the considerations lawyers must take into account, in deciding a particular issue of legal rights and duties, would include propositions having the form and force of principles, and that judges and lawyers themselves, when justifying their conclusions, often use propositions which must be understood in that way. Nothing in this, I believe, commits me to a legal ontology that assumes any particular theory of individuation.

I did say that a 'full' statement of a legal rule would include its exceptions, and that a statement of a rule that neglected the exceptions would be 'incomplete'. I would not have put the point that way had I been aware of Raz's objection. I would have made plain that an exception can be stated in the form of a distinct rule, like the rule about self-defense, as well as in the form of a revised statement of the original rule. But if I had I would also have made plain that the difference is largely a matter of exposition. The distinction between rules and principles remains untouched. I might summarize a body of law by stating a rule, like the rule that an assault is a crime, and a list of established exceptions. If my summary is complete then anyone who commits an assault is guilty of a crime unless an exception I stated applies; if he is not guilty, then either I was wrong or the law has changed. It is otherwise in the case of a principle. Suppose I say that in principle someone may not profit from his own wrong but someone does. My statement need not be corrected, or even brought up-to-date, because someone may properly profit from his own wrong, as these terms must be understood, not only when a recognized exception applies, but when special features of his case invoke some other, newly-recognized, principle or policy that makes a difference.

It is his second, ontological, mood about the individuation of laws that leads Raz to his curious view about conflicts. If one takes seriously the idea that rules of law are in certain forms 'whole' and 'complete', then one may be tempted to think that whole and complete laws are also independent of one another, so that the rule defining assault must then be taken as a flat direction that men who do certain acts be punished. But if we take the statement of a rule of law as an attempt merely to describe the legal effect of certain institutional decisions, we are not tempted to suppose any such conflict. We shall then say merely that the rule about assault, like many of the rules about crimes, is subject to an exception in cases of self-defense; we shall not then worry about whether we have described one rule or two.

Raz has another argument against my distinction, which I do not fully understand. He argues that the distinction is undercut by the fact that rules may conflict with principles; the rules of adverse possession, for example, may be thought to conflict with the principle that no man may profit from his own wrong. I do not think it illuminating to describe the relationship between these rules and that principle as one of conflict. The fact that such rules exist, is, as I said, evidence that the principle about not profiting from one's wrong is indeed a principle and not a rule. If the rules of adverse possession are some day amended, either by explicit legislative enactment or by judicial reinterpretation, then one reason might be that the principle is then recognized as being more important than it was when the rules were adopted. Nevertheless, the rules governing adverse possession may even now be said to *reflect* the principle, rather than *conflict* with it, because these rules have a different shape than they would have had if the principle had not been given any weight in the decision at all. The long length of time generally required for acquiring title by adverse possession might have been much shorter, for example, had this not been thought to conflict with the principle. Indeed, one of my reasons for drawing the distinction between rules and principles was just to show how rules often represent a kind of compromise amongst competing principles in this way, and that point may be lost or submerged if we speak too freely about rules conflicting with principles.

In any event, I cannot see how this phenomenon casts doubt upon the distinction I want to draw between rules and principles. Raz thinks that it shows that rules as well as principles have weight, because he thinks that when rules and principles conflict a decision must be made as to which of them to prefer, and this decision must be made by assigning a weight to the rule which is then set against the weight of the principle. But this description surely misrepresents the interaction between rules and principles. Suppose a court decides to overrule an established common law rule that there can be no legal liability for negligent misstatements, and appeals to a number of principles to justify this decision, including the principle that it is unjust that one man suffer because of another man's wrong. The court must be understood as deciding that the set of principles calling for the overruling of the established rule, including the principle of justice just mentioned, are as a group of greater weight under the circumstances than the set of principles, including the principle of stare decisis, that call for maintaining the rule as before. The court weighs two sets of principles in deciding whether to maintain the rule; it is therefore misleading to say that the court weighs the rule itself against one or the other set of these principles. Indeed, when Raz describes the weighing of either a legal or a moral rule, he in fact talks about weighing the principles and policies that the rule serves, because that must be what he means when he speaks of the 'goal' of the rule.

I cannot reply to all the further points of detail Raz makes in his article, but I should like to comment briefly on some of them.

(1) Raz endorses a different distinction between rules and principles from the one I drew.[1] He prefers a distinction according to which rules prescribe relatively specific acts and principles relatively unspecific acts.[2] 'An act is highly unspecific,' Raz says, 'if it can be performed on different occasions by the performance of a great many heterogeneous generic acts on each occasion.'[3] But this is unsatisfactory, for he fails to specify, except by example, his criteria for the heterogeneity of 'generic acts', and his examples confuse rather than illuminate. He says that the proposition that one must keep one's promises is a rule, and he uses that proposition to illustrate his thesis that rules may conflict with one another. But the most varied sorts of acts can each, in different circumstances, be acts that keep promises, because anything that a man may do he may also promise to do. Raz says, on the other hand, that 'a law instructing the courts and all public officials to protect freedom of speech' would be a principle. But the acts that officials would be required to perform in the light of this principle would all be acts of giving orders or casting votes, and those would seem more homogeneous, and certainly not less homogeneous, than the acts they would be required to do to keep all their promises as individuals. Of course, all acts of promise-keeping are alike in being acts of promise-keeping. But all acts of protecting free speech or even promoting equality are alike in the same way. Whether a group of acts is homogeneous depends upon the description under which they are considered, and until Raz offers a theory of canonical description his distinction is one we cannot use.

---

[1] Raz at 838 ff.
[2] Raz at 838.
[3] *Ibid.*

(2) Raz is right that some statements that begin 'It is a principle of our law that . . .' should be understood as merely summaries of other standards.[4] But he is wrong in supposing that a court's reference to the principle of freedom of contract, for example in the *Henningsen* case I discussed, should be understood in that way. On the contrary, these references recognize the force of a principle in determining particular legal rights and duties, and attempt to assess and sometimes to limit that force.

(3) Raz misunderstands the point I made about the use of words like 'reasonable' in rules.[1] I did not mean that it was the function of such words to 'immunize the law' against general considerations embodied in certain principles.[2] I meant rather that it was their function to open rules to the effect of certain principles, but only certain principles. The rule that unreasonable restraints of trade are invalid remains a rule if every restraint that is unreasonable is invalid, even if other reasons for enforcing it, not mitigating its unreasonableness, might be found. The principle that Raz cites as on all fours with such a rule, that the courts generally refuse to enforce unjust bargains, is by its own terms different in that sense. This principle contemplates that unjust bargains may indeed be enforced when unusual circumstances require; for example, perhaps, when no other way to protect innocent third parties can be found. It would be otherwise if the legislature had enacted a rule that unjust bargains are void and unenforceable.

(4) Raz is right in supposing that very few large communities share a consistent code of moral beliefs, but he misunderstands those judges who appeal to community morality, whom he accuses of propagating a harmful fiction.[3] He fails to distinguish between two concepts of the moral standards of a community. That phrase may refer to a consensus of belief about a particular issue, as might be elicited by a Gallup poll. Or it may refer to moral principles that underlie the community's institutions and laws, in the sense that these principles would figure in a sound theory of law of the sort discussed earlier in this chapter. Whether a principle is a principle of the community in this sense would be a matter for argument, not report, though typically the weight of the principle, not its standing, would be at issue. The judges Raz criticizes use the concept in this second sense, though they sometimes do so in language that is consistent with the first. Raz mistakes their failure to notice a sophisticated distinc-

---

[1] Raz at 837-8.
[2] See Raz at 837.
[3] Raz at 850-1.
[4] Raz at 828-9.

tion for hypocrisy. Is it far-fetched to suppose that his own failure to notice that distinction reflects his reliance on the social rule theory? If the strong version of that theory were right then one could not argue that a community was committed to any morality of duty, by its traditions and institutions, except the morality recognized in its uniform social practices, which generally embrace little of much significance. This is, I think, the most important consequence of the social rule theory for jurisprudence, and the most compelling reason for insisting that that theory is wrong.

4

Hard Cases

I. INTRODUCTION

Legal positivism provides a theory of hard cases. When a particular lawsuit cannot be brought under a clear rule of law, laid down by some institution in advance, then the judge has, according to that theory, a 'discretion' to decide the case either way. His opinion is written in language that seems to assume that one or the other party had a pre-existing right to win the suit, but that idea is only a fiction. In reality he has legislated new legal rights, and then applied them retrospectively to the case at hand. In the last two chapters I argued that this theory of adjudication is wholly inadequate; in this chapter I shall describe and defend a better theory.

I shall argue that even when no settled rule disposes of the case, one party may nevertheless have a right to win. It remains the judge's duty, even in hard cases, to discover what the rights of the parties are, not to invent new rights retrospectively. I should say at once, however, that it is no part of this theory that any mechanical procedure exists for demonstrating what the rights of parties are in hard cases. On the contrary, the argument supposes that reasonable lawyers and judges will often disagree about legal rights, just as citizens and statesmen disagree about political rights. This chapter describes the questions that judges and lawyers must put to themselves, but it does not guarantee that they will all give these questions the same answer.

Some readers may object that, if no procedure exists, even in principle, for demonstrating what legal rights the parties have in hard cases, it follows that they have none. That objection presupposes a controversial thesis of general philosophy, which is that no proposition can be true unless it can, at least in principle, be demonstrated to be true. There is no reason to accept that thesis as part of a general theory of truth, and good reason to reject its specific application to propositions about legal rights.[1]

[1] See Chapter 13.

2. THE RIGHTS THESIS

A. Principles and policies

Theories of adjudication have become more sophisticated, but the most popular theories still put judging in the shade of legislation. The main outlines of this story are familiar. Judges should apply the law that other institutions have made; they should not make new law. That is the ideal, but for different reasons it cannot be realized fully in practice. Statutes and common law rules are often vague and must be interpreted before they can be applied to novel cases. Some cases, moreover, raise issues so novel that they cannot be decided even by stretching or reinterpreting existing rules. So judges must sometimes make new law, either covertly or explicitly. But when they do, they should act as deputy to the appropriate legislature, enacting the law that they suppose the legislature would enact if seized of the problem.

That is perfectly familiar, but there is buried in this common story a further level of subordination not always noticed. When judges make law, so the expectation runs, they will act not only as deputy to the legislature but as a deputy legislature. They will make law in response to evidence and arguments of the same character as would move the superior institution if it were acting on its own. This is a deeper level of subordination, because it makes any understanding of what judges do in hard cases parasitic on a prior understanding of what legislators do all the time. This deeper subordination is thus conceptual as well as political.

In fact, however, judges neither should be nor are deputy legislators, and the familiar assumption, that when they go beyond political decisions already made by someone else they are legislating, is misleading. It misses the importance of a fundamental distinction within political theory, which I shall now introduce in a crude form. This is the distinction between arguments of principle on the one hand and arguments of policy on the other.[1]

Arguments of policy justify a political decision by showing that the decision advances or protects some collective goal of the community as a whole. The argument in favor of a subsidy for aircraft manufacturers, that the subsidy will protect national defense, is an argument of policy. Arguments of principle justify a political decision by showing that the decision respects or secures some individual or group right. The argument in favor of anti-discrimination statutes, that a minority has a right to equal respect and concern, is an argument of principle. These two

---

[1] I discussed the distinction between principles and policies in Chapter 2. The more elaborate formulation in this chapter is an improvement: among other virtues it prevents the collapse of the distinction under the (artificial) assumptions described in the earlier chapter.

sorts of argument do not exhaust political argument. Sometimes, for example, a political decision, like the decision to allow extra income tax exemptions for the blind, may be defended as an act of public generosity or virtue rather than on grounds of either policy or principle. But principle and policy are the major grounds of political justification.

The justification of a legislative program of any complexity will ordinarily require both sorts of argument. Even a program that is chiefly a matter of policy, like a subsidy program for important industries, may require strands of principle to justify its particular design. It may be, for example, that the program provides equal subsidies for manufacturers of different capabilities, on the assumption that weaker aircraft manufacturers have some right not to be driven out of business by government intervention, even though the industry would be more efficient without them. On the other hand, a program that depends chiefly on principle, like an antidiscrimination program, may reflect a sense that rights are not absolute and do not hold when the consequences for policy are very serious. The program may provide, for example, that fair employment practice rules do not apply when they might prove especially disruptive or dangerous. In the subsidy case we might say that the rights conferred are generated by policy and qualified by principle; in the antidiscrimination case they are generated by principle and qualified by policy.

It is plainly competent for the legislature to pursue arguments of policy and to adopt programs that are generated by such arguments. If courts are deputy legislatures, then it must be competent for them to do the same. Of course, unoriginal judicial decisions that merely enforce the clear terms of some plainly valid statute are always justified on arguments of principle, even if the statute itself was generated by policy. Suppose an aircraft manufacturer sues to recover the subsidy that the statute provides. He argues his right to the subsidy; his argument is an argument of principle. He does not argue that the national defense would be improved by subsidizing him; he might even concede that the statute was wrong on policy grounds when it was adopted, or that it should have been repealed, on policy grounds, long ago. His right to a subsidy no longer depends on any argument of policy because the statute made it a matter of principle.

But if the case at hand is a hard case, when no settled rule dictates a decision either way, then it might seem that a proper decision could be generated by either policy or principle. Consider, for example, the problem of the recent *Spartan Steel* case.[1] The defendant's employees had broken an electrical cable belonging to a power company that supplied power to the plaintiff, and the plaintiff's factory was shut down

[1] *Spartan Steel & Alloys Ltd. v. Martin & Co.*, [1973] 1 Q.B. 27.

while the cable was repaired. The court had to decide whether to allow the plaintiff recovery for economic loss following negligent damage to someone else's property. It might have proceeded to its decision by asking either whether a firm in the position of the plaintiff had a right to a recovery, which is a matter of principle, or whether it would be economically wise to distribute liability for accidents in the way the plaintiff suggested, which is a matter of policy.

If judges are deputy legislators, then the court should be prepared to follow the latter argument as well as the former, and decide in favor of the plaintiff if that argument recommends. That is, I suppose, what is meant by the popular idea that a court must be free to decide a novel case like *Spartan Steel* on policy grounds; and indeed Lord Denning described his own opinion in that case in just that way.[1] I do not suppose he meant to distinguish an argument of principle from an argument of policy in the technical way I have, but he in any event did not mean to rule out an argument of policy in that technical sense.

I propose, nevertheless, the thesis that judicial decisions in civil cases, even in hard cases like *Spartan Steel*, characteristically are and should be generated by principle not policy. That thesis plainly needs much elaboration, but we may notice that certain arguments of political theory and jurisprudence support the thesis even in its abstract form. These arguments are not decisive, but they are sufficiently powerful to suggest the importance of the thesis, and to justify the attention that will be needed for a more careful formulation.

B. Principles and democracy

The familiar story, that adjudication must be subordinated to legislation, is supported by two objections to judicial originality. The first argues that a community should be governed by men and women who are elected by and responsible to the majority. Since judges are, for the most part, not elected, and since they are not, in practice, responsible to the electorate in the way legislators are, it seems to compromise that proposition when judges make law. The second argues that if a judge makes new law and applies it retroactively in the case before him, then the losing party will be punished, not because he violated some duty he had, but rather a new duty created after the event.

These two arguments combine to support the traditional ideal that adjudication should be as unoriginal as possible. But they offer much more powerful objections to judicial decisions generated by policy than to those generated by principle. The first objection, that law should be made by elected and responsible officials, seems unexceptionable when

[1] *Ibid.* 36.

we think of law as policy; that is, as a compromise among individual goals and purposes in search of the welfare of the community as a whole. It is far from clear that interpersonal comparisons of utility or preference, through which such compromises might be made objectively, make sense even in theory; but in any case no proper calculus is available in practice. Policy decisions must therefore be made through the operation of some political process designed to produce an accurate expression of the different interests that should be taken into account. The political system of representative democracy may work only indifferently in this respect, but it works better than a system that allows nonelected judges, who have no mail bag or lobbyists or pressure groups, to compromise competing interests in their chambers.

The second objection is also persuasive against a decision generated by policy. We all agree that it would be wrong to sacrifice the rights of an innocent man in the name of some new duty created after the event; it does, therefore, seem wrong to take property from one individual and hand it to another in order just to improve overall economic efficiency. But that is the form of the policy argument that would be necessary to justify a decision in *Spartan Steel*. If the plaintiff had no right to the recovery and the defendant no duty to offer it, the court could be justified in taking the defendant's property for the plaintiff only in the interest of wise economic policy.

But suppose, on the other hand, that a judge successfully justifies a decision in a hard case, like *Spartan Steel*, on grounds not of policy but of principle. Suppose, that is, that he is able to show that the plaintiff has a *right* to recover its damages. The two arguments just described would offer much less of an objection to the decision. The first is less relevant when a court judges principle, because an argument of principle does not often rest on assumptions about the nature and intensity of the different demands and concerns distributed throughout the community. On the contrary, an argument of principle fixes on some interest presented by the proponent of the right it describes, an interest alleged to be of such a character as to make irrelevant the fine discriminations of any argument of policy that might oppose it. A judge who is insulated from the demands of the political majority whose interests the right would trump is, therefore, in a better position to evaluate the argument.

The second objection to judicial originality has no force against an argument of principle. If the plaintiff has a right against the defendant, then the defendant has a corresponding duty, and it is that duty, not some new duty created in court, that justifies the award against him. Even if the duty has not been imposed upon him by explicit prior legislation, there is, but for one difference, no more injustice in enforcing the duty than if it had been.

The difference is, of course, that if the duty had been created by statute the defendant would have been put on much more explicit notice of that duty, and might more reasonably have been expected to arrange his affairs so as to provide for its consequences. But an argument of principle makes us look upon the defendant's claim, that it is unjust to take him by surprise, in a new light. If the plaintiff does indeed have a right to a judicial decision in his favor, then he is entitled to rely upon that right. If it is obvious and uncontroversial that he has the right, the defendant is in no position to claim unfair surprise just because the right arose in some way other than by publication in a statute. If, on the other hand, the plaintiff's claim is doubtful, then the court must, to some extent, surprise one or another of the parties; and if the court decides that on balance the plaintiff's argument is stronger, then it will also decide that the plaintiff was, on balance, more justified in his expectations. The court may, of course, be mistaken in this conclusion; but that possibility is not a consequence of the originality of its argument, for there is no reason to suppose that a court hampered by the requirement that its decisions be unoriginal will make fewer mistakes of principle than a court that is not.

C. Jurisprudence

We have, therefore, in these political considerations, a strong reason to consider more carefully whether judicial arguments cannot be understood, even in hard cases, as arguments generated by principle. We have an additional reason in a familiar problem of jurisprudence. Lawyers believe that when judges make new law their decisions are constrained by legal traditions but are nevertheless personal and original. Novel decisions, it is said, reflect a judge's own political morality, but also reflect the morality that is embedded in the traditions of the common law, which might well be different. This is, of course, only law school rhetoric, but it nevertheless poses the problem of explaining how these different contributions to the decision of a hard case are to be identified and reconciled.

One popular solution relies on a spatial image; it says that the traditions of the common law contract the area of a judge's discretion to rely upon his personal morality, but do not entirely eliminate that area. But this answer is unsatisfactory on two grounds. First, it does not elucidate what is at best a provocative metaphor, which is that some morality is embedded in a mass of particular decisions other judges have reached in the past. Second, it suggests a plainly inadequate phenomenological account of the judicial decision. Judges do not decide hard cases in two stages, first checking to see where the institutional constraints end, and then setting the books aside to stride off on their own. The institutional constraints they sense are pervasive and endure to the decision itself. We therefore need an account of the interaction of personal and institutional morality that is less metaphorical and explains more successfully that pervasive interaction.

The rights thesis, that judicial decisions enforce existing political rights, suggests an explanation that is more successful on both counts. If the thesis holds, then institutional history acts not as a constraint on the political judgment of judges but as an ingredient of that judgment, because institutional history is part of the background that any plausible judgment about the rights of an individual must accommodate. Political rights are creatures of both history and morality : what an individual is entitled to have, in civil society, depends upon both the practice and the justice of its political institutions. So the supposed tension between judicial originality and institutional history is dissolved : judges must make fresh judgments about the rights of the parties who come before them, but these political rights reflect, rather than oppose, political decisions of the past. When a judge chooses between the rule established in precedent and some new rule thought to be fairer, he does not choose between history and justice. He rather makes a judgment that requires some compromise between considerations that ordinarily combine in any calculation of political right, but here compete.

The rights thesis therefore provides a more satisfactory explanation of how judges use precedent in hard cases than the explanation provided by any theory that gives a more prominent place to policy. Judges, like all political officials, are subject to the doctrine of political responsibility. This doctrine states, in its most general form, that political officials must make only such political decisions as they can justify within a political theory that also justifies the other decisions they propose to make. The doctrine seems innocuous in this general form; but it does, even in this form, condemn a style of political administration that might be called, following Rawls, intuitionistic.[1] It condemns the practice of making decisions that seem right in isolation, but cannot be brought within some comprehensive theory of general principles and policies that is consistent with other decisions also thought right. Suppose a Congressman votes to prohibit abortion, on the ground that human life in any form is sacred, but then votes to permit the parents of babies born deformed to withhold medical treatment that will keep such babies alive. He might say that he feels that there is some difference, but the principle of responsibility, strictly applied, will not allow him these two votes unless he can in corporate the difference within some general political theory he sincerely holds.

[1] See Chapter 10.

The doctrine demands, we might say, articulate consistency. But this demand is relatively weak when policies are in play. Policies are aggregative in their influence on political decisions and it need not be part of a responsible strategy for reaching a collective goal that individuals be treated alike. It does not follow from the doctrine of responsibility, therefore, that if the legislature awards a subsidy to one aircraft manufacturer one month it must award a subsidy to another manufacturer the next. In the case of principles, however, the doctrine insists on distributional consistency from one case to the next, because it does not allow for the idea of a strategy that may be better served by unequal distribution of the benefit in question. If an official, for example, believes that sexual liberty of some sort is a right of individuals, then he must protect that liberty in a way that distributes the benefit reasonably equally over the class of those whom he supposes to have the right. If he allows one couple to use contraceptives on the ground that this right would otherwise be invaded, then he must, so long as he does not recant that earlier decision, allow the next couple the same liberty. He cannot say that the first decision gave the community just the amount of sexual liberty it needed, so that no more is required at the time of the second.

Judicial decisions are political decisions, at least in the broad sense that attracts the doctrine of political responsibility. If the rights thesis holds, then the distinction just made would account, at least in a very general way, for the special concern that judges show for both precedents and hypothetical examples. An argument of principle can supply a justification for a particular decision, under the doctrine of responsibility, only if the principle cited can be shown to be consistent with earlier decisions not recanted, and with decisions that the institution is prepared to make in the hypothetical circumstances. That is hardly surprising, but the argument would not hold if judges based their decisions on arguments of policy. They would be free to say that some policy might be adequately served by serving it in the case at bar, providing, for example, just the right subsidy to some troubled industry, so that neither earlier decisions nor hypothetical future decisions need be understood as serving the same policy.

Consistency here, of course, means consistency in the application of the principle relied upon, not merely in the application of the particular rule announced in the name of that principle. If, for example, the principle that no one has the duty to make good remote or unexpected losses flowing from his negligence is relied upon to justify a decision for the defendant in *Spartan Steel*, then it must be shown that the rule laid down in other cases, which allows recovery for negligent misstatements, is consistent with that principle; not merely that the rule about negligent misstatement is a different rule from the rule in *Spartan Steel*.

D. *Three problems*

We therefore find, in these arguments of political theory and jurisprudence, some support for the rights thesis in its abstract form. Any further defense, however, must await a more precise statement. The thesis requires development in three directions. It relies, first, on a general distinction between individual rights and social goals, and that distinction must be stated with more clarity than is provided simply by examples. The distinction must be stated, moreover, so as to respond to the following problem. When politicians appeal to individual rights, they have in mind grand propositions about very abstract and fundamental interests, like the right to freedom or equality or respect. These grand rights do not seem apposite to the decision of hard cases at law, except, perhaps, constitutional law; and even when they are apposite they seem too abstract to have much argumentative power. If the rights thesis is to succeed, it must demonstrate how the general distinction between arguments of principle and policy can be maintained between arguments of the character and detail that do figure in legal argument. In Section 3 of this chapter I shall try to show that the distinction between abstract and concrete rights, suitably elaborated, is sufficient for that purpose.

The thesis provides, second, a theory of the role of precedent and institutional history in the decision of hard cases. I summarized that theory in the last section, but it must be expanded and illustrated before it can be tested against our experience of how judges actually decide cases. It must be expanded, moreover, with an eye to the following problem. No one thinks that the law as it stands is perfectly just. Suppose that some line of precedents is in fact unjust, because it refuses to enforce, as a legal right, some political right of the citizens. Even though a judge deciding some hard case disapproves of these precedents for that reason, the doctrine of articulate consistency nevertheless requires that he allow his argument to be affected by them. It might seem that his argument cannot be an argument of principle, that is, an argument designed to establish the political rights of the parties, because the argument is corrupted, through its attention to precedent, by a false opinion about what these rights are. If the thesis is to be defended, it must be shown why this first appearance is wrong. It is not enough to say that the argument may be an argument of principle because it establishes the legal, as distinguished from the political, rights of the litigants. The rights thesis supposes that the right to win a law suit is a genuine political right, and though that right is plainly different from other forms of political rights, like the right of all citizens to be treated as equals, just noticing that difference does not explain why the former right may be altered by misguided earlier decisions. It is necessary, in order to understand that feature of legal argument, to consider the special qualities of institutional rights in general, which I consider in Section 4, and the particular qualities of legal rights, as a species of institutional rights, which I consider in Section 5.

But the explanation I give of institutional and legal rights exposes a third and different problem for the rights thesis. This explanation makes plain that judges must sometimes make judgments of political morality in order to decide what the legal rights of litigants are. The thesis may therefore be thought open, on that ground, to the first challenge to judicial originality that I mentioned earlier. It might be said that the thesis is indefensible because it cheats the majority of its right to decide questions of political morality for itself. I shall consider that challenge in Section 6.

These, then, are three problems that any full statement of the rights thesis must face. If that full statement shows these objections to the thesis misconceived, then it will show the thesis to be less radical than it might first have seemed. The thesis presents, not some novel information about what judges do, but a new way of describing what we all know they do; and the virtues of this new description are not empirical but political and philosophical.

3. RIGHTS AND GOALS

A. Types of rights

Arguments of principle are arguments intended to establish an individual right; arguments of policy are arguments intended to establish a collective goal. Principles are propositions that describe rights; policies are propositions that describe goals. But what are rights and goals and what is the difference? It is hard to supply any definition that does not beg the question. It seems natural to say, for example, that freedom of speech is a right, not a goal, because citizens are entitled to that freedom as a matter of political morality, and that increased munitions manufacture is a goal, not a right, because it contributes to collective welfare, but no particular manufacturer is entitled to a government contract. This does not improve our understanding, however, because the concept of entitlement uses rather than explains the concept of a right.

In this chapter I shall distinguish rights from goals by fixing on the distributional character of claims about rights, and on the force of these claims, in political argument, against competing claims of a different distributional character. I shall make, that is, a formal distinction that does not attempt to show which rights men and women actually have, or indeed that they have any at all. It rather provides a guide for discovering which rights a particular political theory supposes men and women to have. The formal distinction does suggest, of course, an approach to the more fundamental question : it suggests that we discover what rights people actually have by looking for arguments that would justify claims having the appropriate distributional character. But the distinction does not itself supply any such arguments.

I begin with the idea of a political aim as a generic political justification. A political theory takes a certain state of affairs as a political aim if, for that theory, it counts in favor of any political decision that the decision is likely to advance, or to protect, that state of affairs, and counts against the decision that it will retard or endanger it. A political right is an individuated political aim. An individual has a right to some opportunity or resource or liberty if it counts in favor of a political decision that the decision is likely to advance or protect the state of affairs in which he enjoys the right, even when no other political aim is served and some political aim is disserved thereby, and counts against that decision that it will retard or endanger that state of affairs, even when some other political aim is thereby served.[1] A goal is a nonindividuated political aim, that is, a state of affairs whose specification does not in this way call for any particular opportunity or resource or liberty for particular individuals.

Collective goals encourage trade-offs of benefits and burdens within a community in order to produce some overall benefit for the community as a whole. Economic efficiency is a collective goal : it calls for such distribution of opportunities and liabilities as will produce the greatest aggregate economic benefit defined in some way. Some conception of equality may also be taken as a collective goal; a community may aim at a distribution such that maximum wealth is no more than double minimum wealth, or, under a different conception, so that no racial or ethnic group is much worse off than other groups. Of course, any collective goal will suggest a particular distribution, given particular facts. Economic efficiency as a goal will suggest that a particular industry be subsidized in some circumstances, but taxed punitively in others. Equality as a goal will suggest immediate and complete redistribution in some circumstances, but partial and discriminatory redistribution in others. In each case distributional principles are subordinate to some conception of aggregate collective good, so that offering less of some benefit to one man can be justified simply by showing that this will lead to a greater benefit overall.

Collective goals may, but need not, be absolute. The community may

---

[1] I count legal persons as individuals, so that corporations may have rights; a political theory that counts special groups, like racial groups, as having some corporate standing within the community may therefore speak of group rights.

pursue different goals at the same time, and it may compromise one goal for the sake of another. It may, for example, pursue economic efficiency, but also military strength. The suggested distribution will then be determined by the sum of the two policies, and this will increase the permutations and combinations of possible trade-offs. In any case, these permutations and combinations will offer a number of competing strategies for serving each goal and both goals in combination. Economic efficiency may be well served by offering subsidies to all farmers, and to no manufacturers, and better served by offering double the subsidy to some farmers and none to others. There will be alternate strategies of pursuing any set of collective goals, and, particularly as the number of goals increases, it will be impossible to determine in a piecemeal or case-by-case way the distribution that best serves any set of goals. Whether it is good policy to give double subsidies to some farmers and none to others will depend upon a great number of other political decisions that have been or will be made in pursuit of very general strategies into which this particular decision must fit.

Rights also may be absolute : a political theory which holds a right to freedom of speech as absolute will recognize no reason for not securing the liberty it requires for every individual; no reason, that is, short of impossibility. Rights may also be less than absolute; one principle might have to yield to another, or even to an urgent policy with which it competes on particular facts. We may define the weight of a right, assuming it is not absolute, as its power to withstand such competition. It follows from the definition of a right that it cannot be outweighed by all social goals. We might, for simplicity, stipulate not to call any political aim a right unless it has a certain threshold weight against collective goals in general; unless, for example, it cannot be defeated by appeal to any of the ordinary routine goals of political administration, but only by a goal of special urgency. Suppose, for example, some man says he recognizes the right of free speech, but adds that free speech must yield whenever its exercise would inconvenience the public. He means, I take it, that he recognizes the pervasive goal of collective welfare, and only such distribution of liberty of speech as that collective goal recommends in particular circumstances. His political position is exhausted by the collective goal; the putative right adds nothing and there is no point to recognizing it as a right at all.

These definitions and distinctions make plain that the character of a political aim – its standing as a right or goal – depends upon its place and function within a single political theory. The same phrase might describe a right within one theory and a goal within another, or a right that is absolute or powerful within one theory but relatively weak within another. If a public official has anything like a coherent political

theory that he uses, even intuitively, to justify the particular decisions
he reaches, then this theory will recognize a wide variety of different types
of rights, arranged in some way that assigns rough relative weight to
each.

Any adequate theory will distinguish, for example, between background rights, which are rights that provide a justification for political
decisions by society in the abstract, and institutional rights, that provide
a justification for a decision by some particular and specified political
institution. Suppose that my political theory provides that every man
has a right to the property of another if he needs it more. I might yet
concede that he does not have a legislative right to the same effect; I
might concede, that is, that he has no institutional right that the
present legislature enact legislation that would violate the Constitution,
as such a statute presumably would. I might also concede that he has no
institutional right to a judicial decision condoning theft. Even if I did
make these concessions, I could preserve my initial background claim
by arguing that the people as a whole would be justified in amending
the Constitution to abolish property, or perhaps in rebelling and over-
throwing the present form of government entirely. I would claim that
each man has a residual background right that would justify or require
these acts, even though I concede that he does not have the right to
specific institutional decisions as these institutions are now constituted.

Any adequate theory will also make use of a distinction between
abstract and concrete rights, and therefore between abstract and concrete
principles. This is a distinction of degree, but I shall discuss relatively
clear examples at two poles of the scale it contemplates, and therefore
treat it as a distinction in kind. An abstract right is a general political
aim the statement of which does not indicate how that general aim is to
be weighed or compromised in particular circumstances against other
political aims. The grand rights of political rhetoric are in this way
abstract. Politicians speak of a right to free speech or dignity or equality,
with no suggestion that these rights are absolute, but with no attempt
to suggest their impact on particular complex social situations.

Concrete rights, on the other hand, are political aims that are more
precisely defined so as to express more definitely the weight they have
against other political aims on particular occasions. Suppose I say, not
simply that citizens have a right to free speech, but that a newspaper has
a right to publish defense plans classified as secret provided this publication will not create an immediate physical danger to troops. My principle
declares for a particular resolution of the conflict it acknowledges
between the abstract right of free speech, on the one hand, and competing rights of soldiers to security or the urgent needs of defense on the
other. Abstract rights in this way provide arguments for concrete rights,

but the claim of a concrete right is more definitive than any claim of abstract right that supports it.[1]

B. Principles and utility

The distinction between rights and goals does not deny a thesis that is part of popular moral anthropology. It may be entirely reasonable to think, as this thesis provides, that the principles the members of a particular community find persuasive will be causally determined by the collective goals of that community. If many people in a community believe that each individual has a right to some minimal concern on the part of others, then this fact may be explained, as a matter of cultural history, by the further fact that their collective welfare is advanced by that belief. If some novel arrangement of rights would serve their collective welfare better, then we should expect, according to this thesis, that in due time their moral convictions will alter in favor of that new arrangement.

I do not know how far this anthropological theory holds in our own society, or any society. It is certainly untestable in anything like the simple form in which I have put it, and I do not see why its claim, that rights are psychologically or culturally determined by goals, is a priori more plausible than the contrary claim. Perhaps men and women choose collective goals to accommodate some prior sense of individual rights, rather than delineating rights according to collective goals. In either case, however, there must be an important time lag, so that at any given time most people will recognize the conflict between rights and goals, at

---

[1] A complete political theory must also recognize two other distinctions that I use implicitly in this chapter. The first is the distinction between rights against the state and rights against fellow citizens. The former justify a political decision that requires some agency of the government to act; the latter justify a decision to coerce particular individuals. The right to minimum housing, if accepted at all, is accepted as a right against the state. The right to recover damages for a breach of contract, or to be saved from great danger at minimum risk of a rescuer, is a right against fellow citizens. The right to free speech is, ordinarily, both. It seems strange to define the rights that citizens have against one another as political rights at all; but we are now concerned with such rights only insofar as they justify political decisions of different sorts. The present distinction cuts across the distinction between background and institutional rights; the latter distinguishes among persons or institutions that must make a political decision, the former between persons or institutions whom that decision directs to act or forbear. Ordinary civil cases at law, which are the principal subject of this essay, involve rights against fellow citizens; but I also discuss certain issues of constitutional and criminal law and so touch on rights against the state as well.

The second distinction is between universal and special rights; that is, between rights that a political theory provides for all individuals in the community, with exceptions only for phenomena like incapacity or punishment, and rights it provides for only one section of the community, or possibly only one member. I shall assume, in this essay, that all political rights are universal.

least in particular cases, that the general distinction between these two kinds of political aims presupposes.

The distinction presupposes, that is, a further distinction between the force of a particular right within a political theory and the causal explanation of why the theory provides that right. This is a formal way of putting the point, and it is appropriate only when, as I am now supposing, we can identify a particular political theory and so distinguish the analytical question of what it provides from the historical question of how it came to provide it. The distinction is therefore obscured when we speak of the morality of a *community* without specifying which of the many different conceptions of a community morality we have in mind. Without some further specification we cannot construct even a vague or abstract political theory as the theory of the community at any particular time, and so we cannot make the distinction between reasons and force that is analytically necessary to understand the concepts of principle and policy. We are therefore prey to the argument that the anthropological thesis destroys the distinction between the two; we speak as if we had some coherent theory in mind, as the community's morality; but we deny that it distinguishes principle from policy on the basis of an argument that seems plausible just because we do not have any particular theory in mind. Once we do make plain what we intend by some reference to the morality of a community, and proceed to identify, even crudely, what we take the principles of that morality to be, the anthropological argument is tamed.

There are political theories, however, that unite rights and goals not causally but by making the force of a right contingent upon its power, as a right, to promote some collective goal. I have in mind various forms of the ethical theory called rule utilitarianism. One popular form of that theory, for example, holds that an act is right if the general acceptance of a rule requiring that act would improve the average welfare of members of the community.[1] A political theory might provide for a right to free speech, for example, on the hypothesis that the general acceptance of that right by courts and other political institutions would promote the highest average utility of the community in the long run.

But we may nevertheless distinguish institutional rights, at least, from collective goals within such a theory. If the theory provides that an official of a particular institution is justified in making a political decision, and not justified in refusing to make it, whenever that decision is necessary to protect the freedom to speak of any individual, without regard to the impact of the decision on collective goals, the theory pro-

[1] See Brandt, 'Toward a Credible Form of Utilitarianism', in H. Castenada and G. Nakhnikian (eds.), *Morality and the Language of Conduct* (1963) 107.

vides free speech as a right. It does not matter that the theory stipulates this right on the hypothesis that if all political institutions do enforce the right in that way an important collective goal will in fact be promoted. What is important is the commitment to a scheme of government that makes an appeal to the right decisive in particular cases.

So neither the anthropological thesis nor rule utilitarianism offers any objection to the distinction between arguments of principle and arguments of policy. I should mention, out of an abundance of caution, one further possible challenge to that distinction. Different arguments of principle and policy can often be made in support of the same political decision. Suppose that an official wishes to argue in favor of racial segregation in public places. He may offer the policy argument that mixing races causes more overall discomfort than satisfaction. Or he may offer an argument of principle appealing to the rights of those who might be killed or maimed in riots that desegregation would produce. It might be thought that the substitutibility of these arguments defeats the distinction between arguments of principle and policy, or in any case makes the distinction less useful, for the following reason. Suppose it is conceded that the right to equality between races is sufficiently strong that it must prevail over all but the most pressing argument of policy, and be compromised only as required by competing arguments of principle. That would be an empty concession if arguments of principle could always be found to substitute for an argument of policy that might otherwise be made.

But it is a fallacy to suppose that because some argument of principle can always be found to substitute for an argument of policy, it will be as cogent or as powerful as the appropriate argument of policy would have been. If some minority's claim to an antidiscrimination statute were itself based on policy, and could therefore be defeated by an appeal to overall general welfare or utility, then the argument that cites the majority's discomfort or annoyance might well be powerful enough. But if the claim cites a right to equality that must prevail unless matched by a competing argument of principle, the only such argument available may be, as here, simply too weak. Except in extraordinary cases, the danger to any particular man's life that flows from desegregation adequately managed and policed will be very small. We might therefore concede that the competing right to life offers some argument countervailing against the right to equality here, and yet maintain that that argument is of negligible weight; strong enough, perhaps to slow the pace of desegregation but not strong enough even to slow it very much.

C. *Economics and principle*

The rights thesis, in its descriptive aspect, holds that judicial decisions in hard cases are characteristically generated by principle not policy. Recent research into the connections between economic theory and the common law might be thought to suggest the contrary: that judges almost always decide on grounds of policy rather than principle. We must, however, be careful to distinguish between two propositions said to be established by that research. It is argued, first, that almost every rule developed by judges in such disparate fields as tort, contract and property can be shown to serve the collective goal of making resource allocation more efficient.[1] It is argued, second, that in certain cases judges explicitly base their decisions on economic policy.[2] Neither of these claims subverts the rights thesis.

The first claim makes no reference to the intentions of the judges who decided the cases establishing rules that improve economic efficiency. It does not suppose that these judges were aware of the economic value of their rules, or even that they would have acknowledged that value as an argument in favor of their decisions. The evidence, for the most part, suggests the contrary. The courts that nourished the unfortunate fellow-servant doctrine, for example, thought that the rule was required by fairness, not utility, and when the rule was abolished it was because the argument from fairness, not the argument from utility, was found wanting by a different generation of lawyers.[3]

If this first claim is sound, it might seem to some an important piece of evidence for the anthropological thesis described in the last section. They will think that it suggests that judges and lawyers, reflecting the general moral attitudes of their time, thought that corporations and individuals had just those rights that an explicit rule utilitarian would legislate to serve the general welfare. But the first claim might equally well suggest the contrary conclusion I mentioned, that our present ideas of general welfare reflect our ideas of individual right. Professor Posner, for example, argues for that claim by presupposing a particular conception of efficient resource allocation. He says that the value of some scarce resource to a particular individual is measured by the amount of money he is willing to pay for it, so that community welfare is maximized when each resource is in the hands of someone who would pay more than anyone else to have it.[4] But that is hardly a self-evident or neutral conception of value. It is congenial to a political theory that celebrates competition, but far less congenial to a more egalitarian theory, because it demotes the claims of the poor who are willing to spend less because they have less to spend. Posner's conception of value, therefore, seems

---

[1] See, e.g., R. Posner, *Economic Analysis of Law* (1972) 10-104.
[2] See, e.g., Coase, 'The Problem of Social Cost', 3 *J. Law & Econ.* 1, 19-28 (1960).
[3] See Posner, 'A Theory of Negligence', 1 *J. Legal Stud.* (1972) 29, 71.
[4] Posner, *Economic Analysis*, 4.

as much the consequence as the cause of a theory of individual rights. In any case, however, the anthropological thesis of the first claim offers no threat to the rights thesis. Even if we concede that a judge's theory of rights is determined by some instinctive sense of economic value, rather than the other way about, we may still argue that he relies on that theory, and not economic analysis, to justify decisions in hard cases.

The second claim we distinguished, however, may seem to present a more serious challenge. If judges explicitly refer to economic policy in some cases, then these cases cannot be understood simply as evidence for the anthropological thesis. Learned Hand's theory of negligence is the most familiar example of this explicit reference to economics. He said, roughly, that the test of whether the defendant's act was unreasonable and therefore actionable, is the economic test which asks whether the defendant could have avoided the accident at less cost to himself than the plaintiff was likely to suffer if the accident occurred, discounted by the improbability of the accident.[1] It may be said that this economic test provides an argument of policy rather than principle, because it makes the decision turn on whether the collective welfare would have been advanced more by allowing the accident to take place or by spending what was necessary to avoid it. If so, then cases in which some test like Hand's is explicitly used, however few they might be, would stand as counterexamples to the rights thesis.

But the assumption that an economic calculation of any sort must be an argument of policy overlooks the distinction between abstract and concrete rights. Abstract rights, like the right to speak on political matters, take no account of competing rights; concrete rights, on the other hand, reflect the impact of such competition. In certain kinds of cases the argument from competing abstract principles to a concrete right can be made in the language of economics. Consider the principle that each member of a community has a right that each other member treat him with the minimal respect due a fellow human being.[2] That is a very abstract principle : it demands some balance, in particular cases, between the interests of those to be protected and the liberty of those from whom the principle demands an unstated level of concern and respect. It is natural, particularly when economic vocabulary is in fashion, to define the proper balance by comparing the sum of the utilities of these

---

[1] *United States v. Carroll Towing Co.*, 159 F.2d 169, 173 (2d Cir. 1947). Coase, 22-3, gives other examples, mostly of nuisance cases interpreting the doctrine that a 'reasonable' interference with the plaintiff's use of his property is not a nuisance.

[2] A more elaborate argument of principle might provide a better justification for Hand's test than does this simple principle. I described a more elaborate argument in a set of Rosenthal Lectures delivered at Northwestern University Law School in March, 1975. The simple principle, however, provides a sufficiently good justification for the present point.

two parties under different conditions. If one man acts in a way that he can foresee will injure another so that the collective utility of the pair will be sharply reduced by his act, he does not show the requisite care and concern. If he can guard or insure against the injury much more cheaply or effectively than the other can, for example, then he does not show care and concern unless he takes these precautions or arranges that insurance.

That character of argument is by no means novel, though perhaps its economic dress is. Philosophers have for a long time debated hypothetical cases testing the level of concern that one member of a community owes to another. If one man is drowning, and another may save him at minimal risk to himself, for example, then the first has a moral right to be saved by the second. That proposition might easily be put in economic form : if the collective utility of the pair is very sharply improved by a rescue, then the drowning man has a right to that rescue and the rescuer a duty to make it. The parallel legal proposition may, of course, be much more complex than that. It may specify special circumstances in which the crucial question is not whether the collective utility of the pair will be sharply advanced, but only whether it will be marginally advanced. It might put the latter question, for example, when one man's positive act, as distinct from a failure to act, creates a risk of direct and foreseeable physical injury to the person or property of another. If the rights thesis is sound, of course, then no judge may appeal to that legal proposition unless he believes that the principle of minimal respect states an abstract legal right; but if he does, then he may cast his argument in economic form without thereby changing its character from principle to policy.

Since Hand's test, and the parallel argument about rescuing a drowning man, are methods of compromising competing rights, they consider only the welfare of those whose abstract rights are at stake. They do not provide room for costs or benefits to the community at large, except as these are reflected in the welfare of those whose rights are in question. We can easily imagine an argument that does not concede these restrictions. Suppose someone argued that the principle requiring rescue at minimal risk should be amended so as to make the decision turn, not on some function of the collective utilities of the victim and rescuer, but on marginal utility to the community as a whole, so that the rescuer must take into account not only the relative risks to himself and the victim, but the relative social importance of the two. It might follow that an insignificant man must risk his life to save a bank president, but that a bank president need not even tire himself to save a nobody. The argument is no longer an argument of principle, because it supposes the victim to have a right to nothing but his expectations under general utility. Hand's formula, and more sophisticated variations, are not arguments of that character; they do not subordinate an individual right to some collective goal, but provide a mechanism for compromising competing claims of abstract right.

Negligence cases are not the only cases in which judges compromise abstract rights in defining concrete ones. If a judge appeals to public safety or the scarcity of some vital resource, for example, as a ground for limiting some abstract right, then his appeal might be understood as an appeal to the competing rights of those whose security will be sacrificed, or whose just share of that resource will be threatened if the abstract right is made concrete. His argument is an argument of principle if it respects the distributional requirements of such arguments, and if it observes the restriction mentioned in the last section : that the weight of a competing principle may be less than the weight of the appropriate parallel policy. We find a different sort of example in the familiar argument that certain sorts of law suits should not be allowed because to do so would 'swamp' the courts with litigation. The court supposes that if it were to allow that type of suit it would lack the time to consider promptly enough other law suits aiming to vindicate rights that are, taken together, more important than the rights it therefore proposes to bar.

This is an appropriate point to notice a certain limitation of the rights thesis. It holds in standard civil cases, when the ruling assumption is that one of the parties has a right to win; but it holds only asymmetrically when that assumption cannot be made. The accused in a criminal case has a right to a decision in his favor if he is innocent, but the state has no parallel right to a conviction if he is guilty. The court may therefore find in favor of the accused, in some hard case testing rules of evidence, for example, on an argument of policy that does not suppose that the accused has any right to be acquitted. The Supreme Court in *Linkletter v. Walker*[1] said that its earlier decision in *Mapp v. Ohio*[2] was such a decision. The Court said it had changed the rules permitting the introduction of illegally obtained evidence, not because Miss Mapp had any right that such evidence not be used if otherwise admissible, but in order to deter policemen from collecting such evidence in the future. I do not mean that a constitutional decision on such grounds is proper, or even that the Court's later description of its earlier decision was accurate. I mean only to point out how the geometry of a criminal prosecution, which does not set opposing rights in a case against one another, differs from the standard civil case in which the rights thesis holds symmetrically.

[1] 381 U.S. 618 (1965).
[2] 367 U.S. 643 (1961).

4. INSTITUTIONAL RIGHTS

The rights thesis provides that judges decide hard cases by confirming or denying concrete rights. But the concrete rights upon which judges rely must have two other characteristics. They must be institutional rather than background rights, and they must be legal rather than some other form of institutional rights. We cannot appreciate or test the thesis, therefore, without further elaboration of these distinctions.

Institutional rights may be found in institutions of very different character. A chess player has a 'chess' right to be awarded a point in a tournament if he checkmates an opponent. A citizen in a democracy has a legislative right to the enactment of statutes necessary to protect his free speech. In the case of chess, institutional rights are fixed by constitutive and regulative rules that belong distinctly to the game, or to a particular tournament. Chess is, in this sense, an autonomous institution; I mean that it is understood, among its participants, that no one may claim an institutional right by direct appeal to general morality. No one may argue, for example, that he has earned the right to be declared the winner by his general virtue. But legislation is only partly autonomous in that sense. There are special constitutive and regulative rules that define what a legislature is, and who belongs to it, and how it votes, and that it may not establish a religion. But these rules belonging distinctly to legislation are rarely sufficient to determine whether a citizen has an institutional right to have a certain statute enacted; they do not decide, for example, whether he has a right to minimum wage legislation. Citizens are expected to repair to general considerations of political morality when they argue for such rights.

The fact that some institutions are fully and others partly autonomous has the consequence mentioned earlier, that the institutional rights a political theory acknowledges may diverge from the background rights it provides. Institutional rights are nevertheless genuine rights. Even if we suppose that the poor have an abstract background right to money taken from the rich, it would be wrong, not merely unexpected, for the referees of a chess tournament to award the prize money to the poorest contestant rather than the contestant with the most points. It would provide no excuse to say that since tournament rights merely describe the conditions necessary for calling the tournament a chess tournament, the referee's act is justified so long as he does not use the word 'chess' when he hands out the award. The participants entered the tournament with the understanding that chess rules would apply; they have genuine rights to the enforcement of these rules and no others.

Institutional autonomy insulates an official's institutional duty from the greater part of background political morality. But how far does the force of this insulation extend? Even in the case of a fully insulated institution like chess some rules will require interpretation or elaboration before an official may enforce them in certain circumstances. Suppose some rule of a chess tournament provides that the referee shall declare a game forfeit if one player 'unreasonably' annoys the other in the course of play. The language of the rule does not define what counts as 'unreasonable' annoyance; it does not decide whether, for example, a player who continually smiles at his opponent in such a way as to unnerve him, as the Russian grandmaster Tal once smiled at Fischer, annoys him unreasonably.

The referee is not free to give effect to his background convictions in deciding this hard case. He might hold, as a matter of political theory, that individuals have a right to equal welfare without regard to intellectual abilities. It would nevertheless be wrong for him to rely upon that conviction in deciding difficult cases under the forfeiture rule. He could not say, for example, that annoying behavior is reasonable so long as it has the effect of reducing the importance of intellectual ability in deciding who will win the game. The participants, and the general community that is interested, will say that his duty is just the contrary. Since chess is an intellectual game, he must apply the forfeiture rule in such a way as to protect, rather than jeopardize, the role of intellect in the contest.

We have, then, in the case of the chess referee, an example of an official whose decisions about institutional rights are understood to be governed by institutional constraints even when the force of these constraints is not clear. We do not think that he is free to legislate interstitially within the 'open texture' of imprecise rules.[1] If one interpretation of the forfeiture rule will protect the character of the game, and another will not, then the participants have a right to the first interpretation. We may hope to find, in this relatively simple case, some general feature of institutional rights in hard cases that will bear on the decision of a judge in a hard case at law.

I said that the game of chess has a character that the referee's decisions must respect. What does that mean? How does a referee know that chess is an intellectual game rather than a game of chance or an exhibition of digital ballet? He may well start with what everyone knows. Every institution is placed by its participants in some very rough category of institution; it is taken to be a game rather than a religious ceremony or a form of exercise or a political process. It is, for that reason, definitional of chess that it is a game rather than an exercise in digital skill. These conventions, exhibited in attitudes and manners and in history, are decisive. If everyone takes chess to be a game of chance,

---

[1] See generally H. L. A. Hart, *The Concept of Law* (1961) 121-32.

so that they curse their luck and nothing else when a piece *en prise* happens to be taken, then chess is a game of chance, though a very bad one.

But these conventions will run out, and they may run out before the referee finds enough to decide the case of Tal's smile. It is important to see, however, that the conventions run out in a particular way. They are not incomplete, like a book whose last page is missing, but abstract, so that their full force can be captured in a concept that admits of different conceptions; that is, in a *contested* concept.[1] The referee must select one or another of these conceptions, not to supplement the convention but to enforce it. He must *construct* the game's character by putting to himself different sets of questions. Given that chess is an intellectual game, is it, like poker, intellectual in some sense that includes ability at psychological intimidation? Or is it, like mathematics, intellectual in some sense that does not include that ability? This first set of questions asks him to look more closely at the game, to determine whether its features support one rather than the other of these conceptions of intellect. But he must also ask a different set of questions. Given that chess is an intellectual game of some sort, what follows about reasonable behavior in a chess game? Is ability at psychological intimidation, or ability to resist such intimidation, really an intellectual quality? These questions ask him to look more closely at the concept of intellect itself.

The referee's calculations, if they are self-conscious, will oscillate between these two sets of questions, progressively narrowing the questions to be asked at the next stage. He might first identify, by reflecting on the concept, different conceptions of intellect. He might suppose at this first stage, for example, that physical grace of the sort achieved in ballet is one form of intelligence. But he must then test these different conceptions against the rules and practices of the game. That test will rule out any physical conception of intelligence. But it may not discriminate between a conception that includes or a conception that rejects psychological intimidation, because either of these conceptions would provide an account of the rules and practices that is not plainly superior, according to any general canons of explanation, to the account provided by the other. He must then ask himself which of these two accounts offers a deeper or more successful account of what intellect really is. His calculations, so conceived, oscillate between philosophy of mind and the facts of the institution whose character he must elucidate.

[1] See Gallie, 'Essentially Contested Concepts', 56 *Proceedings of the Aristotelian Society* (1965) 167, 167-8. See also Chapter 10.

This is, of course, only a fanciful reconstruction of a calculation that will never take place; any official's sense of the game will have developed over a career, and he will employ rather than expose that sense in his judgments. But the reconstruction enables us to see how the concept of the game's character is tailored to a special institutional problem. Once an autonomous institution is established, such that participants have institutional rights under distinct rules belonging to that institution, then hard cases may arise that must, in the nature of the case, be supposed to have an answer. If Tal does not have a right that the game be continued, it must be because the forfeiture rule, properly understood, justifies the referee's intervention; if it does, then Fischer has a right to win at once. It is not useful to speak of the referee's 'discretion' in such a case. If some weak sense of discretion is meant, then the remark is unhelpful; if some strong sense is meant, such that Tal no longer has a right to win, then this must be, again, because the rule properly understood destroys the right he would otherwise have.[1] Suppose we say that in such a case all the parties have a right to expect is that the referee will use his best judgment. That is, in a sense, perfectly true, because they can have no more, by way of the referee's judgment, than his best judgment. But they are nevertheless entitled to his best judgment about which behavior is, in the circumstances of the game, unreasonable; they are entitled, that is, to his best judgment about what their rights are. The proposition that there is some 'right' answer to that question does not mean that the rules of chess are exhaustive and unambiguous; rather it is a complex statement about the responsibilities of its officials and participants.

But if the decision in a hard case must be a decision about the rights of the parties, then an official's reason for that judgment must be the sort of reason that justifies recognizing or denying a right. He must bring to his decision a general theory of why, in the case of his institution, the rules create or destroy any rights at all, and he must show what decision that general theory requires in the hard case. In chess the general ground of institutional rights must be the tacit consent or understanding of the parties. They consent, in entering a chess tournament, to the enforcement of certain and only those rules, and it is hard to imagine any other general ground for supposing that they have any institutional rights. But if that is so, and if the decision in a hard case is a decision about which rights they actually have, then the argument for the decision must apply that general ground to the hard case.

The hard case puts, we might say, a question of political theory. It asks what it is fair to suppose that the players have done in consenting

[1] See Chapter 2.

to the forfeiture rule. The concept of a game's character is a conceptual device for framing that question. It is a contested concept that internalizes the general justification of the institution so as to make it available for discriminations within the institution itself. It supposes that a player consents not simply to a set of rules, but to an enterprise that may be said to have a character of its own; so that when the question is put – To what did he consent in consenting to that? – the answer may study the enterprise as a whole and not just the rules.

5. LEGAL RIGHTS

A. *Legislation*

Legal argument, in hard cases, turns on contested concepts whose nature and function are very much like the concept of the character of a game. These include several of the substantive concepts through which the law is stated, like the concepts of a contract and of property. But they also include two concepts of much greater relevance to the present argument. The first is the idea of the 'intention' or 'purpose' of a particular statute or statutory clause. This concept provides a bridge between the political justification of the general idea that statutes create rights and those hard cases that ask what rights a particular statute has created. The second is the concept of principles that 'underlie' or are 'embedded in' the positive rules of law. This concept provides a bridge between the political justification of the doctrine that like cases should be decided alike and those hard cases in which it is unclear what that general doctrine requires. These concepts together define legal rights as a function, though a very special function, of political rights. If a judge accepts the settled practices of his legal system – if he accepts, that is, the autonomy provided by its distinct constitutive and regulative rules – then he must, according to the doctrine of political responsibility, accept some general political theory that justifies these practices. The concepts of legislative purpose and common law principles are devices for applying that general political theory to controversial issues about legal rights.

We might therefore do well to consider how a philosophical judge might develop, in appropriate cases, theories of what legislative purpose and legal principles require. We shall find that he would construct these theories in the same manner as a philosophical referee would construct the character of a game. I have invented, for this purpose, a lawyer of superhuman skill, learning, patience and acumen, whom I shall call Hercules. I suppose that Hercules is a judge in some representative American jurisdiction. I assume that he accepts the main uncontroversial constitutive and regulative rules of the law in his jurisdiction. He accepts, that is, that statutes have the general power to create and extinguish legal rights, and that judges have the general duty to follow earlier decisions of their court or higher courts whose rationale, as lawyers say, extends to the case at bar.

1. The constitution. Suppose there is a written constitution in Hercules' jurisdiction which provides that no law shall be valid if it establishes a religion. The legislature passes a law purporting to grant free busing to children in parochial schools. Does the grant establish a religion?[1] The words of the constitutional provision might support either view. Hercules must nevertheless decide whether the child who appears before him has a right to her bus ride.

He might begin by asking why the constitution has any power at all to create or destroy rights. If citizens have a background right to salvation through an established church, as many believe they do, then this must be an important right. Why does the fact that a group of men voted otherwise several centuries ago prevent this background right from being made a legal right as well? His answer must take some form such as this. The constitution sets out a general political scheme that is sufficiently just to be taken as settled for reasons of fairness. Citizens take the benefit of living in a society whose institutions are arranged and governed in accordance with that scheme, and they must take the burdens as well, at least until a new scheme is put into force either by discrete amendment or general revolution. But Hercules must then ask just what scheme of principles has been settled. He must construct, that is, a constitutional theory; since he is Hercules we may suppose that he can develop a full political theory that justifies the constitution as a whole. It must be a scheme that fits the particular rules of this constitution, of course. It cannot include a powerful background right to an established church. But more than one fully specified theory may fit the specific provision about religion sufficiently well. One theory might provide, for example, that it is wrong for the government to enact any legislation that will cause great social tension or disorder; so that since the establishment of a church will have that effect, it is wrong to empower the legislature to establish one. Another theory will provide a background right to religious liberty, and therefore argue that an established church is wrong, not because it will be socially disruptive, but because it violates that background right. In that case Hercules must turn to the remaining constitutional rules and settled practices under these rules to see which of these two theories provides a smoother fit with the constitutional scheme as a whole.

But the theory that is superior under this test will nevertheless be in-

[1] See *Everson v. Board of Educ.*, 330 U.S. 1 (1947).

sufficiently concrete to decide some cases. Suppose Hercules decides that the establishment provision is justified by a right to religious liberty rather than any goal of social order. It remains to ask what, more precisely, religious liberty is. Does a right to religious liberty include the right not to have one's taxes used for any purpose that helps a religion to survive? Or simply not to have one's taxes used to benefit one religion at the expense of another? If the former, then the free transportation legislation violates that right, but if the latter it does not. The institutional structure of rules and practice may not be sufficiently detailed to rule out either of these two conceptions of religious liberty, or to make one a plainly superior justification of that structure. At some point in his career Hercules must therefore consider the question not just as an issue of fit between a theory and the rules of the institution, but as an issue of political philosophy as well. He must decide which conception is a more satisfactory elaboration of the general idea of religious liberty. He must decide that question because he cannot otherwise carry far enough the project he began. He cannot answer in sufficient detail the question of what political scheme the constitution establishes.

So Hercules is driven, by this project, to a process of reasoning that is much like the process of the self-conscious chess referee. He must develop a theory of the constitution, in the shape of a complex set of principles and policies that justify that scheme of government, just as the chess referee is driven to develop a theory about the character of his game. He must develop that theory by referring alternately to political philosophy and institutional detail. He must generate possible theories justifying different aspects of the scheme and test the theories against the broader institution. When the discriminating power of that test is exhausted, he must elaborate the contested concepts that the successful theory employs.

2. *Statutes.* A statute in Hercules' jurisdiction provides that it is a federal crime for someone knowingly to transport in interstate commerce 'any person who shall have been unlawfully seized, confined, inveigled, decoyed, kidnapped, abducted, or carried away by any means whatsoever. . . .' Hercules is asked to decide whether this statute makes a federal criminal of a man who persuaded a young girl that it was her religious duty to run away with him, in violation of a court order, to consummate what he called a celestial marriage.[1] The statute had been passed after a famous kidnapping case, in order to enable federal authorities to join in the pursuit of kidnappers. But its words are sufficiently broad to apply to this case, and there is nothing in the legislative

[1] See *Chatwin v. United States,* 326 U.S. 455 (1946).

record or accompanying committee reports that says they do not.

Do they apply? Hercules might himself despise celestial marriage, or abhor the corruption of minors, or celebrate the obedience of children to their parents. The groom nevertheless has a right to his liberty, unless the statute properly understood deprives him of that right; it is inconsistent with any plausible theory of the constitution that judges have the power retroactively to make conduct criminal. Does the statute deprive him of that right? Hercules must begin by asking why any statute has the power to alter legal rights. He will find the answer in his constitutional theory: this might provide, for example, that a democratically elected legislature is the appropriate body to make collective decisions about the conduct that shall be criminal. But that same constitutional theory will impose on the legislature certain responsibilities: it will impose not only constraints reflecting individual rights, but also some general duty to pursue collective goals defining the public welfare. That fact provides a useful test for Hercules in this hard case. He might ask which interpretation more satisfactorily ties the language the legislature used to its constitutional responsibilities. That is, like the referee's question about the character of a game. It calls for the construction, not of some hypothesis about the mental state of particular legislators, but of a special political theory that justifies this statute, in the light of the legislature's more general responsibilities, better than any alternative theory.[1]

Which arguments of principle and policy might properly have persuaded the legislature to enact just that statute? It should not have pursued a policy designed to replace state criminal enforcement by federal enforcement whenever constitutionally possible. That would represent an unnecessary interference with the principle of federalism

---

[1] One previous example of the use of policy in statutory interpretations illustrates this form of constitution. In *Charles River Bridge v. Warren Bridge*, 24 Mass. (7 Pick.) 344 (1830), *aff'd*, 36 U.S. (11 Pet.) 420 (1837), the court had to decide whether a charter to construct a bridge across the Charles River was to be taken to be exclusive, so that no further charters could be granted. Justice Morton of the Supreme Judicial Court held that the grant was not to be taken as exclusive, and argued, in support of that interpretation, that:

[I]f consequences so inconsistent with the improvement and prosperity of the state result from the liberal and extended construction of the charters which have been granted, we ought, if the terms used will admit of it, rather to adopt a more limited and restricted one, than to impute such improvidence to the legislature.

. . . .

. . [Construing the grant as exclusive] would amount substantially to a covenant, that during the plaintiffs' charter an important portion of our commonwealth, as to facilities for travel and transportation, should remain *in statu quo*. I am on the whole irresistibly brought to the conclusion, that this construction is neither consonant with sound reason, with judicial authorities, with the course of legislation, nor with the principles of our free institutions. Ibid. 460.

that must be part of Hercules' constitutional theory. It might, however, responsibly have followed a policy of selecting for federal enforcement all crimes with such an interstate character that state enforcement was hampered. Or it could responsibly have selected just specially dangerous or widespread crimes of that character. Which of these two responsible policies offers a better justification of the statute actually drafted? If the penalties provided by the statute are large, and therefore appropriate to the latter but not the former policy, the latter policy must be preferred. Which of the different interpretations of the statute permitted by the language serves that policy better? Plainly a decision that inveiglement of the sort presented by the case is not made a federal crime by the statute.

I have described a simple and perhaps unrepresentative problem of statutory interpretation, because I cannot now develop a theory of statutory interpretation in any detail. I want only to suggest how the general claim, that calculations judges make about the purposes of statutes are calculations about political rights, might be defended. There are, however, two points that must be noticed about even this simple example. It would be inaccurate, first, to say that Hercules supplemented what the legislature did in enacting the statute, or that he tried to determine what it would have done if it had been aware of the problem presented by the case. The act of a legislature is not, as these descriptions suggest, an event whose force we can in some way measure so as to say it has run out at a particular point; it is rather an event whose content is contested in the way in which the content of an agreement to play a game is contested. Hercules constructs his political theory as an argument about what the legislature has, on this occasion, done. The contrary argument, that it did not actually do what he said, is not a realistic piece of common sense, but a competitive claim about the true content of that contested event.

Second, it is important to notice how great a role the canonical terms of the actual statute play in the process described. They provide a limit to what must otherwise be, in the nature of the case, unlimited. The political theory Hercules developed to interpret the statute, which featured a policy of providing federal enforcement for dangerous crimes, would justify a great many decisions that the legislature did not, on any interpretation of the language, actually make. It would justify, for example, a statute making it a federal crime for a murderer to leave the state of his crime. The legislature has no general duty to follow out the lines of any particular policy, and it would plainly be wrong for Hercules to suppose that the legislature had in some sense enacted that further statute. The words of the statute they did enact enables this process of interpretation to operate without absurdity; it permits Hercules to say that the legislature pushed some policy to the limits of the language it used, without also supposing that it pushed that policy to some indeterminate further point.

B. *The common law*

1. Precedent. One day lawyers will present a hard case to Hercules that does not turn upon any statute; they will argue whether earlier common law decisions of Hercules' court, properly understood, provide some party with a right to a decision in his favor. *Spartan Steel* was such a case. The plaintiff did not argue that any statute provided it a right to recover its economic damages; it pointed instead to certain earlier judicial decisions that awarded recovery for other sorts of damage, and argued that the principle behind these cases required a decision for it as well.

Hercules must begin by asking why arguments of that form are ever, even in principle, sound. He will find that he has available no quick or obvious answer. When he asked himself the parallel question about legislation he found, in general democratic theory, a ready reply. But the details of the practices of precedent he must now justify resist any comparably simple theory.

He might, however, be tempted by this answer. Judges, when they decide particular cases at common law, lay down general rules that are intended to benefit the community in some way. Other judges, deciding later cases, must therefore enforce these rules so that the benefit may be achieved. If this account of the matter were a sufficient justification of the practices of precedent, then Hercules could decide these hard common law cases as if earlier decisions were statutes, using the techniques he worked out for statutory interpretation. But he will encounter fatal difficulties if he pursues that theory very far. It will repay us to consider why, in some detail, because the errors in the theory will be guides to a more successful theory.

Statutory interpretation, as we just noticed, depends upon the availability of a canonical form of words, however vague or unspecific, that set limits to the political decisions that the statute may be taken to have made. Hercules will discover that many of the opinions that litigants cite as precedents do not contain any special propositions taken to be a canonical form of the rule that the case lays down. It is true that it was part of Anglo-American judicial style, during the last part of the nineteenth century and the first part of this century, to attempt to compose such canonical statements, so that one could thereafter refer, for example, to the rule in *Rylands v. Fletcher*.[1] But even in this period, lawyers and

---

[1] [1866] L.R. 1 Ex. 265, *aff'd,* (1868) L.R. 3 H.L. 330.

textbook writers disagreed about which parts of famous opinions should be taken to have that character. Today, in any case, even important opinions rarely attempt that legislative sort of draftsmanship. They cite reasons, in the form of precedents and principles, to justify a decision, but it is the decision, not some new and stated rule of law, that these precedents and principles are taken to justify. Sometimes a judge will acknowledge openly that it lies to later cases to determine the full effect of the case he has decided.

Of course, Hercules might well decide that when he does find, in an earlier case, a canonical form of words, he will use his techniques of statutory interpretation to decide whether the rule composed of these words embraces a novel case.[1] He might well acknowledge what could be called an enactment force of precedent. He will nevertheless find that when a precedent does have enactment force, its influence on later cases is not taken to be limited to that force. Judges and lawyers do not think that the force of precedents is exhausted, as a statute would be, by the linguistic limits of some particular phrase. If *Spartan Steel* were a New York case, counsel for the plaintiff would suppose that Cardozo's earlier decision in *MacPherson v. Buick*,[2] in which a woman recovered damages for injuries from a negligently manufactured automobile, counted in favor of his client's right to recover, in spite of the fact that the earlier decision contained no language that could plausibly be interpreted to enact that right. He would urge that the earlier decision exerts a gravitational force on later decisions even when these later decisions lie outside its particular orbit.

This gravitational force is part of the practice Hercules' general theory of precedent must capture. In this important respect, judicial practice differs from the practice of officials in other institutions. In chess, officials conform to established rules in a way that assumes full institutional autonomy. They exercise originality only to the extent required by the fact that an occasional rule, like the rule about forfeiture, demands that originality. Each decision of a chess referee, therefore, can be said to be directly required and justified by an established rule of chess, even though some of these decisions must be based on an interpretation, rather than on simply the plain and unavoidable meaning, of that rule.

---

[1] But since Hercules will be led to accept the rights thesis, see pp. 115-16 *infra*, his 'interpretation' of judicial enactments will be different from his interpretation of statutes in one important respect. When he interprets statutes he fixes to some statutory language, as we saw, arguments of principle or policy that provide the best justification of that language in the light of the legislature's responsibilities. His argument remains an argument of principle; he uses policy to determine what rights the legislature has already created. But when he 'interprets' judicial enactments he will fix to the relevant language only arguments of principle, because the rights thesis argues that only such arguments acquit the responsibility of the 'enacting' court.

[2] *MacPherson v. Buick Motor Co.*, 217 N.Y. 382, 111 N.E. 1050 (1916).

Some legal philosophers write about common law adjudication as if it were in this way like chess, except that legal rules are much more likely than chess rules to require interpretation. That is the spirit, for example, of Professor Hart's argument that hard cases arise only because legal rules have what he calls 'open texture'.[1] In fact, judges often disagree not simply about how some rule or principle should be interpreted, but whether the rule or principle one judges cites should be acknowledged to be a rule or principle at all. In some cases both the majority and the dissenting opinions recognize the same earlier cases as relevant, but disagree about what rule or principle these precedents should be understood to have established. In adjudication, unlike chess, the argument *for* a particular rule may be more important than the argument *from* that rule to the particular case; and while the chess referee who decides a case by appeal to a rule no one has ever heard of before is likely to be dismissed or certified, the judge who does so is likely to be celebrated in law school lectures.

Nevertheless, judges seem agreed that earlier decisions do contribute to the formulation of new and controversial rules in some way other than by interpretation; they are agreed that earlier decisions have gravitational force even when they disagree about what that force is. The legislator may very often concern himself only with issues of background morality or policy in deciding how to cast his vote on some issue. He need not show that his vote is consistent with the votes of his colleagues in the legislature, or with those of past legislatures. But the judge very rarely assumes that character of independence. He will always try to connect the justification he provides for an original decision with decisions that other judges or officials have taken in the past.

In fact, when good judges try to explain in some general way how they work, they search for figures of speech to describe the constraints they feel even when they suppose that they are making new law, constraints that would not be appropriate if they were legislators. They say, for example, that they find new rules immanent in the law as a whole, or that they are enforcing an internal logic of the law through some method that belongs more to philosophy than to politics, or that they are the agents through which the law works itself pure, or that the law has some life of its own even though this belongs to experience rather than logic. Hercules must not rest content with these famous metaphors and personifications, but he must also not be content with any description of the judicial process that ignores their appeal to the best lawyers.

The gravitational force of precedent cannot be captured by any theory that takes the full force of precedent to be its enactment force as a piece of legislation. But the inadequacy of that approach suggests a superior

[1] H. L. A. Hart, *The Concept of Law*, 121-32.

theory. The gravitational force of a precedent may be explained by appeal, not to the wisdom of enforcing enactments, but to the fairness of treating like cases alike. A precedent is the report of an earlier political decision; the very fact of that decision, as a piece of political history, provides some reason for deciding other cases in a similar way in the future. This general explanation of the gravitational force of precedent accounts for the feature that defeated the enactment theory, which is that the force of a precedent escapes the language of its opinion. If the government of a community has forced the manufacturer of defective motor cars to pay damages to a woman who was injured because of the defect, then that historical fact must offer some reason, at least, why the same government should require a contractor who has caused economic damage through the defective work of his employees to make good that loss. We may test the weight of that reason, not by asking whether the language of the earlier decision, suitably interpreted, requires the contractor to pay damages, but by asking the different question whether it is fair for the government, having intervened in the way it did in the first case, to refuse its aid in the second.

Hercules will conclude that this doctrine of fairness offers the only adequate account of the full practice of precedent. He will draw certain further conclusions about his own responsibilities when deciding hard cases. The most important of these is that he must limit the gravitational force of earlier decisions to the extension of the arguments of principle necessary to justify those decisions. If an earlier decision were taken to be entirely justified by some argument of policy, it would have no gravitational force. Its value as a precedent would be limited to its enactment force, that is, to further cases captured by some particular words of the opinion. The distributional force of a collective goal, as we noticed earlier, is a matter of contingent fact and general legislative strategy. If the government intervened on behalf of Mrs MacPherson, not because she had any right to its intervention, but only because wise strategy suggested that means of pursuing some collective goal like economic efficiency, there can be no effective argument of fairness that it therefore ought to intervene for the plaintiff in *Spartan Steel*.

We must remind ourselves, in order to see why this is so, of the slight demands we make upon legislatures in the name of consistency when their decisions are generated by arguments of policy.[1] Suppose the legisla-

---

[1] In *Williamson v. Lee Optical Co.*, 348 U.S. 483 (1955), Justice Douglas suggested that legislation generated by policy need not be uniform or consistent:
> The problem of legislative classification is a perennial one, admitting of no doctrinaire definition. Evils in the same field may be of different dimensions and proportions, requiring different remedies. Or so the legislature may think. Or the reform may take one step at a time, addressing itself to the phase of the problem which seems most acute to the legislative mind. The legislature

ture wishes to stimulate the economy and might do so, with roughly the same efficiency, either by subsidizing housing or by increasing direct government spending for new roads. Road construction companies have no right that the legislature choose road construction; if it does, then home construction firms have no right, on any principle of consistency, that the legislature subsidize housing as well. The legislature may decide that the road construction program has stimulated the economy just enough, and that no further programs are needed. It may decide this even if it now concedes that subsidized housing would have been the more efficient decision in the first place. Or it might concede even that more stimulation of the economy is needed, but decide that it wishes to wait for more evidence – perhaps evidence about the success of the road program – to see whether subsidies provide an effective stimulation. It might even say that it does not now wish to commit more of its time and energy to economic policy. There is, perhaps, some limit to the arbitrariness of the distinctions the legislature may make in its pursuit of collective goals. Even if it is efficient to build all shipyards in southern California, it might be thought unfair, as well as politically unwise, to do so. But these weak requirements, which prohibit grossly unfair distributions, are plainly compatible with providing sizeable incremental benefits to one group that are withheld from others.

There can be, therefore, no general argument of fairness that a government which serves a collective goal in one way on one occasion must serve it that way, or even serve the same goal, whenever a parallel opportunity arises. I do not mean simply that the government may change its mind, and regret either the goal or the means of its earlier decision. I mean that a responsible government may serve different goals in a piecemeal and occasional fashion, so that even though it does not regret, but continues to enforce, one rule designed to serve a particular goal, it may reject other rules that would serve that same goal just as well. It might legislate the rule that manufacturers are responsible for damages flowing from defects in their cars, for example, and yet properly refuse to legislate the same rule for manufacturers of washing machines, let alone contractors who cause economic damage like the damage of

---

may select one phase of one field and apply a remedy there, neglecting the others. The prohibition of the Equal Protection Clause goes no further than the invidious discrimination.
Ibid. 489 (citations omitted).

Of course the point of the argument here, that the demands of consistency are different in the cases of principle and policy, is of great importance in understanding the recent history of the equal protection clause. It is the point behind attempts to distinguish 'old' from 'new' equal protection, or to establish 'suspect' classifications, and it provides a more accurate and intelligible distinction than these attempts have furnished.

Spartan Steel. Government must, of course, be rational and fair; it must make decisions that overall serve a justifiable mix of collective goals and nevertheless respect whatever rights citizens have. But that general requirement would not support anything like the gravitational force that the judicial decision in favour of Mrs MacPherson was in fact taken to have.

So Hercules, when he defines the gravitational force of a particular precedent, must take into account only the arguments of principle that justify that precedent. If the decision in favour of Mrs MacPherson supposes that she has a right to damages, and not simply that a rule in her favor supports some collective goal, then the argument of fairness, on which the practice of precedent relies, takes hold. It does not follow, of course, that anyone injured in any way by the negligence of another must have the same concrete right to recover that she has. It may be that competing rights require a compromise in the later case that they did not require in hers. But it might well follow that the plaintiff in the later case has the same abstract right, and if that is so then some special argument citing the competing rights will be required to show that a contrary decision in the later case would be fair.

2. *The seamless web.* Hercules' first conclusion, that the gravitational force of a precedent is defined by the arguments of principle that support the precedent, suggests a second. Since judicial practice in his community assumes that earlier cases have a *general* gravitational force, then he can justify that judicial practice only by supposing that the rights thesis holds in his community. It is never taken to be a satisfactory argument against the gravitational force of some precedent that the goal that precedent served has now been served sufficiently, or that the courts would now be better occupied in serving some other goal that has been relatively neglected, possibly returning to the goal the precedent served on some other occasion. The practices of precedent do not suppose that the *rationales* that recommend judicial decisions can be served piecemeal in that way. If it is acknowledged that a particular precedent is justified for a particular reason; if that reason would also recommend a particular result in the case at bar; if the earlier decision has not been recanted or in some other way taken as a matter of institutional regret; then that decision must be reached in the later case.

Hercules must suppose that it is understood in his community, though perhaps not explicitly recognized, that judicial decisions must be taken to be justified by arguments of principle rather than arguments of policy. He now sees that the familiar concept used by judges to explain their reasoning from precedent, the concept of certain principles that underlie or are embedded in the common law, is itself only a metaphorical statement of the rights thesis. He may henceforth use that concept in his decisions of hard common law cases. It provides a general test for deciding such cases that is like the chess referee's concept of the character of a game, and like his own concept of a legislative purpose. It provides a question – What set of principles best justifies the precedents? – that builds a bridge between the general justification of the practice of precedent, which is fairness, and his own decision about what that general justification requires in some particular hard case.

Hercules must now develop his concept of principles that underlie the common law by assigning to each of the relevant precedents some scheme of principle that justifies the decision of that precedent. He will now discover a further important difference between this concept and the concept of statutory purpose that he used in statutory interpretation. In the case of statutes, he found it necessary to choose some theory about the purpose of the particular statute in question, looking to other acts of the legislature only insofar as these might help to select between theories that fit the statute about equally well. But if the gravitational force of precedent rests on the idea that fairness requires the consistent enforcement of rights, then Hercules must discover principles that fit, not only the particular precedent to which some litigant directs his attention, but all other judicial decisions within his general jurisdiction and, indeed, statutes as well, so far as these must be seen to be generated by principle rather than policy. He does not satisfy his duty to show that his decision is consistent with established principles, and therefore fair, if the principles he cites as established are themselves inconsistent with other decisions that his court also proposes to uphold.

Suppose, for example, that he can justify Cardozo's decision in favour of Mrs MacPherson by citing some abstract principle of equality, which argues that whenever an accident occurs then the richest of the various persons whose acts might have contributed to the accident must bear the loss. He nevertheless cannot show that that principle has been respected in other accident cases, or, even if he could, that it has been respected in other branches of the law, like contract, in which it would also have great impact if it were recognized at all. If he decides against a future accident plaintiff who is richer than the defendant, by appealing to this alleged right of equality, that plaintiff may properly complain that the decision is just as inconsistent with the government's behavior in other cases as if *MacPherson* itself had been ignored. The law may not be a seamless web; but the plaintiff is entitled to ask Hercules to treat it as if it were.

You will now see why I called our judge Hercules. He must construct a scheme of abstract and concrete principles that provides a coherent justification for all common law precedents and, so far as these are to be justified on principle, constitutional and statutory provisions as well. We may grasp the magnitude of this enterprise by distinguishing, within the vast material of legal decisions that Hercules must justify, a vertical and a horizontal ordering. The vertical ordering is provided by distinguishing layers of authority; that is, layers at which official decisions might be taken to be controlling over decisions made at lower levels. In the United States the rough character of the vertical ordering is apparent. The constitutional structure occupies the highest level, the decisions of the Supreme Court and perhaps other courts interpreting that structure the next, enactments of the various legislatures the next and decisions of the various courts developing the common law different levels below that. Hercules must arrange justification of principle at each of these levels so that the justification is consistent with principles taken to provide the justification of higher levels. The horizontal ordering simply requires that the principles taken to justify a decision at one level must also be consistent with the justification offered for other decisions at that level.

Suppose Hercules, taking advantage of his unusual skills, proposed to work out this entire scheme in advance, so that he would be ready to confront litigants with an entire theory of law should this be necessary to justify any particular decision. He would begin, deferring to vertical ordering, by setting out and refining the constitutional theory he has already used. That constitutional theory would be more or less different from the theory that a different judge would develop, because a constitutional theory requires judgments about complex issues of institutional fit, as well as judgments about political and moral philosophy, and Hercules' judgments will inevitably differ from those other judges would make. These differences at a high level of vertical ordering will exercise considerable force on the scheme each judge would propose at lower levels. Hercules might think, for example, that certain substantive constitutional constraints on legislative power are best justified by postulating an abstract right to privacy against the state, because he believes that such a right is a consequence of the even more abstract right to liberty that the constitution guarantees. If so, he would regard the failure of the law of tort to recognize a parallel abstract right to privacy against fellow citizens, in some concrete form, as an inconsistency. If another judge did not share his beliefs about the connection between privacy and liberty, and so did not accept his constitutional interpretation as persuasive, that judge would also disagree about the proper development of tort.

So the impact of Hercules' own judgments will be pervasive, even though some of these will be controversial. But they will not enter his calculations in such a way that different parts of the theory he constructs can be attributed to his independent convictions rather than to the body of law that he must justify. He will not follow those classical theories of adjudication I mentioned earlier, which suppose that a judge follows statutes or precedent until the clear direction of these runs out, after which he is free to strike out on his own. His theory is rather a theory about what the statute or the precedent itself requires, and though he will, of course, reflect his own intellectual and philosophical convictions in making that judgment, that is a very different matter from supposing that those convictions have some independent force in his argument just because they are his.[1]

3. Mistakes. I shall not now try to develop, in further detail, Hercules' theory of law. I shall mention, however, two problems he will face. He must decide, first, how much weight he must give, in constructing a scheme of justification for a set of precedents, to the arguments that the judges who decided these cases attached to their decisions. He will not always find in these opinions any proposition precise enough to serve as a statute he might then interpret. But the opinions will almost always contain argument, in the form of propositions that the judge takes to recommend his decision. Hercules will decide to assign these only an initial or prima facie place in his scheme of justification. The purpose of that scheme is to satisfy the requirement that the government must extend to all, the rights it supposes some to have. The fact that one officer of the government offers a certain principle as the ground of his decision, may be taken to establish prima facie that the government does rely that far upon that principle.

But the main force of the underlying argument of fairness is forward-looking, not backward-looking. The gravitational force of Mrs Mac-Pherson's case depends not simply on the fact that she recovered for her Buick, but also on the fact that the government proposes to allow others in just her position to recover in the future. If the courts proposed to overrule the decision, no substantial argument of fairness, fixing on the actual decision in the case, survives in favor of the plaintiff in *Spartan Steel.* If, therefore, a principle other than the principle Cardozo cited can be found to justify *MacPherson,* and if this other principle also justifies a great deal of precedent that Cardozo's does not, or if it provides a smoother fit with arguments taken to justify decisions of a higher rank in vertical order, then this new principle is a more satisfactory basis for further decisions. Of course, this argument for not copying Cardozo's principle is unnecessary if the new principle is more abstract, and if Cardozo's principle can be seen as only a concrete form of that more abstract principle. In that case Hercules incorporates, rather than rejects, Cardozo's account of his decision. Cardozo, in fact, used the opinion in the earlier case of *Thomas v. Winchester,*[2] on which case he relied,

---

[1] See below, pp. 123-30.   [2] 6 N.Y. 397 (1852).

in just that fashion. It may be, however, that the new principle strikes out on a different line, so that it justifies a precedent or a series of precedents on grounds very different from what their opinions propose. Brandeis and Warren's famous argument about the right to privacy[1] is a dramatic illustration : they argued that this right was not unknown to the law but was, on the contrary, demonstrated by a wide variety of decisions, in spite of the fact that the judges who decided these cases mentioned no such right. It may be that their argument, so conceived, was unsuccessful, and that Hercules in their place, would have reached a different result. Hercules' theory nevertheless shows why their argument, sometimes taken to be a kind of brilliant fraud, was at least sound in its ambition.

Hercules must also face a different and greater problem. If the history of his court is at all complex, he will find, in practice, that the requirement of total consistency he has accepted will prove too strong, unless he develops it further to include the idea that he may, in applying this requirement, disregard some part of institutional history as a mistake. For he will be unable, even with his superb imagination, to find any set of principles that reconciles all standing statutes and precedents. This is hardly surprising : the legislators and judges of the past did not all have Hercules' ability or insight, nor were they men and women who were all of the same mind and opinion. Of course, any set of statutes and decisions can be explained historically, or psychologically, or sociologically, but consistency requires justification, not explanation, and the justification must be plausible and not sham. If the justification he constructs makes distinctions that are arbitrary and deploys principles that are unappealing, then it cannot count as a justification at all.

Suppose the law of negligence and accidents in Hercules' jurisdiction has developed in the following simplified and imaginary way. It begins with specific common law decisions recognizing a right to damages for bodily injury caused by very dangerous instruments that are defectively manufactured. These cases are then reinterpreted in some landmark decision, as they were in *MacPherson*, as justified by the very abstract right of each person to the reasonable care of others whose actions might injure his person or property. This principle is then both broadened and pinched in different ways. The courts, for example, decide that no concrete right lies against an accountant who has been negligent in the preparation of financial statements. They also decide that the right cannot be waived in certain cases; for example, in a standard form contract of automobile purchase. The legislature adds a statute providing that in certain cases of industrial accident, recovery will be allowed unless the

---

[1] Warren & Brandeis, 'The Right of Privacy', 4 *Harv. L. Rev.* (1890) 193.

defendant affirmatively establishes that the plaintiff was entirely to blame. But it also provides that in other cases, for example in airplane accidents, recovery will be limited to a stipulated amount, which might be much less than the actual loss; and it later adds that the guest in an automobile cannot sue his host even if the host drives negligently and the guest is injured. Suppose now, against this background, that Hercules is called upon to decide *Spartan Steel*.

Can he find a coherent set of principles that justifies this history in the way fairness requires? He might try the proposition that individuals have no right to recover for damages unless inflicted intentionally. He would argue that they are allowed to recover damages in negligence only for policy reasons, not in recognition of any abstract right to such damages, and he would cite the statutes limiting liability to protect airlines and insurance companies, and the cases excluding liability against accountants, as evidence that recovery is denied when policy argues the other way. But he must concede that this analysis of institutional history is incompatible with the common law decisions, particularly the landmark decision recognizing a general right to recovery in negligence. He cannot say, compatibly with the rest of his theory, that these decisions may themselves be justified on policy grounds, if he holds, by virtue of the rights thesis, that courts may extend liability only in response to arguments of principle and not policy. So he must set these decisions aside as mistakes.

He might try another strategy. He might propose some principle according to which individuals have rights to damages in just the circumstances of the particular cases that decided they did, but have no general right to such damages. He might concede, for example, a legal principle granting a right to recover for damages incurred within an automobile owned by the plaintiff, but deny a principle that would extend to other damage. But though he could in this way tailor his justification of institutional history to fit that history exactly, he would realize that this justification rests on distinctions that are arbitrary. He can find no room in his political theory for a distinction that concedes an abstract right if someone is injured driving his own automobile but denies it if he is a guest or if he is injured in an airplane. He has provided a set of arguments that cannot stand as a coherent justification of anything.

He might therefore concede that he can make no sense of institutional history except by supposing some general abstract right to recover for negligence: but he might argue that it is a relatively weak right and so will yield to policy considerations of relatively minor force. He will cite the limiting statutes and cases in support of his view that the right is a weak one. But he will then face a difficulty if, though the statute limiting liability in airplane accidents has never been repealed, the airlines have become sufficiently secure, and the mechanisms of insurance available to airlines so efficient and inexpensive, that a failure to repeal the statute can only be justified by taking the abstract right to be so weak that relatively thin arguments of policy are sufficient to defeat it. If Hercules takes the right to be that weak then he cannot justify the various common law decisions that support the right, as a concrete right, against arguments of policy much stronger than the airlines are now able to press. So he must choose either to take the failure to repeal the airline accident limitation statute, or the common law decisions that value the right much higher, as mistakes.

In any case, therefore, Hercules must expand his theory to include the idea that a justification of institutional history may display some part of that history as mistaken. But he cannot make impudent use of this device, because if he were free to take any incompatible piece of institutional history as a mistake, with no further consequences for his general theory, then the requirement of consistency would be no genuine requirement at all. He must develop some theory of institutional mistakes, and this theory of mistakes must have two parts. It must show the consequences for further arguments of taking some institutional event to be mistaken; and it must limit the number and character of the events that can be disposed of in that way.

He will construct the first part of this theory of mistakes by means of two sets of distinctions. He will first distinguish between the specific authority of any institutional event, which is its power as an institutional act to effect just the specific institutional consequences it describes, and its gravitational force. If he classifies some event as a mistake, then he does not deny its specific authority but he does deny its gravitational force, and he cannot consistently appeal to that force in other arguments. He will also distinguish between embedded and corrigible mistakes; embedded mistakes are those whose specific authority is fixed so that it survives their loss of gravitational force; corrigible mistakes are those whose specific authority depends on gravitational force in such a way that it cannot survive this loss.

The constitutional level of his theory will determine which mistakes are embedded. His theory of legislative supremacy, for example, will insure that any statutes he treats as mistakes will lose their gravitational force but not their specific authority. If he denies the gravitational force of the aircraft liability limitation statute, the statute is not thereby repealed; the mistake is embedded so that the specific authority survives. He must continue to respect the limitations the statute imposes upon liability, but he will not use it to argue in some other case for a weaker right. If he accepts some strict doctrine of precedent, and designates some judicial decision, like the decision denying a right in negligence against an accountant, a mistake, then the strict doctrine may preserve the specific authority of that decision, which might be limited to its enactment force, but the decision will lose its gravitational force; it will become in Justice Frankfurter's phrase, a piece of legal flotsam or jetsam. It will not be necessary to decide which.

That is fairly straightforward, but Hercules must take more pains with the second part of his theory of mistakes. He is required, by the justification he has fixed to the general practice of precedent, to compose a more detailed justification, in the form of a scheme of principle, for the entire body of statutes and common law decisions. But a justification that designates part of what is to be justified as mistaken is prima facie weaker than one that does not. The second part of his theory of mistakes must show that it is nevertheless a stronger justification than any alternative that does not recognize any mistakes, or that recognizes a different set of mistakes. That demonstration cannot be a deduction from simple rules of theory construction, but if Hercules bears in mind the connection he earlier established between precedent and fairness, this connection will suggest two guidelines for his theory of mistakes. In the first place, fairness fixes on institutional history, not just as history but as a political program that the government proposed to continue into the future; it seizes, that is, on forward-looking, not the backward-looking implications of precedent. If Hercules discovers that some previous decision, whether a statute or a judicial decision, is now widely regretted within the pertinent branch of the profession, that fact in itself distinguishes that decision as vulnerable. He must remember, second, that the argument from fairness that demands consistency is not the only argument from fairness to which government in general, or judges in particular, must respond. If he believes, quite apart from any argument of consistency, that a particular statute or decision was wrong because unfair, within the community's own concept of fairness, then that belief is sufficient to distinguish the decision, and make it vulnerable. Of course, he must apply the guidelines with a sense of the vertical structure of his overall justification, so that decisions at a lower level are more vulnerable than decisions at a higher.

Hercules will therefore apply at least two maxims in the second part of his theory of mistakes. If he can show, by arguments of history or by appeal to some sense of the legal community, that a particular principle, though it once had sufficient appeal to persuade a legislature or court to a legal decision, has now so little force that it is unlikely to generate any further such decisions, then the argument from fairness that supports that principle is undercut. If he can show by arguments of political morality that such a principle, apart from its popularity, is unjust, then the argument from fairness that supports that principle is overridden. Hercules will be delighted to find that these discriminations are familiar in the practice of other judges. The jurisprudential importance of his career does not lie in the novelty, but just in the familiarity, of the theory of hard cases that he has now created.

6. POLITICAL OBJECTIONS

The rights thesis has two aspects. Its descriptive aspect explains the present structure of the institution of adjudication. Its normative aspect offers a political justification for that structure. The story of Hercules shows how familiar judicial practice might have developed from a general acceptance of the thesis. This at once clarifies the thesis by showing its implications in some detail, and offers powerful, if special, argument for its descriptive aspect. But the story also provides a further political argument in favour of its normative aspect. Hercules began his calculations with the intention, not simply to replicate what other judges do, but to enforce the genuine institutional rights of those who came to his court. If he is able to reach decisions that satisfy our sense of justice, then that argues in favor of the political value of the thesis.

It may now be said, however, by way of rebuttal, that certain features of Hercules' story count against the normative aspect of the thesis. In the introductory part of this chapter, I mentioned a familiar objection to judicial originality : this is the argument from democracy that elected legislators have superior qualifications to make political decisions. I said that this argument is weak in the case of decisions of principle, but Hercules' story may give rise to fresh doubts on that score. The story makes plain that many of Hercules' decisions about legal rights depend upon judgments of political theory that might be made differently by different judges or by the public at large. It does not matter, to this objection, that the decision is one of principle rather than policy. It matters only that the decision is one of political conviction about which reasonable men disagree. If Hercules decides cases on the basis of such judgments, then he decides on the basis of his own convictions and preferences, which seems unfair, contrary to democracy, and offensive to the rule of law.

That is the general form of the objection I shall consider in this final section. It must first be clarified in one important respect. The objection charges Hercules with relying upon his own convictions in matters of political morality. That charge is ambiguous, because there are two ways in which an official might rely upon his own opinions in making such a decision. One of these, in a judge, is offensive, but the other is inevitable. Sometimes an official offers, as a reason for his decision, the fact that some person or group holds a particular belief or opinion. A legislator might offer, as a reason for voting for an anti-abortion statute, the fact that his constituents believe that abortion is wrong. That is a form of appeal to authority: the official who makes that appeal does not himself warrant the substance of the belief to which he appeals, nor does he count the soundness of the belief as part of his argument. We might imagine a judge appealing, in just this way, to the fact that he *himself* has a particular political preference. He might be a philosophical skeptic in matters of political morality. He might say that one man's opinion in such matters is worth no more than another's because neither has any objective standing, but that, since he himself happens to favor abortion, he will hold anti-abortion statutes unconstitutional.

That judge relies upon the naked fact that he holds a particular political view as itself a justification for his decision. But a judge may rely upon his own belief in the different sense of relying upon the truth or soundness of that belief. Suppose he believes, for example, that the due process clause of the Constitution, as a matter of law, makes invalid any constraint of a fundamental liberty, and that anti-abortion statutes constrain a fundamental liberty. He might rely upon the soundness of those convictions, not the fact that he, as opposed to others, happens to hold them. A judge need not rely upon the soundness of any *particular* belief in this way. Suppose the majority of his colleagues, or the editors of a prominent law journal, or the majority of the community voting in some referendum, holds a contrary view about abortion. He may decide that it is his duty to defer to their judgment of what the Constitution requires, in spite of the fact that their view is, as he thinks, unsound. But in that case he relies upon the soundness of his own conviction that his institutional duty is to defer to the judgment of others in this matter. He must, that is, rely upon the substance of his own judgment at some point, in order to make any judgment at all.

Hercules does not rely upon his own convictions in the first of these two ways. He does not count the fact that he himself happens to favor a particular conception of religious liberty, for example, as providing an argument in favor of a decision that advances that conception. If the objection we are considering is pertinent, therefore, it must be an objection to his relying upon his own convictions in the second way. But in that case the objection cannot be a blanket objection to his relying upon any of his convictions, because he must, inevitably, rely on some. It is rather an objection to his relying on the soundness of certain of his own convictions; it argues that he ought to defer to others in certain judgments even though their judgments are, as he thinks, wrong.

It is difficult, however, to see *which* of his judgments the objection supposes he should remand to others. We would not have any such problem if Hercules had accepted, rather than rejected, a familiar theory of adjudication. Classical jurisprudence supposes, as I said earlier, that judges decide cases in two steps : they find the limit of what the explicit law requires, and they then exercise an independent discretion to legislate on issues which the law does not reach. In the recent abortion cases,[1] according to this theory, the Supreme Court justices first determined that the language of the due process clause and of prior Supreme Court decisions did not dictate a decision either way. They then set aside the Constitution and the cases to decide whether, in their opinion, it is fundamentally unfair for a state to outlaw abortion in the first trimester.

Let us imagine another judge, called Herbert, who accepts this theory of adjudication and proposes to follow it in his decisions. Herbert might believe both that women have a background right to abort fetuses they carry, and that the majority of citizens think otherwise. The present objection argues that he must resolve that conflict in favor of democracy, so that, when he exercises his discretion to decide the abortion cases, he must decide in favor of the prohibitive statutes. Herbert might agree, in which case we should say that he has set aside his morality in favor of the people's morality. That is, in fact, a slightly misleading way to put the point. His own morality made the fact that the people held a particular view decisive; it did not withdraw in favor of the substance of that view. On the other hand, Herbert might disgree. He might believe that background rights in general, or this right in particular, must prevail against popular opinion even in the legislature, so that he has a duty, when exercising a legislative discretion, to declare the statutes unconstitutional. In that case, the present objection argues that he is mistaken, because he insufficiently weighs the principle of democracy in his political theory.

In any case, however, these arguments that seem tailor-made for Herbert are puzzling as arguments against Hercules. Hercules does not first find the limits of law and then deploy his own political convictions to supplement what the law requires. He uses his own judgment to determine what legal rights the parties before him have, and when that judgment is made nothing remains to submit to either his own or the public's convictions. The difference is not simply a difference in ways of describing the same thing : we saw in Section 4 that a judgment of institutional right, like the chess referee's judgment about the forfeiture rule, is very different from an independent judgment of political morality made in the interstices provided by the open texture of rules.

Herbert did not consider whether to consult popular morality until he had fixed the legal rights of the parties. But when Hercules fixes legal rights he has already taken the community's moral traditions into

[1] *Roe v. Wade*, 410 U.S. 113 (1973); *Doe v. Bolton*, 410 U.S. 179 (1973).

account, at least as these are captured in the whole institutional record that it is his office to interpret. Suppose two coherent justifications can be given for earlier Supreme Court decisions enforcing the due process clause. One justification contains some principle of extreme liberality that cannot be reconciled with the criminal law of most of the states, but the other contains no such principle. Hercules cannot seize upon the former justification as license for deciding the abortion cases in favor of abortion, even if he is himself an extreme liberal. His own political convictions, which favor the more liberal justification of the earlier cases, must fall, because they are inconsistent with the popular traditions that have shaped the criminal law that his justification must also explain.

Of course, Hercules' techniques may sometimes require a decision that opposes popular morality on some issue. Suppose no justification of the earlier constitutional cases can be given that does not contain a liberal principle sufficiently strong to require a decision in favor of abortion. Hercules must then reach that decision, no matter how strongly popular morality condemns abortion. He does not, in this case, enforce his own convictions against the community's. He rather judges that the community's morality is inconsistent on this issue : its constitutional morality, which is the justification that must be given for its constitution as interpreted by its judges, condemns its discrete judgment on the particular issue of abortion. Such conflicts are familiar within individual morality; if we wish to use the concept of a community morality in political theory, we must acknowledge conflicts within that morality as well. There is no question, of course, as to how such a conflict must be resolved. Individuals have a right to the consistent enforcement of the principles upon which their institutions rely. It is this institutional right, as defined by the community's constitutional morality, that Hercules must defend against any inconsistent opinion however popular.

These hypothetical cases show that the objection designed for Herbert is poorly cast as an objection against Hercules. Hercules' theory of adjudication at no point provides for any choice between his own political convictions and those he takes to be the political convictions of the community at large. On the contrary, his theory identifies a particular conception of community morality as decisive of legal issues; that conception holds that community morality is the political morality presupposed by the laws and institutions of the community. He must, of course, rely on his own judgment as to what the principles of that morality are, but this form of reliance is the second form we distinguished, which at some level is inevitable.

It is perfectly true that in some cases Hercules' decision about the content of this community morality, and thus his decision about legal rights, will be controversial. This will be so whenever institutional history must be justified by appeal to some contested political concept, like fairness or liberality or equality, but it is not sufficiently detailed so that it can be justified by only one among different conceptions of that concept. I offered, earlier, Hercules' decision of the free busing case as an example of such a decision; we may now take a more topical example. Suppose the earlier due process cases can be justified only by supposing some important right to human dignity, but do not themselves force a decision one way or the other on the issue of whether dignity requires complete control over the use of one's uterus. If Hercules sits in the abortion cases, he must decide that issue and must employ his own understanding of dignity to do so.

It would be silly to deny that this is a political decision, or that different judges, from different subcultures, would make it differently. Even so, it is nevertheless a very different decision from the decision whether women have, all things considered, a background right to abort their fetuses. Hercules might think dignity an unimportant concept; if he were to attend a new constitutional convention he might vote to repeal the due process clause, or at least to amend it so as to remove any idea of dignity from its scope. He is nevertheless able to decide whether that concept, properly understood, embraces the case of abortion. He is in the shoes of the chess referee who hates meritocracy, but is nevertheless able to consider whether intelligence includes psychological intimidation.

It is, of course, necessary that Hercules have some understanding of the concept of dignity, even if he denigrates that concept; and he will gain that understanding by noticing how the concept is used by those to whom it is important. If the concept figures in the justification of a series of constitutional decisions, then it must be a concept that is prominent in the political rhetoric and debates of the time. Hercules will collect his sense of the concept from its life in these contexts. He will do the best he can to understand the appeal of the idea to those to whom it does appeal. He will devise, so far as he can, a conception that explains that appeal to them.

This is a process that can usefully be seen as occupying two stages. Hercules will notice, simply as a matter of understanding his language, which are the clear, settled cases in which the concept holds. He will notice, for example, that if one man is thought to treat another as his servant, though he is not in fact that man's employer, then he will be thought to have invaded his dignity. He will next try to put himself, so far as he can, within the more general scheme of beliefs and attitudes of those who value the concept, to look at these clear cases through their eyes. Suppose, for example, that they believe in some Aristotelian doctrine of the urgency of self-fulfillment or they take self-reliance to be a very great virtue. Hercules must construct some general theory of the concept that explains why those who hold that belief, or accept that virtue, will also prize dignity; if his theory also explains why he, who does not accept the belief or the virtue, does not prize dignity, then the theory will be all the more successful for that feature.

Hercules will then use his theory of dignity to answer questions that institutional history leaves open. His theory of dignity may connect dignity with independence, so that someone's dignity is comprised whenever he is forced, against his will, to devote an important part of his activity to the concerns of others. In that case, he may well endorse the claim that women have a constitutional liberty of abortion, as an aspect of their conceded constitutional right to dignity.

That is how Hercules might interpret a concept he does not value, to reach a decision that, as a matter of background morality, he would reject. It is very unlikely, however, that Hercules will often find himself in that position; he is likely to value most of the concepts that figure in the justification of the institutions of his own community. In that case his analysis of these concepts will not display the same self-conscious air of sociological inquiry. He will begin within, rather than outside, the scheme of values that approves the concept, and he will be able to put to himself, rather than to some hypothetical self, questions about the deep morality that gives the concept value. The sharp distinction between background and institutional morality will fade, not because institutional morality is displaced by personal convictions, but because personal convictions have become the most reliable guide he has to institutional morality.

It does not follow, of course, that Hercules will even then reach exactly the same conclusions that any other judge would reach about disputed cases of the concept in question. On the contrary, he will then become like any reflective member of the community willing to debate about what fairness or equality or liberty requires on some occasion. But we now see that it is wrong to suppose that reflective citizens, in such debates, are simply setting their personal convictions against the convictions of others. They too are contesting different conceptions of a concept they suppose they hold in common; they are debating which of different theories of that concept best explains the settled or clear cases that fix the concept. That character of their debate is obscured by the fact that they do value the concepts they contest, and therefore reason intuitively or introspectively rather than in the more sociological mode that an outsider might use; but, so long as they put their claims as claims about concepts held in common, these claims will have the same structure as the outsider's. We may summarize these important points this way: the community's morality, on these issues at least, is not some sum or combination or function of the competing claims of its members; it is rather what each of the competing claims claims to be. When Hercules relies upon his own conception of dignity, in the second sense of reliance we distinguished, he is still relying on his own sense of what the community's morality provides.

It is plain, therefore, that the present objection must be recast if it is to be a weapon against Hercules. But it cannot be recast to fit Hercules better without losing its appeal. Suppose we say that Hercules must defer, not to his own judgment of the institutional morality of his community, but to the judgment of most members of that community about what that is. There are two apparent objections to tht recommendation. It is unclear, in the first place, how he could discover what that popular judgment is. It does not follow from the fact that the man in the street disapproves of abortion, or supports legislation making it criminal, that he has considered whether the concept of dignity presupposed by the Constitution, consistently applied, supports his political position. That is a sophisticated question requiring some dialectical skill, and though that skill may be displayed by the ordinary man when he self-consciously defends his position, it is not to be taken for granted that his political preferences, expressed casually or in the ballot, have been subjected to that form of examination.

But even if Hercules is satisfied that the ordinary man has decided that dignity does not require the right to abortion, the question remains why Hercules should take the ordinary man's opinion on that issue as decisive. Suppose Hercules thinks that the ordinary man is wrong; that he is wrong, that is, in his philosophical opinions about what the community's concepts require. If Herbert were in that position, he would have good reason to defer to the ordinary man's judgments. Herbert thinks that when the positive rules of law are vague or indeterminate, the litigants have no institutional right at all, so that any decision he might reach is a piece of fresh legislation. Since nothing he decides will cheat the parties of what they have a right to have at his hands, the argument is plausible, at least, that when he legislates he should regard himself as the agent of the majority. But Hercules cannot take that view of the matter. He knows that the question he must decide is the question of the parties' institutional rights. He knows that if he decides wrongly, as he would do if he followed the ordinary man's lead, he cheats the parties of what they are entitled to have. Neither Hercules nor Herbert would submit an ordinary legal question to popular opinion; since Hercules thinks that parties have rights in hard cases as well as in easy ones, he will not submit to popular opinion in hard cases either.

Of course, any judge's judgment about the rights of parties in hard cases may be wrong, and the objection may try, in one final effort, to capitalize on that fact. It might concede, *arguendo,* that Hercules' technique is appropriate to Hercules, who by hypothesis has great moral insight. But it would deny that the same technique is appropriate for judges generally, who do not. We must be careful, however, in assessing this challenge, to consider the alternatives. It is a matter of injustice when judges make mistakes about legal rights, whether these mistakes are in favor of the plaintiff or defendant. The objection points out that they will sometimes make such mistakes, because they are fallible and in any event disagree. But of course, though we, as social critics, know that mistakes will be made, we do not know when because we are not Hercules either. We must commend techniques of adjudication that might be expected to reduce the number of mistakes overall based on some judgment of the relative capacities of men and women who might occupy different roles.

Hercules' technique encourages a judge to make his own judgments about institutional rights. The argument from judicial fallibility might be thought to suggest two alternatives. The first argues that since judges are fallible they should make no effort at all to determine the institutional rights of the parties before them, but should decide hard cases only on grounds of policy, or not at all. But that is perverse; it argues that because judges will often, by misadventure, produce unjust decisions they should make no effort to produce just ones. The second alternative argues that since judges are fallible they should submit questions of institutional right raised by hard cases to someone else. But to whom? There is no reason to credit any other particular group with better facilities of moral argument; or, if there is, then it is the process of selecting judges, not the techniques of judging that they are asked to use, that must be changed. So this form of skepticism does not in itself argue against Hercules' technique of adjudication, though of course it serves as a useful reminder to any judge that he might well be wrong in his political judgments, and that he should therefore decide hard cases with humility.

5

Constitutional Cases

When Richard Nixon was running for President he promised that he would appoint to the Supreme Court men who represented his own legal philosophy, that is, who were what he called 'strict constructionists'. The nominations he subsequently made and talked about, however, did not all illuminate that legal philosophy; jurisprudence played little part in the nation's evaluation of Haynesworth and Carswell, let alone those almost nominated, Hershell Friday and Mildred Lilly. But the President presented his successful choices, Lewis Powell and William Rehnquist, as examples of his theory of law, and took the occasion to expand on that theory for a national television audience. These men, he said, would enforce the law as it is, and not 'twist or bend' it to suit their own personal convictions, as Nixon accused the Warren Court of doing.

Nixon claimed that his opposition to the Warren Court's desegregation decisions, and to other decisions it took, were not based simply on a personal or political distaste for the results. He argued that the decisions violated the standards of adjudication that the Court should follow. The Court was usurping, in his views, powers that rightly belong to other institutions, including the legislatures of the various states whose school systems the Court sought to reform. He was, of course, not alone in this view. It has for some time been part of general conservative attitudes that the Supreme Court has exceeded its rightful authority. Nixon, Ford and many Congressmen and representatives have canvassed ways to limit the Court's authority by legislation. Nixon, for example, asked for a Congressional statute that would have purported to reverse important decisions, including the decision in *Swann v. Charlotte-Mecklenburg Board of Education* which gave federal courts wide powers to use busing orders as a remedy for certain forms of *de facto* segregation, and Senator Jackson and others have for some time campaigned for a constitutional amendment to the same point.

I shall not be concerned with the correctness of any of the Court's controversial decisions, nor with the wisdom of these various attempts, so far unsuccessful, to check its powers by some form of legislation or amendment. I am concerned rather with the philosophy of constitutional adjudication that the politicians who oppose the Court suppose that they hold. I shall argue that there is in fact no coherent philosophy to which such politicians may consistently appeal. I shall also try to show how the general theory of adjudication I described and defended in Chapter 4 supports the constitutional philosophy, if not the particular decisions, of the Warren Court.

Nixon is no longer president, and his crimes were so grave that no one is likely to worry very much any more about the details of his own legal philosophy. Nevertheless in what follows I shall use the name 'Nixon' to refer, not to Nixon, but to any politician holding the set of attitudes about the Supreme Court that he made explicit in his political campaigns. There was, fortunately, only one real Nixon, but there are, in the special sense in which I use the name, many Nixons.

What can be the basis of this composite Nixon's opposition to the controversial decisions of the Warren Court? He cannot object to these decisions simply because they went beyond prior law, or say that the Supreme Court must never change its mind. Indeed the Burger Court itself seems intent on limiting the liberal decisions of the Warren Court, like *Miranda*. The Constitution's guarantee of 'equal protection of the laws', it is true, does not in plain words determine that 'separate but equal' school facilities are unconstitutional, or that segregation was so unjust that heroic measures are required to undo its effects. But neither does it provide that as a matter of constitutional law the Court would be wrong to reach these conclusions. It leaves these issues to the Court's judgment, and the Court would have made law just as much if it had, for example, refused to hold the North Carolina statute unconstitutional. It would have made law by establishing, as a matter of precedent, that the equal protection clause does not reach that far.

So we must search further to find a theoretical basis for Nixon's position. It may be silly, of course, to suppose that Nixon has a jurisprudence. He might simply have strung together catch phrases of conservative rhetoric, or he might be recording a distaste for any judicial decision that seems to extend the rights of individuals against constituted authority. But Nixon is, after all, a lawyer, and in any event his conservative views are supported by a great many lawyers and some very distinguished legal scholars. It is therefore important to see how far this conservative position can be defended as a matter of principle and not simply of prejudice.

2.

The constitutional theory on which our government rests is not a simple majoritarian theory. The Constitution, and particularly the Bill of Rights, is designed to protect individual citizens and groups against certain decisions that a majority of citizens might want to make, even when that majority acts in what it takes to be the general or common interest. Some of these constitutional restraints take the form of fairly precise rules, like the rule that requires a jury trial in federal criminal proceedings or, perhaps, the rule that forbids the national Congress to abridge freedom of speech. But other constraints take the form of what are often called 'vague' standards, for example, the provision that the government shall not deny men due process of law, or equal protection of the laws.

This interference with democratic practice requires a justification. The draftsmen of the Constitution assumed that these restraints could be justified by appeal to moral rights which individuals possess against the majority, and which the constitutional provisions, both 'vague' and precise, might be said to recognize and protect.

The 'vague' standards were chosen deliberately, by the men who drafted and adopted them, in place of the more specific and limited rules that they might have enacted. But their decision to use the language they did has caused a great deal of legal and political controversy, because even reasonable men of good will differ when they try to elaborate, for example, the moral rights that the due process clause or the equal protection clause brings into the law. They also differ when they try to apply these rights, however defined, to complex matters of political administration, like the educational practices that were the subject of the segregation cases.

The practice has developed of referring to a 'strict' and a 'liberal' side to these controversies, so that the Supreme Court might be said to have taken the 'liberal' side in the segregation cases and its critics the 'strict' side. Nixon has this distinction in mind when he calls himself a 'strict constructionist'. But the distinction is in fact confusing, because it runs together two different issues that must be separated. Any case that arises under the 'vague' constitutional guarantees can be seen as posing two questions: (1) Which decision is required by strict, that is to say faithful, adherence to the text of the Constitution or to the intention of those who adopted that text? (2) Which decision is required by a political philosophy that takes a strict, that is to say narrow, view of the moral rights that individuals have against society? Once these questions are distinguished, it is plain that they may have different answers. The text of the First Amendment, for example, says that Congress shall make *no* law abridging the freedom of speech, but a narrow view of individual rights would permit many such laws, ranging from libel and obscenity laws to the Smith Act.

In the case of the 'vague' provisions, however, like the due process and equal protection clauses, lawyers have run the two questions together because they have relied, largely without recognizing it, on a theory of meaning that might be put this way : If the framers of the Constitution used vague language, as they did when they condemned violations of 'due process of law', then what they 'said' or 'meant' is limited to the instances of official action that they had in mind as violations, or, at least, to those instances that they would have thought were violations if they had had them in mind. If those who were responsible for adding the due process clause to the Constitution believed that it was fundamentally unjust to provide separate education for different races, or had detailed views about justice that entailed that conclusion, then the segregation decisions might be defended as an application of the principle they had laid down. Otherwise they could not be defended in this way, but instead would show that the judges had substituted their own ideas of justice for those the constitutional drafters meant to lay down.

This theory makes a strict interpretation of the text yield a narrow view of constitutional rights, because it limits such rights to those recognized by a limited group of people at a fixed date of history. It forces those who favor a more liberal set of rights to concede that they are departing from strict legal authority, a departure they must then seek to justify by appealing only to the desirability of the results they reach.

But the theory of meaning on which this argument depends is far too crude; it ignores a distinction that philosophers have made but lawyers have not yet appreciated. Suppose I tell my children simply that I expect them not to treat others unfairly. I no doubt have in mind examples of the conduct I mean to discourage, but I would not accept that my 'meaning' was limited to these examples, for two reasons. First I would expect my children to apply my instructions to situations I had not and could not have thought about. Second, I stand ready to admit that some particular act I had thought was fair when I spoke was in fact unfair, or vice versa, if one of my children is able to convince me of that later; in that case I should want to say that my instructions covered the case he cited, not that I had changed my instructions. I might say that I meant the family to be guided by the *concept* of fairness, not by any specific *conception* of fairness I might have had in mind.

This is a crucial distinction which it is worth pausing to explore. Suppose a group believes in common that acts may suffer from a special moral defect which they call unfairness, and which consists in a wrongful division of benefits and burdens, or a wrongful attribution of praise or blame. Suppose also that they agree on a great number of standard cases of unfairness and use these as benchmarks against which to test other, more controversial cases. In that case, the group has a concept of unfairness, and its members may appeal to that concept in moral instruction or argument. But members of that group may nevertheless differ over a large number of these controversial cases, in a way that suggests that each either has or acts on a different theory of *why* the standard cases are acts of unfairness. They may differ, that is, on which more fundamental principles must be relied upon to show that a particular division or attribution is unfair. In that case, the members have different conceptions of fairness.

If so, then members of this community who give instructions or set standards in the name of fairness may be doing two different things. First they may be appealing to the concept of fairness, simply by instructing others to act fairly; in this case they charge those whom they instruct with the responsibility of developing and applying their own conception of fairness as controversial cases arise. That is not the same thing, of course, as granting them a discretion to act as they like; it sets a standard which they must try – and may fail – to meet, because it assumes that one conception is superior to another. The man who appeals to the concept in this way may have his own conception, as I did when I told my children to act fairly; but he holds this conception only as his own theory of how the standard he set must be met, so that when he changes his theory he has not changed that standard.

On the other hand, the members may be laying down a particular conception of fairness; I would have done this, for example, if I had listed my wishes with respect to controversial examples or if, even less likely, I had specified some controversial and explicit theory of fairness, as if I had said to decide hard cases by applying the utilitarian ethics of Jeremy Bentham. The difference is a difference not just in the *detail* of the instructions given but in the *kind* of instructions given. When I appeal to the concept of fairness I appeal to what fairness means, and I give my views on that issue no special standing. When I lay down a conception of fairness, I lay down what I mean by fairness, and my view is therefore the heart of the matter. When I appeal to fairness I pose a moral issue; when I lay down my conception of fairness I try to answer it.

Once this distinction is made it seems obvious that we must take what I have been calling 'vague' constitutional clauses as representing appeals to the concepts they employ, like legality, equality, and cruelty. The Supreme Court may soon decide, for example, whether capital punishment is 'cruel' within the meaning of the constitutional clause that prohibits 'cruel and unusual punishment'. It would be a mistake for the Court to be much influenced by the fact that when the clause was adopted capital punishment was standard and unquestioned. That would be decisive if the framers of the clause had meant to lay down a particular conception of cruelty, because it would show that the conception did not extend so far.

But it is not decisive of the different question the Court now faces, which is this : Can the Court, responding to the framers' appeal to the concept of cruelty, now defend a conception that does not make death cruel?

Those who ignore the distinction between concepts and conceptions, but who believe that the Court ought to make a fresh determination of whether the death penalty is cruel, are forced to argue in a vulnerable way. They say that ideas of cruelty change over time, and that the Court must be free to reject out-of-date conceptions; this suggests that the Court must change what the Constitution enacted. But in fact the Court can enforce what the Constitution says only by making up its own mind about what is cruel, just as my children, in my example, can do what I said only by making up their own minds about what is fair. If those who enacted the broad clauses had meant to lay down particular conceptions, they would have found the sort of language conventionally used to do this, that is, they would have offered particular theories of the concepts in question.

Indeed the very practice of calling these clauses 'vague', in which I have joined, can now be seen to involve a mistake. The clauses are vague only if we take them to be botched or incomplete or schematic attempts to lay down particular conceptions. If we take them as appeals to moral concepts they could not be made more precise by being more detailed.[1]

The confusion I mentioned between the two senses of 'strict' construction' is therefore very misleading indeed. If courts try to be faithful to the text of the Constitution, they will for that very reason be forced to decide between competing conceptions of political morality. So it is wrong to attack the Warren Court, for example, on the ground that it failed to treat the Constitution as a binding text. On the contrary, if we wish to treat fidelity to that text as an overriding requirement of constitutional interpretation, then it is the conservative critics of the Warren Court who are at fault, because their philosophy ignores the direction to face issues of moral principle that the logic of the text demands.

I put the matter in a guarded way because we may *not* want to accept fidelity to the spirit of the text as an overriding principle of constitutional adjudication. It may be more important for courts to decide constitutional cases in a manner that respects the judgments of other institutions of government, for example. Or it may be more important for courts to protect established legal doctrines, so that citizens

---

[1] It is less misleading to say that the broad clauses of the Constitution 'delegate' power to the Court to enforce its own conceptions of political morality. But even this is inaccurate if it suggests that the Court need not justify its conception by arguments showing the connections between its conception and standard cases, as described in the text. If the Court finds that the death penalty is cruel, it must do so on the basis of some principles or groups of principles that unite the death penalty with the thumbscrew and the rack.

and the government can have confidence that the courts will hold to what they have said before. But it is crucial to recognize that these other policies compete with the principle that the Constitution is the fundamental and imperative source of constitutional law. They are not, as the 'strict constructionists' suppose, simply consequences of that principle.

3.

Once the matter is put in this light, moreover, we are able to assess these competing claims of policy, free from the confusion imposed by the popular notion of 'strict construction'. For this purpose I want now to compare and contrast two very general philosophies of how the courts should decide difficult or controversial constitutional issues. I shall call these two philosophies by the names they are given in the legal literature – the programs of 'judicial activism' and 'judicial restraint' – though it will be plain that these names are in certain ways misleading.

The program of judicial activism holds that courts should accept the directions of the so-called vague constitutional provisions in the spirit I described, in spite of competing reasons of the sort I mentioned. They should work out principles of legality, equality, and the rest, revise these principles from time to time in the light of what seems to the Court fresh moral insight, and judge the acts of Congress, the states, and the President accordingly. (This puts the program in its strongest form; in fact its supporters generally qualify it in ways I shall ignore for the present.)

The program of judicial restraint, on the contrary, argues that courts should allow the decisions of other branches of government to stand, even when they offend the judges' own sense of the principles required by the broad constitutional doctrines, except when these decisions are so offensive to political morality that they would violate the provisions on any plausible interpretation, or, perhaps, when a contrary decision is required by clear precedent. (Again, this put the program in a stark form; those who profess the policy qualify it in different ways.)

The Supreme Court followed the policy of activism rather than restraint in cases like the segregation cases because the words of the equal protection clause left it open whether the various educational practices of the states concerned should be taken to violate the Constitution, no clear precedent held that they did, and reasonable men might differ on the moral issues involved. If the Court had followed the program of judicial restraint, it would therefore have held in favor of the North Carolina statute in *Swann*, not against it. But the program of restraint would not always act to provide decisions that would please political conservatives. In the early days of the New Deal, as critics of the Warren Court are quick to point out, it was the liberals who objected to Court decisions that struck down acts of Congress in the name of the due process clause.

It may seem, therefore, that if Nixon has a legal theory it depends crucially on some theory of judicial restraint. We must now, however, notice a distinction between two forms of judicial restraint, for there are two different, and indeed incompatible, grounds on which that policy might be based.

The first is a theory of political *skepticism* that might be described in this way. The policy of judicial activism presupposes a certain objectivity of moral principle; in particular it presupposes that citizens do have certain moral rights against the state, like a moral right to equality of public education or to fair treatment by the police. Only if such moral rights exist in some sense can activism be justified as a program based on something beyond the judge's personal preferences. The skeptical theory attacks activism at its roots; it argues that in fact individuals have no such moral rights against the state. They have only such *legal* rights as the Constitution grants them, and these are limited to the plain and uncontroversial violations of public morality that the framers must have had actually in mind, or that have since been established in a line of precedent.

The alternative ground of a program of restraint is a theory of judicial *deference*. Contrary to the skeptical theory, this assumes that citizens do have moral rights against the state beyond what the law expressly grants them, but it points out that the character and strength of these rights are debatable and argues that political institutions other than courts are responsible for deciding which rights are to be recognized.

This is an important distinction, even though the literature of constitutional law does not draw it with any clarity. The skeptical theory and the theory of deference differ dramatically in the kind of justification they assume, and in their implications for the more general moral theories of the men who profess to hold them. These theories are so different that most American politicians can consistently accept the second, but not the first.

A skeptic takes the view, as I have said, that men have no moral rights against the state and only such legal rights as the law expressly provides. But what does this mean, and what sort of argument might the skeptic make for his view? There is, of course, a very lively dispute in moral philosophy about the nature and standing of moral rights, and considerable disagreement about what they are, if they are anything at all. I shall rely, in trying to answer these questions, on a low-keyed theory of moral rights against the state which I develop in Chapter 7. Under that theory, a man has a moral right against the state if for some reason the state would do wrong to treat him in a certain way, even though it would be in the general interest to do so. So a black child has a moral right to an equal education, for example, if it is wrong for the state not to provide that education, even if the community as a whole suffers thereby.

I want to say a word about the virtues of this way of looking at moral rights against the state. A great many lawyers are wary of talking about moral rights, even though they find it easy to talk about what is right or wrong for government to do, because they suppose that rights, if they exist at all, are spooky sorts of things that men and women have in much the same way as they have non-spooky things like tonsils. But the sense of rights I propose to use does not make ontological assumptions of that sort : it simply shows a claim of right to be a special, in the sense of a restricted, sort of judgment about what is right or wrong for governments to do.

Moreover, this way of looking at rights avoids some of the notorious puzzles associated with the concept. It allows us to say, with no sense of strangeness, that rights may vary in strength and character from case to case, and from point to point in history. If we think of rights as things, these metamorphoses seem strange, but we are used to the idea that moral judgments about what it is right or wrong to do are complex and are affected by considerations that are relative and that change.

The skeptic who wants to argue against the very possibility of rights against the state of this sort has a difficult brief. He must rely, I think, on one of three general positions : (a) He might display a more pervasive moral skepticism, which holds that even to speak of an act being morally right or wrong makes no sense. If no act is morally wrong, then the government of North Carolina cannot be wrong to refuse to bus school children. (b) He might hold a stark form of utilitarianism, which assumes that the only reason we ever have for regarding an act as right or wrong is its impact on the general interest. Under that theory, to say that busing may be morally required even though it does not benefit the community generally would be inconsistent. (c) He might accept some form of totalitarian theory, which merges the interests of the individual in the good of the general community, and so denies that the two can conflict.

Very few American politicians would be able to accept any of these three grounds. Nixon, for example, could not, because he presents himself as a moral fundamentalist who knows in his heart that pornography is wicked and that some of the people of South Vietnam have rights of self-determination in the name of which they and we may properly kill many others.

I do not want to suggest, however, that no one would in fact argue for judicial restraint on grounds of skepticism; on the contrary, some of the best known advocates of restraint have pitched their arguments entirely on skeptical grounds. In 1957, for example, the great judge Learned Hand delivered the Oliver Wendell Holmes lectures at Harvard. Hand was a student of Santayana and a disciple of Holmes, and skepticism in morals was his only religion. He argued for judicial restraint, and said that the Supreme Court had done wrong to declare school segregation illegal in the *Brown* case. It is wrong to suppose, he said, that claims about moral rights express anything more than the speakers' preferences. If the Supreme Court justifies its decisions by making such claims, rather than by relying on positive law, it is usurping the place of the legislature, for the job of the legislature, representing the majority, is to decide whose preferences shall govern.

This simple appeal to democracy is successful if one accepts the skeptical premise. Of course, if men have no rights against the majority, if political decision is simply a matter of whose preferences shall prevail, then democracy does provide a good reason for leaving that decision to more democratic institutions than courts, even when these institutions make choices that the judges themselves hate. But a very different, and much more vulnerable, argument from democracy is needed to support judicial restraint if it is based not on skepticism but on deference, as I shall try to show.

4.

If Nixon holds a coherent constitutional theory, it is a theory of restraint based not on skepticism but on deference. He believes that courts ought not to decide controversial issues of political morality because they ought to leave such decisions to other departments of government. If we ascribe this policy to Nixon, we can make sense of his charge that the Warren Court 'twisted and bent' the law. He would mean that they twisted and bent the principle of judicial deference, which is an understatement, because he would be more accurate if he said that they ignored it. But are there any good reasons for holding this policy of deference? If the policy is in fact unsound, then Nixon's jurisprudence is undermined, and he ought to be dissuaded from urging further Supreme Court appointments, or encouraging Congress to oppose the Court, in its name.

There is one very popular argument in favor of the policy of deference, which might be called the argument from democracy. It is at least debatable, according to this argument, whether a sound conception of equality forbids segregated education or requires measures like busing to break it down. Who ought to decide these debatable issues of moral and political theory? Should it be a majority of a court in Washington, whose members are appointed for life and are not politically responsible to the public whose lives will be affected by the decision? Or should it be the elected and responsible state or national legislators? A democrat, so this argument supposes, can accept only the second answer.

But the argument from democracy is weaker than it might first appear. The argument assumes, for one thing, that state legislatures are in fact responsible to the people in the way that democratic theory assumes. But in all the states, though in different degrees and for different reasons, that is not the case. In some states it is very far from the case. I want to pass that point, however, because it does not so much undermine the argument from democracy as call for more democracy, and that is a different matter. I want to fix attention on the issue of whether the appeal to democracy in this respect is even right in principle.

The argument assumes that in a democracy all unsettled issues, including issues of moral and political principle, must be resolved only by institutions that are politically responsible in the way that courts are not. Why should we accept that view of democracy? To say that that is what democracy means does no good, because it is wrong to suppose that the word, as a word, has anything like so precise a meaning. Even if it did, we should then have to rephrase our question to ask why we should have democracy, if we assume that is what it means. Nor is it better to say that that view of democracy is established in the American Constitution, or so entrenched in our political tradition that we are committed to it. We cannot argue that the Constitution, which provides no rule limiting judicial review to clear cases, establishes a theory of democracy that excludes wider review, nor can we say that our courts have in fact consistently accepted such a restriction. The burden of Nixon's argument is that they have.

So the argument from democracy is not an argument to which we are committed either by our words or our past. We must accept it, if at all, on the strength of its own logic. In order to examine the arguments more closely, however, we must make a further distinction. The argument as I have set it out might be continued in two different ways: one might argue that judicial deference is required because democratic institutions, like legislatures, are in fact likely to make *sounder* decisions than courts about the underlying issues that constitutional cases raise, that is, about the nature of an individual's moral rights against the state.

Or one might argue that it is for some reason *fairer* that a democratic institution rather than a court should decide such issues, even though there is no reason to believe that the institution will reach a sounder decision. The distinction between these two arguments would make no sense to a skeptic, who would not admit that someone could do a better or worse job at identifying moral rights against the state, any more than someone could do a better or worse job of identifying ghosts. But a lawyer who believes in judicial deference rather than skepticism must acknowledge the distinction, though he can argue both sides if he wishes.

I shall start with the second argument, that legislatures and other democratic institutions have some special title to make constitutional decisions, apart from their ability to make better decisions. One might say that the nature of this title is obvious, because it is always fairer to allow a majority to decide any issue than a minority. But that, as has often been pointed out, ignores the fact that decisions about rights against the majority are not issues that in fairness ought to be left to the majority. Constitutionalism – the theory that the majority must be restrained to protect individual rights – may be a good or bad political theory, but the United States has adopted that theory, and to make the majority judge in its own cause seems inconsistent and unjust. So principles of fairness seem to speak against, not for, the argument from democracy.

Chief Justice Marshall recognized this in his decision in *Marbury v. Madison,* the famous case in which the Supreme Court first claimed the power to review legislative decisions against constitutional standards. He argued that since the Constitution provides that the Constitution shall be the supreme law of the land, the courts in general, and the Supreme Court in the end, must have power to declare statutes void that offend that Constitution. Many legal scholars regard his argument as a *non sequitur,* because, they say, although constitutional constraints are part of the law, the courts, rather than the legislature itself, have not necessarily been given authority to decide whether in particular cases that law has been violated.[1] But the argument is not a *non sequitur* if we take the principle that no man should be judge in his own cause to be so fundamental a part of the idea of legality that Marshall would have been entitled to disregard it only if the Constitution had expressly denied judicial review.

Some might object that it is simple-minded to say that a policy of

---

[1] I distinguish this objection to Marshall's argument from the different objection, not here relevant, that the Constitution should be interpreted to impose a legal *duty* on Congress not, for example, to pass laws abridging freedom of speech, but it should not be interpreted to detract from the legal *power* of Congress to make such a law valid if it breaks its duty. In this view, Congress is in the legal position of a thief who has a legal duty not to sell stolen goods, but retains legal power to make a valid transfer if he does. This interpretation has little to recommend it since Congress, unlike the thief, cannot be disciplined except by denying validity to its wrongful acts, at least in a way that will offer protection to the individuals the Constitution is designed to protect.

deference leaves the majority to judge its own cause. Political decisions are made, in the United States, not by one stable majority but by many different political institutions each representing a different constituency which itself changes its composition over time. The decision of one branch of government may well be reviewed by another branch that is also politically responsible, but to a larger or different constituency. The acts of the Arizona police which the Court held unconstitutional in *Miranda*, for example, were in fact subject to review by various executive boards and municipal and state legislatures of Arizona, as well as by the national Congress. It would be naïve to suppose that all of these political institutions are dedicated to the same policies and interests, so it is wrong to suppose that if the Court had not intervened the Arizona police would have been free to judge themselves.

But this objection is itself too glib, because it ignores the special character of disputes about individual moral rights as distinct from other kinds of political disputes. Different institutions do have different constituencies when, for example, labor or trade or welfare issues are involved, and the nation often divides sectionally on such issues. But this is not generally the case when individual constitutional rights, like the rights of accused criminals, are at issue. It has been typical of these disputes that the interests of those in political control of the various institutions of the government have been both homogeneous and hostile. Indeed that is why political theorists have conceived of constitutional rights as rights against the 'state' or the 'majority' as such, rather than against any particular body or branch of government.

The early segregation cases are perhaps exceptions to that generality, for one might argue that the only people who wanted *de jure* segregation were white Southerners. But the fact remains that the national Congress had not in fact checked segregation, either because it believed it did not have the legal power to do so or because it did not want to; in either case the example hardly argues that the political process provides an effective check on even local violations of the rights of politically ineffective minorities. In the dispute over busing, moreover, the white majority mindful of its own interests has proved to be both national and powerful. And of course decisions of the national government, like executive decisions to wage war or congressional attempts to define proper police policy, as in the Crime Control Act of 1968, are subject to no review if not court review.

It does seem fair to say, therefore, that the argument from democracy asks that those in political power be invited to be the sole judge of their own decisions, to see whether they have the right to do what they have decided they want to do. That is not a final proof that a policy of judicial activism is superior to a program of deference. Judicial activism involves risks of tyranny; certainly in the stark and simple form I set out. It might even be shown that these risks override the unfairness of asking the majority to be judge in its own cause. But the point does undermine the argument that the majority, in fairness, must be allowed to decide the limits of its own power.

We must therefore turn to the other continuation of the argument from democracy, which holds that democratic institutions, like legislatures, are likely to reach *sounder* results about the moral rights of individuals than would courts. In 1969 the late Professor Alexander Bickel of the Yale Law School delivered his Holmes Lectures at Harvard and argued for the program of judicial restraint in a novel and ingenious way. He allowed himself to suppose, for purposes of argument, that the Warren Court's program of activism could be justified if in fact it produced desirable results.[1] He appeared, therefore, to be testing the policy of activism on its own grounds, because he took activism to be precisely the claim that the courts have the moral right to improve the future, whatever legal theory may say. Learned Hand and other opponents of activism had challenged that claim. Bickel accepted it, as least provisionally, but he argued that activism fails its own test.

The future that the Warren Court sought has already begun not to work, Bickel said. The philosophy of racial integration it adopted was too crude, for example, and has already been rejected by the more imaginative leaders of the black community. Its thesis of simple and radical equality has proved unworkable in many other ways as well; its simple formula of one-man-one-vote for passing on the fairness of election districting, for instance, has produced neither sense nor fairness.

Why should a radical Court that aims at improving society fail even on its own terms? Bickel has this answer: Courts, including the Supreme Court, must decide blocks of cases on principle, rather than responding in a piecemeal way to a shifting set of political pressures. They must do so not simply because their institutional morality requires it, but because their institutional structure provides no means by which they might gauge political forces even if they wanted to. But government by principle is an inefficient and in the long run fatal form of government, no matter how able and honest the statesmen who try to administer it. For there is a limit to the complexity that any principle can contain and remain a recognizable principle, and this limit falls short of the complexity of social organization.

The Supreme Court's reapportionment decisions, in Bickel's view,

[1] Professor Bickel also argued, with his usual very great skill, that many of the Warren Court's major decisions could not even be justified on conventional grounds, that is, by the arguments the Court advanced in its opinions. His criticism of these opinions is often persuasive, but the Court's failures of craftsmanship do not affect the argument I consider in the text. (His Holmes lectures were amplified in his book *The Supreme Court and the Idea of Progress,* 1970.)

were not mistaken just because the Court chose the wrong principle. One-man-one-vote is too simple, but the Court could not have found a better, more sophisticated principle that would have served as a successful test for election districting across the country, or across the years, because successful districting depends upon accommodation with thousands of facts of political life, and can be reached, if at all, only by the chaotic and unprincipled development of history. Judicial activism cannot work as well as government by the more-or-less democratic institutions, not because democracy is required by principle, but, on the contrary, because democracy works without principle, forming institutions and compromises as a river forms a bed on its way to the sea.

What are we to make of Bickel's argument? His account of recent history can be, and has been, challenged. It is by no means plain, certainly not yet, that racial integration will fail as a long-term strategy; and he is wrong if he thinks that black Americans, of whom more still belong to the NAACP than to more militant organizations, have rejected it. No doubt the nation's sense of how to deal with the curse of racism swings back and forth as the complexity and size of the problem become more apparent, but Bickel may have written at a high point of one arc of the pendulum.

He is also wrong to judge the Supreme Court's effect on history as if the Court were the only institution at work, or to suppose that if the Court's goal has not been achieved the country is worse off than if it had not tried. Since 1954, when the Court laid down the principle that equality before the law requires integrated education, we have not had, except for a few years of the Johnson Administration, a national executive willing to accept that principle as an imperative. For the past several years we have had a national executive that seems determined to undermine it. Nor do we have much basis for supposing that the racial situation in America would now be more satisfactory, on balance, if the Court had not intervened, in 1954 and later, in the way that it did.

But there is a very different, and for my purpose much more important, objection to take to Bickel's theory. His theory is novel because it appears to concede an issue of principle to judicial activism, namely, that the Court is entitled to intervene if its intervention produces socially desirable results. But the concession is an illusion, because his sense of what is socially desirable is inconsistent with the presupposition of activism that individuals have moral rights against the state. In fact, Bickel's argument cannot succeed, even if we grant his facts and his view of history, except on a basis of a skepticism about rights as profound as Learned Hand's.

I presented Bickel's theory as an example of one form of the argument from democracy, the argument that since men disagree about rights, it is safer to leave the final decision about rights to the political process, safer in the sense that the results are likely to be sounder. Bickel suggests a reason why the political process is safer. He argues that the endurance of a political settlement about rights is some evidence of the political morality of that settlement. He argues that this evidence is better than the sorts of argument from principle that judges might deploy if the decision were left to them.

There is a weak version of this claim, which cannot be part of Bickel's argument. This version argues that no political principle establishing rights can be sound, whatever abstract arguments might be made in its favor, unless it meets the test of social acceptance in the long run; so that, for example, the Supreme Court cannot be right in its views about the rights of black children, or criminal suspects, or atheists, if the community in the end will not be persuaded to recognize these rights.

This weak version may seem plausible for different reasons. It will appeal, for instance, to those who believe both in the fact and in the strength of the ordinary man's moral sense, and in his willingness to entertain appeals to that sense. But it does not argue for judicial restraint except in the very long run. On the contrary, it supposes what lawyers are fond of calling a dialogue between the judges and the nation, in which the Supreme Court is to present and defend its reflective view of what the citizen's rights are, much as the Warren Court tried to do, in the hope that the people will in the end agree.

We must turn, therefore, to the strong version of the claim. This argues that the organic political process will secure the genuine rights of men more certainly if it is not hindered by the artificial and rationalistic intrusion of the courts. On this view, the rights of blacks, suspects, and atheists will emerge through the process of political institutions responding to political pressures in the normal way. If a claim of right cannot succeed in this way, then for that reason it is, or in any event it is likely to be, an improper claim of right. But this bizarre proposition is only a disguised form of the skeptical point that there are in fact no rights against the state.

Perhaps, as Burke and his modern followers argue, a society will produce the institutions that best suit it only by evolution and never by radical reform. But rights against the state are claims that, if accepted, require society to settle for institutions that may not suit it so comfortably. The nerve of a claim of right, even on the demythologized analysis of rights I am using, is that an individual is entitled to protection against the majority even at the cost of the general interest. Of course the comfort of the majority will require some accommodation for minorities but only to the extent necessary to preserve order; and that is usually an accommodation that falls short of recognizing their rights.

Indeed the suggestion that rights can be demonstrated by a process of history rather than by an appeal to principle shows either a confusion or no real concern about what rights are. A claim of right presupposes a moral argument and can be established in no other way. Bickel paints the judicial activists (and even some of the heroes of judicial restraint, like Brandeis and Frankfurter, who had their lapses) as eighteenth-century philosophers who appeal to principle because they hold the optimistic view that a blueprint may be cut for progress. But this picture confuses two grounds for the appeal to principle and reform, and two senses of progress.

It is one thing to appeal to moral principle in the silly faith that ethics as well as economics moves by an invisible hand, so that individual rights and the general good will coalesce, and law based on principle will move the nation to a frictionless utopia where everyone is better off than he was before. Bickel attacks that vision by his appeal to history, and by his other arguments against government by principle. But it is quite another matter to appeal to principle *as* principle, to show, for example, that it is unjust to force black children to take their public education in black schools, even if a great many people *will* be worse off if the state adopt the measures needed to prevent this.

This is a different version of progress. It is moral progress, and though history may show how difficult it is to decide where moral progress lies, and how difficult to persuade others once one has decided, it cannot follow from this that those who govern us have no responsibility to face that decision or to attempt that persuasion.

5.

This has been a complex argument, and I want to summarize it. Our constitutional system rests on a particular moral theory, namely, that men have moral rights against the state. The difficult clauses of the Bill of Rights, like the due process and equal protection clauses, must be understood as appealing to moral concepts rather than laying down particular conceptions; therefore a court that undertakes the burden of applying these clauses fully as law must be an activist court, in the sense that it must be prepared to frame and answer questions of political morality.

It may be necessary to compromise that activist posture to some extent, either for practical reasons or for competing reasons of principle. But Nixon's public statements about the Supreme Court suggest that the activist policy must be abandoned altogether, and not merely compromised, for powerful reasons of principle. If we try to state these reasons of principle, we find that they are inconsistent with the assumption of a constitutional system, either because they leave the majority to judge its own cause, or because they rest on a skepticism about moral rights that neither Nixon nor most American politicians can consistently embrace.

So Nixon's jurisprudence is a pretense and no genuine theory at all. It cannot be supported by arguments he can accept, let alone by arguments he has advanced. Nixon abused his legal credentials by endorsing an incoherent philosophy of law and by calling into question the good faith of other lawyers because they do not accept what he cannot defend.

The academic debate about the Supreme Court's power of judicial review must, however, have contributed to Nixon's confusion. The failure to draw the distinctions I have described, between appealing to a concept and laying down a conception, and between skepticism and deference, has posed a false choice between judicial activism as the program of moral crusade and judicial restraint as the program of legality. Why has a sophisticated and learned profession posed a complex issue in this simple and misleading way?

The issue at the heart of the academic debate might be put this way. If we give the decisions of principle that the Constitution requires to the judges, instead of to the people, we act in the spirit of legality, so far as our institutions permit. But we run a risk that the judges may make the wrong decisions. Every lawyer thinks that the Supreme Court has gone wrong, even violently wrong, at some point in its career. If he does not hate the conservative decisions of the early 1930s, which threatened to block the New Deal, he is likely to hate the liberal decisions of the last decade.

We must not exaggerate the danger. Truly unpopular decisions will be eroded because public compliances will be grudging, as it has been in the case of public school prayers, and because old judges will die or retire and be replaced by new judges appointed because they agree with a President who has been elected by the people. The decisions against the New Deal did not stand, and the more daring decisions of recent years are now at the mercy of the Nixon Court. Nor does the danger of wrong decisions lie entirely on the side of excess; the failure of the Court to act in the McCarthy period, epitomized by its shameful decision upholding the legality of the Smith Act in the *Dennis* case, may be thought to have done more harm to the nation than did the Court's conservative bias in the early Roosevelt period.

Still, we ought to design our institutions to reduce the risk of error, so far as this is possible. But the academic debate has so far failed to produce an adequate account of where error lies. For the activists, the segregation decisions were right because they advanced a social goal they think desirable, or they were wrong because they advanced a social goal they dislike. For the advocates of restraint they were wrong, whether they approve or disapprove that social goal, because they violated the principle that the Court is not entitled to impose its own view of the social good on the nation.

Neither of these tests forces lawyers to face the special sort of moral issue I described earlier, the issue of what moral rights an individual has against the state. The activists rest their case, when they argue it at all, on the assumption either that their social goals are self-evidently good or that they will in the long run work for the benefit of everybody; this optimism exposes them to Bickel's argument that this is not necessarily so. Those who want restraint argue that some principle of legality protects constitutional lawyers from facing any moral issues at all.

Constitutional law can make no genuine advance until it isolates the problem of rights against the state and makes that problem part of its own agenda. That argues for a fusion of constitutional law and moral theory, a connection that, incredibly, has yet to take place. It is perfectly understandable that lawyers dread contamination with moral philosophy, and particularly with those philosophers who talk about rights, because the spooky overtones of that concept threaten the graveyard of reason. But better philosophy is now available than the lawyers may remember. Professor Rawls of Harvard, for example, has published an abstract and complex book about justice which no constitutional lawyer will be able to ignore.[1] There is no need for lawyers to play a passive role in the development of a theory of moral rights against the state, however, any more than they have been passive in the development of legal sociology and legal economics. They must recognize that law is no more independent from philosophy than it is from these other disciplines.

---

[1] *A Theory of Justice*, 1972. See Chapter 6.

6

Justice and Rights

I trust that it is not necessary to describe John Rawls's famous idea of the original position in any great detail.[1] It imagines a group of men and women who come together to form a social contract. Thus far it resembles the imaginary congresses of the classical social contract theories. The original position differs, however, from these theories in its description of the parties. They are men and women with ordinary tastes, talents, ambitions, and convictions, but each is temporarily ignorant of these features of his own personality, and must agree upon a contract before his self-awareness returns.

Rawls tries to show that if these men and women are rational, and act only in their own self-interest, they will choose his two principles of justice. These provide, roughly, that every person must have the largest political liberty compatible with a like liberty for all, and that inequalities in power, wealth, income, and other resources must not exist except in so far as they work to the absolute benefit of the worst-off members of society. Many of Rawls's critics disagree that men and women in the original position would inevitably choose these two principles. The principles are conservative, and the critics believe they would be chosen only by men who were conservative by temperament, and not by men who were natural gamblers. I do not think this criticism is well-taken, but in this essay, at least, I mean to ignore the point. I am interested in a different issue.

Suppose that the critics are wrong, and that men and women in the original position would in fact choose Rawls's two principles as being in their own best interest. Rawls seems to think that that fact would provide an argument in favor of these two principles as a standard of justice against which to test actual political institutions. But it is not immediately plain why this should be so.

If a group contracted in advance that disputes amongst them would be settled in a particular way, the fact of that contract would be a powerful argument that such disputes should be settled in that way

<hr>

[1] John Rawls, *A Theory of Justice*, 1972.

when they do arise. The contract would be an argument in itself, independent of the force of the reasons that might have led different people to enter the contract. Ordinarily, for example, each of the parties supposes that a contract he signs is in his own interest; but if someone has made a mistake in calculating his self-interest, the fact that he did contract is a strong reason for the fairness of holding him nevertheless to the bargain.

Rawls does not suppose that any group ever entered into a social contract of the sort he describes. He argues only that if a group of rational men did find themselves in the predicament of the original position, they would contract for the two principles. His contract is hypothetical, and hypothetical contracts do not supply an independent argument for the fairness of enforcing their terms. A hypothetical contract is not simply a pale form of an actual contract; it is no contract at all.

If, for example, I am playing a game, it may be that I would have agreed to any number of ground rules if I had been asked in advance of play. It does not follow that these rules may be enforced against me if I have not, in fact, agreed to them. There must be reasons, of course, why I would have agreed if asked in advance, and these may also be reasons why it is fair to enforce these rules against me even if I have not agreed. But my hypothetical agreement does not count as a reason, independent of these other reasons, for enforcing the rules against me, as my actual agreement would have.

Suppose that you and I are playing poker and we find, in the middle of a hand, that the deck is one card short. You suggest that we throw the hand in, but I refuse because I know I am going to win and I want the money in the pot. You might say that I would certainly have agreed to that procedure had the possibility of the deck being short been raised in advance. But your point is not that I am somehow committed to throwing the hand in by an agreement I never made. Rather you use the device of a hypothetical agreement to make a point that might have been made without that device, which is that the solution recommended is so obviously fair and sensible that only someone with an immediate contrary interest could disagree. Your main argument is that your solution is fair and sensible, and the fact that I would have chosen it myself adds nothing of substance to that argument. If I am able to meet the main argument nothing remains, rising out of your claim that I would have agreed, to be answered or excused.

In some circumstances, moreover, the fact that I would have agreed does not even suggest an independent argument of this character. Everything depends on your reasons for supposing that I would have agreed. Suppose you say that I would have agreed, if you had brought up the point and insisted on your solution, because I very much wanted to play and would have given in rather than miss my chance. I might concede that I would have agreed for that reason, and then add that I am lucky that you did not raise the point. The fact that I would have agreed if you had insisted neither adds nor suggests any argument why I should agree now. The point is not that it would have been unfair of you to insist on your proposal as a condition of playing; indeed, it would not have been. If you had held out for your proposal, and I had agreed, I could not say that my agreement was in any way nullified or called into question because of duress. But if I had not in fact agreed, the fact that I would have in itself means nothing.

I do not mean that it is never relevant, in deciding whether an act affecting someone is fair, that he would have consented if asked. If a doctor finds a man unconscious and bleeding, for example, it might be important for him to ask whether the man would consent to a transfusion if he were conscious. If there is every reason to think that he would, that fact is important in justifying the transfusion if the patient later, perhaps because he has undergone a religious conversion, condemns the doctor for having proceeded. But this sort of case is beside the present point, because the patient's hypothetical agreement shows that his will was inclined towards the decision at the time and in the circumstances that the decision was taken. He has lost nothing by not being consulted at the appropriate time, because he would have consented if he had been. The original position argument is very different. If we take it to argue for the fairness of applying the two principles we must take it to argue that because a man would have consented to certain principles if asked in advance, it is fair to apply those principles to him later, under different circumstances, when he does not consent.

But that is a bad argument. Suppose I did not know the value of my painting on Monday; if you had offered me $100 for it then I would have accepted. On Tuesday I discovered it was valuable. You cannot argue that it would be fair for the courts to make me sell it to you for $100 on Wednesday. It may be my good fortune that you did not ask me on Monday, but that does not justify coercion against me later.

We must therefore treat the argument from the original position as we treat your argument in the poker game; it must be a device for calling attention to some independent argument for the fairness of the two principles – an argument that does not rest on the false premise that a hypothetical contract has some pale binding force. What other argument is available? One might say that the original position shows that the two principles are in the best interests of every member of any political community, and that it is fair to govern in accordance with them for that reason. It is true that if the two principles could be shown to be in everyone's interest, that would be a sound argument for their fairness, but it is hard to see how the original position can be used to show that they are.

We must be careful to distinguish two senses in which something might be said to be in my interest. It is in my *antecedent* interest to make a bet on a horse that, all things considered, offers the best odds, even if, in the event, the horse loses. It is in my *actual* interest to bet on the horse that wins, even if the bet was, at the time I made it, a silly one. If the original position furnishes an argument that it is in everyone's interest to accept the two principles over other possible bases for a constitution, it must be an argument that uses the idea of antecedent and not actual interest. It is not in the actual best interests of everyone to choose the two principles, because when the veil of ignorance is lifted some will discover that they would have been better off if some other principle, like the principle of average utility, had been chosen.

A judgment of antecedent interest depends upon the circumstances under which the judgment is made, and, in particular, upon the knowledge available to the man making the judgment. It might be in my antecedent interest to bet on a certain horse at given odds before the starting gun, but not, at least at the same odds, after he has stumbled on the first turn. The fact, therefore, that a particular choice is in my interest at a particular time, under conditions of great uncertainty, is not a good argument for the fairness of enforcing that choice against me later under conditions of much greater knowledge. But that is what, on this interpretation, the original position argument suggests, because it seeks to justify the contemporary use of the two principles on the supposition that, under conditions very different from present conditions, it would be in the antecedent interest of everyone to agree to them. If I have bought a ticket on a longshot it might be in my antecedent interest, before the race, to sell the ticket to you for twice what I paid; it does not follow that it is fair for you to take it from me for that sum when the longshot is about to win.

Someone might now say that I have misunderstood the point of the special conditions of uncertainty in the original position. The parties are made ignorant of their special resources and talents to prevent them from bargaining for principles that are inherently unfair because they favor some collection of resources and talents over others. If the man in the original position does not know his special interests, he cannot negotiate to favor them. In that case, it might be said, the uncertainty of the original position does not vitiate the argument from antecedent interest as I have suggested, but only limits the range within which self-interest might operate. The argument shows that the two principles are in everyone's interest once obviously unfair principles are removed from consideration by the device of uncertainty. Since the only additional knowledge contemporary men and women have over men and women in the original position is knowledge that they ought not to rely upon in choosing principles of justice, their antecedent interest is, so far as it is relevant, the same, and if that is so the original position argument does offer a good argument for applying the two principles to contemporary politics.

But surely this confuses the argument that Rawls makes with a different argument that he might have made. Suppose his men and women had full knowledge of their own talents and tastes, but had to reach agreement under conditions that ruled out, simply by stipulation, obviously unfair principles like those providing special advantage for named individuals. If Rawls could show that, once such obviously unfair principles had been set aside, it would be in the interest of everyone to settle for his two principles, that would indeed count as an argument for the two principles. My point – that the antecedent self-interest of men in the original position is different from that of contemporary men – would no longer hold because both groups of men would then have the same knowledge about themselves, and be subject to the same moral restrictions against choosing obviously unfair principles.

Rawls's actual argument is quite different, however. The ignorance in which his men must choose affects their calculations of self-interest, and cannot be described merely as setting boundaries within which these calculations must be applied. Rawls supposes, for example, that his men would inevitably choose conservative principles because this would be the only rational choice, in their ignorance, for self-interested men to make. But some actual men, aware of their own talents, might well prefer less conservative principles that would allow them to take advantage of the resources they know they have. Someone who considers the original position an argument for the conservative principles, therefore, is faced with this choice. If less conservative principles, like principles that favor named individuals, are to be ruled out as obviously unfair, then the argument for the conservative principles is complete at the outset, on grounds of obvious fairness alone. In that case neither the original position nor any considerations of self-interest it is meant to demonstrate play any role in the argument. But if less conservative principles cannot be ruled out in advance as obviously unfair, then imposing ignorance on Rawls's men, so that they prefer the more conservative principles, cannot be explained simply as ruling out obviously unfair choices. And since this affects the antecedent self-interest of these men, the argument that the original position demonstrates the antecedent self-interest of actual men must therefore fail. This same dilemma can, of course, be constructed for each feature of the two principles.

I recognize that the argument thus far seems to ignore a distinctive feature of Rawls's methodology, which he describes as the technique of seeking a 'reflective equilibrium' between our ordinary, unreflective moral beliefs and some theoretical structure that might unify and justify these ordinary beliefs.[1] It might now be said that the idea of an original position plays a part in this reflective equilibrium, which we will miss if we insist, as I have, on trying to find a more direct, one-way argument from the original position to the two principles of justice.

The technique of equilibrium does play an important role in Rawls's argument, and it is worth describing that technique briefly here. The technique assumes that Rawls's readers have a sense, which we draw upon in our daily life, that certain particular political arrangements or decisions, like conventional trials, are just and others, like slavery, are unjust. It assumes, moreover, that we are each able to arrange these immediate intuitions or convictions in an order that designates some of them as more certain than others. Most people, for example, think that it is more plainly unjust for the state to execute innocent citizens of its own than to kill innocent foreign civilians in war. They might be prepared to abandon their position on foreign civilians in war, on the basis of some argument, but would be much more reluctant to abandon their view on executing innocent countrymen.

It is the task of moral philosophy, according to the technique of equilibrium, to provide a structure of principles that supports these immediate convictions about which we are more or less secure, with two goals in mind. First, this structure of principles must explain the convictions by showing the underlying assumptions they reflect; second it must provide guidance in those cases about which we have either no convictions or weak or contradictory convictions. If we are unsure, for example, whether economic institutions that allow great disparity of wealth are unjust, we may turn to the principles that explain our confident convictions, and then apply these principles to that difficult issue.

But the process is not simply one of finding principles that accommodate our more-or-less settled judgments. These principles must support, and not merely account for, our judgments, and this means that the principles must have independent appeal to our moral sense. It might be, for example, that a cluster of familiar moral convictions could be shown to serve an undeserving policy – perhaps, that the

---

[1] pp. 48 ff.

standard judgments we make without reflection serve the purpose of maintaining one particular class in political power. But this discovery would not vouch for the principle of class egoism; on the contrary, it would discredit our ordinary judgments, unless some other principle of a more respectable sort could be found that also fits our intuitions, in which case it would be this principle and not the class-interest principle that our intuitions would recommend.

It might be that no coherent set of principles could be found that has independent appeal and that supports the full set of our immediate convictions; indeed it would be surprising if this were not often the case. If that does happen, we must compromise, giving way on both sides. We might relax, though we could not abandon, our initial sense of what might be an acceptable principle. We might come to accept, for example, after further reflection, some principle that seemed to us initially unattractive, perhaps the principle that men should sometimes be made to be free. We might accept this principle if we were satisfied that no less harsh principle could support the set of political convictions we were especially reluctant to abandon. On the other hand, we must also be ready to modify or adjust, or even to give up entirely, immediate convictions that cannot be accommodated by any principle that meets our relaxed standards; in adjusting these immediate convictions we will use our initial sense of which seem to us more and which less certain, though in principle no immediate conviction can be taken as immune from reinspection or abandonment if that should prove necessary. We can expect to proceed back and forth between our immediate judgments and the structure of explanatory principles in this way, tinkering first with one side and then the other, until we arrive at what Rawls calls the state of reflective equilibrium in which we are satisfied, or as much satisfied as we can reasonably expect.

It may well be that, at least for most of us, our ordinary political judgments stand in this relation of reflective equilibrium with Rawls's two principles of justice, or, at least, that they could be made to do so through the process of adjustment just described. It is nevertheless unclear how the idea of the original position fits into this structure or, indeed, why it has any role to play at all. The original position is not among the ordinary political convictions that we find we have, and that we turn to reflective equilibrium to justify. If it has any role, it must be in the process of justification, because it takes its place in the body of theory we construct to bring our convictions into balance. But if the two principles of justice are themselves in reflective equilibrium with our convictions, it is unclear why we need the original position to supplement the two principles on the theoretical side of the balance. What can the idea contribute to a harmony already established?

We should consider the following answer. It is one of the conditions we impose on a theoretical principle, before we allow it to figure as a justification of our convictions, that the people the principle would govern would have accepted that principle, at least under certain conditions, if they had been asked, or at least that the principle can be shown to be in the antecedent interest of every such person. If this is so, then the original position plays an essential part in the process of justification through equilibrium. It is used to show that the two principles conform to this established standard of acceptability for political principles. At the same time, the fact that the two principles, which do conform to that standard, justify our ordinary convictions in reflective equilibrium reinforces our faith in the standard and encourages us to apply it to other issues of political or moral philosophy.

This answer does not advance the case that the original position furnishes an argument for the two principles, however; it merely restates the ideas we have already considered and rejected. It is certainly not part of our established political traditions or ordinary moral understanding that principles are acceptable only if they would be chosen by men in the particular predicament of the original position. It is, of course, part of these traditions that principles are fair if they have in fact been chosen by those whom they govern, or if they can at least be shown to be in their antecedent common interest. But we have already seen that the original position device cannot be used to support either of these arguments in favor of applying the two principles to contemporary politics. If the original position is to play any role in a structure of principles and convictions in reflective equilibrium, it must be by virtue of assumptions we have not yet identified.

It is time to reconsider an earlier assumption. So far I have been treating the original position construction as if it were either the foundation of Rawls's argument or an ingredient in a reflective equilibrium established between our political intuitions and his two princples of justice. But, in fact, Rawls does not treat the original position that way. He describes the construction in these words:

I have emphasized that this original position is purely hypothetical. It is natural to ask why, if this agreement is never actually entered into, we should take any interest in these principles, moral or otherwise. The answer is that the conditions embodied in the description of the original position are ones that we do in fact accept. Or if we do not, then perhaps we can be persuaded to do so by philosophical reflection. Each aspect of the contractual situation can be given supporting grounds. . . . On the other hand, this conception is also an intuitive notion that suggests its own elaboration, so that led on by it we are drawn to define more clearly the standpoint from which we can best interpret moral relationships. We need a conception that enables us to envision our objective from afar: the intuitive notion of the original position is to do this for us.[1]

This description is taken from Rawls's first statement of the original position. It is recalled and repeated in the very last paragraph of the book.[2] It is plainly of capital importance, and it suggests that the original position, far from being the foundation of his argument, or an expository device for the technique of equilibrium, is one of the major substantive products of the theory as a whole. Its importance is reflected in another crucial passage. Rawls describes his moral theory as a type of psychology. He wants to characterize the structure of our (or, at least, one person's) capacity to make moral judgments of a certain sort, that is, judgments about justice. He thinks that the conditions embodied in the original position are the fundamental 'principles governing our moral powers, or, more specifically, our sense of justice'.[3] The original position is therefore a schematic representation of a particular mental process of at least some, and perhaps most, human beings, just as depth grammar, he suggests, is a schematic presentation of a different mental capacity.

All this suggests that the original position is an intermediate conclusion, a halfway point in a deeper theory that provides philosophical arguments for its conditions. In the next part of this essay I shall try to describe at least the main outlines of this deeper theory. I shall distinguish three features of the surface argument of the book – the technique of equilibrium, the social contract, and the original position itself – and try to discern which of various familiar philosophical principles or positions these represent.

First, however, I must say a further word about Rawls's exciting, if imprecise, idea that the principles of this deeper theory are constitutive of our moral capacity. That idea can be understood on different levels of profundity. It may mean, at its least profound, that the principles that support the original position as a device for reasoning about justice are so widely shared and so little questioned within a particular community, for whom the book is meant, that the community could not abandon these principles without fundamentally changing its patterns of reasoning and arguing about political morality. It may mean, at its most profound, that these principles are innate categories of morality common to all men, imprinted in their neural structure, so that man

[1] pp. 21-2.
[2] p. 587.
[3] p. 51.

could not deny these principles short of abandoning the power to reason about morality at all.

I shall be guided, in what follows, by the less profound interpretation, though what I shall say, I think, is consistent with the more profound. I shall assume, then, that there is a group of men and women who find, on reading Rawls, that the original position does strike them as a proper 'intuitive notion' from which to think about problems of justice, and who would find it persuasive, if it could be demonstrated that the parties to the original position would in fact contract for the two principles he describes. I suppose, on the basis of experience and the literature, that this group contains a very large number of those who think about justice at all, and I find that I am a member myself. I want to discover the hidden assumptions that bend the inclinations of this group that way, and I shall do so by repeating the question with which I began. Why does Rawls's argument support his claim that his two principles are principles of justice? My answer is complex and it will take us, at times, far from his text, but not, I think, from its spirit.

2.

A. Equilibrium

I shall start by considering the philosophical basis of the technique of equilibrium I just described. I must spend several pages in this way, but it is important to understand what substantive features of Rawls's deep theory are required by his method. This technique presupposes, as I said, a familiar fact about our moral lives. We all entertain beliefs about justice that we hold because they seem right, not because we have deduced or inferred them from other beliefs. We may believe in this way, for example, that slavery is unjust, and that the standard sort of trial is fair.

These different sorts of beliefs are, according to some philosophers, direct perceptions of some independent and objective moral facts. In the view of other philosophers they are simply subjective preferences, not unlike ordinary tastes, but dressed up in the language of justice to indicate how important they seem to us. In any event, when we argue with ourselves or each other about justice we use these accustomed beliefs – which we call 'intuitions' or 'convictions' – in roughly the way Rawls's equilibrium technique suggests. We test general theories about justice against our own institutions, and we try to confound those who disagree with us by showing how their own intuitions embarrass their own theories.

Suppose we try to justify this process by setting out a philosophical position about the connection between moral theory and moral intuition. The technique of equilibrium supposes what might be called a 'coherence' theory of morality.[1] But we have a choice between two general models that define coherence and explain why it is required, and the choice between these is significant and consequential for our moral philosophy. I shall describe these two models, and then argue that the equilibrium technique makes sense on one but not the other.

I call the first a 'natural' model. It presupposes a philosophical position that can be summarized in this way. Theories of justice, like Rawls's two principles, describe an objective moral reality; they are not, that is, created by men or societies but are rather discovered by them, as they discover laws of physics. The main instrument of this discovery is a moral faculty possessed by at least some men, which produces concrete intuitions of political morality in particular situations, like the intuition that slavery is wrong. These intuitions are clues to the nature and existence of more abstract and fundamental moral principles, as physical observations are clues to the existence and nature of fundamental physical laws. Moral reasoning or philosophy is a process of reconstructing the fundamental principles by assembling concrete judgments in the right order, as a natural historian reconstructs the shape of the whole animal from the fragments of its bones that he has found.

The second model is quite different. It treats intuitions of justice not as clues to the existence of independent principles, but rather as stipulated features of a general theory to be constructed, as if a sculptor set himself to carve the animal that best fits a pile of bones he happened to find together. This 'constructive' model does not assume, as the natural model does, that principles of justice have some fixed, objective existence, so that descriptions of these principles must be true or false in some standard way. It does not assume that the animal it matches to the bones actually exists. It makes the different, and in some ways more complex, assumption that men and women have a responsibility to fit the particular judgments on which they act into a coherent program of action, or, at least, that officials who exercise power over other men have that sort of responsibility.

This second, constructive, model is not unfamiliar to lawyers. It is analogous to one model of common law adjudication. Suppose a judge is faced with a novel claim – for example, a claim for damages based on a legal right to privacy that courts have not heretofore recognized.[2] He

---

[1] See Feinberg, 'Justice, Fairness and Rationality', 81 *Yale L. J.* 1004, 1018-21 (1972).

[2] I have here in mind the famous argument of Brandeis and Warren. See Brandeis & Warren, 'The Right to Privacy', 4 *Harv. L. Rev.* 193 (1890), which is a paradigm of argument in the constructive model. See Chapter 4, pp. 118-19.

must examine such precedents as seem in any way relevant to see whether any principles that are, as we might say, 'instinct' in these precedents bear upon the claimed right to privacy. We might treat this judge as being in the position of a man arguing from moral intuitions to a general moral theory. The particular precedents are analogous to intuitions; the judge tries to reach an accommodation between these precedents and a set of principles that might justify them and also justify further decisions that go beyond them. He does not suppose, however, that the precedents are glimpses into a moral reality, and therefore clues to objective principles he ends by declaring. He does not believe that the principles are 'instinct' in the precedents in that sense. Instead, in the spirit of the constructive model, he accepts these precedents as specifications for a principle that he must construct, out of a sense of responsibility for consistency with what has gone before.

I want to underline the important difference between the two models. Suppose that an official holds, with reasonable conviction, some intuition that cannot be reconciled with his other intuitions by any set of principles he can now fashion. He may think, for example, that it is unjust to punish an attempted murder as severely as a successful one, and yet be unable to reconcile that position with his sense that a man's guilt is properly assessed by considering only what he intended, and not what actually happened. Or he may think that a particular minority race, as such, is entitled to special protection, and be unable to reconcile that view with his view that distinctions based on race are inherently unfair to individuals. When an official is in this position the two models give him different advice.

The natural model supports a policy of following the troublesome intuition, and submerging the apparent contradiction, in the faith that a more sophisticated set of principles, which reconciles that intuition does in fact exist though it has not been discovered. The official, according to this model, is in the position of the astronomer who has clear observational data that he is as yet unable to reconcile in any coherent account, for example, of the origin of the solar system. He continues to accept and employ his observational data, placing his faith in the idea that some reconciling explanation does exist though it has not been, and for all he knows may never be, discovered by men.

The natural model supports this policy because it is based on a philosophical position that encourages the analogy between moral intuitions and observational data. It makes perfect sense, on that assumption, to suppose that direct observations, made through a moral faculty, have outstripped the explanatory powers of those who observe. It also makes sense to suppose that some correct explanation, in the shape of principles of morality, does in fact exist in spite of this failure; if the direct observations are sound, some explanation must exist for why matters are as they have been observed to be in the moral universe, just as some explanation must exist for why matters are as they have been observed to be in the physical universe.

The constructive model, however, does not support the policy of submerging apparent inconsistency in the faith that reconciling principles must exist. On the contrary, it demands that decisions taken in the name of justice must never outstrip an official's ability to account for these decisions in a theory of justice, even when such a theory must compromise some of his intuitions. It demands that we act on principle rather than on faith. Its engine is a doctrine of responsibility that requires men to integrate their intuitions and subordinate some of these, when necessary, to that responsibility. It presupposes that articulated consistency, decisions in accordance with a program that can be made public and followed until changed, is essential to any conception of justice. An official in the position I describe, guided by this model, must give up his apparently inconsistent position; he must do so even if he hopes one day, by further reflection, to devise better principles that will allow all his initial convictions to stand as principles.[1]

The constructive model does not presuppose skepticism or relativism. On the contrary, it assumes that the men and women who reason within the model will each hold sincerely the convictions they bring to it, and that this sincerity will extend to criticizing as unjust political acts or systems that offend the most profound of these. The model does not deny, any more than it affirms, the objective standing of any of these convictions; it is therefore consistent with, though as a model of reasoning it does not require, the moral ontology that the natural model presupposes.

It does not require that ontology because its requirements are independent of it. The natural model insists on consistency with conviction, on the assumption that moral intuitions are accurate observations; the requirement of consistency follows from that assumption. The constructive model insists on consistency with conviction as an independent requirement, flowing not from the assumption that these convictions are accurate reports, but from the different assumption that it is unfair for officials to act except on the basis of a general public theory that will constrain them to consistency, provide a public standard for testing or debating or predicting what they do, and not allow appeals to

---

[1] The famous debate between Professor Wechsler, 'Toward Neutral Principles in Constitutional Law', 73 *Hart. L. Rev.* 1 (1959), and his critics may be illuminated by this distinction. Wechsler proposes a constructive model for constitutional adjudication, while those who favor a more tentative or intuitive approach to constitutional law are following the natural model.

unique intuitions that might mask prejudice or self-interest in particular cases. The constructive model requires coherence, then, for independent reasons of political morality; it takes convictions held with the requisite sincerity as given, and seeks to impose conditions on the acts that these intuitions might be said to warrant. If the constructive model is to constitute morality, in either of the senses I have distinguished these independent reasons of political morality are at the heart of our political theories.

The two models, therefore, represent different standpoints from which theories of justice might be developed. The natural model, we might say, looks at intuitions from the personal standpoint of the individual who holds them, and who takes them to be discrete observations of moral reality. The constructive model looks at these intuitions from a more public standpoint; it is a model that someone might propose for the governance of a community each of whose members has strong convictions that differ, though not too greatly, from the convictions of others.

The constructive model is appealing, from this public standpoint, for an additional reason. It is well suited to group consideration of problems of justice, that is, to developing a theory that can be said to be the theory of a community rather than of particular individuals, and this is an enterprise that is important, for example, in adjudication. The range of initial convictions to be assessed can be expanded or contracted to accommodate the intuitions of a larger or smaller group, either by including all convictions held by any members, or by excluding those not held by all, as the particular calculation might warrant. This process would be self-destructive on the natural model, because every individual would believe that either false observations were being taken into account or accurate observations disregarded, and hence that the inference to objective morality was invalid. But on the constructive model that objection would be unavailable; the model, so applied, would be appropriate to identify the program of justice that best accommodates the community's common convictions, for example, with no claim to a description of an objective moral universe.

Which of these two models, then, better supports the technique of equilibrium? Some commentators seem to have assumed that the technique commits Rawls to the natural model.[1] But the alliance between that model and the equilibrium technique turns out to be only superficial; when we probe deeper we find that they are incompatible. In

---

[1] See e.g., Hare, 'Rawls' Theory of Justice – 1', 23 *Philosophical Quarterly* 144 (1973).

the first place, the natural model cannot explain one distinctive feature of the technique. It explains why our theory of justice must fit our intuitions about justice, but it does not explain why we are justified in amending these intuitions to make the fit more secure.

Rawls's notion of equilibrium, as I said earlier, is a two-way process; we move back and forth between adjustments to theory and adjustments to conviction until the best fit possible is achieved. If my settled convictions can otherwise be captured by, for example, a straightforward utilitarian theory of justice, that may be a reason, within the technique, for discarding my intuition that slavery would be wrong even if it advanced utility. But on the natural model this would be nothing short of cooking the evidence, as if a naturalist rubbed out the footprints that embarrassed his efforts to describe the animal that left them, or the astronomer just set aside the observations that his theory could not accommodate.

We must be careful not to lose this point in false sophistication about science. It is common to say — Rawls himself draws the comparison[1] — that scientists also adjust their evidence to achieve a smooth set of explanatory principles. But if this is true at all, their procedures are very different from those recommended by the technique of equilibrium. Consider, to take a familiar example, optical illusions or hallucinations. It is perfectly true that the scientist who sees water in the sand does not say that the pond was really there until he arrived at it, so that physics must be revised to provide for disappearing water; on the contrary, he uses the apparent disappearing as evidence of an illusion, that is, as evidence that, contrary to his observation, there was never any water there at all.

The scientists, of course, cannot leave the matter at that. He cannot dismiss mirages unless he supplements the laws of physics with laws of optics that explain them. It may be that he has, in some sense, a choice amongst competing sets of explanations of all his observations taken together. He may have a choice, for example, between either treating mirages as physical objects of a special sort and then amending the laws of physics to allow for disappearing objects of this sort, or treating mirages as optical illusions and then developing laws of optics to explain such illusions. He has a choice in the sense that his experience does not absolutely force either of these explanations upon him; the former is a possible choice, though it would require wholesale revision of both physics and common sense to carry it off.

This is, I take it, what is meant by philosophers like Quine who suppose that our concepts and our theories face our experience as a whole,

---

[1] Rawls draws attention to the distinction, p. 49.

so that we might react to recalcitrant or surprising experience by making different revisions at different places in our theoretical structures if we wish.[1] Regardless of whether this is an accurate picture of scientific reasoning, it is not a picture of the procedure of equilibrium, because this procedure argues not simply that alternative structures of principle are available to explain the same phenomena, but that some of the phenomena, in the form of moral convictions, may simply be ignored the better to serve some particular theory.

It is true that Rawls sometimes describes the procedure in a more innocent way. He suggests that if our tentative theories of justice do not fit some particular intuition, this should act as a warning light requiring us to reflect on whether the conviction is really one we hold.[2] If my convictions otherwise support a principle of utility, but I feel that slavery would be unjust even if utility were improved, I might think about slavery again, in a calmer way, and this time my intuitions might be different and consistent with that principle. In this case, the initial inconsistency is used as an occasion for reconsidering the intuition, but not as a reason for abandoning it.

Still, this need not happen. I might continue to receive the former intuition, no matter how firmly I steeled myself against it. In that case the procedure nevertheless authorizes me to set it aside if that is required to achieve the harmony of equilibrium. But if I do, I am not offering an alternative account of the evidence, but simply disregarding it. Someone else, whose intuitions are different, may say that mine are distorted, perhaps because of some childhood experience, or because I am insufficiently imaginative to think of hypothetical cases in which slavery might actually improve utility. He may say, that is, that my sensibilties are defective here, so that my intuitions are not genuine perceptions of moral reality, and may be set aside like the flawed reports of a color-blind man.

But I cannot accept that about myself, as an explanation for my own troublesome convictions, so long as I hold these convictions and they seem to me sound, indistinguishable in their moral quality from my other convictions. I am in a different position from the color-blind man who need only come to understand that others' perceptions differ from his. If I believe that my intuitions are a direct report from some moral reality, I cannot accept that one particular intuition is false until I come to feel or sense that it is false. The bare fact that others disagree, if they do, may be an occasion for consulting my intuitions again, but if my convictions remain the same, the fact that others may explain them in

---

[1] W. V. Quine, 'Two Dogmas of Empiricism', in *From a Logical Point of View* 20 (2d ed. rev. 1964).

[2] p. 48.

a different way cannot be a reason for my abandoning them, instead of retaining them in the faith that a reconciliation of these with my other convictions does in fact exist.

Thus, the natural model does not offer a satisfactory explanation of the two-way feature of equilibrium. Even if it did, however, it would leave other features of that technique unexplained; it would leave unexplained, for example, the fact that the results of the technique, at least in Rawls's hands, are necessarily and profoundly practical. Rawlsian men and women in the original position seek to find principles that they and their successors will find it easy to understand and publicize and observe; principles otherwise appealing are to be rejected or adjusted because they are too complex or are otherwise impractical in this sense. But principles of justice selected in this spirit are compromises with infirmity, and are contingent in the sense that they will change as the general condition and education of people change. This seems inconsistent with the spirit, at least, of the natural model, according to which principles of justice are timeless features of some independent moral reality, to which imperfect men and women must attempt to conform at best they can.

The equilibrium technique, moreover, is designed to produce principles that are relative in at least two ways. First, it is designed to select the best theory of justice from a list of alternative theories that must not only be finite, but short enough to make comparisons among them feasible. This limitation is an important one; it leads Rawls himself to say that he has no doubt that an initial list of possible theories expanded well beyond the list he considers would contain a better theory of justice than his own two principles.[1] Second, it yields results that are relative to the area of initial agreement among those who jointly conduct the speculative experiments it recommends. It is designed, as Rawls says, to reconcile men who disagree by fixing on what is common ground among them.[2] The test concededly will yield different results for different groups, and for the same group at different times, as the common ground of confident intuition shifts.

If the equilibrium technique were used within the natural model, the authority of its conclusions would be seriously compromised by both forms of relativism. If the equilibrium argument for Rawls's two principles, for example, shows only that a better case can be made for them than for any other principles on a restricted short list, and if Rawls himself is confident that further study would produce a better theory, then we have very little reason to suppose that these two principles are

[1] p. 581.
[2] pp. 580-1.

an accurate description of moral reality. It is hard to see, on the natural model, why they then should have any authority at all.

Indeed, the argument provides no very good ground for supposing even that the two principles are a better description of moral reality than other theories on the short list. Suppose we are asked to choose, among five theories of justice, the theory that best unites our convictions in reflective equilibrium, and we pick, from among these, the fifth. Let us assume that there is some sixth theory that we would have chosen had it appeared on the list. This sixth theory might be closer to, for example, the first on our original list than to the fifth, at least in the following sense : over a long term, a society following the first might reach more of the decisions that a society following the sixth would reach than would a society following the fifth.

Suppose, for example, that our original list included, as available theories of justice, classical utilitarianism and Rawls's two principles, but did not include average utilitarianism. We might have rejected classical utilitarianism on the ground that the production of pleasure for its own sake, unrelated to any increase in the welfare of particular human beings or other animals, makes little sense, and then chosen Rawls's two principles as the best of the theories left. We might nevertheless have chosen average utilitarianism as superior to the two principles, if it had been on the list, because average utilitarianism does not suppose that just any increase in the total quantity of pleasure is good. But classical utilitarianism, which we rejected, might be closer to average utilitarianism, which we would have chosen if we could have, than are the two principles which we did choose. It might be closer, in the sense described, because it would dictate more of the particular decisions that average utilitarianism would require, and thus be a better description of ultimate moral reality, than would the two principles. Of course, average utilitarianism might itself be rejected in a still larger list, and the choice we should then make might indicate that another member of the original list was better than either classical utilitarianism or the two principles.

The second sort of relativism would be equally damaging on the natural model, for reasons I have already explained. If the technique of equilibrium is used by a single person, and the intuitions allowed to count are just his and all of his, then the results may be authoritative for him. Others, whose intuitions differ, will not be able to accept his conclusions, at least in full, but he may do so himself. If, however, the technique is used in a more public way, for example, by fixing on what is common amongst the intuitions of a group, then the results will be those that no one can accept as authoritative, just as no one could accept as authoritative a scientific result reached by disregarding what he believed to be evidence at least as pertinent as the evidence used.

So the natural model turns out to be poor support for the equilibrium technique. None of the difficulties just mentioned count, however, if we assume the technique to be in the service of the constructive model. It is, within that model, a reason for rejecting even a powerful conviction that it cannot be reconciled with other convictions by a plausible and coherent set of principles; the conviction is rejected not as a false report, but simply as ineligible within a program that meets the demands of the model. Nor does either respect in which the technique is relative embarrass the constructive model. It is not an embarrassment that some theory not considered might have been deemed superior if it had been considered. The model requires officials or citizens to proceed on the best program they can now fashion, for reasons of consistency that do not presuppose, as the natural model does, that the theory chosen is in any final sense true. It does not undermine a particular theory that a different group, or a different society, with different culture and experience, would produce a different one. It may call into question whether any group is entitled to treat its moral intuitions as in any sense objective or transcendental, but not that a particular society, which does treat particular convictions in that way, is therefore required to follow them in a principled way.

I shall assume, therefore, at least tentatively, that Rawls's methodology presupposes the constructive model of reasoning from particular convictions to general theories of justice, and I shall use that assumption in my attempt to show the further postulates of moral theory that lie behind his theory of justice.

B. The Contract

I come, then, to the second of the three features of Rawls's methodology that I want to discuss, which is the use he makes of the old idea of a social contract. I distinguish, as does Rawls, the general idea that an imaginary contract is an appropriate device for reasoning about justice, from the more specific features of the original position, which count as a particular application of that general idea. Rawls thinks that all theories that can be seen to rest on a hypothetical social contract of some sort are related and are distinguished as a class from theories that cannot; he supposes, for example, that average utilitarianism, which can be seen as the product of a social contract on a particular interpretation, is more closely related to his own theory than either is to classical utilitarianism, which cannot be seen as the product of a contract on any interpretation.[1] In the next section I shall consider the theoretical basis

[1] Chapter 30.

of the original position. In this section I want to consider the basis of the more general idea of the contract itself.

Rawls says that the contract is a powerful argument for his principles because it embodies philosophical principles that we accept, or would accept if we thought about them. We want to find out what these principles are, and we may put our problem this way. The two principles comprise a theory of justice that is built up from the hypothesis of a contract. But the contract cannot sensibly be taken as the fundamental premise or postulate of that theory, for the reasons I described in the first part of this article. It must be seen as a kind of halfway point in a larger argument, as itself the product of a deeper political theory that argues for the two principles *through* rather than *from* the contract. We must therefore try to identify the features of a deeper theory that would recommend the device of a contract as the engine for a theory of justice, rather than the other theoretical devices Rawls mentions, like the device of the impartial spectator.[1]

We shall find the answer, I think, if we attend to and refine the familiar distinction philosophers make between two types of moral theories, which they call teleological theories and deontological theories.[2] I shall argue that any deeper theory that would justify Rawls's use of the contract must be a particular form of deontological theory, a theory that takes the idea of rights so seriously as to make them fundamental in political morality. I shall try to show how such a theory would be distinguished, as a type, from other types of political theories, and why only such a theory could give the contract the role and prominence Rawls does.

I must begin this argument, however, by explaining how I shall use some familiar terms. (1) I shall say that some state of affairs is a *goal* within a particular political theory if it counts in favor of a political act, within that theory, that the act will advance or preserve that state of affairs, and counts against an act that it will retard or threaten it. Goals may be relatively specific, like full employment or respect for authority, or relatively abstract, like improving the general welfare, advancing the power of a particular nation, or creating a utopian society according to a particular concept of human goodness or of the good life. (2) I shall say that an individual has a *right* to a particular political act, within a political theory, if the failure to provide that act, when he calls for it, would be unjustified within that theory even if the goals of the theory would, on the balance, be disserviced by that act. The strength of a particular right, within a particular theory, is a function of the degree of disservice to the goals of the theory, beyond a mere

[1] p. 144 ff.
[2] Rawls defines these terms at pp. 24-5 and 30.

disservice on the whole, that is necessary to justify refusing an act called for under the right. In the popular political theory apparently prevailing in the United States, for example, individuals have rights to free public speech on political matters and to a certain minimum standard of living, but neither right is absolute and the former is much stronger than the latter. (3) I shall say that an individual has a *duty* to act in a particular way, within a political theory, if a political decision constraining such act is justified within that theory notwithstanding that no goal of the system would be served by that decision. A theory may provide, for example, that individuals have a duty to worship God, even though it does not stipulate any goal served by requiring them to do so.[1]

The three concepts I have described work in different ways, but they all serve to justify or to condemn, at least pro tanto, particular political decisions. In each case, the justification provided by citing a goal, a right, or a duty is in principle complete, in the sense that nothing need be added to make the justification effective, if it is not undermined by some competing considerations. But, though such a justification is in this sense complete, it need not, within the theory, be ultimate. It remains open to ask why the particular goal, right, or duty is itself justified, and the theory may provide an answer by deploying a *more basic* goal, right, or duty that is served by accepting this less basic goal, right, or duty as a complete justification in particular cases.

A particular goal, for example, might be justified as contributing to a more basic goal; thus, full employment might be justified as contributing to greater average welfare. Or a goal might be justified as serving a more basic right or duty; a theory might argue, for example, that improving the gross national product, which is a goal, is necessary to enable the state to respect the rights of individuals to a decent minimum standard of living, or that improving the efficiency of the police process is necessary to enforce various individual duties not to sin. On the other hand, rights and duties may be justified on the ground that, by acting as a complete justification on particular occasions, they in fact serve more fundamental goals; the duty of individuals to drive carefully may be justified, for example, as serving the more basic goal of improving the general welfare. This form of justification does not, of course, suggest that the less basic right or duty itself justifies political decisions only when these decisions, considered one by one, advance the more basic goal. The point is rather the familiar one of rule utilitarianism, that treating the right or duty as a complete justification in particular cases,

---

[1] I do not count, as goals, the goal of respecting rights or enforcing duties. In this and other apparent ways my use of the terms I define is narrower than ordinary language permits.

without reference to the more basic goal, will in fact advance the goal in the long run.

So goals can be justified by other goals or by rights or duties, and rights or duties can be justified by goals. Rights and duties can also be justified, of course, by other, more fundamental duties or rights. Your duty to respect my privacy, for example, may be justified by my right to privacy. I do not mean merely that rights and duties may be correlated, as opposite sides of the same coin. That may be so when, for example, a right and the corresponding duty are justified as serving a more fundamental goal, as when your right to property and my corresponding duty not to trespass are together justified by the more fundamental goal of socially efficient land use. In many cases, however, corresponding rights and duties are not correlative, but one is derivative from the other, and it makes a difference which is derivative from which. There is a difference between the idea that you have a duty not to lie to me because I have a right not to be lied to, and the idea that I have a right that you not lie to me because you have a duty not to tell lies. In the first case I justify a duty by calling attention to a right; if I intend any further justification it is the right that I must justify, and I cannot do so by calling attention to the duty. In the second case it is the other way around. The difference is important because, as I shall shortly try to show, a theory that takes rights as fundamental is a theory of a different character from one that takes duties as fundamental.

Political theories will differ from one another, therefore, not simply in the particular goals, rights, and duties each sets out, but also in the way each connects the goals, rights, and duties it employs. In a well-formed theory some consistent set of these, internally ranked or weighted, will be taken as fundamental or ultimate within the theory. It seems reasonable to suppose that any particular theory will give ultimate pride of place to just one of these concepts; it will take some overriding goal, or some set of fundamental rights, or some set of transcendent duties, as fundamental, and show other goals, rights, and duties as subordinate and derivative.[1]

We may therefore make a tentative initial classification of the political theories we might produce, on the constructive model, as deep theories that might contain a contract as an intermediate device. Such a theory might be *goal-based*, in which case it would take some goal, like improving the general welfare, as fundamental; it might be *right-based*, taking some right, like the right of all men to the greatest possible overall liberty, as fundamental; or it might be *duty-based*, taking some duty, like the duty to obey God's will as set forth in the Ten Commandments,

---

[1] But an 'intuitionist' theory, as Rawls uses that term, need not. See p. 34.

as fundamental. It is easy to find examples of pure, or nearly pure, cases of each of these types of theory. Utilitarianism is, as my example suggested, a goal-based theory; Kant's categorical imperatives compose a duty-based theory; and Tom Paine's theory of revolution is right-based.

Theories within each of these types are likely to share certain very general characteristics. The types may be contrasted, for example, by comparing the attitudes they display towards individual choice and conduct. Goal-based theories are concerned with the welfare of any particular individual only in so far as this contributes to some state of affairs stipulated as good quite apart from his choice of that state of affairs. This is plainly true of totalitarian goal-based theories, like fascism, that take the interest of a political organization as fundamental. It is also true of the various forms of utilitarianism, because, though they count up the impact of political decisions on distinct individuals, and are in this way concerned with individual welfare, they merge these impacts into overall totals or averages and take the improvement of these totals or averages as desirable quite apart from the decision of any individual that it is. It is also true of perfectionist theories, like Aristotle's, that impose upon individuals an ideal of excellence and take the goal of politics to be the culture of such excellence.

Right-based and duty-based theories, on the other hand, place the individual at the center, and take his decision or conduct as of fundamental importance. But the two types put the individual in a different light. Duty-based theories are concerned with the moral quality of his acts, because they suppose that it is wrong, without more, for an individual to fail to meet certain standards of behavior. Kant thought that it was wrong to tell a lie no matter how beneficial the consequences, not because having this practice promoted some goal, but just because it was wrong. Right-based theories are, in contrast, concerned with the independence rather than the conformity of individual action. They presuppose and protect the value of individual thought and choice. Both types of theory make use of the idea of moral rules, codes of conduct to be followed, on individual occasions, without consulting self-interest. Duty-based theories treat such codes of conduct as of the essence, whether set by society to the individual or by the individual to himself. The man at their center is the man who must conform to such a code, or be punished or corrupted if he does not. Right-based theories, however, treat codes of conduct as instrumental, perhaps necessary to protect the rights of others, but having no essential value in themselves. The man at their center is the man who benefits from others' compliance, not the man who leads the life of virtue by complying himself.

We should, therefore, expect that the different types of theories would be associated with different metaphysical or political temperaments, and that one or another would be dominant in certain sorts of political economy. Goal-based theories, for example, seem especially compatible with homogeneous societies, or those at least temporarily united by an urgent, overriding goal, like self-defense or economic expansion. We should also expect that these differences between types of theory would find echoes in the legal systems of the communities they dominate. We should expect, for example, that a lawyer would approach the question of punishing moral offenses through the criminal law in a different way if his inchoate theory of justice were goal-, right- or duty-based. If his theory were goal-based he would consider the full effect of enforcing morality upon his overriding goal. If this goal were utilitarian, for example, he would entertain, though he might in the end reject, Lord Devlin's arguments that the secondary effects of punishing immorality may be beneficial.[1] If his theory were duty-based, on the other hand, he would see the point of the argument, commonly called retributive, that since immorality is wrong the state must punish it even if it harms no one. If his theory were right-based, however, he would reject the retributive argument, and judge the utilitarian argument against the background of his own assumption that individual rights must be served even at some cost to the general welfare.

All this is, of course, superficial and trivial as ideological sociology. My point is only to suggest that these differences in the character of a political theory are important quite apart from the details of position that might distinguish one theory from another of the same character. It is for this reason that the social contract is so important a feature of Rawls's methodology. It signals that his deep theory is a right-based theory, rather than a theory of either of the other two types.

The social contract provides every potential party with a veto : unless he agrees, no contract is formed. The importance, and even the existence, of this veto is obscured in the particular interpretation of the contract that constitutes the original position. Since no one knows anything about himself that would distinguish him from anyone else, he cannot rationally pursue any interest that is different. In these circumstances nothing turns on each man having a veto, or, indeed, on there being more than one potential party to the contract in the first place. But the original position is only one interpretation of the contract, and in any other interpretation in which the parties do have some knowledge with which to distinguish their situation or ambitions from those of others, the veto that the contract gives each party becomes crucial. The force of the veto each individual has depends, of course, upon his knowledge, that is to say, the particular interpretation of the contract we in the end

[1] See Chapter 10.

choose. But the fact that individuals should have any veto at all is in itself remarkable.

It can have no place in a purely goal-based theory, for example. I do not mean that the parties to a social contract could not settle on a particular social goal and make that goal henceforth the test of the justice of political decisions. I mean that no goal-based theory could make a contract the proper device for deciding upon a principle of justice in the first place; that is, the deep theory we are trying to find could not itself be goal-based.

The reason is straightforward. Suppose some particular overriding goal, like the goal of improving the average welfare in a community, or increasing the power and authority of a state, or creating a utopia according to a particular conception of the good, is taken as fundamental within a political theory. If any such goal is fundamental, then it authorizes such distribution of resources, rights, benefits, and burdens within the community as will best advance that goal, and condemns any other. The contract device, however, which supposes each individual to pursue his own interest and gives each a veto on the collective decision, applies a very different test to determine the optimum distribution. It is designed to produce the distribution that each individual deems in his own best interest, given his knowledge under whatever interpretation of the contract is specified, or at least to come as close to that distribution as he thinks he is likely to get. The contract, therefore, offers a very different test of optimum distribution than a direct application of the fundamental goal would dictate. There is no reason to suppose that a system of individual vetoes will produce a good solution to a problem in which the fairness of a distribution, considered apart from the contribution of the distribution to an overall goal, is meant to count for nothing.

It might be, of course, that a contract would produce the result that some fundamental goal dictates. Some critics, in fact, think that men in the original position, Rawls's most favored interpretation of the contract, would choose a theory of justice based on principles of average utility, that is, just the principles that a deep theory stipulating the fundamental goal of average utility would produce.[1] But if this is so, it is either because of coincidence or because the interpretation of the contract has been chosen to produce this result; in either case the contract is supererogatory, because the final result is determined by the fundamental goal and the contract device adds nothing.

One counterargument is available. Suppose it appears that the fundamental goal will in fact be served only if the state is governed in accord-

---

[1] John Mackie presented a forceful form of this argument to an Oxford seminar in the fall of 1972.

ance with principles that all men will see to be, in some sense, in their own interest. If the fundamental goal is the aggrandizement of the state, for example, it may be that this goal can be reached only if the population does not see that the government acts for this goal, but instead supposes that it acts according to principles shown to be in their individual interests through a contract device; only if they believe this will they work in the state's interest at all. We cannot ignore this devious, if unlikely, argument, but it does not support the use that Rawls makes of the contract. The argument depends upon a deception, like Sidgewick's famous argument that utilitarianism can best be served by keeping the public ignorant of that theory.[1] A theory that includes such a deception is ineligible on the constructivist model we are pursuing, because our aim, on that model, is to develop a theory that unites our convictions and can serve as a program for public action; publicity is as much a requirement of our deep theory as of the conception of justice that Rawls develops within it.

So a goal-based deep theory cannot support the contract, except as a useless and confusing appendage. Neither can a duty-based deep theory, for much the same reasons. A theory that takes some duty or duties to be fundamental offers no ground to suppose that just institutions are those seen to be in everyone's self-interest under some description. I do not deny, again, that the parties to the contract may decide to impose certain duties upon themselves and their successors, just as they may decide to adopt certain goals, in the exercise of their judgment of their own self-interest. Rawls describes the duties they would impose upon themselves under his most favored interpretation, the original position, and calls these natural duties.[2] But this is very different from supposing that the deep theory, which makes this decision decisive of what these duties are, can itself be duty-based.

It is possible to argue, of course, as many philosophers have, that a man's self-interest lies in doing his duty under the moral law, either because God will punish him otherwise, or because fulfilling his role in the natural order is his most satisfying activity, or, as Kant thought, because only in following rules he could consistently wish universal can he be free. But that says a man's duties define his self-interest, and not the other way round. It is an argument not for deciding upon a man's particular duties by letting him consult his own interest, but rather for his setting aside any calculations of self-interest except calculations of duty. It could not, therefore, support the role of a Rawlsian contract in a duty-based deep theory.

1 H. Sidgwick, *The Methods of Ethics* 489 ff. (7th ed. 1907).
2 Chapter 19.

It is true that if a contract were a feature of a duty-based deep theory, an interpretation of the contract could be chosen that would dissolve the apparent conflict between self-interest and duty. It might be a feature of the contract situation, for example, that all parties accepted the idea just mentioned, that their self-interest lay in ascertaining and doing their duty. This contract would produce principles that accurately described their duties, at least if we add the supposition that they are proficient, for some reason, in discovering what their duties are. But then, once again, we have made the contract supererogatory, a march up the hill and then back down again. We would have done better simply to work out principles of justice from the duties the deep theory takes as fundamental.

The contract does, however, make sense in a right-based deep theory. Indeed, it seems a natural development of such a theory. The basic idea of a right-based theory is that distinct individuals have interests that they are entitled to protect if they so wish. It seems natural, in developing such a theory, to try to identify the institutions an individual would veto in the exercise of whatever rights are taken as fundamental. The contract is an excellent device for this purpose, for at least two reasons. First, it allows us to distinguish between a veto in the exercise of these rights and a veto for the sake of some interest that is not so protected, a distinction we can make by adopting an interpretation of the contract that reflects our sense of what these rights are. Second, it enforces the requirements of the constructive model of argument. The parties to the contract face a practical problem; they must devise a constitution from the options available to them, rather than postponing their decision to a day of later moral insight, and they must devise a program that is both practical and public in the sense I have described.

It seems fair to assume, then, that the deep theory behind the original position must be a right-based theory of some sort. There is another way to put the point, which I have avoided until now. It must be a theory that is based on the concepts of rights that are *natural,* in the sense that they are not the product of any legislation, or convention, or hypothetical contract. I have avoided that phrase because it has, for many people, disqualifying metaphysical associations. They think that natural rights are supposed to be spectral attributes worn by primitive men like amulets, which they carry into civilization to ward off tyranny. Mr. Justice Black, for example, thought it was a sufficient refutation of a judicial philosophy he disliked simply to point out that it seemed to rely on this preposterous notion.[1]

But on the constructive model, at least, the assumption of natural

---

[1] *Griswold v. Connecticut*, 381 U.S. 479, 507 (1964) (dissenting opinion).

rights is not a metaphysically ambitious one. It requires no more than the hypothesis that the best political program, within the sense of that model, is one that takes the protection of certain individual choices as fundamental, and not properly subordinated to any goal or duty or combination of these. This requires no ontology more dubious or controversial than any contrary choice of fundamental concepts would be and, in particular, no more than the hypothesis of a fundamental goal that underlies the various popular utilitarian theories would require. Nor is it disturbing that a Rawlsian deep theory makes these rights natural rather than legal or conventional. Plainly, any right-based theory must presume rights that are not simply the product of deliberate legislation or explicit social custom, but are independent grounds for judging legislation and custom. On the constructive model, the assumption that rights are in this sense natural is simply one assumption to be made and examined for its power to unite and explain our political convictions, one basic programmatic decision to submit to this test of coherence and experience.

C. The original position

I said that the use of a social contract, in the way that Rawls uses it, presupposes a deep theory that assumes natural rights. I want now to describe, in somewhat more detail, how the device of a contract applies that assumption. It capitalizes on the idea, mentioned earlier, that some political arrangements might be said to be in the antecedent interest of every individual even though they are not, in the event, in his actual interest.

Everyone whose consent is necessary to a contract has a veto over the terms of that contract, but the worth of that veto, to him, is limited by the fact that his judgment must be one of antecedent rather than actual self-interest. He must commit himself, and so abandon his veto, at a time when his knowledge is sufficient only to allow him to estimate the best odds, not to be certain of his bet. So the contract situation is in one way structurally like the situation in which an individual with specific political rights confronts political decisions that may disadvantage him. He has a limited, political right to veto these, a veto limited by the scope of the rights he has. The contract can be used as a model for the political situation by shaping the degree or character of a party's ignorance in the contractual situation so that this ignorance has the same force on his decision as the limited nature of his rights would have in the political situation.

This shaping of ignorance to suit the limited character of political rights is most efficiently done simply by narrowing the individual goals that the parties to the contract know they wish to pursue. If we take Hobbes's deep theory, for example, to propose that men have a fundamental natural right to life, so that it is wrong to take their lives, even for social goals otherwise proper, we should expect a contract situation of the sort he describes. Hobbes's men and women, in Rawls's phrase, have lexically ordered security of life over all other individual goals; the same situation would result if they were simply ignorant of any other goals they might have and unable to speculate about the chances that they have any particular one or set of these.

The ignorance of the parties in the original position might thus be seen as a kind of limiting case of the ignorance that can be found, in the form of a distorted or eccentric ranking of interests, in classical contract theories and that is natural to the contract device. The original position is a limiting case because Rawls's men are not simply ignorant of interests beyond a chosen few; they are ignorant of all the interests they have. It would be wrong to suppose that this makes them incapable of any judgments of self-interest. But the judgments they make must nevertheless be very abstract; they must allow for any combination of interests, without the benefit of any supposition that some of these are more likely than others.

The basic right of Rawls's deep theory, therefore, cannot be a right to any particular individual goal, like a right to security of life, or a right to lead a life according to a particular conception of the good. Such rights to individual goals may be produced by the deep theory, as rights that men in the original position would stipulate as being in their best interest. But the original position cannot itself be justified on the assumption of such a right, because the parties to the contract do not know that they have any such interest or rank it lexically ahead of others.

So the basic right of Rawls's deep theory must be an abstract right, that is, not a right to any particular individual goal. There are two candidates, within the familiar concepts of political theory, for this role. The first is the right to liberty, and it may strike many readers as both plausible and comforting to assume that Rawls's entire structure is based on the assumption of a fundamental natural right to liberty – plausible because the two principles that compose his theory of justice give liberty an important and dominant place, and comforting because the argument attempting to justify that place seems uncharacteristically incomplete.[1]

Nevertheless, the right to liberty cannot be taken as the fundamental right in Rawls's deep theory. Suppose we define general liberty as the

---

[1] See Hart, 'Rawls on Liberty and Its Priority', 40 *U. Chi. L. Rev.* 534 (1973).

overall minimum possible constraints, imposed by government or by other men, on what a man might want to do.[1] We must then distinguish this general liberty from particular liberties, that is, freedom from such constraints on particular acts thought specially important, like participation in politics. The parties to the original position certainly have, and know that they have, an interest in general liberty, because general liberty will, *pro tanto*, improve their power to achieve any particular goals they later discover themselves to have. But the qualification is important, because they have no way of knowing that general liberty will in fact improve this power overall, and every reason to suspect that it will not. They know that they might have other interests, beyond general liberty, that can be protected only by political constraints on acts of others.

So if Rawlsian men must be supposed to have a right to liberty of some sort, which the contract situation is shaped to embody, it must be a right to particular liberties. Rawls does name a list of basic liberties, and it is these that his men do choose to protect through their lexically ordered first principle of justice.[2] But Rawls plainly casts this principle as the product of the contract rather than as a condition of it. He argues that the parties to the original position would select these basic liberties to protect the basic goods they decide to value, like self-respect, rather than taking these liberties as goals in themselves. Of course they might, in fact, value the activities protected as basic liberties for their own sake, rather than as means to some other goal or interest. But they certainly do not know that they do.

The second familiar concept of political theory is even more abstract than liberty. This is equality, and in one way Rawlsian men and women cannot choose other than to protect it. The state of ignorance in the original position is so shaped that the antecedent interest of everyone must lie, as I said, in the same solution. The right of each man to be treated equally without regard to his person or character or tastes is enforced by the fact that no one else can secure a better position by virtue of being different in any such respect. In other contract situations, when ignorance is less complete, individuals who share the same goal may nevertheless have different antecedent interests. Even if two men value life above everything else, for example, the antecedent interest of the weaker might call for a state monopoly of force rather than some provision for private vengeance, but the antecedent interest of the stronger might not. Even if two men value political participation above all else, the knowledge that one's views are likely to be more unorthodox or unpopular than those of the other will suggest that his antecedent

---

[1] Cf. Rawls's definition of liberty at p. 202.
[2] p. 61.

interest calls for different arrangements. In the original position no such discrimination of antecedent interests can be made.

It is true that, in two respects, the principles of justice that Rawls thinks men and women would choose in the original position may be said to fall short of an egalitarian ideal. First, they subordinate equality in material resources, when this is necessary, to liberty of political activity, by making the demands of the first principle prior to those of the second. Second, they do not take account of relative deprivation, because they justify any inequality when those worse off are better off than they would be, in absolute terms, without that inequality.

Rawls makes plain that these inequalities are required, not by some competing notion of liberty or some overriding goal, but by a more basic sense of equality itself. He accepts a distinction between what he calls two conceptions of equality :

> Some writers have distinguished between equality as it is invoked in connection with the distribution of certain goods, some of which will almost certainly give higher status or prestige to those who are more favored, and equality as it applies to the respect which is owed to persons irrespective of their social position. Equality of the first kind is defined by the second principle of justice . . . . But equality of the second kind is fundamental.[1]

We may describe a right to equality of the second kind, which Rawls says is fundamental, in this way. We might say that individuals have a right to equal concern and respect in the design and administration of the political institutions that govern them. This is a highly abstract right. Someone might argue, for example, that it is satisfied by political arrangements that provide equal opportunity for office and position on the basis of merit. Someone else might argue, to the contrary, that it is satisfied only by a system that guarantees absolute equality of income and status, without regard to merit. A third man might argue that equal concern and respect is provided by that system, whatever it is, that improves the average welfare of all citizens counting the welfare of each on the same scale. A fourth might argue, in the name of this fundamental equality, for the priority of liberty, and for the other apparent inequalities of Rawls's two principles.

The right to equal concern and respect, then, is more abstract than the standard conceptions of equality that distinguish different political theories. It permits arguments that this more basic right requires one or another of these conceptions as a derivative right or goal.

---

[1] p. 511.

The original portion may now be seen as a device for testing these competing arguments. It supposes, reasonably, that political arrangements that do not display equal concern and respect are those that are established and administered by powerful men and women who, whether they recognize it or not, have more concern and respect for members of a particular class, or people with particular talents or ideals, than they have for others. It relies on this supposition in shaping the ignorance of the parties to the contract. Men who do not know to which class they belong cannot design institutions, consciously or unconsciously, to favor their own class. Men who have no idea of their own conception of the good cannot act to favor those who hold one ideal over those who hold another. The original position is well designed to enforce the abstract right to equal concern and respect, which must be understood to be the fundamental concept of Rawls's deep theory.

If this is right, then Rawls must not use the original position to argue for this right in the same way that he uses it, for example, to argue for the rights to basic liberties embodied in the first principle. The text confirms that he does not. It is true that he once says that equality of respect is 'defined' by the first principle of justice.[1] But he does not mean, and in any case he does not argue, that the parties choose to be respected equally in order to advance some more basic right or goal. On the contrary, the right to equal respect is not, on his account, a product of the contract, but a condition of admission to the original position. This right, he says, is 'owed to human beings as moral persons', and follows from the moral personality that distinguishes humans from animals. It is possessed by all men who can give justice, and only such men can contract.[2] This is one right, therefore, that does not emerge from the contract, but is assumed, as the fundamental right must be, in its design.

Rawls is well aware that his argument for equality stands on a different footing from his argument for the other rights within his theory:

> Now of course none of this is literally argument. I have not set out the premises from which this conclusion follows, as I have tried to do, albeit not very rigorously, with the choice of conceptions of justice in the original position. Nor have I tried to prove that the characterization of the parties must be used as the basis of equality. Rather this interpretation seems to be the natural completion of justice as fairness.[3]

[1] *Id.*
[2] Chapter 77.
[3] p. 509.

It is the 'natural completion', that is to say, of the theory as a whole. It completes the theory by providing the fundamental assumption that charges the original position, and makes it an 'intuitive notion' for developing and testing theories of justice.

We may therefore say that justice as fairness rests on the assumption of a natural right of all men and women to equality of concern and respect, a right they possess not by virtue of birth or characteristic or merit or excellence but simply as human beings with the capacity to make plans and give justice. Many readers will not be surprised by this conclusion, and it is, as I have said, reasonably clear from the text. It is an important conclusion, nevertheless, because some forms of criticism of the theory, already standard, ignore it. I shall close this long essay with one example.

One form of criticism has been expressed to me by many colleagues and students, particularly lawyers. They point out that the particular political institutions and arrangements that Rawls says men in the original position would choose are merely idealized forms of those now in force in the United States. They are the institutions, that is, of liberal constitutional democracy. The critics conclude that the fundamental assumptions of Rawls's theory must, therefore, be the assumptions of classical liberalism, however they define these, and that the original position, which appears to animate the theory, must somehow be an embodiment of these assumptions. Justice as fairness therefore seems to them, in its entirety, a particularly subtle rationalization of the political status quo, which may safely be disregarded by those who want to offer a more radical critique of the liberal tradition.

If I am right, this point of view is foolish, and those who take it lose an opportunity, rare for them, to submit their own political views to some form of philosophical examination. Rawls's most basic assumption is not that men have a right to certain liberties that Locke or Mill thought important, but that they have a right to equal respect and concern in the design of political institutions. This assumption may be contested in many ways. It will be denied by those who believe that some goal, like utility or the triumph of a class or the flowering of some conception of how men should live, is more fundamental than any individual right, including the right to equality. But it cannot be denied in the name of any more radical concept of equality, because none exists.

Rawls does argue that this fundamental right to equality requires a liberal constitution, and supports an idealized form of present economic and social structures. He argues, for example, that men in the original position would protect the basic liberties in the interest of their right to equality, once a certain level of material comfort has been reached, because they would understand that a threat to self-respect, which the basic liberties protect, is then the most serious threat to equal respect. He also argues that these men would accept the second principle in preference to material equality because they would understand that sacrifice out of envy for another is a form of subordination to him. These arguments may, of course, be wrong. I have certainly said nothing in their defense here. But the critics of liberalism now have the responsibility to show that they are wrong. They cannot say that Rawls's basic assumptions and attitudes are too far from their own to allow a confrontation.

7

Taking Rights Seriously

The language of rights now dominates political debate in the United States. Does the Government respect the moral and political rights of its citizens? Or does the Government's foreign policy, or its race policy, fly in the face of these rights? Do the minorities whose rights have been violated have the right to violate the law in return? Or does the silent majority itself have rights, including the right that those who break the law be punished? It is not surprising that these questions are now prominent. The concept of rights, and particularly the concept of rights against the Government, has its most natural use when a political society is divided, and appeals to co-operation or a common goal are pointless.

The debate does not include the issue of whether citizens have *some* moral rights against their Government. It seems accepted on all sides that they do. Conventional lawyers and politicians take it as a point of pride that our legal system recognizes, for example, individual rights of free speech, equality, and due process. They base their claim that our law deserves respect, at least in part, on that fact, for they would not claim that totalitarian systems deserve the same loyalty.

Some philosophers, of course, reject the idea that citizens have rights apart from what the law happens to give them. Bentham thought that the idea of moral rights was 'nonsense on stilts'. But that view has never been part of our orthodox political theory, and politicians of both parties appeal to the rights of the people to justify a great part of what they want to do. I shall not be concerned, in this essay, to defend the thesis that citizens have moral rights against their governments; I want instead to explore the implications of that thesis for those, including the present United States Government, who profess to accept it.

It is much in dispute, of course, what *particular* rights citizens have. Does the acknowledged right to free speech, for example, include the right to participate in nuisance demonstrations? In practice the Government will have the last word on what an individual's rights are, because its police will do what its officials and courts say. But that does not mean that the Government's view is necessarily the correct view; anyone who thinks it does must believe that men and women have only such moral rights as Government chooses to grant, which means that they have no moral rights at all.

All this is sometimes obscured in the United States by the constitutional system. The American Constitution provides a set of individual *legal* rights in the First Amendment, and in the due process, equal protection, and similar clauses. Under present legal practice the Supreme Court has the power to declare an act of Congress or of a state legislature void if the Court finds that the act offends these provisions. This practice has led some commentators to suppose that individual moral rights are fully protected by this system, but that is hardly so, nor could it be so.

The Constitution fuses legal and moral issues, by making the validity of a law depend on the answer to complex moral problems, like the problem of whether a particular statute respects the inherent equality of all men. This fusion has important consequences for the debates about civil disobedience; I have described these elsewhere[1] and I shall refer to them later. But it leaves open two prominent questions. It does not tell us whether the Constitution, even properly interpreted, recognizes all the moral rights that citizens have, and it does not tell us whether, as many suppose, citizens would have a duty to obey the law even if it did invade their moral rights.

Both questions become crucial when some minority claims moral rights which the law denies, like the right to run its local school system, and which lawyers agree are not protected by the Constitution. The second question becomes crucial when, as now, the majority is sufficiently aroused so that Constitutional amendments to eliminate rights, like the right against self-incrimination, are seriously proposed. It is also crucial in nations, like the United Kingdom, that have no constitution of a comparable nature.

Even if the Constitution were perfect, of course, and the majority left it alone, it would not follow that the Supreme Court could guarantee the individual rights of citizens. A Supreme Court decision is still a legal decision, and it must take into account precedent and institutional considerations like relations between the Court and Congress, as well as morality. And no judicial decision is necessarily the right decision. Judges stand for different positions on controversial issues of law and morals and, as the fights over Nixon's Supreme Court nominations showed, a President is entitled to appoint judges of his own persuasion, provided that they are honest and capable.

[1] See Chapter 8.

So, though the constitutional system adds something to the protection of moral rights against the Government, it falls far short of guaranteeing these rights, or even establishing what they are. It means that, on some occasions, a department other than the legislature has the last word on these issues, which can hardly satisfy someone who thinks such a department profoundly wrong.

It is of course inevitable that some department of government will have the final say on what law will be enforced. When men disagree about moral rights, there will be no way for either side to prove its case, and some decision must stand if there is not to be anarchy. But that piece of orthodox wisdom must be the beginning and not the end of a philosophy of legislation and enforcement. If we cannot insist that the Government reach the right answers about the rights of its citizens, we can insist at least that it try. We can insist that it take rights seriously, follow a coherent theory of what these rights are, and act consistently with its own professions. I shall try to show what that means, and how it bears on the present political debates.

2. RIGHTS AND THE RIGHT TO BREAK THE LAW

I shall start with the most violently argued issue. Does an American ever have the moral right to break a law? Suppose someone admits a law is valid; does he therefore have a duty to obey it? Those who try to give an answer seem to fall into two camps. The conservatives, as I shall call them, seem to disapprove of any act of disobedience; they appear satisfied when such acts are prosecuted, and disappointed when convictions are reversed. The other group, the liberals, are much more sympathetic to at least some cases of disobedience; they sometimes disapprove of prosecutions and celebrate acquittals. If we look beyond these emotional reactions, however, and pay attention to the arguments the two parties use, we discover an astounding fact. Both groups give essentially the same answer to the question of principle that supposedly divides them.

The answer that both parties give is this. In a democracy, or at least a democracy that in principle respects individual rights, each citizen has a general moral duty to obey all the laws, even though he would like some of them changed. He owes that duty to his fellow citizens, who obey laws that they do not like, to his benefit. But this general duty cannot be an absolute duty, because even a society that is in principle just may produce unjust laws and policies, and a man has duties other than his duties to the State. A man must honour his duties to his God and to his conscience, and if these conflict with his duty to the State, then he is entitled, in the end, to do what he judges to be right. If he decides that he must break the law, however, then he must submit to the judgment and punishment that the State imposes, in recognition of the fact that his duty to his fellow citizens was overwhelmed but not extinguished by his religious or moral obligation.

Of course this common answer can be elaborated in very different ways. Some would describe the duty to the State as fundamental, and picture the dissenter as a religious or moral fanatic. Others would describe the duty to the State in grudging terms, and picture those who oppose it as moral heroes. But these are differences in tone, and the position I described represents, I think, the view of most of those who find themselves arguing either for or against civil disobedience in particular cases.

I do not claim that it is everyone's view. There must be some who put the duty to the State so high that they do not grant that it can ever be overcome. There are certainly some who would deny that a man ever has a moral duty to obey the law, at least in the United States today. But these two extreme positions are the slender tails of a bell curve, and all those who fall in between hold the orthodox position I described — that men have a duty to obey the law but have the right to follow their consciences when it conflicts with that duty.

But if that is so, then we have a paradox in the fact that men who give the same answer to a question of principle should seem to disagree so much, and to divide so fiercely, in particular cases. The paradox goes even deeper, for each party, in at least some cases, takes a position that seems flatly inconsistent with the theoretical position they both accept. This position was tested, for example, when someone evaded the draft on grounds of conscience, or encouraged others to commit this crime. Conservatives argued that such men must be prosecuted, even though they are sincere. Why must they be prosecuted? Because society cannot tolerate the decline in respect for the law that their act constitutes and encourages. They must be prosecuted, in short, to discourage them and others like them from doing what they have done.

But there seems to be a monstrous contradiction here. If a man has a right to do what his conscience tells him he must, then how can the State be justified in discouraging him from doing it? Is it not wicked for a state to forbid and punish what it acknowledges that men have a right to do?

Moreover, it is not just conservatives who argue that those who break the law out of moral conviction should be prosecuted. The liberal is notoriously opposed to allowing racist school officials to go slow on desegregation, even though he acknowledges that these school officials think they have a moral right to do what the law forbids. The liberal does not often argue, it is true, that the desegregation laws must be enforced to encourage general respect for law. He argues instead that the desegregation laws must be enforced because they are right. But his position also seems inconsistent: can it be right to prosecute men for doing what their conscience requires, when we acknowledge their right to follow their conscience?

We are therefore left with two puzzles. How can two parties to an issue of principle, each of which thinks it is in profound disagreement with the other, embrace the same position on that issue? How can it be that each side urges solutions to particular problems which seem flatly to contradict the position of principle that both accept? One possible answer is that some or all of those who accept the common position are hypocrites, paying lip service to rights of conscience which in fact they do not grant.

There is some plausibility in this charge. A sort of hypocrisy must have been involved when public officials who claim to respect conscience denied Muhammad Ali the right to box in their states. If Ali, in spite of his religious scruples, had joined the Army, he would have been allowed to box even though, on the principles these officials say they honour, he would have been a worse human being for having done so. But there are few cases that seem so straightforward as this one, and even here the officials did not seem to recognize the contradiction between their acts and their principles. So we must search for some explanation beyond the truth that men often do not mean what they say.

The deeper explanation lies in a set of confusions that often embarrass arguments about rights. These confusions have clouded all the issues I mentioned at the outset and have crippled attempts to develop a coherent theory of how a government that respects rights must behave.

In order to explain this, I must call attention to the fact, familiar to philosophers, but often ignored in political debate, that the word 'right' has different force in different contexts. In most cases when we say that someone has 'right' to do something, we imply that it would be wrong to interfere with his doing it, or at least that some special grounds are needed for justifying any interference. I use this strong sense of right when I say that you have the right to spend your money gambling, if you wish, though you ought to spend it in a more worthwhile way. I mean that it would be wrong for anyone to interfere with you even though you propose to spend your money in a way that I think is wrong.

There is a clear difference between saying that someone has a right to do something in this sense and saying that it is the 'right' thing for him to do, or that he does no 'wrong' in doing it. Someone may have the right to do something that is the wrong thing for him to do, as might be the case with gambling. Conversely, something may be the right thing for him to do and yet he may have no right to do it, in the sense that it would not be wrong for someone to interfere with his trying. If our army captures an enemy soldier, we might say that the right thing for him to do is to try to escape, but it would not follow that it is wrong for us to try to stop him. We might admire him for trying to escape, and perhaps even think less of him if he did not. But there is no suggestion here that it is wrong of us to stand in his way; on the contrary, if we think our cause is just, we think it right for us to do all we can to stop him.

Ordinarily this distinction, between the issues of whether a man has a right to do something and whether it is the right thing for him to do, causes no trouble. But sometimes it does, because sometimes we say that a man has a right to do something when we mean only to deny that it is the wrong thing for him to do. Thus we say that the captured soldier has a 'right' to try to escape when we mean, not that we do wrong to stop him, but that he has no duty not to make the attempt. We use 'right' this way when we speak of someone having the 'right' to act on his own principles, or the 'right' to follow his own conscience. We mean that he does no wrong to proceed on his honest convictions, even though we disagree with these convictions, and even though, for policy or other reasons, we must force him to act contrary to them.

Suppose a man believes that welfare payments to the poor are profoundly wrong, because they sap enterprise, and so declares his full income-tax each year but declines to pay half of it. We might say that he has a right to refuse to pay, if he wishes, but that the Government has a right to proceed against him for the full tax, and to fine or jail him for late payment if that is necessary to keep the collection system working efficiently. We do not take this line in most cases; we do not say that the ordinary thief has a right to steal, if he wishes, so long as he pays the penalty. We say a man has the right to break the law, even though the State has a right to punish him, only when we think that, because of his convictions, he does no wrong in doing so.[1]

These distinctions enable us to see an ambiguity in the orthodox question : Does a man ever have a right to break the law? Does that question mean to ask whether he ever has a right to break the law in the strong sense, so that the Government would do wrong to stop him, by arresting and prosecuting him? Or does it mean to ask whether he ever does the

---

[1] It is not surprising that we sometimes use the concept of having a right to say that others must not interfere with an act and sometimes to say that the act is not the wrong thing to do. Often, when someone has *no* right to do something, like attacking another man physically, it is true *both* that it is the wrong thing to do and that others are entitled to stop it, by demand, if not by force. It is therefore natural to say that someone has a right when we mean to deny *either* of these consequences, as well as when we mean to deny both.

right thing to break the law, so that we should all respect him even though the Government should jail him?

If we take the orthodox position to be an answer to the first – and most important – question, then the paradoxes I described arise. But if we take it as an answer to the second, they do not. Conservatives and liberals do agree that sometimes a man does not do the wrong thing to break a law, when his conscience so requires. They disagree, when they do, over the different issue of what the State's response should be. Both parties do think that sometimes the State should prosecute. But this is not inconsistent with the proposition that the man prosecuted did the right thing in breaking the law.

The paradoxes seem genuine because the two questions are not usually distinguished, and the orthodox position is presented as a general solution to the problem of civil disobedience. But once the distinction is made, it is apparent that the position has been so widely accepted only because, when it is applied, it is treated as an answer to the second question but not the first. The crucial distinction is obscured by the troublesome idea of a right to conscience; this idea has been at the centre of most recent discussions of political obligation, but it is a red herring drawing us away from the crucial political questions. The state of a man's conscience may be decisive, or central, when the issue is whether he does something morally wrong in breaking the law; but it need not be decisive or even central when the issue is whether he has a right, in the strong sense of that term, to do so. A man does not have the right, in that sense, to do whatever his conscience demands, but he may have the right, in that sense, to do something even though his conscience does not demand it.

If that is true, then there has been almost no serious attempt to answer the questions that almost everyone means to ask. We can make a fresh start by stating these questions more clearly. Does an American ever have the right, in a strong sense, to do something which is against the law? If so, when? In order to answer these questions put in that way, we must try to become clearer about the implications of the idea, mentioned earlier, that citizens have at least some rights against their government.

I said that in the United States citizens are supposed to have certain fundamental rights against their Government, certain moral rights made into legal rights by the Constitution. If this idea is significant, and worth bragging about, then these rights must be rights in the strong sense I just described. The claim that citizens have a right to free speech must imply that it would be wrong for the Government to stop them from speaking, even when the Government believes that what they will say will cause more harm than good. The claim cannot mean, on the prisoner-of-war analogy, only that citizens do no wrong in speaking their minds, though the Government reserves the right to prevent them from doing so.

This is a crucial point, and I want to labour it. Of course a responsible government must be ready to justify anything it does, particularly when it limits the liberty of its citizens. But normally it is a sufficient justification, even for an act that limits liberty, that the act is calculated to increase what the philosophers call general utility – that it is calculated to produce more over-all benefit than harm. So, though the New York City government needs a justification for forbidding motorists to drive up Lexington Avenue, it is sufficient justification if the proper officials believe, on sound evidence, that the gain to the many will outweigh the inconvenience to the few. When individual citizens are said to have rights against the Government, however, like the right of free speech, that must mean that this sort of justification is not enough. Otherwise the claim would not argue that individuals have special protection against the law when their rights are in play, and that is just the point of the claim.

Not all legal rights, or even Constitutional rights, represent moral rights against the Government. I now have the legal right to drive either way on Fifty-seventh Street, but the Government would do no wrong to make that street one-way if it thought it in the general interest to do so. I have a Constitutional right to vote for a congressman every two years, but the national and state governments would do no wrong if, following the amendment procedure, they made a congressman's term four years instead of two, again on the basis of a judgment that this would be for the general good.

But those Constitutional rights that we call fundamental like the right of free speech, are supposed to represent rights against the Government in the strong sense; that is the point of the boast that our legal system respects the fundamental rights of the citizen. If citizens have a moral right of free speech, then governments would do wrong to repeal the First Amendment that guarantees it, even if they were persuaded that the majority would be better off if speech were curtailed.

I must not overstate the point. Someone who claims that citizens have a right against the Government need not go so far as to say that the State is *never* justified in overriding that right. He might say, for example, that although citizens have a right to free speech, the Government may override that right when necessary to protect the rights of others, or to prevent a catastrophe, or even to obtain a clear and major public benefit (though if he acknowledged this last as a possible justification he would be treating the right in question as not among the most important or fundamental). What he cannot do is to say that the Government is justified in overriding a right on the minimal grounds that would be sufficient if no such right existed. He cannot say that the Government is entitled to act on no more than a judgment that its act is likely to produce, overall, a benefit to the community. That admission would make his claim of a right pointless, and would show him to be using some sense of 'right' other than the strong sense necessary to give his claim the political importance it is normally taken to have.

But then the answers to our two questions about disobedience seem plain, if unorthodox. In our society a man does sometimes have the right, in the strong sense, to disobey a law. He has that right whenever that law wrongly invades his rights against the Government. If he has a moral right to free speech, that is, then he has a moral right to break any law that the Government, by virtue of his right, had no right to adopt. The right to disobey the law is not a separate right, having something to do with conscience, additional to other rights against the Government. It is simply a feature of these rights against the Government, and it cannot be denied in principle without denying that any such rights exist.

These answers seem obvious once we take rights against the Government to be rights in the strong sense I described. If I have a right to speak my mind on political issues, then the Government does wrong to make it illegal for me to do so, even if it thinks this is in the general interest. If, nevertheless, the Government does make my act illegal, then it does a further wrong to enforce that law against me. My right against the Government means that it is wrong for the Government to stop me from speaking; the Government cannot make it right to stop me just by taking the first step.

This does not, of course, tell us exactly what rights men do have against the Government. It does not tell us whether the right of free speech includes the right of demonstration. But it does mean that passing a law cannot affect such rights as men do have, and that is of crucial importance, because it dictates the attitude that an individual is entitled to take toward his personal decision when civil disobedience is in question.

Both conservatives and liberals suppose that in a society which is generally decent everyone has a duty to obey the law, whatever it is. That is the source of the 'general duty' clause in the orthodox position, and though liberals believe that this duty can sometimes be 'overridden', even they suppose, as the orthodox position maintains, that the duty of obedience remains in some submerged form, so that a man does well to accept punishment in recognition of that duty. But this general duty is almost incoherent in a society that recognizes rights. If a man believes he has a right to demonstrate, then he must believe that it would be wrong for the Government to stop him, with or without benefit of a law.

If he is entitled to believe that, then it is silly to speak of a duty to obey the law as such, or of a duty to accept the punishment that the State has no right to give.

Conservatives will object to the short work I have made of their point. They will argue that even if the Government was wrong to adopt some law, like a law limiting speech, there are independent reasons why the Government is justified in enforcing the law once adopted. When the law forbids demonstration, then, so they argue, some principle more important than the individual's right to speak is brought into play, namely the principle of respect for law. If a law, even a bad law, is left unenforced, then respect for law is weakened, and society as a whole suffers. So an individual loses his moral right to speak when speech is made criminal, and the Government must, for the common good and for the general benefit, enforce the law against him.

But this argument, though popular, is plausible only if we forget what it means to say that an individual has a right against the State. It is far from plain that civil disobedience lowers respect for law, but even if we suppose that it does, this fact is irrelevant. The prospect of utilitarian gains cannot justify preventing a man from doing what he has a right to do, and the supposed gains in respect for law are simply utilitarian gains. There would be no point in the boast that we respect individual rights unless that involved some sacrifice, and the sacrifice in question must be that we give up whatever marginal benefits our country would receive from overriding these rights when they prove inconvenient. So the general benefit cannot be a good ground for abridging rights, even when the benefit in question is a heightened respect for law.

But perhaps I do wrong to assume that the argument about respect for law is only an appeal to general utility. I said that a state may be justified in overriding or limiting rights on other grounds, and we must ask, before rejecting the conservative position, whether any of these apply. The most important – and least well understood – of these other grounds invokes the notion of *competing rights* that would be jeopardized if the right in question were not limited. Citizens have personal rights to the State's protection as well as personal rights to be free from the State's interference, and it may be necessary for the Government to choose between these two sorts of rights. The law of defamation, for example, limits the personal right of any man to say what he thinks, because it requires him to have good grounds for what he says. But this law is justified, even for those who think that it does invade a personal right, by the fact that it protects the right of others not to have their reputations ruined by a careless statement.

The individual rights that our society acknowledges often conflict in this way, and when they do it is the job of government to discriminate.

If the Government makes the right choice, and protects the more important at the cost of the less, then it has not weakened or cheapened the notion of a right; on the contrary it would have done so had it failed to protect the more important of the two. So we must acknowledge that the Government has a reason for limiting rights if it plausibly believes that a competing right is more important.

May the conservative seize on this fact? He might argue that I did wrong to characterize his argument as one that appeals to the general benefit, because it appeals instead to competing rights, namely the moral right of the majority to have its laws enforced, or the right of society to maintain the degree of order and security it wishes. These are the rights, he would say, that must be weighed against the individual's right to do what the wrongful law prohibits.

But this new argument is confused, because it depends on yet another ambiguity in the language of rights. It is true that we speak of the 'right' of society to do what it wants, but this cannot be a 'competing right' of the sort that may justify the invasion of a right against the Government. The existence of rights against the Government would be jeopardized if the Government were able to defeat such a right by appealing to the right of a democratic majority to work its will. A right against the Government must be a right to do something even when the majority thinks it would be wrong to do it, and even when the majority would be worse off for having it done. If we now say that society has a right to do whatever is in the general benefit, or the right to preserve whatever sort of environment the majority wishes to live in, and we mean that these are the sort of rights that provide justification for overruling any rights against the Government that may conflict, then we have annihilated the latter rights.

In order to save them, we must recognize as competing rights only the rights of other members of the society as individuals. We must distinguish the 'rights' of the majority as such, which cannot count as a justification for overruling individual rights, and the personal rights of members of a majority, which might well count. The test we must use is this. Someone has a competing right to protection, which must be weighed against an individual right to act, if that person would be entitled to demand that protection from his government on his own title, as an individual, without regard to whether a majority of his fellow citizens joined in the demand.

It cannot be true, on this test, that anyone has a right to have all the laws of the nation enforced. He has a right to have enforced only those criminal laws, for example, that he would have a right to have enacted if they were not already law. The laws against personal assault may well fall into that class. If the physically vulnerable members of the community – those who need police protection against personal violence – were only a small minority, it would still seem plausible to say that they were entitled to that protection. But the laws that provide a certain level of quiet in public places, or that authorize and finance a foreign war, cannot be thought to rest on individual rights. The timid lady on the streets of Chicago is not entitled to just the degree of quiet that now obtains, nor is she entitled to have boys drafted to fight in wars she approves. There are laws – perhaps desirable laws – that provide these advantages for her, but the justification for these laws, if they can be justified at all, is the common desire of a large majority, not her personal right. If, therefore, these laws do abridge someone else's moral right to protest, or his right to personal security, she cannot urge a competing right to justify the abridgement. She has no personal right to have such laws passed, and she has no competing right to have them enforced either.

So the conservative cannot advance his argument much on the ground of competing rights, but he may want to use another ground. A government, he may argue, may be justified in abridging the personal rights of its citizens in an emergency, or when a very great loss may be prevented, or perhaps, when some major benefit can clearly be secured. If the nation is at war, a policy of censorship may be justified even though it invades the right to say what one thinks on matters of political controversy. But the emergency must be genuine. There must be what Oliver Wendell Holmes described as a clear and present danger, and the danger must be one of magnitude.

Can the conservative argue that when any law is passed, even a wrongful law, this sort of justification is available for enforcing it? His argument might be something of this sort. If the Government once acknowledges that it may be wrong – that the legislature might have adopted, the executive approved, and the courts left standing, a law that in fact abridges important rights – then this admission will lead not simply to a marginal decline in respect for law, but to a crisis of order. Citizens may decide to obey only those laws they personally approve, and that is anarchy. So the Government must insist that whatever a citizen's rights may be before a law is passed and upheld by the courts, his rights thereafter are determined by that law.

But this argument ignores the primitive distinction between what may happen and what will happen. If we allow speculation to support the justification of emergency or decisive benefit, then, again, we have annihilated rights. We must, as Learned Hand said, discount the gravity of the evil threatened by the likelihood of reaching that evil. I know of no genuine evidence to the effect that tolerating some civil disobedience, out of respect for the moral position of its authors, will increase such disobedience, let alone crime in general. The case that it will must be based on vague assumptions about the contagion of ordinary crimes, assumptions that are themselves unproved, and that are in any event largely irrelevant. It seems at least as plausible to argue that tolerance will increase respect for officials and for the bulk of the laws they promulgate, or at least retard the rate of growing disrespect.

If the issue were simply the question whether the community would be marginally better off under strict law enforcement, then the Government would have to decide on the evidence we have, and it might not be unreasonable to decide, on balance, that it would. But since rights are at stake, the issue is the very different one of whether tolerance would destroy the community or threaten it with great harm, and it seems to me simply mindless to suppose that the evidence makes that probable or even conceivable.

The argument from emergency is confused in another way as well. It assumes that the Government must take the position either that a man never has the right to break the law, or that he always does. I said that any society that claims to recognize rights at all must abandon the notion of a general duty to obey the law that holds in all cases. This is important, because it shows that there are no short cuts to meeting a citizen's claim to right. If a citizen argues that he has a moral right not to serve in the Army, or to protest in a way he finds effective, then an official who wants to answer him, and not simply bludgeon him into obedience, must respond to the particular point he makes, and cannot point to the draft law or a Supreme Court decision as having even special, let alone decisive, weight. Sometimes an official who considers the citizen's moral arguments in good faith will be persuaded that the citizen's claim is plausible, or even right. It does not follow, however, that he will always be persuaded or that he always should be.

I must emphasize that all these propositions concern the strong sense of right, and they therefore leave open important questions about the right thing to do. If a man believes he has the right to break the law, he must then ask whether he does the right thing to exercise that right. He must remember that reasonable men can differ about whether he has a right against the Government, and therefore the right to break the law, that he thinks he has; and therefore that reasonable men can oppose him in good faith. He must take into account the various consequences his acts will have, whether they involve violence, and such other considerations as the context makes relevant; he must not go beyond the rights he can in good faith claim, to acts that violate the rights of others.

On the other hand, if some official, like a prosecutor, believes that the citizen does *not* have the right to break the law, then *he* must ask whether he does the right thing to enforce it. In Chapter 8 I argue that certain features of our legal system, and in particular the fusion of legal and moral issues in our Constitution, mean that citizens often do the right thing in exercising what they take to be moral rights to break the law, and that prosecutors often do the right thing in failing to prosecute them for it. I will not anticipate those arguments here; instead I want to ask whether the requirement that Government take its citizens' rights seriously has anything to do with the crucial question of what these rights are.

3. CONTROVERSIAL RIGHTS

The argument so far has been hypothetical: if a man has a particular moral right against the Government, that right survives contrary legislation or adjudication. But this does not tell us what rights he has, and it is notorious that reasonable men disagree about that. There is wide agreement on certain clearcut cases; almost everyone who believes in rights at all would admit, for example, that a man has a moral right to speak his mind in a non-provocative way on matters of political concern, and that this is an important right that the State must go to great pains to protect. But there is great controversy as to the limits of such paradigm rights, and the so-called 'anti-riot' law involved in the famous Chicago Seven trial of the last decade is a case in point.

The defendants were accused of conspiring to cross state lines with the intention of causing a riot. This charge is vague – perhaps unconstitutionally vague – but the law apparently defines as criminal emotional speeches which argue that violence is justified in order to secure political equality. Does the right of free speech protect this sort of speech? That, of course, is a legal issue, because it invokes the free-speech clause of the First Amendment of the Constitution. But it is also a moral issue, because, as I said, we must treat the First Amendment as an attempt to protect a moral right. It is part of the job of governing to 'define' moral rights through statutes and judicial decisions, that is, to declare officially the extent that moral rights will be taken to have in law. Congress faced this task in voting on the anti-riot bill, and the Supreme Court has faced it in countless cases. How should the different departments of government go about defining moral rights?

They should begin with a sense that whatever they decide might be wrong. History and their descendants may judge that they acted unjustly when they thought they were right. If they take their duty seriously, they must try to limit their mistakes, and they must therefore try to discover where the dangers of mistake lie.

They might choose one of two very different models for this purpose. The first model recommends striking a balance between the rights of the individual and the demands of society at large. If the Government *infringes* on a moral right (for example, by defining the right of free speech more narrowly than justice requires), then it has done the individual a wrong. On the other hand, if the Government *inflates* a right (by defining it more broadly than justice requires) then it cheats society of some general benefit, like safe streets, that there is no reason it should not have. So a mistake on one side is as serious as a mistake on the other. The course of government is to steer to the middle, to balance the general good and personal rights, giving to each its due.

When the Government, or any of its branches, defines a right, it must bear in mind, according to the first model, the social cost of different proposals and make the necessary adjustments. It must not grant the same freedom to noisy demonstrations as it grants to calm political discussion, for example, because the former causes much more trouble than the latter. Once it decides how much of a right to recognize, it must enforce its decision to the full. That means permitting an individual to act within his rights, as the Government has defined them, but not beyond, so that if anyone breaks the law, even on grounds of conscience, he must be punished. No doubt any government will make mistakes, and will regret decisions once taken. That is inevitable. But this middle policy will ensure that errors on one side will balance out errors on the other over the long run.

The first model, described in this way, has great plausibility, and most laymen and lawyers, I think, would respond to it warmly. The metaphor of balancing the public interest against personal claims is established in our political and judicial rhetoric, and this metaphor gives the model both familiarity and appeal. Nevertheless, the first model is a false one, certainly in the case of rights generally regarded as important, and the metaphor is the heart of its error.

The institution of rights against the Government is not a gift of God, or an ancient ritual, or a national sport. It is a complex and troublesome practice that makes the Government's job of securing the general benefit more difficult and more expensive, and it would be a frivolous and wrongful practice unless it served some point. Anyone who professes to take rights seriously, and who praises our Government for respecting them, must have some sense of what that point is. He must accept, at the minimum, one or both of two important ideas. The first is the vague but powerful idea of human dignity. This idea, associated with Kant, but defended by philosophers of different schools, supposes that there are ways of treating a man that are inconsistent with recognizing him as a full member of the human community, and holds that such treatment is profoundly unjust.

The second is the more familiar idea of political equality. This supposes that the weaker members of a political community are entitled to the same concern and respect of their government as the more powerful members have secured for themselves, so that if some men have freedom of decision whatever the effect on the general good, then all men must have the same freedom. I do not want to defend or elaborate these ideas here, but only to insist that anyone who claims that citizens have rights must accept ideas very close to these.[1]

It makes sense to say that a man has a fundamental right against the Government, in the strong sense, like free speech, if that right is necessary to protect his dignity, or his standing as equally entitled to concern and respect, or some other personal value of like consequence. It does not make sense otherwise.

So if rights make sense at all, then the invasion of a relatively important right must be a very serious matter. It means treating a man as less than a man, or as less worthy of concern than other men. The institution of rights rests on the conviction that this is a grave injustice, and that it is worth paying the incremental cost in social policy or efficiency that is necessary to prevent it. But then it must be wrong to say that inflating rights is as serious as invading them. If the Government errs on the side of the individual, then it simply pays a little more in social efficiency than it has to pay; it pays a little more, that is, of the same coin that it has already decided must be spent. But if it errs against the individual it inflicts an insult upon him that, on its own reckoning, it is worth a great deal of that coin to avoid.

So the first model is indefensible. It rests, in fact, on a mistake I discussed earlier, namely the confusion of society's rights with the rights of members of society. 'Balancing' is appropriate when the Government must choose between competing claims of right – between the Southerner's claim to freedom of association, for example, and the black man's claim to an equal education. Then the Government can do nothing but estimate the merits of the competing claims, and act on its estimate. The first model assumes that the 'right' of the majority is a competing right that must be balanced in this way; but that, as I argued before, is a confusion that threatens to destroy the concept of individual rights. It is worth noticing that the community rejects the first model in that area

---

[1] He need not consider these ideas to be axiomatic. He may, that is, have reasons for insisting that dignity or equality are important values, and these reasons may be utilitarian. He may believe, for example, that the general good will be advanced, *in the long run*, only if we treat indignity or inequality as very great injustices, and never allow our *opinions* about the general good to justify them. I do not know of any good arguments for or against this sort of 'institutional' utilitarianism, but it is consistent with my point, because it argues that we must treat violations of dignity and equality as special moral crimes, beyond the reach of ordinary utilitarian justification.

where the stakes for the individual are highest, the criminal process. We say that it is better that a great many guilty men go free than that one innocent man be punished, and that homily rests on the choice of the second model for government.

The second model treats abridging a right as much more serious than inflating one, and its recommendations follow from that judgment. It stipulates that once a right is recognized in clear-cut cases, then the Government should act to cut off that right only when some compelling reason is presented, some reason that is consistent with the suppositions on which the original right must be based. It cannot be an argument for curtailing a right, once granted, simply that society would pay a further price for extending it. There must be something special about that further cost, or there must be some other feature of the case, that makes it sensible to say that although great social cost is warranted to protect the original right, this particular cost is not necessary. Otherwise, the Government's failure to extend the right will show that its recognition of the right in the original case is a sham, a promise that it intends to keep only until that becomes inconvenient.

How can we show that a particular cost is not worth paying without taking back the initial recognition of a right? I can think of only three sorts of grounds that can consistently be used to limit the definition of a particular right. First, the Government might show that the values protected by the original right are not really at stake in the marginal case, or are at stake only in some attenuated form. Second, it might show that if the right is defined to include the marginal case, then some competing right, in the strong sense I described earlier, would be abridged. Third, it might show that if the right were so defined, then the cost to society would not be simply incremental, but would be of a degree far beyond the cost paid to grant the original right, a degree great enough to justify whatever assault on dignity or equality might be involved.

It is fairly easy to apply these grounds to one group of problems the Supreme Court faced, imbedded in constitutional issues. The draft law provided an exemption for conscientious objectors, but this exemption, as interpreted by the draft boards, has been limited to those who object to *all* wars on *religious* grounds. If we suppose that the exemption is justified on the ground that an individual has a moral right not to kill in violation of his own principles, then the question is raised whether it is proper to exclude those whose morality is not based on religion, or whose morality is sufficiently complex to distinguish among wars. The Court held, as a matter of Constitutional law, that the draft boards were wrong to exclude the former, but competent to exclude the latter.

None of the three grounds I listed can justify either of these exclusions as a matter of political morality. The invasion of personality in forcing men to kill when they believe killing immoral is just as great when these beliefs are based on secular grounds, or take account of the fact that wars differ in morally relevant ways, and there is no pertinent difference in competing rights or in national emergency. There are differences among the cases, of course, but they are insufficient to justify the distinction. A government that is secular on principle cannot prefer a religious to a non-religious morality as such. There are utilitarian arguments in favour of limiting the exception to religious or universal grounds – an exemption so limited may be less expensive to administer, and may allow easier discrimination between sincere and insincere applicants. But these utilitarian reasons are irrelevant, because they cannot count as grounds for limiting a right.

What about the anti-riot law, as applied in the Chicago trial? Does the law represent an improper limitation of the right to free speech, supposedly protected by the First Amendment? If we were to apply the first model for government to this issue, the argument for the anti-riot law would look strong. But if we set aside talk of balancing as inappropriate, and turn to the proper grounds for limiting a right, then the argument becomes a great deal weaker. The original right of free speech must suppose that it is an assault on human personality to stop a man from expressing what he honestly believes, particularly on issues affecting how he is governed. Surely the assault is greater, and not less, when he is stopped from expressing those principles of political morality that he holds most passionately, in the face of what he takes to be outrageous violations of these principles.

It may be said that the anti-riot law leaves him free to express these principles in a non-provocative way. But that misses the point of the connection between expression and dignity. A man cannot express himself freely when he cannot match his rhetoric to his outrage, or when he must trim his sails to protect values he counts as nothing next to those he is trying to vindicate. It is true that some political dissenters speak in ways that shock the majority, but it is arrogant for the majority to suppose that the orthodox methods of expression are the proper ways to speak, for this is a denial of equal concern and respect. If the point of the right is to protect the dignity of dissenters, then we must make judgments about appropriate speech with the personalities of the dissenters in mind, not the personality of the 'silent' majority for whom the anti-riot law is no restraint at all.

So the argument fails, that the personal values protected by the original right are less at stake in this marginal case. We must consider whether competing rights, or some grave threat to society, nevertheless justify the anti-riot law. We can consider these two grounds together, because the only plausible competing rights are rights to be free from violence, and violence is the only plausible threat to society that the context provides.

I have no right to burn your house, or stone you or your car, or swing a bicycle chain against your skull, even if I find these to be natural means of expression. But the defendants in the Chicago trial were not accused of direct violence; the argument runs that the acts of speech they planned made it likely that others would do acts of violence, either in support of or out of hostility to what they said. Does this provide a justification?

The question would be different if we could say with any confidence how much and what sort of violence the anti-riot law might be expected to prevent. Will it save two lives a year, or two hundred, or two thousand? Two thousand dollars of property, or two hundred thousand, or two million? No one can say, not simply because prediction is next to impossible, but because we have no firm understanding of the process by which demonstration disintegrates into riot, and in particular of the part played by inflammatory speech, as distinct from poverty, police brutality, blood lust, and all the rest of human and economic failure. The Government must try, of course, to reduce the violent waste of lives and property, but it must recognize that any attempt to locate and remove a cause of riot, short of a reorganization of society, must be an exercise in speculation, trial, and error. It must make its decisions under conditions of high uncertainty, and the institution of rights, taken seriously, limits its freedom to experiment under such conditions.

It forces the Government to bear in mind that preventing a man from speaking or demonstrating offers him a certain and profound insult, in return for a speculative benefit that may in any event be achieved in other if more expensive ways. When lawyers say that rights may be limited to protect other rights, or to prevent catastrophe, they have in mind cases in which cause and effect are relatively clear, like the familiar example of a man falsely crying 'Fire!' in a crowded theater.

But the Chicago story shows how obscure the causal connections can become. Were the speeches of Hoffman or Rubin necessary conditions of the riot? Or had thousands of people come to Chicago for the purposes of rioting anyway, as the Government also argues? Were they in any case sufficient conditions? Or could the police have contained the violence if they had not been so busy contributing to it, as the staff of the President's Commission on Violence said they were?

These are not easy questions, but if rights mean anything, then the Government cannot simply assume answers that justify its conduct. If a man has a right to speak, if the reasons that support that right extend to provocative political speech, and if the effects of such speech on violence are unclear, then the Government is not entitled to make its first attack on that problem by denying that right. It may be that abridging the right to speak is the least expensive course, or the least damaging to police morale, or the most popular politically. But these are utilitarian arguments in favor of starting one place rather than another, and such arguments are ruled out by the concept of rights.

This point may be obscured by the popular belief that political activists look forward to violence and 'ask for trouble' in what they say. They can hardly complain, in the general view, if they are taken to be the authors of the violence they expect, and treated accordingly. But this repeats the confusion I tried to explain earlier between having a right and doing the right thing. The speaker's motives may be relevant in deciding whether he does the right thing in speaking passionately about issues that may inflame or enrage the audience. But if he has a right to speak, because the danger in allowing him to speak is speculative, his motives cannot count as independent evidence in the argument that justifies stopping him.

But what of the individual rights of those who will be destroyed by a riot, of the passer-by who will be killed by a sniper's bullet or the shop-keeper who will be ruined by looting? To put the issue in this way, as a question of competing rights, suggests a principle that would undercut the effect of uncertainty. Shall we say that some rights to protection are so important that the Government is justified in doing all it can to maintain them? Shall we therefore say that the Government may abridge the rights of others to act when their acts might simply increase the risk, by however slight or speculative a margin, that some person's right to life or property will be violated?

Some such principle is relied on by those who oppose the Supreme Court's recent liberal rulings on police procedure. These rulings increase the chance that a guilty man will go free, and therefore marginally increase the risk that any particular member of the community will be murdered, raped, or robbed. Some critics believe that the Court's decisions must therefore be wrong.

But no society that purports to recognize a variety of rights, on the ground that a man's dignity or equality may be invaded in a variety of ways, can accept such a principle. If forcing a man to testify against himself, or forbidding him to speak, does the damage that the rights against self-incrimination and the right of free speech assume, then it would be contemptuous for the State to tell a man that he must suffer this damage against the possibility that other men's risk of loss may be marginally reduced. If rights make sense, then the degrees of their importance cannot be so different that some count not at all when others are mentioned.

Of course the Government may discriminate and may stop a man from exercising his right to speak when there is a clear and substantial risk that his speech will do great damage to the person or property of others, and no other means of preventing this are at hand, as in the case of the man shouting 'Fire!' in a theater. But we must reject the suggested principle that the Government can simply ignore rights to speak when life and property are in question. So long as the impact of speech on these other rights remains speculative and marginal, it must look elsewhere for levers to pull.

4. WHY TAKE RIGHTS SERIOUSLY?

I said at the beginning of this essay that I wanted to show what a government must do that professes to recognize individual rights. It must dispense with the claim that citizens never have a right to break its law, and it must not define citizens' rights so that these are cut off for supposed reasons of the general good. Any Government's harsh treatment of civil disobedience, or campaign against vocal protest, may therefore be thought to count against its sincerity.

One might well ask, however, whether it is wise to take rights all that seriously after all. America's genius, at least in her own legend, lies in not taking any abstract doctrine to its logical extreme. It may be time to ignore abstractions, and concentrate instead on giving the majority of our citizens a new sense of their Government's concern for their welfare, and of their title to rule.

That, in any event, is what former Vice-President Agnew seemed to believe. In a policy statement on the issue of 'weirdos' and social misfits, he said that the liberals' concern for individual rights was a headwind blowing in the face of the ship of state. That is a poor metaphor, but the philosophical point it expresses is very well taken. He recognized, as many liberals do not, that the majority cannot travel as fast or as far as it would like if it recognizes the rights of individuals to do what, in the majority's terms, is the wrong thing to do.

Spiro Agnew supposed that rights are divisive, and that national unity and a new respect for law may be developed by taking them more skeptically. But he is wrong. America will continue to be divided by its social and foreign policy, and if the economy grows weaker again the divisions will become more bitter. If we want our laws and our legal institutions to provide the ground rules within which these issues will be contested then these ground rules must not be the conqueror's law that the dominant class imposes on the weaker, as Marx supposed the law of a capitalist society must be. The bulk of the law – that part which defines and implements social, economic, and foreign policy – cannot be neutral. It must state, in its greatest part, the majority's view of the common good. The institution of rights is therefore crucial, because it represents the majority's promise to the minorities that their dignity and equality will be respected. When the divisions among the groups are most violent, then this gesture, if law is to work, must be most sincere.

The institution requires an act of faith on the part of the minorities, because the scope of their rights will be controversial whenever they are important, and because the officers of the majority will act on their own notions of what these rights really are. Of course these officials will disagree with many of the claims that a minority makes. That makes it all the more important that they take their decisions gravely. They must show that they understand what rights are, and they must not cheat on the full implications of the doctrine. The Government will not re-establish respect for law without giving the law some claim to respect. It cannot do that if it neglects the one feature that distinguishes law from ordered brutality. If the Government does not take rights seriously, then it does not take law seriously either.

8

Civil Disobedience

How should the government deal with those who disobey the draft laws out of conscience? Many people think the answer is obvious: The government must prosecute the dissenters, and if they are convicted it must punish them. Some people reach this conclusion easily, because they hold the mindless view that conscientious disobedience is the same as lawlessness. They think that the dissenters are anarchists who must be punished before their corruption spreads. Many lawyers and intellectuals come to the same conclusion, however, on what looks like a more sophisticated argument. They recognize that disobedience to law may be *morally* justified, but they insist that it cannot be *legally* justified, and they think that it follows from this truism that the law must be enforced. Erwin Griswold, once Solicitor General of the United States, and before that Dean of the Harvard Law School, appears to have adopted this view. '[It] is of the essence of law,' he said, 'that it is equally applied to all, that it binds all alike, irrespective of personal motive. For this reason, one who contemplates civil disobedience out of moral conviction should not be surprised and must not be bitter if a criminal conviction ensues. And he must accept the fact that organized society cannot endure on any other basis.'

The New York Times applauded that statement. A thousand faculty members of several universities had signed a *Times* advertisement calling on the Justice Department to quash the indictments of the Rev. William Sloane Coffin, Dr. Benjamin Spock, Marcus Raskin, Mitchell Goodman, and Michael Ferber, for conspiring to counsel various draft offenses. The *Times* said that the request to quash the indictments 'confused moral rights with legal responsibilties'.

But the argument that, because the government believes a man has committed a crime, it must prosecute him is much weaker than it seems. Society 'cannot endure' if it tolerates all disobedience; it does not follow, however, nor is there evidence, that it will collapse if it tolerates some. In the United States prosecutors have discretion whether to enforce criminal laws in particular cases. A prosecutor may properly decide not to press charges if the lawbreaker is young, or inexperienced, or the sole support of a family, or is repentant, or turns state's evidence, or if the law is unpopular or unworkable or generally disobeyed, or if the courts are clogged with more important cases, or for dozens of other reasons. This discretion is not license – we expect prosecutors to have good reasons for exercising it – but there are, at least *prima facie*, some good reasons for not prosecuting those who disobey the draft laws out of conscience. One is the obvious reason that they act out of better motives than those who break the law out of greed or a desire to subvert government. If motive can count in distinguishing between thieves, then why not in distinguishing between draft offenders? Another is the practical reason that our society suffers a loss if it punishes a group that includes – as the group of draft dissenters does – some of its most loyal and law-respecting citizens. Jailing such men solidifies their alienation from society, and alienates many like them who are deterred by the threat. If practical consequences like these argued for not enforcing prohibition, why do they not argue for tolerating offenses of conscience?

Those who think that conscientious draft offenders should always be punished must show that these are not good reasons for exercising discretion, or they must find contrary reasons that outweigh them. What arguments might they produce? There are practical reasons for enforcing draft laws, and I shall consider some of these later. But Dean Griswold and those who agree with him seem to rely on a fundamental moral argument that it would be unfair, not merely impractical, to let the dissenters go unpunished. They think it would be unfair, I gather, because society could not function if everyone disobeyed laws he disapproved of or found disadvantageous. If the government tolerates those few who will not 'play the game', it allows them to secure the benefits of everyone else's deference to law, without shouldering the burdens, such as the burden of the draft.

This argument is a serious one. It cannot be answered simply by saying that the dissenters would allow everyone else the privilege of disobeying a law he believed immoral. In fact, few draft dissenters would accept a changed society in which sincere segregationists were free to break civil rights laws they hated. The majority want no such change, in any event, because they think that society would be worse off for it; until they are shown this is wrong, they will expect their officials to punish anyone who assumes a privilege which they, for the general benefit, do not assume.

There is, however, a flaw in the argument. The reasoning contains a hidden assumption that makes it almost entirely irrelevant to the draft cases, and indeed to any serious case of civil disobedience in the United States. The argument assumes that the dissenters know that they are breaking a valid law, and that the privilege they assert is the privilege to do that. Of course, almost everyone who discusses civil disobedience recognizes that in America a law may be invalid because it is unconstitutional. But the critics handle this complexity by arguing on separate hypotheses: If the law is invalid, then no crime is committed, and society may not punish. If the law is valid, then a crime has been committed, and society must punish. This reasoning hides the crucial fact that the validity of the law may be doubtful. The officials and judges may believe that the law is valid, the dissenters may disagree, and both sides may have plausible arguments for their positions. If so, then the issues are different from what they would be if the law were clearly valid or clearly invalid, and the argument of fairness, designed for these alternatives, is irrelevant.

Doubtful law is by no means special or exotic in cases of civil disobedience. On the contrary. In the United States, at least, almost any law which a significant number of people would be tempted to disobey on moral grounds would be doubtful – if not clearly invalid – on constitutional grounds as well. The constitution makes our conventional political morality relevant to the question of validity; any statute that appears to compromise that morality raises constitutional questions, and if the compromise is serious, the constitutional doubts are serious also.

The connection between moral and legal issues was especially clear in the draft cases of the last decade. Dissent was based at the time on the following moral objections: (a) The United States is using immoral weapons and tactics in Vietnam. (b) The war has never been endorsed by deliberate, considered, and open vote of the peoples' representatives. (c) The United States has no interest at stake in Vietnam remotely strong enough to justify forcing a segment of its citizens to risk death there. (d) If an army is to be raised to fight that war, it is immoral to raise it by a draft that defers or exempts college students, and thus discriminates against the economically underprivileged. (e) The draft exempts those who object to all wars on religious grounds, but not those who object to particular wars on moral grounds; there is no relevant difference between these positions, and so the draft, by making the distinction, implies that the second group is less worthy of the nation's respect than the first. (f) The law that makes it a crime to counsel draft resistance stifles those who oppose the war, because it is morally impossible to argue that the war is profoundly immoral, without encouraging and assisting those who refuse to fight it.

Lawyers will recognize that these moral positions, if we accept them, provide the basis for the following constitutional arguments: (a) The constitution makes treaties part of the law of the land, and the United States is a party to international conventions and covenants that make illegal the acts of war the dissenters charged the nation with committing. (b) The constitution provides that Congress must declare war; the legal issue of whether our action in Vietnam was a 'war' and whether the Tonkin Bay Resolution was a 'declaration' is the heart of the moral issue of whether the government had made a deliberate and open decision. (c) Both the due process clause of the Fifth and Fourteenth Amendments and equal protection clause of the Fourteenth Amendment condemn special burdens placed on a selected class of citizens when the burden or the classification is not reasonable; the burden is unreasonable when it patently does not serve the public interest, or when it is vastly disproportionate to the interest served. If our military action in Vietnam was frivolous or perverse, as the dissenters claimed, then the burden we placed on men of draft age was unreasonable and unconstitutional. (d) In any event, the discrimination in favor of college students denied to the poor the equal protection of the law that is guaranteed by the constitution. (e) If there is no pertinent difference between religious objection to all wars and moral objection to some wars, then the classification the draft made was arbitrary and unreasonable, and unconstitutional on that ground. The 'establishment of religion' clause of the First Amendment forbids governmental pressure in favor of organized religion; if the draft's distinction coerced men in this direction, it was invalid on that count also. (f) The First Amendment also condemns invasions of freedom of speech. If the draft law's prohibition on counseling did inhibit expression of a range of views on the war, it abridged free speech.

The principal counterargument, supporting the view that the courts ought not to have held the draft unconstitutional, also involves moral issues. Under the so-called 'political question' doctrine, the courts deny their own jurisdiction to pass on matters – such as foreign or military policy – whose resolution is best assigned to other branches of the government. The Boston court trying the Coffin, Spock case declared, on the basis of this doctrine, that it would not hear arguments about the legality of the war. But the Supreme Court has shown itself (in the reapportionment cases, for example) reluctant to refuse jurisdiction when it believed that the gravest issues of political morality were at stake and that no remedy was available through the political process. If the dissenters were right, and the war and the draft were state crimes of profound injustice to a group of citizens, then the argument that the courts should have refused jurisdiction is considerably weakened.

We cannot conclude from these arguments that the draft (or any part of it) was unconstitutional. When the Supreme Court was called upon to rule on the question, it rejected some of them, and refused to consider the others on grounds that they were political. The majority of lawyers agreed with this result. But the arguments of unconstitutionality were at least plausible, and a reasonable and competent lawyer might well think that they present a stronger case, on balance, than the counterarguments. If he does, he will consider that the draft was not constitutional, and there will be no way of proving that he is wrong.

Therefore we cannot assume, in judging what should have been done with the draft dissenters, that they were asserting a privilege to disobey valid laws. We cannot decide that fairness demanded their punishment until we try to answer further questions: What should a citizen do when the law is unclear, and when he thinks it allows what others think it does not? I do not mean to ask, of course, what it is *legally* proper for him to do, or what his *legal* rights are – that would be begging the question, because it depends upon whether he is right or they are right. I mean to ask what his proper course is as a citizen, what, in other words, we would consider to be 'playing the game'. That is a crucial question, because it cannot be unfair not to punish him if he is acting as, given his opinions, we think he should.[1]

There is no obvious answer on which most citizens would readily agree, and that is itself significant. If we examine our legal institutions and practices, however, we shall discover some relevant underlying principles and policies. I shall set out three possible answers to the question, and then try to show which of these best fits our practices and expectations. The three possibilities I want to consider are these:

(1) If the law is doubtful, and it is therefore unclear whether it permits someone to do what he wants, he should assume the worst, and act on the assumption that it does not. He should obey the executive authorities who command him, even though he thinks they are wrong, while using the political process, if he can, to change the law.

(2) If the law is doubtful, he may follow his own judgment, that is, he may do what he wants if he believes that the case that the law permits this is stronger than the case that it does not. But he may follow his own judgment only until an authoritative institution, like a court, decides the other way in a case involving him or someone else. Once an institutional decision has been reached, he must abide by that decision, even though he thinks that it was wrong. (There are, in theory, many subdivisions of this second possibility. We may say that the individual's choice is foreclosed by the contrary decision of any court, including the lowest court in the system if the case is not appealed. Or we may require

---

[1] I do not mean to imply that the government should always punish a man who deliberately breaks a law he knows is valid. There may be reasons of fairness or practicality, like those I listed in the third paragraph, for not prosecuting such men. But cases like the draft cases present special arguments for tolerance; I want to concentrate on these arguments and therefore have isolated these cases.

a decision of some particular court or institution. I shall discuss this second possibility in its most liberal form, namely that the individual may properly follow his own judgment until a contrary decision of the highest court competent to pass on the issue, which, in the case of the draft, was the United States Supreme Court.)

(3) If the law is doubtful, he may follow his own judgment, even after a contrary decision by the highest competent court. Of course, he must take the contrary decision of any court into account in making his judgment of what the law requires. Otherwise the judgment would not be an honest or reasonable one, because the doctrine of precedent, which is an established part of our legal system, has the effect of allowing the decision of the courts to *change* the law. Suppose, for example, that a taxpayer believes that he is not required to pay tax on certain forms of income. If the Supreme Court decides to the contrary, he should, taking into account the practice of according great weight to the decisions of the Supreme Court on tax matters, decide that the Court's decision has itself tipped the balance, and that the law now requires him to pay the tax.

Someone might think that this qualification erases the difference between the third and the second models, but it does not. The doctrine of precedent gives different weights to the decisions of different courts, and greatest weight to the decisions of the Supreme Court, but it does not make the decisions of any court conclusive. Sometimes, even after a contrary Supreme Court decision, an individual may still reasonably believe that the law is on his side; such cases are rare, but they are most likely to occur in disputes over constitutional law when civil disobedience is involved. The Court has shown itself more likely to overrule its past decisions if these have limited important personal or political rights, and it is just these decisions that a dissenter might want to challenge.

We cannot assume, in other words, that the Constitution is always what the Supreme Court says it is. Oliver Wendell Holmes, for example, did not follow such a rule in his famous dissent in the *Gitlow* case. A few years before, in *Abrams*, he had lost his battle to persuade the court that the First Amendment protected an anarchist who had been urging general strikes against the government. A similar issue was presented in *Gitlow*, and Holmes once again dissented. 'It is true,' he said, 'that in my opinion this criterion was departed from [in *Abrams*] but the convictions that I expressed in that case are too deep for it to be possible for me as yet to believe that it . . . settled the law.' Holmes voted for acquitting Gitlow, on the ground that what Gitlow had done was no crime, even though the Supreme Court had recently held that it was.

Here then are three possible models for the behavior of dissenters who disagree with the executive authorities when the law is doubtful. Which of them best fits our legal and social practices?

I think it plain that we do not follow the first of these models, that is, that we do not expect citizens to assume the worst. If no court has decided the issue, and a man thinks, on balance, that the law is on his side, most of our lawyers and critics think it perfectly proper for him to follow his own judgment. Even when many disapprove of what he does – such as peddling pornography – they do not think he must desist just because the legality of his conduct is subject to doubt.

It is worth pausing a moment to consider what society would lose if it did follow the first model or, to put the matter the other way, what society gains when people follow their own judgment in cases like this. When the law is uncertain, in the sense that lawyers can reasonably disagree on what a court ought to decide, the reason usually is that different legal principles and policies have collided, and it is unclear how best to accommodate these conflicting principles and policies.

Our practice, in which different parties are encouraged to pursue their own understanding, provides a means of testing relevant hypotheses. If the question is whether a particular rule would have certain undesirable consequences, or whether these consequences would have limited or broad ramifications, then, before the issue is decided, it is useful to know what does in fact take place when some people proceed on that rule. (Much anti-trust and business regulation law has developed through this kind of testing.) If the question is whether and to what degree a particular solution would offend principles of justice or fair play deeply respected by the community, it is useful, again, to experiment by testing the community's response. The extent of community indifference to anti-contraception laws, for example, would never have become established had not some organizations deliberately flouted those laws.

If the first model were followed, we would lose the advantages of these tests. The law would suffer, particularly if this model were applied to constitutional issues. When the validity of a criminal statute is in doubt, the statute will almost always strike some people as being unfair or unjust, because it will infringe some principle of liberty or justice or fairness which they take to be built into the Constitution. If our practice were that whenever a law is doubtful on these grounds, one must act as if it were valid, then the chief vehicle we have for challenging the law on moral grounds would be lost, and over time the law we obeyed would certainly become less fair and just, and the liberty of our citizens would certainly be diminished.

We would lose almost as much if we used a variation of the first model, that a citizen must assume the worst unless he can anticipate that the courts will agree with his view of the law. If everyone deferred to his guess of what the courts would do, society and its law would be poorer. Our assumption in rejecting the first model was that the record a citizen makes in following his own judgment, together with the arguments he makes supporting that judgment when he has the opportunity, are helpful in creating the best judicial decision possible. This remains true even when, at the time the citizen acts, the odds are against his success in court. We must remember, too, that the value of the citizen's example is not exhausted once the decision has been made. Our practices require that the decision be criticized, by the legal profession and the law schools, and the record of dissent may be invaluable here.

Of course a man must consider what the courts will do when he decides whether it would be *prudent* to follow his own judgment. He may have to face jail, bankruptcy, or opprobrium if he does. But it is essential that we separate the calculation of prudence from the question of what, as a good citizen, he may properly do. We are investigating how society ought to treat him when its courts believe that he judged wrong; therefore we must ask what he is justified in doing when his judgment differs from others. We beg the question if we assume that what he may properly do depends on his guess as to how society will treat him.

We must also reject the second model, that if the law is unclear a citizen may properly follow his own judgment until the highest court has ruled that he is wrong. This fails to take into account the fact that any court, including the Supreme Court, may overrule itself. In 1940 the Court decided that a West Virginia law requiring students to salute the Flag was constitutional. In 1943 it reversed itself, and decided that such a statute was unconstitutional after all. What was the duty as citizens, of those people who in 1941 and 1942 objected to saluting the Flag on grounds of conscience, and thought that the Court's 1940 decision was wrong? We can hardly say that their duty was to follow the first decision. They believed that saluting the Flag was unconscionable, and they believed, reasonably, that no valid law required them to do so. The Supreme Court later decided that in this they were right. The Court did not simply hold that after the second decision failing to salute would not be a crime; it held (as in a case like this it almost always would) that it was no crime after the first decision either.

Some will say that the flag-salute dissenters should have obeyed the Court's first decision, while they worked in the legislatures to have the law repealed, and tried in the courts to find some way to challenge the law again without actually violating it. That would be, perhaps, a plausible recommendation if conscience were not involved, because it would then be arguable that the gain in orderly procedure was worth the personal sacrifice of patience. But conscience was involved, and if the dissenters had obeyed the law while biding their time, they would have suffered the irreparable injury of having done what their conscience forbade them to do. It is one thing to say that an individual must sometimes violate his conscience when he knows that the law commands him to do it. It is quite another to say that he must violate his conscience even when he reasonably believes that the law does not require it, because it would inconvenience his fellow citizens if he took the most direct, and perhaps the only, method of attempting to show that he is right and they are wrong.

Since a court may overrule itself, the same reasons we listed for rejecting the first model count against the second as well. If we did not have the pressure of dissent, we would not have a dramatic statement of the degree to which a court decision against the dissenter is felt to be wrong, a demonstration that is surely pertinent to the question of whether it was right. We would increase the chance of being governed by rules that offend the principles we claim to serve.

These considerations force us, I think, from the second model, but some will want to substitute a variation of it. They will argue that once the Supreme Court has decided that a criminal law is valid, then citizens have a duty to abide by that decision until they have a reasonable belief, not merely that the decision is a bad law, but that the Supreme Court is likely to overrule it. Under this view the West Virginia dissenters who refused to salute the Flag in 1942 were acting properly, because they might reasonably have anticipated that the Court would change its mind. But once the Court held laws like the draft laws constitutional, it would be improper to continue to challenge these laws, because there would be no great likelihood that the Court would soon change its mind. This suggestion must also be rejected, however. For once we say that a citizen may properly follow his own judgment of the law, in spite of his judgment that the courts will probably find against him, there is no plausible reason why he should act differently because a contrary decision is already on the books.

Thus the third model, or something close to it, seems to be the fairest statement of a man's social duty in our community. A citizen's allegiance is to the law, not to any particular person's view of what the law is, and he does not behave unfairly so long as he proceeds on his own considered and reasonable view of what the law requires. Let me repeat (because it is crucial) that this is not the same as saying that an individual may disregard what the courts have said. The doctrine of precedent lies near the core of our legal system, and no one can make a reasonable effort to follow the law unless he grants the courts the general power to alter it by their decisions. But if the issue is one touching fundamental personal or political rights, and it is arguable that the Supreme Court has made a mistake, a man is within his social rights in refusing to accept that decision as conclusive.

One large question remains before we can apply these observations to the problems of draft resistance. I have been talking about the case of a man who believes that the law is not what other people think, or what the courts have held. This description may fit some of those who disobey the draft laws out of conscience, but it does not fit most of them. Most of the dissenters are not lawyers or political philosophers; they believe that the laws on the books are immoral, and inconsistent with their country's legal ideals, but they have not considered the question of whether they may be invalid as well. Of what relevance to their situation, then, is the proposition that one may properly follow one's own view of the law?

To answer this, I shall have to return to the point I made earlier. The Constitution, through the due process clause, the equal protection clause, the First Amendment, and the other provisions I mentioned, injects an extraordinary amount of our political morality into the issue of whether a law is valid. The statement that most draft dissenters are unaware that the law is invalid therefore needs qualification. They hold beliefs that, if true, strongly support the view that the law is on their side; the fact that they have not reached that further conclusion can be traced, in at least most cases, to their lack of legal sophistication. If we believe that when the law is doubtful people who follow their own judgment of the law may be acting properly, it would seem wrong not to extend that view to those dissenters whose judgments come to the same thing. No part of the case that I made for the third model would entitle us to distinguish them from their more knowledgeable colleagues.

We can draw several tentative conclusions from the argument so far: When the law is uncertain, in the sense that a plausible case can be made on both sides, then a citizen who follows his own judgment is not behaving unfairly. Our practices permit and encourage him to follow his own judgment in such cases. For that reason, our government has a special responsibility to try to protect him, and soften his predicament, whenever it can do so without great damage to other policies. It does not follow that the government can guarantee him immunity – it cannot adopt the rule that it will prosecute no one who acts out of conscience, or convict no one who reasonably disagrees with the courts. That would paralyze the government's ability to carry out its policies; it would, moreover, throw away the most important benefit of following the third model. If the state never prosecuted, then the courts could not act on the experience and the arguments the dissent has generated. But it does follow that when the practical reasons for prosecuting are relatively weak in a particular case, or can be met in other ways, the path of fairness lies in tolerance. The popular view that the law is the law and must always be enforced refuses to distinguish the man who acts on his own judgment of a doubtful law, and thus behaves as our practices provide, from the common criminal. I know of no reason, short of moral blindness, for not drawing a distinction in principle between the two cases.

I anticipate a philosophical objection to these conclusions: that I am treating law as a 'brooding omnipresence in the sky'. I have spoken of people making judgments about what the law requires, even in cases in which the law is unclear and undemonstrable. I have spoken of cases in which a man might think that the law requires one thing, even though the Supreme Court has said that it requires another, and even when it was not likely that the Supreme Court would soon change its mind. I will therefore be charged with the view that there is always a 'right answer' to a legal problem to be found in natural law or locked up in some transcendental strongbox.

The strongbox theory of law is, of course, nonsense. When I say that people hold views on the law when the law is doubtful, and that these views are not merely predictions of what the courts will hold, I intend no such metaphysics. I mean only to summarize as accurately as I can many of the practices that are part of our legal process.

Lawyers and judges make statements of legal right and duty, even when they know these are not demonstrable, and support them with arguments even when they know that these arguments will not appeal to everyone. They make these arguments to one another, in the professional journals, in the classrooms, and in the courts. They respond to these arguments, when others make them, by judging them good or bad or mediocre. In so doing they assume that some arguments for a given doubtful position are better than others. They also assume that the case on one side of a doubtful proposition may be stronger than the case on the other, which is what I take a claim of law in a doubtful case to mean. They distinguish, without too much difficulty, these arguments from predictions of what the courts will decide.

These practices are poorly represented by the theory that judgments of law on doubtful issues are nonsense, or are merely predictions of what the courts will do. Those who hold such theories cannot deny the fact of these practices; perhaps these theorists mean that the practices are not sensible, because they are based on suppositions that do not hold, or for some other reason. But this makes their objection mysterious, because they never specify what they take the purposes underlying these practices to be; and unless these goals are specified, one cannot decide whether the practices are sensible. I understand these underlying purposes to be those I described earlier: the development and testing of the law through experimentation by citizens and through the adversary process.

Our legal system pursues these goals by inviting citizens to decide the strengths and weaknesses of legal arguments for themselves, or through their own counsel, and to act on these judgments, although that permission is qualified by the limited threat that they may suffer if the courts do not agree. Success in this strategy depends on whether there is sufficient agreement within the community on what counts as good or bad argument, so that, although different people will reach different judgments, these differences will be neither so profound nor so frequent as to make the system unworkable, or dangerous for those who act by their own lights. I believe there is sufficient agreement on the criteria of the argument to avoid these traps, although one of the main tasks of legal philosophy is to exhibit and clarify these criteria. In any event, the practices I have described have not yet been shown to be misguided; they therefore must count in determining whether it is just and fair to be lenient to those who break what others think is the law.

I have said that the government has a special responsibility to those who act on a reasonable judgment that a law is invalid. It should make accommodation for them as far as possible, when this is consistent with other policies. It may be difficult to decide what the government ought to do, in the name of that responsibility, in particular cases. The decision will be a matter of balance, and flat rules will not help. Still, some principles can be set out.

I shall start with the prosecutor's decision whether to press charges. He must balance both his responsibility to be lenient and the risk that convictions will rend the society, against the damage to the law's policy that may follow if he leaves the dissenters alone. In making his calculation he must consider not only the extent to which others will be harmed, but also how the law evaluates that harm; and he must therefore make the following distinction. Every rule of law is supported, and presumably justified, by a set of policies it is supposed to advance and principles it is supposed to respect. Some rules (the laws prohibiting murder and theft, for example) are supported by the proposition that the individuals protected have a moral right to be free from the harm proscribed. Other rules (the more technical anti-trust rules, for example) are not supported by any supposition of an underlying right; their support comes chiefly from the alleged utility of the economic and social policies they promote. These may be supplemented with moral principles (like the view that it is a harsh business practice to undercut a weak competitor's prices) but these fall short of recognizing a moral right against the harm in question.

The point of the distinction here is this: if a particular rule of law represents an official decision that individuals have a moral right to be free from some harm, then that is a powerful argument against tolerating violations that inflict those injuries. Laws protecting people from personal injury or the destruction of their property, for example, do represent that sort of decision, and this is a very strong argument against tolerating civil disobedience that involves violence.

It may be controversial, of course, whether a law does rest on the assumption of a moral right. The question is whether it is reasonable to suppose, from the background and administration of the law, that its authors recognized such a right. There are cases, in addition to rules against violence, where it is plain that they did; the civil rights laws are examples. Many sincere and ardent segregationists believe that the civil rights laws and decisions are unconstitutional, because they compromise principles of local government and of freedom of association. This is an arguable, though not a persuasive, view. But these laws and decisions clearly embody the view that Negroes, as individuals, have a right not to be segregated. They do not rest simply on the judgment that other national policies are best pursued by preventing racial segregation. If we take no action against the man who blocks the school house door, therefore, we violate the moral rights, confirmed by law, of the schoolgirl he blocks. The responsibility of leniency cannot go this far.

The schoolgirl's position is different, however, from that of the draftee who may be called up sooner or given a more dangerous post if draft offenders are not punished. The draft laws, taken as a whole and with an eye to their administration, cannot be said to reflect the judgment that a man has a moral right to be drafted only after certain other men or groups have been called. The draft classifications, and the order-of-call within classifications, are arranged for social and administrative convenience. They also reflect considerations of fairness, like the proposition that a mother who has lost one of two sons in war ought not to be made to risk losing the other. But they presuppose no fixed rights. The draft boards are given considerable discretion in the classification process, and the army, of course, has almost complete discretion in assigning dangerous posts. If the prosecutor tolerates draft offenders, he makes small shifts in the law's calculations of fairness and utility. These may cause disadvantage to others in the pool of draftees but that is a different matter from contradicting their moral rights.

This difference between segregation and the draft is not an accident of how the laws happen to have been written. It would run counter to a century of practice to suppose that citizens have moral rights with respect to the order in which they are called to serve; the lottery system of selection, for example, would be abhorrent under that supposition. If our history had been different, and if the community had recognized such a moral right, it seems fair to suppose that some of the draft dissenters, at least, would have modified their acts so as to try to respect these rights.

So it is wrong to analyze draft cases in the same way as cases of violence or civil rights cases, as many critics do when considering whether tolerance is justified. I do not mean that fairness to others is irrelevant in draft cases; it must be taken into account, and balanced against fairness to dissenters and the long-term benefit to society. But it does not play the commanding role here that it does when rights are at stake.

Where, then, does the balance of fairness and utility lie in the case of those who counseled draft resistance? If these men had encouraged violence or otherwise trespassed on the rights of others, then there would have been a strong case for prosecution. But in the absence of such actions, the balance of fairness and utility seems to me to lie the other way, and I therefore think that the decision to prosecute Coffin, Spock, Raskin, Goodman, and Ferber was wrong. It might have been argued that if those who counsel draft resistance are free from prosecution, the number who resist induction will increase; but not, I think, much beyond the number of those who would resist in any event.

If this is wrong, and there is much greater resistance, then a sense of this residual discontent is of importance to policy makers, and it ought not to have been hidden under a ban on speech. Conscience is deeply involved – it is hard to believe that many who counseled resistance did so on any other grounds. The case is strong that the laws making counseling a crime are unconstitutional; even those who do not find the case persuasive will admit that its arguments have substance. The harm to potential draftees, both those who may have been persuaded to resist and those who may have been called earlier because others have been persuaded, was remote and speculative.

The cases of men who refused induction when drafted are more complicated. The crucial question is whether a failure to prosecute will lead to wholesale refusals to serve. It may not – there were social pressures, including the threat of career disadvantages, that would have forced many young Americans to serve if drafted, even if they knew they would not go to jail if they refused. If the number would not much have increased, then the State should have left the dissenters alone, and I see no great harm in delaying any prosecution until the effect of that policy became clearer. If the number of those who refuse induction turned out to be large, this would argue for prosecution. But it would also make the problem academic, because if there had been sufficient dissent to bring us to that pass, it would have been most difficult to pursue the war in any event, except under a near-totalitarian regime.

There may seem to be a paradox in these conclusions. I argued earlier that when the law is unclear citizens have the right to follow their own judgment, partly on the grounds that this practice helps to shape issues for adjudication; now I propose a course that eliminates or postpones adjudication. But the contradiction is only apparent. It does not follow from the fact that our practice facilitates adjudication, and renders it more useful in developing the law, that a trial should follow whenever citizens do act by their own lights. The question arises in each case whether the issues are ripe for adjudication, and whether adjudication would settle these issues in a manner that would decrease the chance of, or remove the grounds for, further dissent.

In the draft cases, the answer to both these questions was negative : there was much ambivalence about the war, and uncertainty and ignorance about the scope of the moral issues involved in the draft. It was far from the best time for a court to pass on these issues, and tolerating dissent for a time was one way of allowing the debate to continue until it produced something clearer. Moreover, it was plain that an adjudication of the constitutional issues would not settle the law. Those who had doubts whether the draft was constitutional had the same doubts even after the Supreme Court said that it was. This is one of those cases, touching fundamental rights, in which our practices of precedent encourage such doubts.

Even if the prosecutor does not act, however, the underlying problem will be only temporarily relieved. So long as the law appears to make acts of dissent criminal, a man of conscience will face danger. What can Congress, which shares the responsibility of leniency, do to lessen this danger?

Congress can review the laws in question to see how much accommodation can be given the dissenters. Every program a legislature adopts is a mixture of policies and restraining principles. We accept loss of efficiency in crime detection and urban renewal, for example, so that we can respect the rights of accused criminals and compensate property owners for their damages. Congress may properly defer to its responsibility toward the dissenters by adjusting or compromising other policies. The relevant questions are these : What means can be found for allowing the greatest possible tolerance of conscientious dissent while minimizing its impact on policy? How strong is the government's responsibility for leniency in this case – how deeply is conscience involved, and how strong is the case that the law is invalid after all? How important is the policy in question – is interference with that policy too great a price to pay? These questions are no doubt too simple, but they suggest the heart of the choices that must be made.

For the same reasons that those who counseled resistance should not have been prosecuted, I think that the law that makes this a crime should be repealed. The case is strong that this law abridges free speech. It certainly coerces conscience, and it probably serves no beneficial effect. If counseling would persuade only a few to resist who otherwise would not, the value of the restraint is small; if counseling would persuade many, that is an important political fact that should be known.

The issues are more complex, again, in the case of draft resistance itself. Those who believed that the war in Vietnam was itself a grotesque blunder would have favored any change in the law that made peace more likely. But if we take the position of those who think the war was necessary, then we must admit that a policy that continued the draft but wholly exempted dissenters would have been unwise. Two less drastic alternatives should have been considered, however: a volunteer army, and an expanded conscientious objector category that included those who found the war immoral. There is much to be said against both proposals, but once the requirement of respect for dissent is recognized, the balance of principle may be tipped in their favor.

So the case for not prosecuting conscientious draft offenders, and for changing the laws in their favor, was a strong one. It would have been unrealistic to expect this policy to prevail, however, for political pressures opposed it.

We must consider, therefore, what the courts could and should have done. A court might, of course, have upheld the arguments that the draft laws were in some way unconstitutional, in general or as applied to the defendants in the case at hand. Or it might acquit the defendants because the facts necessary for conviction are not proved. I shall not argue the constitutional issues, or the facts of any particular case. I want instead to suggest that a court ought not to convict, at least in some circumstances, even if it sustains the statutes and finds the facts as charged. The Supreme Court had not ruled on the chief arguments that the draft was unconstitutional, nor had it held that these arguments raised political questions that are not within its jurisdiction, when several of the draft cases arose. There are strong reasons why a Court should acquit in these circumstances even if it does then sustain the draft. It ought to acquit on the ground that before its decision the validity of the draft was doubtful, and it is unfair to punish men for disobeying a doubtful law.

There would be precedent for a decision along these lines. The Court has several times reversed criminal convictions, on due process grounds, because the law in question was too vague. (It has overturned convictions, for example, under laws that made it a crime to charge 'unreasonable prices' or to be a member of a 'gang'.) Conviction under a vague criminal law offends the moral and political ideals of due process in two ways. First, it places a citizen in the unfair position of either acting at his peril or accepting a more stringent restriction on his life than the legislature may have authorized: As I argued earlier, it is not acceptable, as a model of social behavior, that in such cases he ought to assume the worst. Second, it gives power to the prosecutor and the courts to make criminal law, by opting for one or the other possible interpretations after the event. This would be a delegation of authority by the legislature that is inconsistent with our scheme of separation of powers.

Conviction under a criminal law whose terms are not vague, but whose constitutional validity is doubtful, offends due process in the first of these ways. It forces a citizen to assume the worst, or act at his peril. It offends due process in something like the second way as well. Most citizens would be deterred by a doubtful statute if they were to risk jail by violating it. Congress, and not the courts, would then be the effective voice in deciding the constitutionality of criminal enactments, and this also violates the separation of powers.

If acts of dissent continue to occur after the Supreme Court has ruled that the laws are valid, or that the political question doctrine applies, then acquittal on the grounds I have described is no longer appropriate. The Court's decision will not have finally settled the law, for the reasons given earlier, but the Court will have done all that can be done to settle it. The courts may still exercise their sentencing discretion, however, and impose minimal or suspended sentences as a mark of respect for the dissenters' position.

Some lawyers will be shocked by my general conclusion that we have a responsibility toward those who disobey the draft laws out of conscience, and that we may be required not to prosecute them, but rather to change our laws or adjust our sentencing procedures to accommodate them. The simple Draconian propositions, that crime must be punished, and that he who misjudges the law must take the consequences, have an extraordinary hold on the professional as well as the popular imagination. But the rule of law is more complex and more intelligent than that and it is important that it survive.

9

Reverse Discrimination

1.

In 1945 a black man named Sweatt applied to the University of Texas Law School, but was refused admission because state law provided that only whites could attend. The Supreme Court declared that this law violated Sweatt's rights under the Fourteenth Amendment to the United States Constitution, which provides that no state shall deny any man the equal protection of its laws.[1] In 1971 a Jew named DeFunis applied to the University of Washington Law School; he was rejected although his test scores and college grades were such that he would have been admitted if he had been a black or a Filipino or a Chicano or an American Indian. DeFunis asked the Supreme Court to declare that the Washington practice, which required less exacting standards of minority groups, violated his rights under the Fourteenth Amendment.[2]

The Washington Law School's admissions procedures were complex. Applications were divided into two groups. The majority – those not from the designated minority groups – were first screened so as to eliminate all applicants whose predicted average, which is a function of college grades and aptitude test scores, fell below a certain level. Majority applicants who survived this initial cut were then placed in categories that received progressively more careful consideration. Minority-group applications, on the other hand, were not screened; each received the most careful consideration by a special committee consisting of a black professor of law and a white professor who had taught in programs to aid black law students. Most of the minority applicants who were accepted in the year in which DeFunis was rejected had predicted averages below the cutoff level, and the law school conceded that any minority applicant with his average would certainly have been accepted.

The *DeFunis* case split those political action groups that have tradi-

[1] *Sweatt v. Painter*, 339 U.S. 629, 70 S. Ct. 848.
[2] *DeFunis v. Odegaard*, 94 S. Ct. 1704 (1974).

tionally supported liberal causes. The B'nai Brith Anti-Defamation League and the AFL-CIO, for example, filed briefs as *amici curiae* in support of DeFunis' claim, while the American Hebrew Women's Council, the UAW, and the UMWA filed briefs against it.

These splits among old allies demonstrate both the practical and the philosophical importance of the case. In the past liberals held, within one set of attitudes, three propositions: that racial classification is an evil in itself; that every person has a right to an educational opportunity commensurate with his abilities; and that affirmative state action is proper to remedy the serious inequalities of American society. In the last decade, however, the opinion has grown that these three liberal propositions are in fact not compatible, because the most effective programs of state action are those that give a competitive advantage to minority racial groups.

That opinion has, of course, been challenged. Some educators argue that benign quotas are ineffective, even self-defeating, because preferential treatment will reinforce the sense of inferiority that many blacks already have. Others make a more general objection. They argue that any racial discrimination, even for the purpose of benefiting minorities, will in fact harm those minorities, because prejudice is fostered whenever racial distinctions are tolerated for any purpose whatever. But these are complex and controversial empirical judgments, and it is far too early, as wise critics concede, to decide whether preferential treatment does more harm or good. Nor is it the business of judges, particularly in constitutional cases, to overthrow decisions of other officials because the judges disagree about the efficiency of social policies. This empirical criticism is therefore reinforced by the moral argument that even if reverse discrimination does benefit minorities and does reduce prejudice in the long run, it is nevertheless wrong because distinctions of race are inherently unjust. They are unjust because they violate the rights of individual members of groups not so favored, who may thereby lose a place as DeFunis did.

DeFunis presented this moral argument, in the form of a constitutional claim, to the courts. The Supreme Court did not, in the end, decide whether the argument was good or bad. DeFunis had been admitted to the law school after one lower court had decided in his favor, and the law school said that he would be allowed to graduate however the case was finally decided. The Court therefore held that the case was moot and dismissed the appeal on that ground. But Mr. Justice Douglas disagreed with this neutral disposition of the case; he wrote a dissenting opinion in which he argued that the Court should have upheld DeFunis's claim on the merits. Many universities and colleges have taken Justice Douglas's opinion as handwriting on the wall, and have changed their practices in anticipation of a later Court decision in which his opinion prevails. In fact, his opinion pointed out that law schools might achieve much the same result by a more sophisticated policy than Washington used. A school might stipulate, for example, that applicants from all races and groups would be considered together, but that the aptitude tests of certain minority applicants would be graded differently, or given less weight in overall predicted average, because experience had shown that standard examinations were for different reasons a poorer test of the actual ability of these applicants. But if this technique is used deliberately to achieve the same result, it is devious, and it remains to ask why the candid program used by the University of Washington was either unjust or unconstitutional.

2.

DeFunis plainly has no Constitutional right that the state provide him a legal education of a certain quality. His rights would not be violated if his state did not have a law school at all, or if it had a law school with so few places that he could not win one on intellectual merit. Nor does to have a right to insist that intelligence be the exclusive test of admission. Law schools do rely heavily on intellectual tests for admission. That seems proper, however, not because applicants have a right to be judged in that way, but because it is reasonable to think that the community as a whole is better off if its lawyers are intelligent. That is, intellectual standards are justified, not because they reward the clever, but because they seem to serve a useful social policy.

Law schools sometimes serve that policy better, moreover, by supplementing intelligence tests with other sorts of standards: they sometimes prefer industrious applicants, for example, to those who are brighter but lazier. They also serve special policies for which intelligence is not relevant. The Washington Law School, for example, gave special preference not only to the minority applicants but also to veterans who had been at the school before entering the military, and neither DeFunis nor any of the briefs submitted in his behalf complained of that preference.

DeFunis does not have an absolute right to a law school place, nor does he have a right that only intelligence be used as a standard for admission. He says he nevertheless has a right that race *not* be used as a standard, no matter how well a racial classification might work to promote the general welfare or to reduce social and economic inequality. He does not claim, however, that he has this right as a distinct and independent political right that is specifically protected by the Constitution, as is his right to freedom of speech and religion. The Constitution does not condemn racial classification directly, as it does condemn

censorship or the establishment of a state religion. DeFunis claims that
his right that race not be used as a criterion of admission follows from
the more abstract right of equality that is protected by the Fourteenth
Amendment, which provides that no state shall deny to any person the
equal protection of the law.

But the legal arguments made on both sides show that neither the
text of the Constitution nor the prior decisions of the Supreme Court
decisively settle the question whether, as a matter of law, the Equal
Protection Clause makes all racial classifications unconstitutional. The
Clause makes the concept of equality a test of legislation, but it
does not stipulate any particular conception of that concept.[1] Those
who wrote the Clause intended to attack certain consequences of slavery
and racial prejudice, but it is unlikely that they intended to outlaw all
racial classifications, or that they expected such a prohibition to be the
result of what they wrote. They outlawed whatever policies would violate
equality, but left it to others to decide, from time to time, what that
means. There cannot be a good legal argument in favor of DeFunis,
therefore, unless there is a good moral argument that all racial classifications, even those that make society as a whole more equal, are inherently offensive to an individual's right to equal protection for himself.

There is nothing paradoxical, of course, in the idea that an individual's right to equal protection may sometimes conflict with an otherwise desirable social policy, including the policy of making the community more equal overall. Suppose a law school were to charge a few
middle-class students, selected by lot, double tuition in order to increase
the scholarship fund for poor students. It would be serving a desirable
policy – equality of opportunity – by means that violated the right of
the students selected by lot to be treated equally with other students
who could also afford the increased fees. It is, in fact, part of the
importance of DeFunis's case that it forces us to acknowledge the
distinction between equality as a policy and equality as a right, a distinction that political theory has virtually ignored. He argues that the
Washington Law School violated his individual right to equality for the
sake of a policy of greater equality overall, in the same way that double
tuition for arbitrarily chosen students would violate their rights for the
same purpose.

We must therefore concentrate our attention on that claim. We must
try to define the central concept on which it turns, which is the concept
of an individual right to equality made a constitutional right by the
Equal Protection Clause. What rights to equality do citizens have as

[1] See Chapter 5.

individuals which might defeat programs aimed at important economic and social policies, including the social policy of improving equality overall?

There are two different sorts of rights they may be said to have. The first is the right to *equal treatment*, which is the right to an equal distribution of some opportunity or resource or burden. Every citizen, for example, has a right to an equal vote in a democracy; that is the nerve of the Supreme Court's decision that one person must have one vote even if a different and more complex arrangement would better secure the collective welfare. The second is the right to *treatment as an equal*, which is the right, not to receive the same distribution of some burden or benefit, but to be treated with the same respect and concern as anyone else. If I have two children, and one is dying from a disease that is making the other uncomfortable, I do not show equal concern if I flip a coin to decide which should have the remaining dose of a drug. This example shows that the right to treatment as an equal is fundamental, and the right to equal treatment, derivative. In some circumstances the right to treatment as an equal will entail a right to equal treatment, but not, by any means, in all circumstances.

DeFunis does not have a right to equal treatment in the assignment of law school places; he does not have a right to a place just because others are given places. Individuals may have a right to equal treatment in elementary education, because someone who is denied elementary education is unlikely to lead a useful life. But legal education is not so vital that everyone has an equal right to it.

DeFunis does have the second sort of right – a right to treatment as an equal in the decision as to which admissions standards should be used. That is, he has a right that his interests be treated as fully and sympathetically as the interests of any others when the law school decides whether to count race as a pertinent criterion for admission. But we must be careful not to overstate what that means.

Suppose an applicant complains that his right to be treated as an equal is violated by tests that place the less intelligent candidates at a disadvantage against the more intelligent. A law school might properly reply in the following way. Any standard will place certain candidates at a disadvantage as against others, but an admission policy may nevertheless be justified if it seems reasonable to expect that the overall gain to the community exceeds the overall loss, and if no other policy that does not provide a comparable disadvantage would produce even roughly the same gain. An individual's right to be treated as an equal means that his potential loss must be treated as a matter of concern, but that loss may nevertheless be outweighed by the gain to the community as a whole. If it is, then the less intelligent applicant cannot claim that he is cheated of his right to be treated as an equal just because he suffers a disadvantage others do not.

Washington may make the same reply to DeFunis. Any admissions policy must put some applicants at a disadvantage, and a policy of preference for minority applicants can reasonably be supposed to benefit the community as a whole, even when the loss to candidates such as DeFunis is taken into account. If there are more black lawyers, they will help to provide better legal services to the black community, and so reduce social tensions. It might well improve the quality of legal education for all students, moreover, to have a greater number of blacks as classroom discussants of social problems. Further, if blacks are seen as successful law students, then other blacks who do meet the usual intellectual standards might be encouraged to apply, and that, in turn, would raise the intellectual quality of the bar. In any case, preferential admissions of blacks should decrease the difference in wealth and power that now exists between different racial groups, and so make the community more equal overall. It is, as I said, controversial whether a preferential admissions program will in fact promote these various policies, but it cannot be said to be implausible that it will. The disadvantage to applicants such as DeFunis is, on that hypothesis, a cost that must be paid for a greater gain; it is in that way like the disadvantage to less intelligent students that is the cost of ordinary admissions policies.[1]

We now see the difference between DeFunis's case and the case we imagined, in which a law school charged students selected at random higher fees. The special disadvantage to these students was not necessary to achieve the gain in scholarship funds, because the same gain would have been achieved by a more equal distribution of the cost amongst all the students who could afford it. That is not true of DeFunis. He did suffer from the Washington policy more than those majority applicants who were accepted. But that discrimination was not arbitrary; it was a consequence of the meritocratic standards he approves. DeFunis's argu-

---

[1] I shall argue later in this Chapter that there are circumstances in which a policy violates someone's right to be treated as an equal in spite of the fact that the social gains from that policy may be said to outweigh the losses. These circumstances arise when the gains that outweigh the losses include the satisfaction of prejudices and other sorts of preferences that it is improper for officials or institutions to take into account at all. But the hypothetical social gains described in this paragraph do not include gains of that character. Of course, if DeFunis had some other right, beyond the right to be treated as an equal, which the Washington policy violated, then the fact that the policy might achieve an overall social gain would not justify the violation (See Chapter 6). If the Washington admissions procedure included a religious test that violated his right to religious freedom, for example, it would offer no excuse that using such a test might make the community more cohesive. But DeFunis does not rely on any distinct right beyond his right to equality protected by the Equal Protection Clause.

ment therefore fails. The Equal Protection Clause gives constitutional standing to the right to be treated as an equal, but he cannot find, in that right, any support for his claim that the clause makes all racial classifications illegal.

3.

If we dismiss DeFunis's claim in this straightforward way, however, we are left with this puzzle. How can so many able lawyers, who supported his claim both in morality and law, have made that mistake? These lawyers all agree that intelligence is a proper criterion for admission to law schools. They do not suppose that anyone's constitutional right to be treated as an equal is compromised by that criterion. Why do they deny that race, in the circumstances of this decade, may also be a proper criterion?

They fear, perhaps, that racial criteria will be misused; that such criteria will serve as an excuse for prejudice against the minorities that are not favored, such as Jews. But that cannot explain their opposition. Any criteria may be misused, and in any case they think that racial criteria are wrong in principle and not simply open to abuse.

Why? The answer lies in their belief that, in theory as well as in practice, *DeFunis* and *Sweatt* must stand or fall together. They believe that it is illogical for liberals to condemn Texas for raising a color barrier against Sweatt, and then applaud Washington for raising a color barrier against DeFunis. The difference between these two cases, they suppose, must be only the subjective preference of liberals for certain minorities now in fashion. If there is something wrong with racial classifications, then it must be something that is wrong with racial classifications as such, not just classifications that work against those groups currently in favor. That is the inarticulate premise behind the slogan, relied on by defendants of DeFunis, that the Constitution is color blind. That slogan means, of course, just the opposite of what it says: it means that the Constitution is so sensitive to color that it makes any institutional racial classification invalid as a matter of law.

It is of the greatest importance, therefore, to test the assumption that Sweatt and DeFunis must stand or fall together. If that assumption is sound, then the straightforward argument against DeFunis must be fallacious after all, for no argument could convince us that segregation of the sort practiced against Sweatt is justifiable or constitutional.[1]

---

[1] In the actual *Sweatt* decision, the Supreme Court applied the old rule which held that segregation was constitutionally permitted if facilities were provided for blacks that were 'separate but equal'. Texas had provided a separate law school for blacks, but the Court held that that school was by no means the equal of the white

Superficially, moreover, the arguments against DeFunis do indeed seem available against Sweatt, because we can construct an argument that Texas might have used to show that segregation benefits the collective welfare, so that the special disadvantage to blacks is a cost that must be paid to achieve an overall gain.

Suppose the Texas admissions committee, though composed of men and women who themselves held no prejudices, decided that the Texas economy demanded more white lawyers than they could educate, but could find no use for black lawyers at all. That might have been, after all, a realistic assessment of the commercial market for lawyers in Texas just after World War II. Corporate law firms needed lawyers to serve booming business but could not afford to hire black lawyers, however skillful, because the firms' practices would be destroyed if they did. It was no doubt true that the black community in Texas had great need of skillful lawyers, and would have preferred to use black lawyers if these were available. But the committee might well have thought that the commercial needs of the state as a whole outweighed that special need.

Or suppose the committee judged, no doubt accurately, that alumni gifts to the law school would fall off drastically if it admitted a black student. The committee might deplore that fact, but nevertheless believe that the consequent collective damage would be greater than the damage to black candidates excluded by the racial restriction.

It may be said that these hypothetical arguments are disingenuous, because any policy of excluding blacks would in fact be supported by a prejudice against blacks as such, and arguments of the sort just described would be rationalization only. But if these arguments are, in fact, sound, then they might be accepted by men who do not have the prejudices the objection assumes. It therefore does not follow from the fact that the admissions officers were prejudiced, if they were, that they would have rejected these arguments if they had not been.

In any case, arguments such as those I describe were in fact used by officials who might have been free from prejudice against those they excluded. Many decades ago, as the late Professor Bickel reminds us in his brief for the B'nai Brith, President Lowell of Harvard University argued in favor of a quota limiting the number of Jews who might be accepted by his university. He said that if Jews were accepted in numbers larger than their proportion of the population, as they certainly would have been if intelligence were the only test, then Harvard would no

---

school. *Sweatt* was decided before the famous *Brown* case in which the Court finally rejected the 'separate but equal' rule, and there is no doubt that an all-white law school would be unconstitutional today, even if an all-black law school were provided that was, in a material sense, the equal of that provided for whites.

longer be able to provide to the world men of the qualities and temperament it aimed to produce, men, that is, who were more well-rounded
and less exclusively intellectual than Jews tended to be, and who, therefore, were better and more likely leaders of other men, both in and out
of government. It was no doubt true, when Lowell spoke, that Jews were
less likely to occupy important places in government or at the heads of
large public companies. If Harvard wished to serve the general welfare
by improving the intellectual qualities of the nation's leaders, it was
rational not to allow its classes to be filled up with Jews. The men who
reached that conclusion might well prefer the company of Jews to that
of the Wasps who were more likely to become senators. Lowell suggested he did, though perhaps the responsibilities of his office prevented
him from frequently indulging his preference.

It might now be said, however, that discrimination against blacks,
even when it does serve some plausible policy, is nevertheless unjustified
because it is invidious and insulting. The briefs opposing DeFunis make
just that argument to distinguish his claim from Sweatt's. Because blacks
were the victims of slavery and legal segregation, they say, any discrimination that excludes blacks will be taken as insulting by them, whatever
arguments of general welfare might be made in its support. But it is not
true, as a general matter, that any social policy is unjust if those whom
it puts at a disadvantage feel insulted. Admission to law school by
intelligence is not unjust because those who are less intelligent feel
insulted by their exclusion. Everything depends upon whether the feeling
of insult is produced by some more objective feature that would disqualify
the policy even if the insult were not felt. If segregation does improve
the general welfare, even when the disadvantage to blacks is fully
taken into account, and if no other reason can be found why segregation
is nevertheless unjustified, then the insult blacks feel, while understandable, must be based on misperception.

It would be wrong, in any case, to assume that men in the position
of DeFunis will not take *their* exclusion to be insulting. They are very
likely to think of themselves, not as members of some other minority,
such as Jews or Poles or Italians, whom comfortable and successful
liberals are willing to sacrifice in order to delay more violent social
change. If we wish to distinguish *DeFunis* from *Sweatt* on some argument that uses the concept of an insult, we must show that the treatment
of the one, but not the other, is in fact unjust.

4.

So these familiar arguments that might distinguish the two cases are
unconvincing. That seems to confirm the view that Sweatt and DeFunis

must be treated alike, and therefore that racial classification must be outlawed altogether. But fortunately a more successful ground of distinction can be found to support our initial sense that the cases are in fact very different. This distinction does not rely, as these unconvincing arguments do, on features peculiar to issues of race or segregation, or even on features peculiar to issues of educational opportunity. It relies instead on further analysis of the idea, which was central to my argument against DeFunis, that in certain circumstances a policy which puts many individuals at a disadvantage is nevertheless justified because it makes the community as a whole better off.

Any institution which uses that idea to justify a discriminatory policy faces a series of theoretical and practical difficulties. There are, in the first place, two distinct senses in which a community may be said to be better off as a whole, in spite of the fact that certain of its members are worse off, and any justification must specify which sense is meant. It may be better off in a *utilitarian* sense, that is, because the average or collective level of welfare in the community is improved even though the welfare of some individuals falls. Or it may be better off in an *ideal* sense, that is, because it is more just, or in some other way closer to an ideal society, whether or not average welfare is improved. The University of Washington might use either utilitarian or ideal arguments to justify its racial classification. It might argue, for example, that increasing the number of black lawyers reduces racial tensions, which improves the welfare of almost everyone in the community. That is a utilitarian argument. Or it might argue that, whatever effect minority preference will have on average welfare, it will make the community more equal and therefore more just. That is an ideal, not a utilitarian, argument.

The University of Texas, on the other hand, cannot make an ideal argument for segregation. It cannot claim that segregation makes the community more just whether it improves the average welfare or not. The arguments it makes to defend segregation must therefore all be utilitarian arguments. The arguments I invented, like the argument that white lawyers could do more than black lawyers to improve commercial efficiency in Texas, are utilitarian, since commercial efficiency makes the community better off only if it improves average welfare.

Utilitarian arguments encounter a special difficulty that ideal arguments do not. What is meant by average or collective welfare? How can the welfare of an individual be measured, even in principle, and how can gains in the welfare of different individuals be added and then compared with losses, so as to justify the claim that gains outweigh losses overall? The utilitarian argument that segregation improves average welfare presupposes that such calculations can be made. But how?

Jeremy Bentham, who believed that only utilitarian arguments could justify political decisions, gave the following answer. He said that the effect of a policy on an individual's welfare could be determined by discovering the amount of pleasure or pain the policy brought him, and that effect of the policy on the collective welfare could be calculated by adding together all the pleasure and subtracting all of the pain it brought to everyone. But, as Bentham's critics insisted, it is doubtful whether there exists a simple psychological state of pleasure common to all those who benefit from a policy or of pain common to all those who lose by it; in any case it would be impossible to identify, measure, and add the different pleasures and pains felt by vast numbers of people.

Philosophers and economists who find utilitarian arguments attractive, but who reject Bentham's psychological utilitarianism, propose a different concept of individual and overall welfare. They suppose that whenever an institution or an official must decide upon a policy, the members of the community will each prefer the consequences of one decision to the consequences of others. DeFunis, for example, prefers the consequences of the standard admissions policy to the policy of minority preference Washington used, while the blacks in some urban ghetto might each prefer the consequences of the latter policy to the former. If it can be discovered what each individual prefers, and how intensely, then it might be shown that a particular policy would satisfy on balance more preferences, taking into account their intensity, than alternative policies. On this concept of welfare, a policy makes the community better off in a utilitarian sense if it satisfies the collection of preferences better than alternative policies would, even though it dissatisfies the preferences of some.[1]

Of course, a law school does not have available any means of making accurate judgments about the preferences of all those whom its admissions policies will affect. It may nevertheless make judgments which, though speculative, cannot be dismissed as implausible. It is, for example, plausible to think that in post-War Texas, the preferences of the people were overall in favor of the consequences of segregation in law schools, even if the intensity of the competing preference for integration, and not simply the number of those holding that preference, is taken into account. The officials of the Texas law school might have relied upon voting behavior, newspaper editorials, and simply their own sense of

[1] Many economists and philosophers challenge the intelligibility of preference utilitarianism as well as psychological utilitarianism. They argue that there is no way, even in principle, to calculate and compare the intensity of individual preferences. Since I wish to establish a different failing in certain utilitarian arguments, I assume, for purposes of this essay, that at least rough and speculative calculations about overall community preferences can be made.

their community in reaching that decision. Though they might have been wrong, we cannot now say, even with the benefit of hindsight, that they were.

So even if Bentham's psychological utilitarianism is rejected, law schools may appeal to preference utilitarianism to provide at least a rough and speculative justification for admissions policies that put some classes of applicants at a disadvantage. But once it is made clear that these utilitarian arguments are based on judgments about the actual preferences of members of the community, a fresh and much more serious difficulty emerges.

The utilitarian argument, that a policy is justified if it satisfies more preferences overall, seems at first sight to be an egalitarian argument. It seems to observe strict impartiality. If the community has only enough medicine to treat some of those who are sick, the argument seems to recommend that those who are sickest be treated first. If the community can afford a swimming pool or a new theater, but not both, and more people want the pool, then it recommends that the community build the pool, unless those who want the theater can show that their preferences are so much more intense that they have more weight in spite of the numbers. One sick man is not to be preferred to another because he is worthier of official concern; the tastes of the theater audience are not to be preferred because they are more admirable. In Bentham's phrase, each man is to count as one and no man is to count as more than one.

These simple examples suggest that the utilitarian argument not only respects, but embodies, the right of each citizen to be treated as the equal of any other. The chance that each individual's preferences have to succeed, in the competition for social policy, will depend upon how important his preference is to him, and how many others share it, compared to the intensity and number of competing preferences. His chance will not be affected by the esteem or contempt of either officials or fellow citizens, and he will therefore not be subservient or beholden to them.

But if we examine the range of preferences that individuals in fact have, we shall see that the apparent egalitarian character of a utilitarian argument is often deceptive. Preference utilitarianism asks officials to attempt to satisfy people's preferences so far as this is possible. But the preferences of an individual for the consequences of a particular policy may be seen to reflect, on further analysis, either a *personal* preference for his own enjoyment of some goods or opportunities, or an *external* preference for the assignment of goods and opportunities to others, or both. A white law school candidate might have a personal preference for the consequences of segregation, for example, because the policy improves his own chances of success, or an external preference for those consequences because he has contempt for blacks and disapproves social situations in which the races mix.

The distinction between personal and external preferences is of great importance for this reason. If a utilitarian argument counts external preferences along with personal preferences, then the egalitarian character of that argument is corrupted, because the chance that anyone's preferences have to succeed will then depend, not only on the demands that the personal preferences of others make on scarce resources, but on the respect or affection they have for him or for his way of life. If external preferences tip the balance, then the fact that a policy makes the community better off in a utilitarian sense would *not* provide a justification compatible with the right of those it disadvantages to be treated as equals.

This corruption of utilitarianism is plain when some people have external preferences because they hold political theories that are themselves contrary to utilitarianism. Suppose many citizens, who are not themselves sick, are racists in political theory, and therefore prefer that scarce medicine be given to a white man who needs it rather than a black man who needs it more. If utilitarianism counts these political preferences at face value, then it will be, from the standpoint of personal preferences, self-defeating, because the distribution of medicine will then not be, from that standpoint, utilitarian at all. In any case, self-defeating or not, the distribution will not be egalitarian in the sense defined. Blacks will suffer, to a degree that depends upon the strength of the racist preference, from the fact that others think them less worthy of respect and concern.

There is a similar corruption when the external preferences that are counted are altruistic or moralistic. Suppose many citizens, who themselves do not swim, prefer the pool to the theater because they approve of sports and admire athletes, or because they think that the theater is immoral and ought to be repressed. If the altruistic preferences are counted, so as to reinforce the personal preferences of swimmers, the result will be a form of double counting : each swimmer will have the benefit not only of his own preference, but also of the preference of someone else who takes pleasure in his success. If the moralistic preferences are counted, the effect will be the same : actors and audiences will suffer because their preferences are held in lower respect by citizens whose personal preferences are not themselves engaged.

In these examples, external preferences are independent of personal preferences. But of course political, altruistic, and moralistic preferences are often not independent, but grafted on to the personal preferences they reinforce. If I am white and sick, I may also hold a racist political theory. If I want a swimming pool for my own enjoyment I may also be altruistic in favor of my fellow athlete, or I may also think that the theater is immoral. The consequences of counting these external preferences will be as grave for equality as if they were independent of personal preference, because those against whom the external preferences run might be unable or unwilling to develop reciprocal external preferences that would right the balance.

External preferences therefore present a great difficulty for utilitarianism. That theory owes much of its popularity to the assumption that it embodies the right of citizens to be treated as equals. But if external preferences are counted in overall preferences, then this asssumption is jeopardized. That is, in itself, an important and neglected point in political theory; it bears, for example, on the liberal thesis, first made prominent by Mill, that the government has no right to enforce popular morality by law. It is often said that this liberal thesis is inconsistent with utilitarianism, because if the preferences of the majority that homosexuality should be repressed, for example, are sufficiently strong, utilitarianism must give way to their wishes. But the preference against homosexuality is an external preference, and the present argument provides a general reason why utilitarians should not count external preferences of any form. If utilitarianism is suitably reconstituted so as to count only personal preferences, then the liberal thesis is a consequence, not an enemy, of that theory.

It is not always possible, however, to reconstitute a utilitarian argument so as to count only personal preferences. Sometimes personal and external preferences are so inextricably tied together, and so mutually dependent, that no practical test for measuring preferences will be able to discriminate the personal and external elements in any individual's overall preference. That is especially true when preferences are affected by prejudice. Consider, for example, the associational preference of a white law student for white classmates. This may be said to be a personal preference for an association with one kind of colleague rather than another. But it is a personal preference that is parasitic upon external preferences : except in very rare cases a white student prefers the company of other whites because he has racist, social, and political convictions, or because he has contempt for blacks as a group. If these associational preferences are counted in a utilitarian argument used to justify segregation, then the egalitarian character of the argument is destroyed just as if the underlying external preferences were counted directly. Blacks would be denied their right to be treated as equals because the chance that their preferences would prevail in the design of admissions policy would be crippled by the low esteem in which others hold them. In any community in which prejudice against a particular minority is strong, then the personal preferences upon which a utilitarian argument must fix will be saturated with that prejudice; it follows that in such a community no utilitarian argument purporting to justify a disadvantage to that minority can be fair.[1]

This final difficulty is therefore fatal to Texas' utilitarian arguments in favor of segregation. The preferences that might support any such argument are either distinctly external, like the preferences of the community at large for racial separation, or are inextricably combined with and dependent upon external preferences, like the associational preferences of white students for white classmates and white lawyers for white colleagues. These external preferences are so widespread that they must corrupt any such argument. Texas' claim, that segregation makes the community better off in a utilitarian sense, is therefore incompatible with Sweatt's right to treatment as an equal guaranteed by the Equal Protection Clause.

It does not matter, to this conclusion, whether external preferences figure in the justification of a fundamental policy or in the justification of derivative policies designed to advance a more fundamental policy. Suppose Texas justifies segregation by pointing to the apparently neutral economic policy of increasing community wealth, which satisfies the personal preferences of everyone for better homes, food, and recreation. If the argument that segregation will improve community wealth depends upon the fact of external preference; if the argument notices, for example, that because of prejudice industry will run more efficiently if factories are segregated; then the argument has the consequence that the black man's personal preferences are defeated by what others think of him. Utilitarian arguments that justify a disadvantage to members of a race against whom prejudice runs will always be unfair arguments, unless it can be shown that the same disadvantage would have been justified in the absence of the prejudice. If the prejudice is widespread and pervasive, as in fact it is in the case of blacks, that can never be shown. The preferences on which any economic argument justifying

[1] The argument of this paragraph is powerful, but it is not, in itself, sufficient to disqualify all utilitarian arguments that produce substantial disadvantages to minorities who suffer from prejudice. Suppose the government decides, on a utilitarian argument, to allow unemployment to increase because the loss to those who lose their jobs is outweighed by the gain to those who would otherwise suffer from inflation. The burden of this policy will fall disproportionately on blacks, who will be fired first because prejudice runs against them. But though prejudice in this way affects the consequences of the policy of unemployment, it does not figure, even indirectly, in the utilitarian argument that supports that policy. (It figures, if at all, as a utilitarian argument against it.) We cannot say, therefore, that the special damage blacks suffer from a high unemployment policy is unjust for the reasons described in this essay. It may well be unjust for other reasons; if John Rawls is right, for example, it is unjust because the policy improves the condition of the majority at the expense of those already worse off.

segregation must be based will be so intertwined with prejudice that they cannot be disentangled to the degree necessary to make any such contrary-to-fact hypothesis plausible.

We now have an explanation that shows why any form of segregation that disadvantages blacks is, in the United States, an automatic insult to them, and why such segregation offends their right to be treated as equals. The argument confirms our sense that utilitarian arguments purporting to justify segregation are not simply wrong in detail but misplaced in principle. This objection to utilitarian arguments is not, however, limited to race or even prejudice. There are other cases in which counting external preferences would offend the rights of citizens to be treated as equals and it is worth briefly noticing these, if only to protect the argument against the charge that it is constructed ad hoc for the racial case. I might have a moralistic preference against professional women, or an altruistic preference for virtuous men. It would be unfair for any law school to count preferences like these in deciding whom to admit to law schools; unfair because these preferences, like racial prejudices, make the success of the personal preferences of an applicant depend on the esteem and approval, rather than on the competing personal preferences, of others.

The same objection does not hold, however, against a utilitarian argument used to justify admission based on intelligence. That policy need not rely, directly or indirectly, on any community sense that intelligent lawyers are intrinsically more worthy of respect. It relies instead upon the law school's own judgment, right or wrong, that intelligent lawyers are more effective in satisfying personal preferences of others, such as the preference for wealth or winning law suits. It is true that law firms and clients prefer the services of intelligent lawyers; that fact might make us suspicious of any utilitarian argument that is said not to depend upon that preference, just as we are suspicious of any argument justifying segregation that is said not to depend upon prejudice. But the widespread preference for intelligent lawyers is, by and large, not parasitic on external preferences : law firms and clients prefer intelligent lawyers because they also hold the opinion that such lawyers will be more effective in serving their personal preferences. Instrumental preferences, of that character, do not themselves figure in utilitarian arguments, though a law school may accept, on its own responsibility, the instrumental hypothesis upon which such preferences depend.[1]

---

[1] No doubt the preference that some men and women have for intellectual companions is parasitic on external preferences; they value these companions not as a means to anything else, but because they think that intelligent people are better, and more worthy of honor, than others. If such preferences were sufficiently strong and

5.

We therefore have the distinctions in hand necessary to distinguish *DeFunis* from *Sweatt*. The arguments for an admissions program that discriminates against blacks are all utilitarian arguments, and they are all utilitarian arguments that rely upon external preferences in such a way as to offend the constitutional right of blacks to be treated as equals. The arguments for an admissions program that discriminates in favor of blacks are both utilitarian and ideal. Some of the utilitarian arguments do rely, at least indirectly, on external preferences, such as the preference of certain blacks for lawyers of their own race; but the utilitarian arguments that do not rely on such preferences are strong and may be sufficient. The ideal arguments do not rely upon preferences at all, but on the independent argument that a more equal society is a better society even if its citizens prefer inequality. That argument does not deny anyone's right to be treated as an equal himself.

We are therefore left, in *DeFunis*, with the simple and straightforward argument with which we began. Racial criteria are not necessarily the right standards for deciding which applicants should be accepted by law schools. But neither are intellectual criteria, nor indeed, any other set of criteria. The fairness – and constitutionality – of any admissions program must be tested in the same way. It is justified if it serves a proper policy that respects the right of all members of the community to be treated as equals, but not otherwise. The criteria used by schools that refused to consider blacks failed that test, but the criteria used by the Washington University Law School do not.

We are all rightly suspicious of racial classifications. They have been used to deny, rather than to respect, the right of equality, and we are all conscious of the consequent injustice. But if we misunderstand the nature of that injustice because we do not make the simple distinctions that are necessary to understand it, then we are in danger of more injustice still. It may be that preferential admissions programs will not, in fact, make a more equal society, because they may not have the effects their advocates believe they will. That strategic question should be at the center of debate about these programs. But we must not corrupt the debate by supposing that these programs are unfair even if they do work. We must take care not to use the Equal Protection Clause to cheat ourselves of equality.

---

pervasive we might reach the same conclusion here that we reached about segregation: that no utilitarian argument purporting to justify discrimination against less intelligent men and women could be trusted to be fair. But there is no reason to assume that the United States is that intellectualistic; certainly no reason to think that it is intellectualistic to the degree that it is racist.

10

Liberty and Moralism

No doubt most Americans and Englishmen think that homosexuality, prostitution, and the publication of pornography are immoral. What part should this fact play in the decision whether to make them criminal? This is a tangled question, full of issues with roots in philosophical and sociological controversy. It is a question lawyers must face, however, and recent and controversial events – publication of the Wolfenden Report in England,[1] followed by a public debate on prostitution and homosexuality, and a series of obscenity decisions in the United States Supreme Court[2] – press it upon us.

Several positions are available, each with its own set of difficulties. Shall we say that public condemnation is sufficient, in and of itself, to justify making an act a crime? This seems inconsistent with our traditions of individual liberty, and our knowledge that the morals of even the largest mob cannot come warranted for truth. If public condemnation is not sufficient, what more is needed? Must there be some demonstration of present harm to particular persons directly affected by the practice in question? Or is it sufficient to show some effect on social customs and institutions which alters the social environment, and thus affects all members of society indirectly? If the latter, must it also be demonstrated that these social changes threaten long-term harm of some standard sort, like an increase in crime or a decrease in productivity? Or would it be enough to show that the vast bulk of the present community would deplore the change? If so, does the requirement of harm add much to the bare requirement of public condemnation?

In 1958 Lord Devlin delivered the second Maccabaean Lecture to the British Academy. He called his lecture 'The Enforcement of Morals', and devoted it to these issues of principle.[3] His conclusions he summarized in these remarks about the practice of homosexuality: 'We should ask

[1] *Report of the Committee on Homosexual Offences and Prostitution*, Cmd. no. 247 (1957).

[2] *Memoirs v. Massachusetts (Fanny Hill)*, 383 U.S. 413 (1966), *Ginzburg v. United States*, 383 463 U.S. (1966), *Mishkin v. New York*, 383 U.S. 502 (1966).

[3] Devlin, *The Enforcement of Morals* (1959). Reprinted in Devlin, *The Enforcement of Morals* (1965). [The latter is hereinafter cited as Devlin.]

ourselves in the first instance whether, looking at it calmly and dis-passionately, we regard it as a vice so abominable that its mere presence is an offence. If that is the genuine feeling of the society in which we live, I do not see how society can be denied the right to eradicate it.'[1]

The lecture, and in particular this hypothetical position on punishing homosexuals, provoked a tide of rebuttal that spilled over from academic journals into the radio and the almost-popular press.[2] Lord Devlin has since republished the Maccabaean Lecture, together with six further essays developing and defending the views there expressed, a preface to the whole, and some important new footnotes to the original lecture.[3]

American lawyers ought to attend to Lord Devlin's arguments. His conclusions will not be popular, although the swaggering insensitivity some of his critics found disappears with careful reading. Popular or not, we have no right to disregard them until we are satisfied that his arguments can be met. One of these arguments – the second of the two I shall discuss – has the considerable merit of focusing our attention on the connection between democratic theory and the enforcement of morals. It provokes us to consider, more closely than we have, the crucial concept upon which this connection depends – the concept of a public morality.

LORD DEVLIN'S DISENCHANTMENT

The preface to the new book contains a revealing account of how Lord Devlin came to his controversial opinions. When he was invited to prepare his Maccabaean Lecture the celebrated Wolfenden Committee had recently published its recommendation that homosexual practices in private between consenting adults no longer be criminal. He had read with complete approval the Committee's expression of the proper division between crime and sin :

> In this field, its [the law's] function, as we see it, is to preserve public order and decency, to protect the citizen from what is offen-sive or injurious, and to provide sufficient safeguards against exploitation and corruption of others . . . . It is not, in our view, the function of the law to intervene in the private lives of citizens, or to seek to enforce any particular pattern of behaviour, further than is necessary to carry out the purposes which we have out-lined . . . .

[1] Devlin 17. This position was carefully stated as hypothetical. Apparently Lord Devlin does not now think that the condition is met, because he has publically urged modification of the laws on homosexuality since the book's publication.

[2] Lord Devlin includes references to these comments in a bibliography. Devlin xiii.

[3] Devlin.

[T]here must remain a realm of private morality and immorality which is, in brief and crude terms, not the law's business.[1]

Lord Devlin believed that these ideals, which he recognized as derived from the teachings of Jeremy Bentham and John Stuart Mill, were unquestionable. He decided to devote his lecture to a painstaking consideration of what further changes, beyond the changes in the crime of homosexuality that the Committee recommended, would be necessary to make the criminal law of England conform to them. But study, in his words, 'destroyed instead of confirming the simple faith in which I had begun my task'[2] and he ended in the conviction that these ideals were not only questionable, but wrong.

The fact of his disenchantment is clear, but the extent of his disenchantment is not. He seems sometimes to be arguing the exact converse of the Committee's position, namely that society has a right to punish conduct of which its members strongly disapprove, even though that conduct has no effects which can be deemed injurious to others, on the ground that the state has a role to play as moral tutor and the criminal law is its proper tutorial technique. Those readers who take this to be his position are puzzled by the fact that distinguished philosophers and lawyers have concerned themselves to reply, for this seems a position that can safely be regarded as eccentric. In fact he is arguing not this position, but positions which are more complex and neither so eccentric nor so flatly at odds with the Wolfenden ideals. They are nowhere summarized in any crisp form (indeed the statement on homosexuality I have already quoted is as good a summary as he gives) but must be taken from the intricate arguments he develops.

There are two chief arguments. The first is set out in structured form in the Maccabaean Lecture. It argues from society's right to protect its own existence. The second, a quite different and much more important argument, develops in disjointed form through various essays. It argues from the majority's right to follow its own moral convictions in defending its social environment from change it opposes. I shall consider these two arguments in turn, but the second at greater length.

THE FIRST ARGUMENT : SOCIETY'S RIGHT TO PROTECT ITSELF

The first argument – and the argument which has received by far the major part of the critics' attention – is this :[3]

[1] *Report of the Committee on Homosexual Offences and Prostitution,* 9-10, 24.
[2] Devlin vii.
[3] It is developed chiefly in Devlin 7-25.

(1) In a modern society there are a variety of moral principles which some men adopt for their own guidance and do not attempt to impose upon others. There are also moral standards which the majority places beyond toleration and imposes upon those who dissent. For us, the dictates of particular religion are an example of the former class, and the practice of monogamy an example of the latter. A society cannot survive unless some standards are of the second class, because some moral conformity is essential to its life. Every society has a right to preserve its own existence, and therefore the right to insist on some such conformity.

(2) If society has such a right, then it has the right to use the institutions and sanctions of its criminal law to enforce the right – '[S]ociety may use the law to preserve morality in the same way it uses it to safeguard anything else if it is essential to its existence.'[1] Just as society may use its law to prevent treason, it may use it to prevent a corruption of that conformity which ties it together.

(3) But society's right to punish immorality by law should not necessarily be exercised against every sort and on every occasion of immorality – we must recognize the impact and the importance of some restraining principles. There are several of these, but the most important is that there 'must be toleration of the maximum individual freedom that is consistent with the integrity of society.'[2] These restraining principles, taken together, require that we exercise caution in concluding that a practice is considered profoundly immoral. The law should stay its hand if it detects any uneasiness or half-heartedness or latent toleration in society's condemnation of the practice. But none of these restraining principles apply, and hence society is free to enforce its rights, when public feeling is high, enduring and relentless, when, in Lord Devlin's phrase, it rises to 'intolerance, indignation and disgust'.[3] Hence the summary conclusion about homosexuality : if it is genuinely regarded as an abominable vice, society's right to eradicate it cannot be denied.

We must guard against a possible, indeed tempting, misconception of this argument. It does not depend upon any assumption that when the vast bulk of a community thinks a practice is immoral they are likely right. What Lord Devlin thinks is at stake, when our public morality is challenged, is the very survival of society, and he believes that society is entitled to preserve itself without vouching for the morality that holds it together.

[1] *Ibid.* 11.
[2] *Ibid.* 16.
[3] *Ibid.* 17.

Is this argument sound? Professor H. L. A. Hart, responding to its appearance at the heart of the Maccabaean lecture,[1] thought that it rested upon a confused conception of what a society is. If one holds anything like a conventional notion of a society, he said, it is absurd to suggest that every practice the society views as profoundly immoral and disgusting threatens its survival. This is as silly as arguing that society's existence is threatened by the death of one of its members or the birth of another, and Lord Devlin, he reminds us, offers nothing by way of evidence to support any such claim. But if one adopts an artificial definition of a society, such that a society consists of that particular complex of moral ideas and attitudes which its members happen to hold at a particular moment in time, it is intolerable that each such moral status quo should have the right to preserve its precarious existence by force. So, Professor Hart argued, Lord Devlin's argument fails whether a conventional or an artificial sense of 'society' is taken.

Lord Devlin replies to Professor Hart in a new and lengthy footnote. After summarizing Hart's criticism he comments, 'I do not assert that *any* deviation from a society's shared morality threatens its existence any more than I assert that *any* subversive activity threatens its existence. I assert that they are both activities which are capable in their nature of threatening the existence of society so that neither can be put beyond the law.'[2] This reply exposes a serious flaw in the architecture of the argument.

It tells us that we must understand the second step of the argument – the crucial claim that society has a right to enforce its public morality by law – as limited to a denial of the proposition that society never has such a right. Lord Devlin apparently understood the Wolfenden Report's statement of a 'realm of private morality . . . not the law's business' to assert a fixed jurisdictional barrier placing private sexual practices forever beyond the law's scrutiny. His arguments, the new footnote tells us, are designed to show merely that no such constitutional barrier should be raised, because it is possible that the challenge to established morality might be so profound that the very existence of a conformity in morals, and hence of the society itself, would be threatened.[3]

We might well remain unconvinced, even of this limited point. We

---

[1] H. L. A. Hart, *Law, Liberty and Morality* 51 (1963).

[2] Devlin 13.

[3] This reading had great support in the text even without the new footnote: 'I think, therefore, that it is not possible to set theoretical limits to the power of the State to legislate against immorality. It is not possible to settle in advance exceptions to the general rule or to define inflexibly areas of morality into which the law is in no circumstances to be allowed to enter.' (Devlin 12-13).

The arguments presented bear out this construction. They are of the *reductio ad absurdum* variety, exploiting the possibility that what is immoral can in theory become might believe that the danger which any unpopular practice can present to the existence of society is so small that it would be wise policy, a prudent protection of individual liberty from transient hysteria, to raise just this sort of constitutional barrier and forbid periodic reassessment of the risk.

But if we were persuaded to forego this constitutional barrier we would expect the third step in the argument to answer the inevitable next question: Granted that a challenge to deep-seated and genuine public morality may conceivably threaten society's existence, and so must be placed above the threshold of the law's concern, how shall we know when the danger is sufficiently clear and present to justify not merely scrutiny but action? What more is needed beyond the fact of passionate public disapproval to show that we are in the presence of an actual threat?

The rhetoric of the third step makes it seem responsive to this question – there is much talk of 'freedom' and 'toleration' and even 'balancing'. But the argument is not responsive, for freedom, toleration and balancing turn out to be appropriate only when the public outrage diagnosed at the second step is shown to be overstated, when the fever, that is, turns out to be feigned. When the fever is confirmed, when the intolerance, indignation and disgust are genuine, the principle that calls for 'the maximum individual freedom consistent with the integrity of society' no longer applies. But this means that nothing more than passionate public disapproval is necessary after all.

In short, the argument involves an intellectual sleight of hand. At the second step, public outrage is presented as a threshold criterion, merely placing the practice in a category which the law is not forbidden to regulate. But offstage, somewhere in the transition to the third step, this threshold criterion becomes itself a dispositive affirmative reason for action, so that when it is clearly met the law may proceed without more. The power of this manoeuvre is proved by the passage on homosexuality.

---

subversive of society. 'But suppose a quarter or a half of the population got drunk every night, what sort of society would it be? You cannot set a theoretical limit to the number of people who can get drunk before society is entitled to legislate against drunkenness. The same may be said of gambling.' (*Ibid.* 14.)

Each example argues that no jurisdictional limit may be drawn, not that every drunk or every act of gambling threatens society. There is no suggestion that society is entitled actually to make drunkenness or gambling crimes if the practice in fact falls below the level of danger. Indeed Lord Devlin quotes the Royal Commission on Betting, Lotteries, and Gaming to support his example on gambling: 'If we were convinced that whatever the degree of gambling this effect [on the character of the gambler as a member of society] must be harmful we should be inclined to think that it was the duty of the state to restrict gambling to the greatest extent practicable.' (Cmd. no. 8190 at para. 159 (1951), quoted in Devlin 14). The implication is that society may scrutinize and be ready to regulate, but should not actually do so until the threat in fact exists.

Lord Devlin concludes that if our society hates homosexuality enough it is justified in outlawing it, and forcing human beings to choose between the miseries of frustration and persecution, because of the danger the practice presents to society's existence. He manages this conclusion without offering evidence that homosexuality presents any danger at all to society's existence, beyond the naked claim that all 'deviations from a society's shared morality . . . are capable in their nature of threatening the existence of society' and so 'cannot be put beyond the law'.[1]

THE SECOND ARGUMENT: SOCIETY'S RIGHT TO FOLLOW ITS OWN LIGHTS

We are therefore justified in setting aside the first argument and turning to the second. My reconstruction includes making a great deal explicit which I believe implicit, and so involves some risk of distortion, but I take the second argument to be this:[2]

(1) If those who have homosexual desires freely indulged them, our social environment would change. What the changes would be cannot be calculated with any precision, but it is plausible to suppose, for example, that the position of the family, as the assumed and natural institution around which the educational, economic and recreational arrangements of men center, would be undermined, and the further ramifications of that would be great. We are too sophisticated to suppose that the effects of an increase in homosexuality would be confined to those who participate in the practice alone, just as we are too sophisticated to suppose that prices and wages affect only those who negotiate them. The environment in which we and our children must live is determined, among other things, by patterns and relationships formed privately by others than ourselves.

(2) This in itself does not give society the right to prohibit homosexual practices. We cannot conserve every custom we like by jailing those who do not want to preserve it. But it means that our legislators must inevitably decide some moral issues. They must decide whether the institutions which seem threatened are sufficiently valuable to protect at the cost of human freedom. And they must decide whether the practices which threaten that institution are immoral, for if they are then the freedom of an individual to pursue them counts for less. We do not need so strong a justification, in terms of the social importance of the institutions being protected, if we are confident that no one has a moral right

---

[1] Devlin 13, n.l.

[2] Most of the argument appears in Devlin chs. 5, 6 and 7. See also an article published after the book: 'Law and Morality', 1 *Manitoba* L.S.J. 243 (1964/65).

to do what we want to prohibit. We need less of a case, that is, to abridge someone's freedom to lie, cheat or drive recklessly, than his freedom to choose his own jobs or to price his own goods. This does not claim that immorality is sufficient to make conduct criminal; it argues, rather, that on occasion it is necessary.

(3) But how shall a legislator decide whether homosexual acts are immoral? Science can give no answer, and a legislator can no longer properly turn to organized religion. If it happens, however, that the vast bulk of the community is agreed upon an answer, even though a small minority of educated men may dissent, the legislator has a duty to act on the consensus. He has such a duty for two closely connected reasons: (a) In the last analysis the decision must rest on some article of moral faith, and in a democracy this sort of issue, above all others, must be settled in accordance with democratic principles. (b) It is, after all, the community which acts when the threats and sanctions of the criminal law are brought to bear. The community must take the moral responsibility, and it must therefore act on its own lights – that is, on the moral faith of its members.

This, as I understand it, is Lord Devlin's second argument. It is complex, and almost every component invites analysis and challenge. Some readers will dissent from its central assumption, that a change in social institutions is the sort of harm a society is entitled to protect itself against. Others who do not take this strong position (perhaps because they approve of laws which are designed to protect economic institutions) will nevertheless feel that society is not entitled to act, however immoral the practice, unless the threatened harm to an institution is demonstrable and imminent rather than speculative. Still others will challenge the thesis that the morality or immorality of an act ought even to count in determining whether to make it criminal (though they would no doubt admit that it does count under present practice), and others still will argue that even in a democracy legislators have the duty to decide moral questions for themselves, and must not refer such issues to the community at large. I do not propose to argue now for or against any of these positions. I want instead to consider whether Lord Devlin's conclusions are valid on his own terms, or the assumption, that is, that society does have a right to protect its central and valued social institutions against conduct which the vast bulk of its members disapproves on moral principle.

I shall argue that his conclusions are not valid, even on these terms, because he misunderstands what it is to disapprove on moral principle. I might say a cautionary word about the argument I shall present. It will consist in part of reminders that certain types of moral language (terms like 'prejudice' and 'moral position', for example) have standard uses in moral argument. My purpose is not to settle issues of political morality by the fiat of a dictionary, but to exhibit what I believe to be mistakes in Lord Devlin's moral sociology. I shall try to show that our conventional moral practices are more complex and more structured than he takes them to be, and that he consequently misunderstands what it means to say that the criminal law should be drawn from public morality. This is a popular and appealing thesis, and it lies near the core not only of Lord Devlin's, but of many other, theories about law and morals. It is crucial that its implications be understood.

THE CONCEPT OF A MORAL POSITION

We might start with the fact that terms like 'moral position' and 'moral conviction' function in our conventional morality as terms of justification and criticism, as well as of description. It is true that we sometimes speak of a group's 'morals', or 'morality', or 'moral beliefs', or 'moral positions' or 'moral convictions', in what might be called an anthropological sense, meaning to refer to whatever attitudes the group displays about the propriety of human conduct, qualities or goals. We say, in this sense, that the morality of Nazi Germany was based on prejudice, or was irrational. But we also use some of these terms, particularly 'moral position' and 'moral conviction', in a discriminatory sense, to contrast the positions they describe with prejudices, rationalizations, matters of personal aversion or taste, arbitrary stands, and the like. One use – perhaps the most characteristic use – of this discriminatory sense is to offer a limited but important sort of justification for an act, when the moral issues surrounding that act are unclear or in dispute.

Suppose I tell you that I propose to vote against a man running for a public office of trust because I know him to be a homosexual and because I believe that homosexuality is profoundly immoral. If you disagree that homosexuality is immoral, you may accuse me of being about to cast my vote unfairly, acting on prejudice or out of a personal repugnance which is irrelevant to the moral issue. I might then try to convert you to my position on homosexuality, but if I fail in this I shall still want to convince you of what you and I will both take to be a separate point – that my vote was based upon *a* moral position, in the discriminatory sense, even though one which differs from yours. I shall want to persuade you of this, because if I do I am entitled to expect that you will alter your opinion of me and of what I am about to do. Your judgment of my character will be different – you might still think me eccentric (or puritanical or unsophisticated) but these are types of character and not faults of character. Your judgment of my act will also be different, in this respect. You will admit that so long as I hold my moral position, I have a moral right to vote against the homosexual, because I have a right (indeed a duty) to vote my own convictions. You would not admit such a right (or duty) if you were still persuaded that I was acting out of a prejudice or a personal taste.

I am entitled to expect that your opinion will change in these ways, because these distinctions are a part of the conventional morality you and I share, and which forms the background for our discussion. They enforce the difference between positions we must respect, although we think them wrong, and positions we need not respect because they offend some ground rule of moral reasoning. A great deal of debate about moral issues (in real life, although not in philosophy texts) consists of arguments that some position falls on one or the other side of this crucial line.

It is this feature of conventional morality that animates Lord Devlin's argument that society has the right to follow its own lights. We must therefore examine that discriminatory concept of a moral position more closely, and we can do so by pursuing our imaginary conversation. What must I do to convince you that my position is a moral position?

(a) I must produce some reasons for it. This is not to say that I have to articulate a moral principle I am following or a general moral theory to which I subscribe. Very few people can do either, and the ability to hold a moral position is not limited to those who can. My reason need not be a principle or theory at all. It must only point out some aspect or feature of homosexuality which moves me to regard it as immoral: the fact that the Bible forbids it, for example, or that one who practices homosexuality becomes unfit for marriage and parenthood. Of course, any such reason would presuppose my acceptance of some general principle or theory, but I need not be able to state what it is, or realize that I am relying upon it.

Not every reason I might give will do, however. Some will be excluded by general criteria stipulating sorts of reasons which do not count. We might take note of four of the most important such criteria:

(i) If I tell you that homosexuals are morally inferior because they do not have heterosexual desires, and so are not 'real men', you would reject that reason as showing one type of prejudice. Prejudices, in general, are postures of judgment that take into account considerations our conventions exclude. In a structured context, like a trial or a contest, the ground rules exclude all but certain considerations, and a prejudice is a basis of judgment which violates these rules. Our conventions stipulate some ground rules of moral judgment which obtain even apart from such special contexts, the most important of which is that a man must not be held morally inferior on the basis of some physical, racial or other characteristic he cannot help having. Thus a man whose moral judgments about Jews, or Negroes, or Southerners, or women, or effeminate men are based on his belief that any member of these classes automatically deserves less respect, without regard to anything he himself has done, is said to be prejudiced against that group.

(ii) If I base my view about homosexuals on a personal emotional reaction ('they make me sick') you would reject that reason as well. We distinguish moral positions from emotional reactions, not because moral positions are supposed to be unemotional or dispassionate – quite the reverse is true – but because the moral position is supposed to justify the emotional reaction, and not vice versa. If a man is unable to produce such reasons, we do not deny the fact of his emotional involvement, which may have important social or political consequences, but we do not take this involvement as demonstrating his moral conviction. Indeed, it is just this sort of position – a severe emotional reaction to a practice or a situation for which one cannot account – that we tend to describe, in lay terms, as a phobia or an obsession.

(iii) If I base my position on a proposition of fact ('homosexual acts are physically debilitating') which is not only false, but is so implausible that it challenges the minimal standards of evidence and argument I generally accept and impose upon others, then you would regard my belief, even though sincere, as a form of rationalization, and disqualify my reason on that ground. (Rationalization is a complex concept, and also includes, as we shall see, the production of reasons which suggest general theories I do not accept.)

(iv) If I can argue for my own position only by citing the beliefs of others ('everyone knows homosexuality is a sin') you will conclude that I am parroting and not relying on a moral conviction of my own. With the possible (though complex) exception of a deity, there is no moral authority to which I can appeal and so automatically make my position a moral one. I must have my own reasons, though of course I may have been taught these reasons by others.

No doubt many readers will disagree with these thumbnail sketches of prejudice, mere emotional reaction, rationalization and parroting. Some may have their own theories of what these are. I want to emphasize now only that these are distinct concepts, whatever the details of the differences might be, and that they have a role in deciding whether to treat another's position as a moral conviction. They are not merely epithets to be pasted on positions we strongly dislike.

(b) Suppose I do produce a reason which is not disqualified on one of these (or on similar) grounds. That reason will presuppose some general moral principle or theory, even though I may not be able to state that principle or theory, and do not have it in mind when I speak. If I offer, as my reason, the fact that the Bible forbids homosexual acts, or that homosexual acts make it less likely that the actor will marry and raise children, I suggest that I accept the theory my reason presupposes, and you will not be satisfied that my position is a moral one if you believe that I do not. It may be a question of my sincerity – do I in fact believe that the injunctions of the Bible are morally binding as such, or that all men have a duty to procreate? Sincerity is not, however, the only issue, for consistency is also in point. I may believe that I accept one of these general positions, and be wrong, because my other beliefs, and my own conduct on other occasions, may be inconsistent with it. I may reject certain Biblical injunctions, or I may hold that men have a right to remain bachelors if they please or use contraceptives all their lives.

Of course, my general moral positions may have qualifications and exceptions. The difference between an exception and an inconsistency is that the former can be supported by reasons which presuppose other moral positions I can properly claim to hold. Suppose I condemn all homosexuals on Biblical authority, but not all fornicators. What reason can I offer for the distinction? If I can produce none which supports it, I cannot claim to accept the general position about Biblical authority. If I do produce a reason which seems to support the distinction, the same sorts of question may be asked about that reason as were asked about my original reply. What general position does the reason for my exception presuppose? Can I sincerely claim to accept that further general position? Suppose my reason, for example, is that fornication is now very common, and has been sanctioned by custom. Do I really believe that what is immoral becomes moral when it becomes popular? If not, and if I can produce no other reason for the distinction, I cannot claim to accept the general position that what the Bible condemns is immoral. Of course, I may be persuaded, when this is pointed out, to change my views on fornication. But you would be alert to the question of whether this is a genuine change of heart, or only a performance for the sake of the argument.

In principle there is no limit to these ramifications of my original claim, though of course, no actual argument is likely to pursue very many of them.

(c) But do I really have to have a reason to make my position a matter of moral conviction? Most men think that acts which cause unnecessary suffering, or break a serious promise with no excuse, are immoral, and yet they could give no reason for these beliefs. They feel that no reason is necessary, because they take it as axiomatic or self-evident that these are immoral acts. It seems contrary to common sense to deny that a position held in this way can be a moral position.

Yet there is an important difference between believing that one's position is self-evident and just not having a reason for one's position. The former presupposes a positive belief that no further reason is necessary, that the immorality of the act in question does not depend upon its social effects, or its effects on the character of the actor, or its proscription by a deity, or anything else, but follows from the nature of the act itself. The claim that a particular position is axiomatic, in other words, does supply a reason of a special sort, namely that the act is immoral in and of itself, and this special reason, like the others we considered, may be inconsistent with more general theories I hold.

The moral arguments we make presuppose not only moral principles, but also more abstract positions about moral reasoning. In particular, they presuppose positions about what kinds of acts can be immoral in and of themselves. When I criticize your moral opinions, or attempt to justify my own disregard of traditional moral rules I think are silly, I will likely proceed by denying that the act in question has any of the several features that can make an act immoral – that it involves no breach of an undertaking or duty, for example, harms no one including the actor, is not proscribed by any organized religion, and is not illegal. I proceed in this way because I assume that the ultimate grounds of immorality are limited to some such small set of very general standards. I may assert this assumption directly or it may emerge from the pattern of my argument. In either event, I will enforce it by calling positions which can claim no support from any of these ultimate standards *arbitrary*, as I should certainly do if you said that photography was immoral, for instance, or swimming. Even if I cannot articulate this underlying assumption, I shall still apply it, and since the ultimate criteria I recognize are among the most abstract of my moral standards, they will not vary much from those my neighbors recognize and apply. Although many who despise homosexuals are unable to say why, few would claim affirmatively that one needs no reason, for this would make their position, on their own standards, an arbitrary one.

(d) This anatomy of our argument could be continued, but it is already long enough to justify some conclusions. If the issue between us is whether my views on homosexuality amount to a moral position, and hence whether I am entitled to vote against a homosexual on that ground, I cannot settle the issue simply by reporting my feelings. You will want to consider the reasons I can produce to support my belief, and whether my other views and behavior are consistent with the theories these reasons presuppose. You will have, of course, to apply your own understanding, which may differ in detail from mine, of what a prejudice or a rationalization is, for example, and of when one view is inconsistent with another. You and I may end in disagreement over whether my position is a moral one, partly because of such differences in understanding, and partly because one is less likely to recognize these illegitimate grounds in himself than in others.

We must avoid the skeptical fallacy of passing from these facts to the conclusion that there is no such thing as a prejudice or a rationalization or an inconsistency, or that these terms mean merely that the one who uses them strongly dislikes the positions he describes this way. That would be like arguing that because different people have different understandings of what jealousy is, and can in good faith disagree about whether one of them is jealous, there is no such thing as jealousy, and one who says another is jealous merely means he dislikes him very much.

LORD DEVLIN'S MORALITY

We may now return to Lord Devlin's second argument. He argues that when legislators must decide a moral issue (as by his hypothesis they must when a practice threatens a valued social arrangement), they must follow any consensus of moral position which the community at large has reached, because this is required by the democratic principle, and because a community is entitled to follow its own lights. The argument would have some plausibility if Lord Devlin meant, in speaking of the moral consensus of the community, those positions which are moral positions in the discriminatory sense we have been exploring.

But he means nothing of the sort. His definition of a moral position shows he is using it in what I called the anthropological sense. The ordinary man whose opinion we must enforce, he says, '. . . is not expected to reason about anything and his judgment may be largely a matter of feeling.'[1] 'If the reasonable man believes,' he adds, 'that a practice is immoral and believes also – no matter whether the belief is right or wrong, so be it that it is honest and dispassionate – that no right-minded member of his society could think otherwise, then for the purpose of the law it is immoral.'[2] Elsewhere he quotes with approval Dean Rostow's attribution to him of the view that 'the common morality of a society at any time is a blend of custom and conviction, of reason

[1] Devlin 15.
[2] *Ibid.* 22-3.

and feeling, of experience and prejudice.'[1] His sense of what a moral conviction is emerges most clearly of all from the famous remark about homosexuals. If the ordinary man regards homosexuality 'as a vice so abominable that its mere presence is an offence',[2] this demonstrates for him that the ordinary man's feelings about homosexuals are a matter of moral conviction.[3]

His conclusions fail because they depend upon using 'moral position' in this anthropological sense. Even if it is true that most men think homosexuality an abominable vice and cannot tolerate its presence, it remains possible that this common opinion is a compound of prejudice (resting on the assumption that homosexuals are morally inferior creatures because they are effeminate), rationalization (based on assumptions of fact so unsupported that they challenge the community's own standards of rationality), and personal aversion (representing no conviction but merely blind hate rising from unacknowledged self-suspicion). It remains possible that the ordinary man could produce no reason for his view, but would simply parrot his neighbor who in turn parrots him, or that he would produce a reason which presupposes a general moral position he could not sincerely or consistently claim to hold. If so, the principles of democracy we follow do not call for the enforcement of the consensus, for the belief that prejudices, personal aversions and rationalizations do not justify restricting another's freedom itself occupies a critical and fundamental position in our popular morality. Nor would the bulk of the community then be entitled to follow its own lights, for the community does not extend that privilege to one who acts on the basis of prejudice, rationalization, or personal aversion. Indeed, the distinction between these and moral convictions, in the discriminatory sense, exists largely to mark off the former as the sort of positions one is not entitled to pursue.

A conscientious legislator who is told a moral consensus exists must test the credentials of that consensus. He cannot, of course, examine

---

[1] Rostow, 'The Enforcement of Morals', 1960 *Camb. L.J.* 174, 197; reprinted in E. V. Rostow, *The Sovereign Prerogative* 45, 78 (1962). Quoted in Devlin 95.

[2] *Ibid.* 17.

[3] In the preface (*Ibid.* viii) Lord Devlin acknowledges that the language of the original lecture might have placed 'too much emphasis on feeling and too little on reason', and he states that the legislator is entitled to disregard 'irrational' beliefs. He gives as an example of the latter the belief that homosexuality causes earthquakes, and asserts that the exclusion of irrationality 'is usually an easy and comparatively unimportant process'. I think it fair to conclude that this is all Lord Devlin would allow him to exclude. If I am wrong, and Lord Devlin would ask him to exclude prejudices, personal aversions, arbitrary stands and the rest as well, he should have said so, and attempted to work some of these distinctions out. If he had, his conclusions would have been different and would no doubt have met with a different reaction.

the beliefs or behavior of individual citizens; he cannot hold hearings on the Clapham omnibus. That is not the point.

The claim that a moral consensus exists is not itself based on a poll. It is based on an appeal to the legislator's sense of how his community reacts to some disfavored practice. But this same sense includes an awareness of the grounds on which that reaction is generally supported. If there has been a public debate involving the editorial columns, speeches of his colleagues, the testimony of interested groups, and his own correspondence, these will sharpen his awareness of what arguments and positions are in the field. He must sift these arguments and positions, trying to determine which are prejudices or rationalizations, which presuppose general principles or theories vast parts of the population could not be supposed to accept, and so on. It may be that when he has finished this process of reflection he will find that the claim of a moral consensus has not been made out. In the case of homosexuality, I expect, it would not be, and that is what makes Lord Devlin's undiscriminating hypothetical so serious a misstatement. What is shocking and wrong is not his idea that the community's morality counts, but his idea of what counts as the community's morality.

Of course the legislator must apply these tests for himself. If he shares the popular views he is less likely to find them wanting, though if he is self-critical the exercise may convert him. His answer, in any event, will depend upon his own understanding of what our shared morality requires. That is inevitable, for whatever criteria we urge him to apply, he can apply them only as he understands them.

A legislator who proceeds in this way, who refuses to take popular indignation, intolerance and disgust as the moral conviction of his community, is not guilty of moral elitism. He is not simply setting his own educated views against those of a vast public which rejects them. He is doing his best to enforce a distinct, and fundamentally important, part of his community's morality, a consensus more essential to society's existence in the form we know it than the opinion Lord Devlin bids him follow.

No legislator can afford to ignore the public's outrage. It is a fact he must reckon with. It will set the boundaries of what is politically feasible, and it will determine his strategies of persuasion and enforcement within these boundaries. But we must not confuse strategy with justice, nor facts of political life with principles of political morality. Lord Devlin understands these distinctions, but his arguments will appeal most, I am afraid, to those who do not.

POSTSCRIPT ON PORNOGRAPHY

I have been discussing homosexuality because that is Lord Devlin's example. I should like to say a word about pornography, if only because it was, at the time of Britain's concern over Lord Devlin's theories, more in the American legal headlines than homosexuality. The Supreme Court had just decided three important cases: *Ginzburg, Mishkin* and *Fanny Hill*.[1] In two of these, convictions (and jail sentences) for the distribution of pornography were upheld, and in the third, while the Court reversed a state ban on an allegedly obscene novel, three justices dissented.

Two of the cases involved review of state procedures for constitutionality, and the third the interpretation and application of a federal statute. The Court therefore had to pass on the constitutional question of how far a state or the nation may legally restrict the publication of erotic literature, and on questions of statutory construction. But each decision nevertheless raised issues of political principle of the sort we have been considering.

A majority of the Court adhered to the constitutional test laid down some years ago by *Roth*.[2] Under that test, a book was obscene and as such not protected by the first amendment, if: '(a) the dominant theme of the material taken as a whole appeals to a prurient interest in sex; (b) the material is patently offensive because it affronts contemporary community standards relating to the description or representation of sexual matters; and (c) the material is utterly without redeeming social value.'[3] We might put the question of political principle this way: What gives the federal government, or any state, the moral right to prohibit the publication of books which are obscene under the *Roth* test?

Justice Brennan's opinion in *Mishkin* floated one answer: erotic literature, he said, incites some readers to crime. If this is true, if in a significant number of such cases the same readers would not have been incited to the same crime by other stimuli, and if the problem cannot effectively be handled in other ways, this might give society a warrant to ban these books. But these are at least speculative hypotheses, and in any event they are not pertinent to a case like *Ginzburg*, in which the Court based its decision not on the obscene character of the publications themselves, but on the fact that they were presented to the public as salacious rather than enlightening. Can any other justification be given for the prohibition of obscene books?

An argument like Lord Devlin's second argument can be constructed, and many of those who feel society is entitled to ban pornography are

[1] Above, n. 2.
[2] *Roth v. United States*, 354 U.S. 476 (1957).
[3] *Memoirs v. Massachusetts (Fanny Hill)*, 383 U.S. 413, 418 (1966).

in fact moved by some such argument. It might take this form :

(1) If we permit obscene books freely to be sold, to be delivered as it were with the morning milk, the whole tone of the community will eventually change. That which is now thought filthy and vulgar in speech and dress, and in public behavior, will become acceptable. A public which could enjoy pornography legally would soon settle for nothing very much tamer, and all forms of popular culture would inevitably move closer to the salacious. We have seen these forces at work already – the same relaxations in our legal attitudes which enabled books like *Tropic of Cancer* to be published have already had an effect on what we find in movies and magazines, on beaches and on the city streets. Perhaps we must pay that price for what many critics plausibly consider works of art, but we need not pay what would be a far greater price for trash – mass-manufactured for profit only.

(2) It is not a sufficient answer to say that social practices will not change unless the majority willingly participates in the change. Social corruption works through media and forces quite beyond the control of the mass of the people, indeed quite beyond the control of any conscious design at all. Of course, pornography attracts while it repels, and at some point in the deterioration of community standards the majority will not object to further deterioration, but that is a mark of the corruption's success, not proof that there has been no corruption. It is precisely that possibility which makes it imperative that we enforce our standards while we still have them. This is an example – it is not the only one – of our wishing the law to protect us from ourselves.

(3) Banning pornography abridges the freedom of authors, publishers and would-be readers. But if what they want to do is immoral, we are entitled to protect ourselves at that cost. Thus we are presented with a moral issue; does one have a moral right to publish or to read 'hardcore' pornography which can claim no value or virtue beyond its erotic effect? This moral issue should not be solved by fiat, nor by self-appointed ethical tutors, but by submission to the public. The public at present believes that hard-core pornography is immoral, that those who produce it are panderers, and that the protection of the community's sexual and related mores is sufficiently important to justify restricting their freedom.

But surely it is crucial to this argument, whatever else one might think of it, that the consensus described in the last sentence be a consensus of moral conviction. If it should turn out that the ordinary man's dislike of pornographers is a matter of taste, or an arbitrary stand, the argument would fail because these are not satisfactory reasons for abridging freedom.

It will strike many readers as paradoxical even to raise the question whether the average man's views on pornography are moral convictions. For most people the heart of morality is a sexual code, and if the ordinary man's views on fornication, adultery, sadism, exhibitionism and the other staples of pornography are not moral positions, it is hard to imagine any beliefs he is likely to have that are. But writing and reading about these adventures is not the same as performing in them, and one may be able to give reasons for condemning the practices (that they cause pain, or are sacrilegious, or insulting, or cause public annoyance) which do not extend to producing or savoring fantasies about them.

Those who claim a consensus of moral conviction on pornography must provide evidence that this exists. They must provide moral reasons or arguments which the average member of society might sincerely and consistently advance in the manner we have been describing. Perhaps this can be done, but it is no substitute simply to report that the ordinary man – within or without the jury box – turns his thumb down on the whole business.

Liberty and Liberalism

John Stuart Mill's famous essay *On Liberty* has on the whole served conservatives better than liberals. From Fitzjames Stephen to Wilmore Kendall and Lord Devlin, critics of liberalism have been pleased to cite the essay as the most cogent philosophical defense of that theory, and then, by noticing the defects in its argument, argue that liberalism is flawed. In *Liberty and Liberalism: The Case of John Stuart Mill*, Miss Gertrude Himmelfarb uses the essay in the same way, but with this difference. She does not attack Mill's arguments, but argues *ad hominem* against Mill himself. She says that he himself condemns, in his other writings, the philosophical premises upon which *On Liberty* is built. Friedrich Hayek made the same point years ago, and Miss Himmelfarb touched upon it in her 1962 edition of Mill's essays. Now she documents her case in great detail.

If, as she believes, *On Liberty* runs against the grain of everything Mill wrote before or after it, then it is necessary to explain why he took such time and care, in that essay, to refute himself. She finds the answer in his long association with Harriet Taylor, who had become his wife when *On Liberty* was written, though she died before it was published. Mill dedicated *On Liberty* to her in extravagant terms; he said that her ideas inspired the essay, and that she was an active collaborator in the long process of revising and polishing it. Miss Himmelfarb argues that this was understatement; that Miss Taylor was so much the dominant partner in the enterprise that she was able to drive him to unnatural intellectual positions. She also thinks that Miss Taylor's outrage, which provoked the essay, was generated by the legal and social subjugation of women in Victorian England, a topic hardly mentioned in the essay, but of great concern to Miss Taylor.

But her only argument in favor of the hypothesis that Miss Taylor took over Mill's mind is that no other explanation of the inconsistency in his thought can be found. There is no direct evidence, either internal or external to the essay. Miss Himmelfarb claims that the lack of internal evidence only shows how intimate the collaboration was, and explains the absence of external evidence by noticing that the Mills lived in isolation from all friends while the essay was being written. If there is in fact no genuine inconsistency between *On Liberty* and Mill's other work, then no evidence remains for Miss Himmelfarb's interesting speculation.

Her argument for the supposed inconsistency is this. Mill discussed liberty not only in the famous essay but in many books and papers, including his autobiography, his early essay 'The Spirt of the Age', his famous essay on Coleridge, and his major work on utilitarianism. In these other works, he argues in favor of both complexity and historicism in political theory. He condemns Bentham, the founder of utilitarianism, for reducing social psychology and political theory to simple axioms. He deploys a pessimistic theory of human nature, emphasizes the value of cultural and historical constraints on egotism, and insists on the role of the state in educating its citizens away from individual appetite and toward social conscience.

But *On Liberty*, in Miss Himmelfarb's view, contradicts each of these propositions. It begins by asserting:

> one very simple principle, as entitled to govern absolutely the dealings of society with the individual in the way of compulsion and control. . . . That principle is, that the sole end for which mankind are warranted, individually or collectively, in interfering with the liberty of action of any of their number, is self-protection. That the only purpose for which power can be rightfully exercised over any member of a civilized community, against his will, is to prevent harm to others. His own good, either physical or moral, is not a sufficient warrant.

She condemns, first, the absolute character of this assertion: Mill is false to his own sophistication, she says, when he asserts that 'one very simple principle' can 'govern absolutely' the complex connections between society and individual. She then characterizes this simple principle as an 'extreme' claim for liberty in defiance of Mill's more characteristic claims for tradition and education. *On Liberty*, she says, encouraged individuals to 'prize and cultivate their personal desires, impulses, inclinations, and wills, to see these as the source of all good, the force behind individual and social well-being'; it supported a philosophy 'which recognized no higher, no more worthy subject than the individual, which made the individual the repository of wisdom and virtue, and which made the freedom of the individual the sole aim of social policy.' It did all this in the face of Mill's own philosophy, developed in other essays, that individuals achieve virtue and excellence through concern for others rather than attention to themselves.

Miss Himmelfarb's argument begins with a blunder from which it does not recover. It confuses the force of a principle with its range. Bentham's theories of human nature and utility, which Mill thought too simple, were absolute in their range. Bentham thought that every human act and decision was motivated by some calculation of pleasures and pains, and thought that every political decision should be made on that same calculation, that is, to maximize the net product of simple pleasure over pain for the community as a whole.

But Mill's principle is of very limited range. It speaks only to those relatively rare occasions when a government is asked to prohibit some act on the sole ground that the act is dangerous to the actor, like driving a motorcycle without a helmet. Or on the ground that it is offensive to community standards of morality, like practicing homosexuality or publishing or reading pornography. Such decisions form a very small part of the business of any responsible government. The principle says nothing about how the government shall distribute scarce resources like income or security or power, or even how it shall decide when to limit liberty for the sake of some other value. It does not counsel government, for example, to respect the liberty of conscience of draft resisters at the cost of military efficiency, or the liberty of protest at the cost of property damage, or the liberty of a land user at the cost of the nuisance he causes.

The more limited the range of a principle, the more plausibly it may be said to be absolute. Even the most sophisticated philosophers might believe, for example, that it is always wrong for the government gratuitously to insult one class of its citizens. Mill thought his principle was also sufficiently limited to be absolute, and though he may have been wrong in this he can hardly be said to be simple-minded or fanatical because he thought so.

Miss Himmelfarb's confusion between the range and force of Mill's principle is responsible for the curious argument of the last part of her book. In recent years, she says, liberals have carried that principle to its logical extreme, with results that show that they have not yet learned that 'absolute liberty may corrupt absolutely' and that 'A populace that cannot respect principles of prudence and moderation is bound to behave so imprudently and immoderately as to violate every other principle, including the principle of liberty.' But her own account hardly suggests any connection between Mill and any social disorder. She says, for example, that the radical 'counterculture' celebrates spontaneity, and she therefore claims it as Mill's creature. But she concedes that the language of this 'counterculture' emphasizes community more than individuality. She might have added that its proponents have held liberalism in general, and Mill in particular, in special contempt, and have much preferred such writers as Marcuse, whose hostility to *On Liberty* they find congenial.

Her other evidence of social corruption is limited to familiar examples of sexual explicitness. It is true that laws punishing homosexuals have been relaxed, that *Deep Throat* was shown uncut in some cities, and that there are more naked bathers on the beach than there used to be. But these are not threats to any principle of justice. The genuine damage we have suffered to liberty, like Harvard's refusal and Yale's inability to allow Professor Shockley to speak, suggest not too much attention to Mill but too little.

Miss Himmelfarb believes that these changes in sexual mores are previews or symptoms of a more general social anarchy and lawlessness. She thinks that Mill introduced a new and consuming *idea* of liberty; that his own distinction, between decisions affecting oneself and decisions affecting others, was simply an arbitrary and illogical line he drew to contain this corrosive idea; that since this line cannot hold, the idea must soon expand into violence and anarchy, into the absolute corruption that absolute liberty guarantees. Only her sense that Mill's principle has this inner logic and inevitable consequence, that its inherent range as well as its force must be absolute, can explain the rhetoric of the last third of her book.

But her argument, whatever its other defects, betrays a huge misunderstanding of *On Liberty*; it confuses two concepts of liberty and assigns the wrong one to Mill's essay. It does not distinguish between the idea of liberty as license, that is, the degree to which a person is free from social or legal constraint to do what he might wish to do, and liberty as independence, that is, the status of a person as independent and equal rather than subservient. These two ideas are of course closely related. If a person is much cramped by legal and social constraints, then that is strong evidence, at least, that he is in a politically inferior position to some group that uses its power over him to impose those constraints. But the two ideas are nevertheless different in very important ways.

Liberty as license is an indiscriminate concept because it does not distinguish among forms of behavior. Every prescriptive law diminishes a citizen's liberty as license: good laws, like laws prohibiting murder, diminish this liberty in the same way, and possibly to a greater degree, as bad laws, like laws prohibiting political speech. The question raised by any such law is not whether it attacks liberty, which it does, but whether the attack is justified by some competing value, like equality or safety or public amenity. If a social philosopher places a very high value on liberty as license, he may be understood as arguing for a lower relative value for these competing values. If he defends freedom of speech, for example, by some general argument in favor of license, then his argument also supports, at least *pro tanto*, freedom to form monopolies or smash storefront windows.

But liberty as independence is not an indiscriminate concept in that way. It may well be, for example, that laws against murder or monopoly do not threaten, but are necessary to protect, the political independence of citizens generally. If a social philosopher places a high value on liberty as independence he is not necessarily denigrating values like safety or amenity, even in a relative way. If he argues for freedom of speech, for example, on some general argument in favor of independence and equality, he does not automatically argue in favor of greater license when these other values are not at stake.

Miss Himmelfarb's argument, that the inner logic of Mill's principle threatens anarchy, assumes that the principle promotes liberty as license. In fact it promotes the more complex idea of liberty as independence. Bentham and Mill's father, John Mill, thought that political independence would be sufficiently secured by wide distribution of the right to vote and other political liberties: that is, by democracy. Mill saw independence as a further dimension of equality; he argued that an individual's independence is threatened, not simply by a political process that denies him equal voice, but by political decisions that deny him equal respect. Laws that recognize and protect common interests, like laws against violence and monopoly, offer no insult to any class or individual; but laws that constrain one man, on the sole ground that he is incompetent to decide what is right for himself, are profoundly insulting to him. They make him intellectually and morally subservient to the conformists who form the majority, and deny him the independence to which he is entitled. Mill insisted on the political importance of these moral concepts of dignity, personality, and insult. It was these complex ideas, not the simpler idea of license, that he tried to make available for political theory, and to use as the basic vocabulary of liberalism.

This distinction between acts that are self-regarding and those that are other-regarding was not an arbitrary compromise between the claims of license and other values. It was intended to define political independence, because it marked the line between regulation that connoted equal respect and regulation that denied it. That explains why he had such difficulty making the distinction, and why he drew it in different ways on different occasions. He conceded what his critics have always labored: that any act, no matter how personal, may have important effects on others. He acknowledged, for example, that if a man drinks himself sick, this act will cause pain to well-meaning men and women who will grieve at the waste of human life. The decision to drink is nevertheless self-regarding, not because these consequences are not real or socially important, but because they work, as Mill says, *through* the personality of the actor. We could not suppose that society has a right to be free from sympathy or regret without supposing that it has a right to decide what sort of personality its members shall have, and it is this right that Mill thought incompatible with freedom.

Once these two concepts of liberty are distinguished then Miss Himmelfarb's argument, that Mill contradicts *On Liberty* in other essays, collapses. She quotes, for example, this passage from one of his early papers:

> Liberty in its original sense, means freedom from restraint. In this sense, every law, and every rule of morals, is contrary to liberty. A despot, who is entirely emancipated from both, is the only person whose freedom of action is complete. A measure of government, therefore, is not necessarily bad, because it is contrary to liberty; and to blame it for that reason leads to confusion of ideas.

The 'original' sense of liberty the youthful Mill had in mind was, of course, liberty as license, and nothing here contradicts *On Liberty*, either in letter or in spirit. She also cites passages from the essay on Coleridge in which Mill includes, as among the functions of education in a good society, 'To train the human being in the habit, and thence the power, of subordinating his personal impulses and aims, to what were considered the ends of society. . . .' But educating men to accept the aims of society is educating them to accept constraints on license in order to respect the interests of others, not to subordinate their own personality when these interests are not in play.

She cites Mill's approval, in the same essay, of the feeling of nationality, that is, of a common public philosophy, and she suggests that that sort of nationality is opposed to the individuality of *On Liberty*. But she fails to mention Mill's immediate proviso that 'the only shape in which [that] feeling is likely to exist hereafter' is as a common respect for 'principles of individual freedom and social equality, as realized in institutions which as yet exist nowhere, or exist only in a rudimentary state.' Nor does she mention that in the Coleridge essay he described education and nationality not as compromises with the *philosophe's* goals of liberty but as conditions under which that goal might be achieved, as conditions necessary, that is, for 'vigor and manliness of character' to be preserved. Each essay Miss Himmelfarb mentions confirms rather than contradicts the point of *On Liberty*, that independence of personality must be distinguished from license and anarchy, and established as a special and distinct condition of a just society.

If she had understood this she would not have repeated the silly proposition that true liberals must respect economic as well as intellectual liberty, nor would she have taxed Mill, who was a socialist, with inconsistency in that respect as well. Economic license and intellectual liberty must stand on the same footing only if liberty means license; they are plainly distinguishable, and at some point inconsistent, if liberty means independence.

The Supreme Court confused these two ideas, decades ago, when it decided, temporarily, that if the Constitution protects liberty at all it must protect the liberty of an employer to hire workers on such terms as he wishes. Conservatives confuse these ideas when they use 'permissiveness' to describe both sexual independence and political violence and to suggest that these differ only in degree. Radicals confuse these ideas when they identify liberalism with capitalism, and therefore suppose that individual rights are responsible for social injustice. Mill's collected works are not the source of that sort of confusion, but its antidote.

12

What Rights Do We Have?

Do we have a right to liberty?[1] Thomas Jefferson thought so, and since his day the right to liberty has received more play than the competing rights he mentioned to life and the pursuit of happiness. Liberty gave its name to the most influential political movement of the last century, and many of those who now despise liberals do so on the ground that they are not sufficiently libertarian. Of course, almost everyone concedes that the right to liberty is not the only political right, and that therefore claims to freedom must be limited, for example, by restraints that protect the security or property of others. Nevertheless the consensus in favor of some right to liberty is a vast one, though it is, as I shall argue in this chapter, misguided.

The right to liberty is popular all over this political spectrum. The rhetoric of liberty fuels every radical movement from international wars of liberation to campaigns for sexual freedom and women's liberation. But liberty has been even more prominent in conservative service. Even the mild social reorganizations of the anti-trust and unionization movements, and of the early New Deal, were opposed on the grounds that they infringed the right to liberty, and just now efforts to achieve some racial justice in America through techniques like the busing of black and white schoolchildren, and social justice in Britain through constraints in private education are bitterly opposed on that ground.

It has become common, indeed, to describe the great social issues of domestic politics, and in particular the racial issue, as presenting a conflict between the demands of liberty and equality. It may be, it is said, that the poor and the black and the uneducated and the unskilled have an abstract right to equality, but the prosperous and the whites and the educated and the able have a right to liberty as well and any efforts at social reorganization in aid of the first set of rights must reckon with and respect the second. Everyone except extremists recognizes, therefore, the need to compromise between equality and liberty. Every

[1] I use 'liberty' in this essay in the sense Isaiah Berlin called 'negative'.

piece of important social legislation, from tax policy to integration plans, is shaped by the supposed tension between these two goals.

I have this supposed conflict between equality and liberty in mind when I ask whether we have a *right* to liberty, as Jefferson and everyone else has supposed. That is a crucial question. If freedom to choose one's schools, or employees, or neighborhood is simply something that we all want, like air conditioning or lobsters, then we are not entitled to hang on to these freedoms in the face of what we concede to be the rights of others to an equal share of respect and resources. But if we can say, not simply that we want these freedoms, but that we are ourselves entitled to them, then we have established at least a basis for demanding a compromise.

There is now a movement, for example, in favor of a proposed amendment to the constitution of the United States that would guarantee every school child the legal right to attend a 'neighborhood school' and thus outlaw busing. The suggestion, that neighborhood schools somehow rank with jury trials as constitutional values, would seem silly but for the sense many Americans have that forcing school children into buses is somehow as much an interference with the fundamental right to liberty as segregated schooling was an insult to equality. But that seems to me absurd; indeed it seems to me absurd to suppose that men and women have any general right to liberty at all, at least as liberty has traditionally been conceived by its champions.

I have in mind the traditional definition of liberty as the absence of constraints placed by a government upon what a man might do if he wants to. Isaiah Berlin, in the most famous modern essay on liberty, put the matter this way: 'The sense of freedom, in which I use this term, entails not simply the absence of frustration but the absence of obstacles to possible choices and activities – absence of obstructions on roads along which a man can decide to walk.' This conception of liberty as license is neutral amongst the various activities a man might pursue, the various roads he might wish to walk. It diminishes a man's liberty when we prevent him from talking or making love as he wishes, but it also diminishes his liberty when we prevent him from murdering or defaming others. These latter constraints may be justifiable, but only because they are compromises necessary to protect the liberty or security of others, and not because they do not, in themselves, infringe the independent value of liberty. Bentham said that any law whatsoever is an 'infraction' of liberty, and though some such infractions might be necessary, it is obscurantist to pretend that they are not infractions after all. In this neutral, all embracing sense of liberty as license, liberty and equality are plainly in competition. Laws are needed to protect equality, and laws are inevitably compromises of liberty.

Liberals like Berlin are content with this neutral sense of liberty, because it seems to encourage clear thinking. It allows us to identify just what is lost, though perhaps unavoidably, when men accept constraints on their actions for some other goal or value. It would be an intolerable muddle, on this view, to use the concept of liberty or freedom in such a way that we counted a loss of freedom only when men were prevented from doing something that we thought they ought to do. It would allow totalitarian governments to masquerade as liberal, simply by arguing that they prevent men from doing only what is wrong. Worse, it would obscure the most distinctive point of the liberal tradition, which is that interfering with a man's free choice to do what he might want to do is in and of itself an insult to humanity, a wrong that may be justified but can never be wiped away by competing considerations. For a true liberal, any constraint upon freedom is something that a decent government must regret, and keep to the minimum necessary to accommodate the other rights of its constituents.

In spite of this tradition, however, the neutral sense of liberty seems to me to have caused more confusion than it has cured, particularly when it is joined to the popular and inspiring idea that men and women have a right to liberty. For we can maintain that idea only by so watering down the idea of a right that the right to liberty is something hardly worth having at all.

The term 'right' is used in politics and philosophy in many different senses, some of which I have tried to disentangle elsewhere.[1] In order sensibly to ask whether we have a right to liberty in the neutral sense, we must fix on some one meaning of 'right'. It would not be difficult to find a sense of that term in which we could say with some confidence that men have a right to liberty. We might say, for example, that someone has a right to liberty if it is in his interest to have liberty, that is, if he either wants it or if it would be good for him to have it. In this sense, I would be prepared to concede that citizens have a right to liberty. But in this sense I would also have to concede that they have a right, at least generally, to vanilla ice cream. My concession about liberty, moreover, would have very little value in political debate. I should want to claim, for example, that people have a right to equality in a much stronger sense, that they do not simply want equality but that they are entitled to it, and I would therefore not recognize the claim that some men and women want liberty as requiring any compromise in the efforts that I believe are necessary to give other men and women the equality to which they are entitled.

If the right to liberty is to play the role cut out for it in political

[1] See Chapter 7.

debate, therefore, it must be a right in a much stronger sense. In Chapter 7 I defined a strong sense of right that seems to me to capture the claims men mean to make when they appeal to political and moral rights. I do not propose to repeat my analysis here, but only to summarize it in this way. A successful claim of right, in the strong sense I described, has this consequence. If someone has a right to something, then it is wrong for the government to deny it to him even though it would be in the general interest to do so. This sense of a right (which might be called the anti-utilitarian concept of a right) seems to me very close to the sense of right principally used in political and legal writing and argument in recent years. It marks the distinctive concept of an individual right against the State which is the heart, for example, of constitutional theory in the United States.

I do not think that the right to liberty would come to very much, or have much power in political argument, if it relied on any sense of the right any weaker than that. If we settle on this concept of a right, however, then it seems plain that there exists no general right to liberty as such. I have no political right to drive up Lexington Avenue. If the government chooses to make Lexington Avenue one-way down town, it is a sufficient justification that this would be in the general interest, and it would be ridiculous for me to argue that for some reason it would nevertheless be wrong. The vast bulk of the laws which diminish my liberty are justified on utilitarian grounds, as being in the general interest or for the general welfare; if, as Bentham supposes, each of these laws diminishes my liberty, they nevertheless do not take away from me any thing that I have a right to have. It will not do, in the one-way street case, to say that although I have a right to drive up Lexington Avenue, nevertheless the government for special reasons is justified in overriding that right. That seems silly because the government needs no special justification – but only *a* justification – for this sort of legislation. So I can have a political right to liberty, such that every act of constraint diminishes or infringes that right, only in such a weak sense of right that the so called right to liberty is not competitive with strong rights, like the right to equality, at all. In any strong sense of right, which would be competitive with the right to equality, there exists no general right to liberty at all.

It may now be said that I have misunderstood the claim that there is a right to liberty. It does not mean to argue, it will be said, that there is a right to all liberty, but simply to important or basic liberties. Every law is, as Bentham said, an infraction of liberty, but we have a right to be protected against only fundamental or serious infractions. If the constraint on liberty is serious or severe enough, then it is indeed true that the government is not entitled to impose that constraint simply because that would be in the general interest; the government is not entitled to constrain liberty of speech, for example, whenever it thinks that would improve the general welfare. So there is, after all, a general right to liberty as such, provided that that right is restricted to important liberties or serious deprivations. This qualification does not affect the political arguments I described earlier, it will be said, because the rights to liberty that stand in the way of full equality are rights to basic liberties like, for example, the right to attend a school of one's choice.

But this qualification raises an issue of great importance for liberal theory, which those who argue for a right to liberty do not face. What does it mean to say that the right to liberty is limited to basic liberties, or that it offers protection only against serious infractions of liberty? That claim might be spelled out in two different ways, with very different theoretical and practical consequences. Let us suppose two cases in which government constrains a citizen from doing what he might want to do: the government prevents him from speaking his mind on political issues; from driving his car uptown on Lexington Avenue. What is the connection between these two cases, and the difference between them, such that though they are both cases in which a citizen is constrained and deprived of liberty, his right to liberty is infringed only in the first, and not in the second?

On the first of the two theories we might consider, the citizen is deprived of the same commodity, namely liberty, in both cases, but the difference is that in the first case the amount of that commodity taken away from him is, for some reason, either greater in amount or greater in its impact than in the second. But that seems bizarre. It is very difficult to think of liberty as a commodity. If we do try to give liberty some operational sense, such that we can measure the relative diminution of liberty occasioned by different sorts of laws or constraints, then the result is unlikely to match our intuitive sense of what are basic liberties and what are not. Suppose, for example, we measure a diminution in liberty by calculating the extent of frustration that it induces. We shall then have to face the fact that laws against theft, and even traffic laws, impose constraints that are felt more keenly by most men than constraints on political speech would be. We might take a different tack, and measure the degree of loss of liberty by the impact that a particular constraint has on future choices. But we should then have to admit that the ordinary criminal code reduces choice for most men more than laws which forbid fringe political activity. So the first theory – that the difference between cases covered and those not covered by our supposed right to liberty is a matter of degree – must fail.

The second theory argues that the difference between the two cases has to do, not with the degree of liberty involved, but with the special character of the liberty involved in the case covered by the right. On this theory, the offense involved in a law that limits free speech is of a different character, and not just different in degree, from a law that prevents a man from driving up Lexington Avenue. That sounds plausible, though as we shall see it is not easy to state what this difference in character comes to, or why it argues for a right in some cases though not in others. My present point, however, is that if the distinction between basic liberties and other liberties is defended in this way, then the notion of a general right to liberty as such has been entirely abandoned. If we have a right to basic liberties not because they are cases in which the commodity of liberty is somehow especially at stake, but because an assault on basic liberties injures us or demeans us in some way that goes beyond its impact on liberty, then what we have a right to is not liberty at all, but to the values or interests or standing that this particular constraint defeats.

This is not simply a question of terminology. The idea of a right to liberty is a misconceived concept that does a dis-service to political thought in at least two ways. First, the idea creates a false sense of a necessary conflict between liberty and other values when social regulation, like the busing program, is proposed. Second, the idea provides too easy an answer to the question of why we regard certain kinds of restraints, like the restraint on free speech or the exercise of religion, as especially unjust. The idea of a right to liberty allows us to say that these constraints are unjust because they have a special impact on liberty as such. Once we recognize that this answer is spurious, then we shall have to face the difficult question of what is indeed at stake in these cases.

I should like to turn at once to that question. If there is no general right to liberty, then why do citizens in a democracy have rights to any specific kind of liberty, like freedom of speech or religion or political activity? It is no answer to say that if individuals have these rights, then the community will be better off in the long run as a whole. This idea – that individual rights may lead to overall utility – may or may not be true, but it is irrelevant to the defence of rights as such, because when we say that someone has a right to speak his mind freely, in the relevant political sense, we mean that he is entitled to do so even if this would not be in the general interest. If we want to defend individual rights in the sense in which we claim them, then we must try to discover something beyond utility that argues for these rights.

I mentioned one possibility earlier. We might be able to make out a case that individuals suffer some special damage when the traditional rights are invaded. On this argument, there is something about the liberty to speak out on political issues such that if that liberty is denied the individual suffers a special kind of damage which makes it wrong to inflict that damage upon him even though the community as a whole would benefit. This line of argument will appeal to those who themselves would feel special deprivation at the loss of their political and civil liberties, but it is nevertheless a difficult argument to pursue for two reasons.

First, there are a great many men and women and they undoubtedly form the majority even in democracies like Britain and the United States, who do not exercise political liberties that they have, and who would not count the loss of these liberties as especially grievous. Second, we lack a psychological theory which would justify and explain the idea that the loss of civil liberties, or any particular liberties, involves inevitable or even likely psychological damage. On the contrary, there is now a lively tradition in psychology, led by psychologists like Ronald Laing, who argue that a good deal of mental instability in modern societies may be traced to the demand for too much liberty rather than too little. In their account, the need to choose, which follows from liberty, is an unnecessary source of destructive tension. These theories are not necessarily persuasive, but until we can be confident that they are wrong, we cannot assume that psychology demonstrates the opposite, however appealing that might be on political grounds.

If we want to argue for a right to certain liberties, therefore, we must find another ground. We must argue on grounds of political morality that it is wrong to deprive individuals of these liberties, for some reason, apart from direct psychological damage, in spite of the fact that the common interest would be served by doing so. I put the matter this vaguely because there is no reason to assume, in advance, that only one kind of reason would support that moral position. It might be that a just society would recognize a variety of individual rights, some grounded on very different sorts of moral considerations from others. In what remains of this chapter I shall try to describe only one possible ground for rights. It does not follow that men and women in civil society have only the rights that the argument I shall make would support; but it does follow that they have at least these rights, and that is important enough.

2. THE RIGHT TO LIBERTIES

The central concept of my argument will be the concept not of liberty but of equality. I presume that we all accept the following postulates of political morality. Government must treat those whom it governs with concern, that is, as human beings who are capable of suffering and frustration, and with respect, that is, as human beings who are capable of forming and acting on intelligent conceptions of how their lives should be lived. Government must not only treat people with concern and respect, but with equal concern and respect. It must not distribute goods or opportunities unequally on the ground that some citizens are entitled to more because they are worthy of more concern. It must not constrain liberty on the ground that one citizen's conception of the good life of one group is nobler or superior to another's. These postulates, taken together, state what might be called the liberal conception of equality; but it is a conception of equality, not of liberty as license, that they state.

The sovereign question of political theory, within a state supposed to be governed by the liberal conception of equality, is the question of what inequalities in goods, opportunities and liberties are permitted in such a state, and why. The beginning of an answer lies in the following distinction. Citizens governed by the liberal conception of equality each have a right to equal concern and respect. But there are two different rights that might be comprehended by that abstract right. The first is the right to equal treatment, that is, to the same distribution of goods or opportunities as anyone else has or is given. The Supreme Court, in the Reapportionment Cases, held that citizens have a right to equal treatment in the distribution of voting power; it held that one man must be given one vote in spite of the fact that a different distribution of votes might in fact work for the general benefit. The second is the right to treatment as an equal. This is the right, not to an equal distribution of some good or opportunity, but the right to equal concern and respect in the political decision about how these goods and opportunities are to be distributed. Suppose the question is raised whether an economic policy that injures long-term bondholders is in the general interest. Those who will be injured have a right that their prospective loss be taken into account in deciding whether the general interest is served by the policy. They may not simply be ignored in that calculation. But when their interest is taken into account it may nevertheless be outweighed by the interests of others who will gain from the policy, and in that case their right to equal concern and respect, so defined, would provide no objection. In the case of economic policy, therefore, we might wish to say that those who will be injured if inflation is permitted have a right to treatment as equals in the decision whether that policy would serve the general interest, but no right to equal treatment that would outlaw the policy even if it passed that test.

I propose that the right to treatment as an equal must be taken to be fundamental under the liberal conception of equality, and that the more restrictive right to equal treatment holds only in those special circumstances in which, for some special reason, it follows from the more fundamental right, as perhaps it does in the special circumstance of the Reapportionment Cases. I also propose that individual rights to distinct liberties must be recognized only when the fundamental right to treatment as an equal can be shown to require these rights. If this is correct, then the right to distinct liberties does not conflict with any supposed competing right to equality, but on the contrary follows from a conception of equality conceded to be more fundamental.

I must now show, however, how the familiar rights to distinct liberties – those established, for example, in the United States constitution – might be thought to be required by that fundamental conception of equality. I shall try to do this, for present purposes, only by providing a skeleton of the more elaborate argument that would have to be made to defend any particular liberty on this basis, and then show why it would be plausible to expect that the more familiar political and civil liberties would be supported by such an argument if it were in fact made.

A government that respects the liberal conception of equality may properly constrain liberty only on certain very limited types of justification. I shall adopt, for purposes of making this point, the following crude typology of political justifications. There are, first, arguments of principle, which support a particular constraint on liberty on the argument that the constraint is required to protect the distinct right of some individual who will be injured by the exercise of the liberty. There are, second, arguments of policy, which support constraints on the different ground that such constraints are required to reach some overall political goal, that is, to realize some state of affairs in which the community as a whole, and not just certain individuals, are better off by virtue of the constraint. Arguments of policy might be further subdivided in this way. Utilitarian arguments of policy argue that the community as a whole will be better off because (to put the point roughly) more of its citizens will have more of what they want overall, even though some of them will have less. Ideal arguments of policy, on the other hand, argue that the community will be better off, not because more of its members will have more of what they want, but because the community will be in some way closer to an ideal community, whether its members desire the improvement in question or not.

The liberal conception of equality sharply limits the extent to which ideal arguments of policy may be used to justify any constraint on liberty. Such arguments cannot be used if the idea in question is itself controversial within the community. Constraints cannot be defended, for example, directly on the ground that they contribute to a culturally sophisticated community, whether the community wants the sophistication or not, because that argument would violate the canon of the liberal conception of equality that prohibits a government from relying on the claim that certain forms of life are inherently more valuable than others.

Utilitarian arguments of policy, however, would seem secure from that objection. They do not suppose that any form of life is inherently more valuable than any other, but instead base their claim, that constraints on liberty are necessary to advance some collective goal of the community, just on the fact that that goal happens to be desired more widely or more deeply than any other. Utilitarian arguments of policy, therefore, seem not to oppose but on the contrary to embody the fundamental right of equal concern and respect, because they treat the wishes of each member of the community on a par with the wishes of any other, with no bonus or discount reflecting the view that that member is more or less worthy of concern, or his views more or less worthy of respect, than any other.

This appearance of egalitarianism has, I think, been the principal source of the great appeal that utilitarianism has had, as a general political philosophy, over the last century. In Chapter 9, however, I pointed out that the egalitarian character of a utilitarian argument is often an illusion. I will not repeat, but only summarize, my argument here.

Utilitarian arguments fix on the fact that a particular constraint on liberty will make more people happier, or satisfy more of their preferences, depending upon whether psychological or preference utilitarianism is in play. But people's overall preference for one policy rather than another may be seen to include, on further analysis, both preferences that are *personal*, because they state a preference for the assignment of one set of goods or opportunities to him and preferences that are *external*, because they state a preference for one assignment of goods or opportunities to others. But a utilitarian argument that assigns critical weight to the external preferences of members of the community will not be egalitarian in the sense under consideration. It will not respect the right of everyone to be treated with equal concern and respect.

Suppose, for example, that a number of individuals in the community holds racist rather than utilitarian political theories. They believe, not that each man is to count for one and no one for more than one in the distribution of goods, but rather that a black man is to count for less and a white man therefore to count for more than one. That is an external preference, but it is nevertheless a genuine preference for one policy rather than another, the satisfaction of which will bring pleasure. Nevertheless if this preference or pleasure is given the normal weight in a utilitarian calculation, and blacks suffer accordingly, then their own assignment of goods and opportunities will depend, not simply on the competition among personal preferences that abstract statements of utilitarianism suggest, but precisely on the fact that they are thought less worthy of concern and respect than others are.

Suppose, to take a different case, that many members of the community disapprove on moral grounds of homosexuality, or contraception, or pornography, or expressions of adherence to the Communist party. They prefer not only that they themselves do not indulge in these activities, but that no one else does so either, and they believe that a community that permits rather than prohibits these acts is inherently a worse community. These are external preferences, but, once again, they are no less genuine, nor less a source of pleasure when satisfied and displeasure when ignored, than purely personal preferences. Once again, however, if these external preferences are counted, so as to justify a constraint on liberty, then those constrained suffer, not simply because their personal preferences have lost in a competition for scarce resources with the personal preferences of others, but precisely because their conception of a proper or desirable form of life is despised by others.

These arguments justify the following important conclusion. If utilitarian arguments of policy are to be used to justify constraints on liberty, then care must be taken to insure that the utilitarian calculations on which the argument is based fix only on personal and ignore external preferences. That is an important conclusion for political theory because it shows, for example, why the arguments of John Stuart Mill in *On Liberty* are not counter-utilitarian but, on the contrary, arguments in service of the only defensible form of utilitarianism.

Important as that conclusion is at the level of political philosophy, however, it is in itself of limited practical significance, because it will be impossible to devise political procedures that will accurately discriminate between personal and external preferences. Representative democracy is widely thought to be the institutional structure most suited, in a complex and diverse society, to the identification and achievement of utilitarian policies. It works imperfectly at this, for the familiar reason that majoritarianism cannot sufficiently take acount of the intensity, as distinct from the number, of particular preferences, and because techniques of political persuasion, backed by money, may corrupt the accuracy with which votes represent the genuine preferences of those who have voted. Nevertheless democracy seems to enforce utilitarianism more satisfactorily, in spite of these imperfections, than any alternative general political scheme would.

But democracy cannot discriminate, within the overall preferences imperfectly revealed by voting, distinct personal and external components, so as to provide a method for enforcing the former while ignoring the latter. An actual vote in an election or referendum must be taken to represent an overall preference rather than some component of the preference that a skilful cross-examination of the individual voter, if time and expense permitted, would reveal. Personal and external preferences are sometimes so inextricably combined, moreover, that the discrimination is psychologically as well as institutionally impossible. That will be true, for example, in the case of the associational preferences that many people have for members of one race, or people of one talent or quality, rather than another, for this is a personal preference so parasitic upon external preferences that it is impossible to say, even as a matter of introspection, what personal preferences would remain if the underlying external preference were removed. It is also true of certain self-denying preferences that many individuals have; that is preferences for less of a certain good on the assumption, or rather proviso, that other people will have more. That is also a preference, however noble, that is parasitic upon external preferences, in the shape of political and moral theories, and they may no more be counted in a defensible utilitarian argument than less attractive preferences rooted in prejudice rather than altruism.

I wish now to propose the following general theory of rights. The concept of an individual political right, in the strong anti-utilitarian sense I distinguished earlier, is a response to the philosophical defects of a utilitarianism that counts external preferences and the practical imposibility of a utilitarianism that does not. It allows us to enjoy the institutions of political democracy, which enforce overall or unrefined utilitarianism, and yet protect the fundamental right of citizens to equal concern and respect by prohibiting decisions that seem, antecedently, likely to have been reached by virtue of the external components of the preferences democracy reveals.

It should be plain how this theory of rights might be used to support the idea, which is the subject of this chapter, that we have distinct rights to certain liberties like the liberty of free expression and of free choice in personal and sexual relations. It might be shown that any utilitarian constraint on these liberties must be based on overall preferences in the community that we know, from our general knowledge of society, are likely to contain large components of external preferences, in the shape of political or moral theories, which the political process cannot discriminate and eliminate. It is not, as I said, my present purpose to frame the arguments that would have to be made to defend particular rights to liberty in this way, but only to show the general character such arguments might have.

I do wish, however, to mention one alleged right that might be called into question by my general argument, which is the supposed individual right to the free use of property. In chapter 11 I complained about the argument, popular in certain quarters, that it is inconsistent for liberals to defend a liberty of speech, for example, and not also concede a parallel right of some sort of property and its use. There might be force in that argument if the claim, that we have a right of free speech, depended on the more general proposition that we have a right to something called liberty as such. But that general idea is untenable and incoherent; there is no such thing as any general right to liberty. The argument for any given specific liberty may therefore be entirely independent of the argument for any other, and there is no antecedent inconsistency or even implausibility in contending for one while disputing the other.

What can be said, on the general theory of rights I offer, for any particular right of property? What can be said, for example, in favor of the right to liberty of contract sustained by the Supreme Court in the famous *Lochner* case, and later regretted, not only by the court, but by liberals generally? I cannot think of any argument that a political decision to limit such a right, in the way in which minimum wage laws limited it, is antecedently likely to give effect to external preferences, and in that way offend the right of those whose liberty is curtailed to equal concern and respect. If, as I think, no such argument can be made out, then the alleged right does not exist; in any case there can be no inconsistency in denying that it exists while warmly defending a right to other liberties.

13

Can Rights be Controversial?

In this final chapter I must defend the arguments of the book against a pervasive and, if successful, destructive objection. My arguments suppose that there is often a single right answer to complex questions of law and political morality. The objection replies that there is sometimes no single right answer, but only answers.

An attractive attitude supports this objection. It is a mixture of tolerance and common sense, expressed in judgments like these. When men and women disagree about whether the right of free speech extends to abusive language, or whether capital punishment is cruel and unusual within the meaning of the constitution, or whether a group of inconclusive precedents establishes a right to recover for merely economic damage in tort, then it is both silly and arrogant to pretend that there is somehow, latent in the controversy, a single right answer. It is wiser and more realistic to concede that though some answers may be plainly wrong, and some arguments plainly bad, there is nevertheless a set of answers and arguments that must be acknowledged to be, from any objective or neutral standpoint, equally good.

If so, then the choice of one of these is just that: a choice rather than a decision forced by reason. If a prosecutor is required to decide whether protesters have a moral right to protest, or whether economic damage is recoverable in tort, then all the public is entitled to expect is that his choice will be made honestly and in a cool moment, free from bias or passion or zeal. It is not entitled to any particular decision, because that supposes that there is a single right answer to the question he must decide.

This book does not respect these modest sentiments. In Chapters 2 and 3, for example, I oppose the popular theory that judges have discretion to decide hard cases. I concede that principles of law are sometimes so well balanced that those favoring a decision for the plaintiff will seem stronger, taken together, to some lawyers but weaker to others. I argue that even so it makes perfect sense for each party to claim that it is entitled to win, and therefore each to deny that the judge has a discretion to find for the other. In Chapter 4 I describe a process of decision that gives content to that claim; but I do not claim (indeed I deny) that that process of decision will always yield the same decision in the hands of different judges. Nevertheless I insist that the process, even in hard cases, can sensibly be said to be aimed at discovering, rather than inventing, the rights of the parties concerned, and that the political justification of the process depends upon the soundness of that characterization.

So the no-right-answer thesis is hostile to the rights thesis I defend. The former is supported by the attractive attitude I described. Is it also supported by argument? We may distinguish two kinds of arguments that might be made. The first of these is practical. It concedes, arguendo, that there may be in principle one right answer to a controversial issue at law. But it insists that it is useless to say that the parties have a right to that answer, or that a judge has a duty to find it, since no one can be sure what the right answer is. Suppose I bet you that *Lear* is a better play than *Endgame*. Even if we are objectivists in aesthetics, and believe that there is, in principle, a right answer to the question, this is nevertheless a silly bet, because it can never be settled to the satisfaction of the losing party. It would be pointless to settle the bet by calling in a third party as umpire. He can offer no more than a third personal opinion, and the fact of that opinion would not (at least should not) convince either of us that he was wrong. So it is with a judge in a hard law suit. Even if there is, in principle, one best theory of law, and so one right answer to a hard case, that right answer is locked in legal philosopher's heaven, inaccessible to laymen, lawyers and judges alike. Each can have only his own opinion, and the opinion of the judge comes no more warranted for truth than the opinion of anyone else.

This practical argument for the 'no right answer' thesis is easily met. It argues that it is pointless to demand that a judge seek to find the right answer, even if there is one, because his answer is no more likely to be right than anyone else's, and because there is no way to prove that his is the right answer even if it is. We must be careful to distinguish the following three questions. (a) Do reasonable lawyers ever disagree whether a litigant in a hard case has a right to win, even after all the facts, including facts of institutional history, are agreed? (b) Is it possible that a litigant may have a right to win a hard case even though reasonable lawyers do disagree after all the facts are agreed? (c) Is it sensible or fair for the state to enforce the decision of a particular group of judges in a hard case, even though a different group, equally reasonable and competent, would have reached a different decision?

What logical relations should hold among positive answers to these three questions? The practical argument assumes that a positive answer to the first excludes a positive answer to the third, even given a positive answer to the second. But that is plainly wrong. It is clear that a positive answer to the second is necessary to a positive answer to the third. If the litigants in a hard case can have no right to a particular decision, it is both pointless and unfair to let the case between them be decided by a controversial (or for that matter uncontroversial) decision about the rights they have. It is also clear that a positive answer to the second is not in itself sufficient for a positive answer to the third. It is necessary also to be satisfied that, though the decision of any particular group of judges is fallible, and may never be proved right to the satisfaction of all other lawyers, it is nevertheless better to let that decision stand than to assign the decision to some other institution, or to ask judges to decide on grounds of policy, or in some other way that does not require their best judgment about the rights of the parties. But of course one might be satisfied of that in some way even after answering the first question 'yes'. There are many reasons (perfectly practical reasons among them) for asking judges to decide hard cases on their best judgment about rights even when that judgment cannot be demonstrated to be true to the satisfaction of all, and may in fact be false.

The practical argument assumes that the answer to the first question is decisive of the third. Let it once be conceded that rights may be controversial; the argument takes hold and insists that controversial rights can have no place in adjudication. But that is simplistic. The third question is comparative. Suppose (which may be contested) that a 'yes' answer to the first question counts against a 'yes' answer to the third. We would be happier with the rights thesis if there were no hard cases. It does not follow that we must reject the rights thesis if hard cases are inevitable. Everything depends on the alternatives. In Chapter 4 I described those alternatives and found them unappealing; none of them was more practical or more dependable than the rights thesis, and they were all a good deal less fair.

The second form of argument we must consider, which is theoretical rather than practical, is more powerful. It argues that the second of the three questions we distinguished must have a negative answer. If it is inherently controversial whether some party has a particular legal or political right, then, according to this argument, it cannot be true that he has this right.

I shall consider, in the balance of this chapter, whether that argument holds for legal rights. I want first to notice, however, how thoroughly the theoretical argument condemns ordinary practice, not only in law, but in a large variety of other enterprises as well. Historians and scientists, for example, suppose that what they say can be true even though it cannot be, in the way the theoretical argument requires, proved to be true. They have arguments to back their judgments, and they make and change opinion through these arguments. But these are not arguments that hang by chains of logic from uncontroversial premises. In Chapter 4 I described the position of a chess referee called upon to apply the rule that players must not annoy each other unreasonably. I said that a referee in that position would have to make a judgment about the character of the game of chess, and that reasonable referees might well disagree about the exact characterization that some particular issue might require. Suppose two referees do disagree: one judges (to recall the example of that chapter) that chess is a game of intelligence in a sense that excludes psychological intimidation and the other disagrees. The theoretical argument holds that neither opinion can be true; that there can be no answer to the question, but only answers, each of which must be as sound as the other. But of course the two referees who debate cannot look upon their argument that way, because that analysis leaves each with a theory about nothing. Each knows that the other disagrees, and that there is no common test that can adjudicate their dispute so as to dissolve the disagreement. But each nevertheless thinks his answer is a superior answer to the question that divides them: if he does not think that, then what does he think?

It adds nothing to say that each knows that his judgment represents a choice rather than a decision forced upon him by reason. His choice is a choice of (what seems to him) the best characterization; it is a choice forced upon him by his judgment just as surely as when the case is controversial, and others disagree, as when it is easy and they do not. Nor is it useful to stress that the choice is just *his* judgment, as if that somehow modified the character of the judgment he makes; indeed the last sentence might be changed by deleting the phrase in parentheses without changing either its sense or its truth. The referees might accept, as a sound piece of common sense, that there is no 'right answer' to their question. But if they take that proposition as a negative answer to the second, and not simply the first, of the three questions I distinguished, then their common sense makes no sense of what they do when they act as professionals and not as philosophers.

It does not follow, of course, that the 'no right answer' thesis is wrong. If some philosophical theory compels us to concede that a proposition cannot be true unless there is some agreed test through which its truth might be demonstrated, then so much the worse for ordinary experience, including ordinary legal experience. But happily the shoe is on the other foot. The theoretical argument is not so compelling that we must reject ordinary experience in its place. On the contrary it is unclear what the 'no right answer' thesis, as interpreted by the theoretical argument, even means.

2.

Suppose the judges of a particular jurisdiction met in convention and determined each to follow the rights thesis, and otherwise to decide cases as Hercules did in Chapter 4. They therefore agree to act as participants in an enterprise which stipulates certain truth conditions for propositions of law, like the proposition that capital punishment is not in itself cruel and unusual punishment, or that those who suffer merely economic damage from negligence may recover in tort. A proposition of law may be asserted as true if it is more consistent with the theory of law that best justifies settled law than the contrary proposition of law. It may be denied as false if it is less consistent with that theory of law than the contrary. Suppose that this enterprise proceeds with the ordinary success of modern legal systems. Judges often agree about the truth values of propositions of law, and when they disagree they understand the arguments of their opponents sufficiently well to be able to locate the level of disagreement, and to rank these arguments in rough order of plausibility.

Suppose now that a philosopher visits the next convention of these judges and tells them that they have made a very serious mistake. They seem to think that there is a right answer to a difficult question of law, whereas in fact there is no right answer but only answers. They are wrong to think that in hard cases any particular proposition of law may be true, so that its contrary is false. It may be (the philosopher adds) that there is some political value in propagating the myth that there is a right answer, and that they therefore have no discretion in deciding hard cases. But the judges must concede (at least among themselves) that the idea is indeed a myth.

Why should the judges be persuaded by what this philosopher says? His arguments are compromised, for a start, by the following consideration. Suppose the judges persuade the philosopher to attend law school for the standard period of three years, and then himself to take up a position on the bench for a period of several years thereafter. He will find that he himself will be able to form judgments of the sort he believes rest on mistake. He will find that one theory of law seems to him to provide a better justification of settled law than competetive theories. He will be able to provide reasons for that belief, even though he knows that others will not find these reasons conclusive. How can he say that, according to arguments he finds persuasive, economic damage may be recovered in tort, and yet deny that such a proposition can be true? How can he have reasons for his belief, and yet deny that anyone can have reasons for such a belief?

Suppose the philosopher says that though he has such beliefs he has these only because he has been trained in law and therefore joined an enterprise whose members have been seduced by their training into a myth. He denies that an independent observer, not himself a participant in the enterprise, would be able to decide that one participant's theories and judgments were superior to another's, at least in controversial cases. But what could he mean, here, by the idea of an independent observer? If he means someone who has had no legal training, then it is neither surprising nor relevant that such an observer would be incompetent to form opinions about what the participants do. If he means, on the other hand, someone who has had the requisite training, but has not been invited to sit as a judge, then it is wholly unclear why that lack of authority should affect that persons's capacity to form the judgments he would form if he had it.

So the philosopher's own capacities will embarrass him. He will have, moreover, a further, though related, problem. He wants to argue that neither of the parties in a hard case has a right to a decision in his favor. He will say, for example, that the plaintiff in *Spartan Steel*[1] does not have a right to recover for its economic damage, and also that the defendant does not have a right to be free from liability for that damage. He thinks that the proposition that a company in the position of the defendant is liable for economic damage is not true, though neither is the proposition that the defendant is not liable. Neither proposition is false (because that would make the other true) but neither is true. That is, presumably, the consequence of the no right answer thesis for the truth values of propositions.

Now none of this will necessarily seem strange or outrageous to the judges of the enterprise. Each of these judgments about the truth value of propositions of law is one that a judge might sensibly make, under certain conditions, *within the ground rules of the enterprise*. Suppose a judge thinks that the case for a theory of the relevant law that makes the defendant liable for economic damage is exactly as strong as the case for a theory that frees him from that liability. The rules of the enterprise, as so far described, acknowledge that situation as a theoretical possibility; and if that possibility is realized, then judges cannot, under these rules, assert either proposition as true or deny it as false. In any particular hard case, therefore, a judge may sensibly make, for that case, the same judgment as the philosopher seems to make for all hard cases.

[1] See Chapter 4.

The judgment that neither of these contrary propositions is true we may call the 'tie' judgment. We may now notice the following features of tie judgments, as judgments within the judge's enterprise. (a) The tie judgment is a judgment of the same character as the judgment that one or the other of these contrary propositions is true and the other false. We may conceive of a hard case as presenting, for each judge, a scale of confidence running from a left-hand point at which the judge is confident that the proposition favoring the plaintiff is true, through points at which he believes that proposition is true, but with progressively less confidence, to a right-hand side with points representing progressively more confidence that the proposition favouring the defendant is true. Then the tie point is the single point at the center of this scale. In a hard case judges may hold one of three views. Some may think that the case should be located at some point to the left of the center, others may think it should be located at some point to the right of center, and some may think that it should be located at the very center itself. But the tie judgment is a positive judgment of the same character as the other two. It is competitive with these, and makes exactly the same epistemological or ontological presuppositions (whatever these might be). We may say that the third judgment is a 'no right answer' judgment if we take that to mean simply that neither of the other two available answers is right; but the third judgment is a judgment that itself claims to be *the* right answer.

(b) Suppose a judge in the enterprise says (I) 'Neither the proposition that the defendant is liable (p) nor the proposition that he is not liable ($-$p) is true.' That does not mean the same thing as (II) 'I cannot see any difference in the case for (p) or ($-$p).' A judge who is in the position described by (II) can do no better, if he must decide while in that position, than to assert (I). It may even be that, for him, (II) counts as evidence of (I). But that is not the same thing as saying that (I) and (II) are identical. 'It seems to me that the case for the plaintiff is the stronger' is not the same as 'The case for the plaintiff is the stronger', even in the mouth of the same judge; so, and in the same way, is (II) different from (I). Suppose a judge says both (I) and (II) but later is persuaded, by a fellow judge, that in fact the case for the plaintiff is stronger than the case for the defendant. He will then say that, at the time of his earlier statements, (I) was false, but not, of course, (II).

I stress the difference between (I) and (II) to reinforce the point just made, that the so-called 'no right answer' answer, as a judgment within the enterprise, is a judgment of the same character, and is equally fallible, as either of the other available answers. It is not a residuary answer, or an answer in default, that is automatically true whenever no persuasive argument is available for any other answer, or whenever good arguments are available for both other answers. The judge who asserts (I) is making a leap from his own analysis to a conclusion that reports more than the fact of that analysis, just as a judge who finds for the plaintiff is making a leap from the fact of his own arguments to the conclusion that they are right.

We can imagine an enterprise in which the difference between (I) and (II) is less clear-cut. Suppose the management of a horse racing track purchases less than the most precise equipment for photo finishes. It might lay down a track rule that if a photograph taken by this equipment is so indistinct that it cannot be clearly established which horse won, then they shall be deemed to have tied, in spite of the fact that superior equipment might well have shown a winner. In that case, the proposition that the machine cannot distinguish a winner and the proposition that there is no winner come to the same thing. But that is not the enterprise the judges have established. Nothing in the rules of the enterprise provides that what strikes a particular judge or a particular group of judges as a tie is therefore a tie.

(c) The judgment, by a particular judge, that a case is a tie, and therefore offers 'no right answer' within the enterprise, is very likely to be controversial. We can speak, nevertheless, about the antecedent probability that the enterprise will produce many or few cases that are in fact ties. Suppose the legal system in which the judges operate is a primitive legal system: there are very few judicial precedents or statutes, and a very rudimentary constitution. It is probable, in advance of any particular judicial term, both that the judges will judge that several cases in that term are ties, and that in fact several cases will be ties. Since there is very little settled law, more than one theory of law, critically different for the result in a hard case, will often offer equally good justifications for the settled law, and will seem to offer equally good justifications to many judges.

But suppose, on the other hand, that the legal system these judges administer is very advanced, and is thick with constitutional rules and practices, and dense with precedents and statutes. The antecedent probability of a tie is very much lower; indeed it might well be so low as to justify a further ground rule of the enterprise which instructs judges to eliminate ties from the range of answers they might give. That instruction does not deny the theoretical possibility of a tie, but it does suppose that, given the complexity of the legal materials at hand, judges will, if they think long and hard enough, come to think that one side or the other has, all things considered and marginally, the better of the case. This further instruction will be rational if the antecedent probability of error in a judicial decision seems to be greater than the antecedent probability that some case will indeed be, in fact, a tie, and if there are advantages of finality or other political advantages to be gained by denying the possibility of tie cases at law. Of course, the instruction will be not rational but silly if the legal system is not sufficiently complex to justify that calculation of antecedent probabilities.

We may now return to the philosopher's claim that the judges are making a profound mistake by assuming that there can be a right answer in a hard case. If we take his claim to be a claim within the enterprise, such as a judge himself might make, then the claim is almost certainly false. It comes to this : the tie judgment is necessarily the right judgment in every single controversial case, that is, in every case in which one answer cannot be proved in a way that can only be challenged by the irrational. Now (unless the special instruction to ignore ties is part of the enterprise) every judge will concede that some hard cases may in fact be ties, but no judge will suppose that they all are ties. The philosopher, to support his claim against their opinion, would have to produce arguments affirmatively establishing that all hard cases will lie at the exact center of the scale we imagined, and that claim is so implausible that it can be set aside at once.

If the enterprise has adopted the special instruction just mentioned, then the philosopher's claim might be taken in a more modest way. He might oppose the rationality or reasonableness of that instruction, by arguing that the antecedent probability of a genuine tie is sufficiently great that it is silly to instruct judges to ignore that possibility. His claim then must be amended : he does not argue that there is no right answer in any hard case, but only that it is irrational to stipulate that there must be a right answer in every hard case. This more modest claim, which is a recommendation that the enterprise be amended so as to allow for ties, will deserve consideration, though the judges might do well to reject that recommendation if their system is sufficiently complex.

So if we take the philosopher's claim to be a claim made within the enterprise, in either of these two versions, then it is not a claim that need trouble the judges very long, for it is a claim that presupposes, rather than challenges, the fundamental soundness of their enterprise. The philosopher might object that his claim must not be construed as a claim within the enterprise; it must not be construed as a claim that the judges, faithful to the enterprise, may themselves make. It is rather a profound attack on the very rationality of the enterprise, and must be understood as such. But we must now face this crucial question. Is there any way to take the philosopher's claim *other than* as a claim within the judge's enterprise? How can we understand it as an external criticism of that entire enterprise?

There are two possibilities that seem open. We might take the philosopher's claim as a claim made from within a different judicial enterprise, which stipulates different truth conditions for propositions of law. Or we may take it as a claim external to all such enterprises, as a claim about facts of the real world which judges, whatever truth conditions they might choose for their propositions, must in the end respect. But neither of these two possibilities will serve the philosopher's purpose at all.

(1) We might easily imagine a legal enterprise in which the philosopher's judgment, that there is never a right answer in a hard case, is perfectly sound. Suppose a group of judges decided to observe the following rules. A proposition of law may be asserted as true if that proposition may be derived from settled law, on facts agreed or stipulated, simply by deduction. A proposition of law may be denied as false if its contrary may be derived from settled law, on facts agreed or stipulated, simply by deduction. Under these rules, in any hard case, neither the proposition of law favoring the plaintiff nor the proposition favoring the defendant may be asserted as true, and neither may be denied as false. There will be, in any hard case, no right answer in that sense.

But the enterprise conducted by the judges we imagine is plainly not that enterprise. So the philosopher's claim, however sound in some other enterprise, is irrelevant to this one. The philosopher may now say that *his* enterprise, just described, is the legal enterprise actually in force in, for example, Britain and the United States, and that the judges' enterprise I described is simply imaginary. In Chapter 4 I argued that the legal systems in force in those countries (and no doubt elsewhere) are actually very like the enterprise I have imagined here. If so, then the philosopher can hardly claim that his enterprise is more faithful to reality. But suppose I was wrong, and that his enterprise is more like those actually in play. The theoretical argument for the no right answer thesis was supposed to show that, in principle, there could be no single right answer to a hard case. But it now argues only that, as a matter of fact, familiar legal systems recognize truth conditions for propositions of law that do not permit a right answer in a hard case. That would be a much more modest claim, even if it were true, which it is not.

(2) Suppose the philosopher claims that he is speaking, not from within some alternate enterprise with different ground rules of assertion and denial, but about the real world. His argument is that there can be no right answer in fact to a hard case at law, so that if any legal enterprise adopts rules which presuppose that there can be, that enterprise is based on a myth. He reports, not a different enterprise, but objective facts that any enterprise must face if it is to be realistic.

But what is this objective reality? It must contain rights and duties, including legal rights and duties, as objective facts, independent of the structure or content of conventional systems. That idea is familiar in the theories of natural lawyers, but it is a surprising toy to find in the hands of the philosopher who argues, in the name of common sense, that there can be no right answer in a hard case. After all, if rights and duties are part of some objective and independent world, then why should we not suppose that someone can have a right even when no one else thinks he does, or when no one can prove he does?

So it is dangerous for our philosopher to claim that he speaks of objective legal reality whose truth conditions are independent of human convention. It is also dangerous in a different way. It threatens to make his most basic claim incomprehensible. He argues that (p) (The defendant is liable for economic damage) and (-p) (The defendant is not liable for economic damage) may neither be true though neither is false. How can we make sense of this? If liability is a matter of objective fact, independent of enterprises like those we have been describing, and if a proposition asserting a right of recovery (like (p)) is not true, it must be false.

We can *only* make sense of the philosopher's claim if we take it to report the special truth conditions of an enterprise. His claim would be sound, as I just conceded, in an enterprise having truth conditions which permitted an assertion or denial of a proposition only in an easy case. Then, in a hard case, a proposition of law could neither be asserted as true nor denied as false. Its falsity would not follow from the failure of its truth. In the enterprise our judges established (but without the special instruction forbidding ties) that condition remains a theoretical possibility, though the probability that it will actually occur, in a very developed legal system, is small. If the special instruction is added, then the rules forbid by fiat the combination of a failure to assert and a failure to deny, relying on a prediction that the failure to allow that combination will not, for the reasons I described, inhibit the operation of the enterprise. But without *some* special truth conditions, which enable us to resist the inference that if a proposition is not true then it is false, the no right answer thesis cannot be maintained at all.

I have made this same argument, but at much greater length, elsewhere, and those interested in the general question of whether there is aways a right answer to a question of law should pursue that longer argument.[1] I should mention, however, one possible objection to this portion of my argument not foreseen in that discussion. This appeals, in a general way, to an argument which is familiar among philosophers of language, namely that propositions about non-existent entities are neither

---

[1] 'No Right Answer', in *Law, Morality and Society: Essays in Honour of H. L. A. Hart*, London 1977.

true nor false. There is a tradition which argues that the proposition that the present King of France is bald is neither true nor false (though there is also a tradition which argues that this proposition, properly understood, is simply false). The proposition about the King of France does not seem to be a proposition which can only be understood within some special enterprise like those we have considered and yet (according to one view) it is neither true nor false. So (I have heard it argued) propositions of law, not meant as propositions within special enterprises, may also be neither true nor false.

But the comparison between propositions of law in hard cases and propositions about non-existent entities is plainly worthless. The latter pose problems only because it is understood that the subject of the proposition does not exist, and the proposition assumes rather than asserts its existence. Controversial propositions of law either assert or deny the existence of a legal right or some other legal relation. The controversy is precisely over whether that assertion or denial is correct. If we once assume that a right to recover for economic damage does not exist, then the proposition that the plaintiff in such a case has a right to recover is not problematical. It is simply false. The comparable proposition is the proposition that there is now a King of France. No one supposes that that proposition is neither true nor false. It is either (as most of us think) false, or (as some extreme supporters of the Comte de Paris believe) true.

3.

What shall we then say, finally, about the general objection which has been the subject of this chapter? It is no longer so clear that either common sense or realism supports the objection that there can be no right answer, but only a range of acceptable answers, in a hard case. The practical argument for that claim is misconceived. The theoretical argument is contradicted by the capacities of those who make the argument, and it cannot even be stated, or so it seems, in a way that does not dissolve its claims into the very background it seeks to challenge. Some readers will remain unconvinced. Surely it *cannot* be that in a genuinely hard case one side is simply right and the other simply wrong. But why not? It may be that the supposition that one side may be right and the other wrong is cemented into our habits of thought at a level so deep that we cannot coherently deny that supposition, no matter how skeptical or hard-headed we wish to be in such matters. That would explain our difficulty in stating the theoretical argument in a coherent way. The 'myth' that there is one right answer in a hard case is both recalcitrant and successful. Its recalcitrance and success count as arguments that it is no myth.

Appendix:

A Reply to Critics*

This appendix is a revised and expanded version of an article, *Seven Critics*, which responded to a number of articles originally published in a single number of the *Georgia Law Review* (vol. 11, Sept. 1977, no 5) discussing various aspects of this book. Several of these articles raised questions that I have found to be of general interest among readers, and I therefore thought it a good idea to add my response, which significantly develops my arguments, to the new impression. I have, however, made certain changes. I have deleted one section of the original article, not because the critics discussed there raised unimportant issues, but because my response to them did not seem of independent interest. I have added new sections discussing problems raised by three other critics. (I do not mean to suggest, however, that these are the only, or indeed the most difficult, problems raised for my arguments in the pleasingly formidable literature, much of which is of very high quality, nor that I either accept, or have no reply to, other objections that have been made.) I have added a further part to section 2, examining an earlier essay of the critic discussed there, and have enlarged several other sections.

In a very few cases this appendix argues that my critics have not understood the points I wish to make. I acknowledge that the responsibility for these misunderstandings is mine. The several essays in the book pursue a general theory of law but, as I stated in the Introduction, they were written separately, contain some repetition and development of ideas, and do not say all that I wish to say on the topics they discuss. Such a book runs a greater risk of misinterpretation than one written as a whole. The reader must often be tempted to fill in gaps between the various parts for himself, perhaps in a way so as to bring the author closer to some standard position with which the reader is already familiar. Passages inconsistent with these more familiar positions may then be more easily overlooked.

I repeated just now that I want to say more than I yet have about several issues, and I shall mention two of these. The first is the distinction between concepts and conceptions, and the idea that an argument defending a conception of a concept is a distinct form of argument. I rely on that idea in Chapter 5 and again in section 5 of this appendix, but my analysis of the idea is so far only intuitive. The second is the claim, described in the Introduction and again below in section 6, that the conception of equality as equal concern and respect not only provides an argument in favour of the familiar constitutional rights described in Chapter 12, and the economic rights described in a further essay,[1] but also provides an account of the idea of autonomy which has figured in classical descriptions of human rights. If this is correct, then the supposed conflict between autonomy and equality, like the familiar conflict between liberty and equality, is spurious. I presently think that both of these issues – the problem of understanding arguments for a conception of a concept and the problem of understanding the connection between equality and autonomy – will lead legal and political philosophy into a further classical problem of philosophy: the problem of personal identity. For the way in which each of us forms a conception of a life is both a paradigm for us of a distinct kind of argument and the source of the idea of autonomy. But this last suggestion is speculative even beyond the generous limits of this paragraph.

I. HART AND A GOOD NIGHT'S SLEEP

It may seem churlish to count Professor Hart's remarks about me, in the course of his elegant Sibley Lecture,[2] as criticism. He offered only predictions of the faults others might find, and did even this so gently, and with such generosity, as to make me realize once again that criticism at his hands always gives pleasure as well as instruction. He says that lawyers will find grave difficulties in my argument that adjudication, even in hard cases when judges create new rules of law, is a matter of principle rather than policy. He also says that they will not be persuaded by my denial of the popular idea that in such cases there is often no right answer to questions of law.

Hart's essay is useful, however, not only in predicting these responses but in reminding us of a familiar picture of law that explains why certain critics have come to understand my claims as they have and to reject them with such confidence. They believe that rules can usefully be said to exist, and they believe in something Hart calls the 'existing law', which consists in a special and numerable list of legal rules (and possibly other sorts of standards) that at a given moment do exist. The existing law, so conceived, has two functions: it alone can provide answers to questions about the legal duties of citizens and other legal persons, and it alone can impose

---

[1] 'Liberalism' in S. Hampshire (ed.), *Public and Private Morality* (forthcoming).
[2] H. L. A. Hart, 'American Jurisprudence through English Eyes: The Nightmare and the Noble Dream', *Ga. L. Rev.* 968, 983 (1977).

obligations upon judges to accept these answers as dispositive of law suits. American jurisprudence, in Hart's view, has taken itself as forced to choose between two extreme theories about the content of the existing law. The first is a nightmare, which is that the existing law is empty: there are in fact no rules in it at all. The second is a noble dream; this supposes, in the extreme version Hart attributes to me, that the existing law is so rich and detailed that the judge

> must always suppose that for every conceivable case there is some solution which is already [existing] law before he decides the case and awaits his discovery. He must not suppose that the law is ever incomplete, inconsistent, or indeterminate; if it appears so, the fault is not in it, but in the judge's limited human powers of discernment . . .[1]

In fact, according to Hart, the sensible lawyer will avoid both the nightmare and the dream and settle for a good night's sleep, which is provided by the familiar intermediate position, that the existing law contains a great many rules which are put there by legislation, precedent, and custom, but that these rules are neither sufficiently numerous nor precise to decide all cases.

Hart is right in thinking that the picture of 'existing law' as some sort of entity has had a terrible hold on jurisprudence. It is responsible for the 'secret book' theory of controversial legal rights I describe below. Hart's own common sense view shares that picture with both of the more extreme positions, differing from them only in the content it ascribes to that existing law. I hope to persuade lawyers to lay the entire picture of existing law aside in favour of a theory of law that takes questions about legal rights as special questions about political rights, so that one may think a plaintiff has a certain legal right without supposing that any rule or principle that already 'exists' provides that right. In place of the misleading question, whether judges find rules in the 'existing law' or make up rules not to be found there, we must ask whether judges try to determine what the parties have a right to have, or whether they create what they take to be new rights to serve social goals. I offer the suggestion that Hart and other critics have tried to force my views into the old picture I reject, and that the dream they find in my work, which I think more silly than noble, is the product of the union. But I do agree that something noble is at stake in whether I am right or wrong in all this, which I try to explain in section 3B below.

[1] *Ibid.*, 983.

2. GREENAWALT AND THE RIGHTS THESIS

A. Principles and policies

Greenawalt takes as his main target my claim that judges in ordinary civil cases characteristically justify their decisions through what I called arguments of principle rather than arguments of policy, and that they not only do decide in this way but should. Greenawalt objects to several features of this claim. He offers, in opposition to its descriptive claim, several counter-examples. These are designed to show that American judges at least, often reach decisions in hard cases on the basis of arguments of policy. He fears that I will try to avoid these counter-examples by 'ingenious' arguments showing that what are apparently arguments of policy in these cases are really, if properly understood, arguments of principle. But he warns me that if I succeed in this sort of defence I shall do so at the cost of erasing the distinction between the two sorts of arguments, or in some other way making my main claim trivial. He also, and independently, challenges my claim that judges ought to use arguments of principle and avoid arguments of policy in hard cases. It is this normative claim, as I understand him, that he takes to be based on a 'political theory that is startlingly and misleadingly simplistic'.[1] He believes that in at least some cases—when the rights of the parties are controversial – it is entirely appropriate and beneficial for judges to make new law justified only by arguments of policy even though they must apply that new law retrospectively to adjudicate the consequences of events in the past.

What are arguments of principle and arguments of policy, and what is the difference? Arguments of principle attempt to justify a political decision that benefits some person or group by showing that the person or group has a right to the benefit. Arguments of policy attempt to justify a decision by showing that, in spite of the fact that those who are benefited do not have a right to the benefit, providing the benefit will advance a collective goal of the political community. It is important not to confuse this distinction, between arguments of principle and arguments of policy, with a different distinction, which is the distinction between consequentialist and non-consequentialist theories of rights.

Consider a paradigm nuisance problem. *A*'s property adjoins *B*'s; *B* operates a factory on his property and the resulting pollution spoils *A*'s enjoyment of his own property. Suppose *A* takes himself to the legislature

---

[1] Greenawalt, 'Policy, Rights and Judicial Decision', 11 *Ga. L. Rev.* 991, 992 (1977).

and asks for a statute prohibiting persons in the position of B from polluting in the way B does, at least unless those in the position of A consent. A might make two different sorts of arguments supporting his request. He might say, first, that he has, all things considered, a right to enjoy his property free from such pollution. That would be an argument of principle, an argument that appeals to rights as a justification for a political decision that enforces or protects those rights. Or he might say that the community as a whole will be better off (because its air will be cleaner) if activities like those of B are prohibited or at least made to pay their way by purchasing the consent of those most immediately affected. That would be an argument of policy, an argument that appeals to some collective goal of the community to justify a political decision that advances or protects that goal.

Suppose that A makes and is asked to defend a claim of principle, that he has a right that B not use B's own property in the way B has. A's argument might be innocent of any appeal to further consequences of B's being allowed to pollute the air. He might say, for instance, that people who buy property in the area in question do so with the understanding, confirmed by convention, that they will be able to breathe entirely uncontaminated air thereon, and that his right arises solely from that general understanding. But on the other hand A might make a more consequentialist argument. He might say, for example, that the pollution of the air will injure his and his family's health, and that his right arises from the fact that B's action threatens an especially vital interest which A has a right to have protected by society. A appeals in this way to the consequences of B's act as an argument that A has a right that that act not take place. This appeal to consequences does not, of course, convert his original argument into an argument of policy. If we thought it did, then we should be making the mistake of supposing that because arguments of policy direct our attention to the consequences of having or not having a particular rule, any argument that directs our attention to consequences must be an argument of policy.

Consequentialist arguments may be introduced into debate about rights not only by the proponent of a right, but by its challenger. Suppose B challenges A's arguments of principle before the legislature. B might meet these arguments directly, by denying, for example, that people who buy land in this section of the community do expect to control the quality of air, or by denying that his pollution does in fact threaten the health of A or his family. Or he might try to establish a competing right of his own, more weighty than the right A has established, so that he might win the conflict of rights thus established. He might, in his turn, use either non-consequentialist or consequentialist arguments to this effect. He might say, in the non-consequentialist way, that purchasers of land in this area share an understanding that they may build factories or may use that land in the most commercially valuable way, with no let or hindrance from neighbours. Or he may say, in a more consequentialist spirit, that if he is not allowed to produce the pollution of which *A* complains, then he will not be able to operate his business at a profit, and will become a bankrupt, with more serious consequences for him than will follow for *A* if the pollution continues. Once again this attention to the relative consequences of allowing or rejecting *A*'s claim of right is made as part of an argument of principle. In this case, the argument supposes that *B* has some competing abstract right, and the appeal to consequences is used to show that the competing right is, in the circumstances, more weighty, so that *A* does not in fact have the concrete right he claims in asking for the statute. If *B* does in fact persuade the legislature to refuse the statute, through a consequentialist argument of this sort, it does not follow that the legislature's decision was generated by arguments of policy. The legislature has not refused to enact the statute as a piece of strategy to improve overall economic efficiency, for example, but rather because it was persuaded that *B* did and *A* did not have the right each said he had.

But *B* may make a different, negative consequentialist argument, intended to defeat *A*'s claim of a right without relying, as the arguments just described do rely, on the idea that *B* has a stronger competing right. *B* may say, for example, that no one can have a right to be protected from nuisance if the cost of that protection to the economic health of the community would be very great, and he may then add that since his factory employs most members of the community's working population, the cost of that protection for *A* would be plainly too high. Suppose the legislature is persuaded by this argument, and refuses to enact the statute *A* wants on that account. There might now be more temptation to say that the legislature's decision was a matter of policy rather than principle, but that would nevertheless be a mistake. The question before the legislature is still the question of whether, all things considered, *A* has the right he claims. If the legislature is persuaded that the answer to that question depends upon some calculation of consequences, that does not change the nature of the question it is trying to answer. It decides that *A* does not have a right to the statute and so rejects that reason for enacting the statute. Of course, the legislature might have wished to consider whether, even absent a right in *A* to the statute, there were not good policy grounds for enacting the statute anyway. In that case *B*'s arguments would have done double duty: they would have rebutted *A*'s claim of a right to a statute, and also rebutted the independent policy arguments, if there were any, that a statute was desirable even if *A* had no right to it. In that case, the legislature has reached two decisions: first, on grounds of principle, that *A* has no right to what he asks, and second, on grounds of policy, that what he asks would be detrimental rather than helpful to the community's goals.

The difference between an argument of principle and an argument of policy, then, is a difference between two kinds of questions that a political institution might put to itself, not a difference in the kinds of facts that can figure in an answer. If an argument is intended to answer the question whether or not some party has a right to a political act or decision, then the argument is an argument of principle, even though the argument is thoroughly consequentialist in its detail. Of course a critic of an argument of principle may want to say that it is a bad argument of principle just because it appeals to consequences in the way it does. Suppose the legislature decides that *A* has no right to the statute because *B* has shown that the cost of modifying factories to reduce pollution, while economically feasible, is nevertheless greater than the loss in real estate values caused by pollution at its present level. *A* might protest that his abstract right to enjoy his own property free from threats to health is too important to yield, in this case, to bare considerations of marginal cost of that character. He might add (as I would myself) that accepting that sort of reason as grounds for refusing to recognize a concrete political right is tantamount to denying that any abstract political right exists at all, so that it is inconsistent to concede the abstract right and yet refuse to enforce it in this sort of case. But these are just different ways of saying that the legislature has made a mistake of principle: the mistake of valuing the abstract right too little, or the mistake of refusing to recognize the abstract right at all. The legislature may reply that the mistake is not theirs but the critic's; the issue thus joined is an issue of principle, not policy.

How shall we tell, as a matter of history, whether a particular political decision has been taken on grounds of principle or policy? It may not be a simple matter. Suppose we take, as examples, the string of early nineteenth-century cases about the rights of riparian owners discussed by Professor Horwitz in his interesting book.[1] If two people or firms own land, one upstream of the other on a stream that may be dammed, either may want to use the water in such a way as to cause disadvantage to the other. Horwitz believes that the courts of Massachusetts and other states took different attitudes to these cases at different times. At one period they allowed one owner to do almost nothing that might damage the prospects of the other, no matter how necessary or valuable the activity so constrained was to the first owner or to the community in general. At another period they applied a test of reasonableness: it was a question of balancing the loss to the defendant if he were unable to use his land in the way he wanted against the loss to the plaintiff if he were so able. At still a different

---

[1] M. Horwitz, *The Transformation of American Law* (1977), Harvard University Press.

time the courts were at the other extreme: one owner might use the water, as it ran through his land, in any way he wished profitable to himself, no matter how great the impact on his neighbour. Horwitz argues that in each of these periods the practice settled upon had the effect of benefiting the expansion of capitalist industry; changes in legal rules followed changes in the way in which water might contribute to the most profitable use of the land. In several of the landmark cases in which the rules of law changed, the court offered consequentialist justifications for its decisions. Often these consequences were, in the first instance, consequences for the plaintiff or defendant and those similarly situated, but in some cases explicit reference was had to the more general economic interests of the community as a whole.

We might tell two very different stories about these cases. The first is the story of policy. In the early nineteenth century, judges seized on the opportunity presented by private litigation to develop rules for the distribution of power over running streams that would promote, better than other rules, the collective goal of developing and strengthening a capitalistic economy. As economic practice and circumstance changed, these judges changed the rules so as to keep pace. No doubt the judges were prepared to concede that each landowner had certain rights over the use of his land, rights that the judges would have been wrong to alter just for that policy. They would not have dreamt, for example, of establishing a rule forbidding landowners to use their land in economically inefficient ways if they wished, or allowing a more efficient user to trespass upon the land of a less efficient user. But they did not see *hard* cases about water as cases requiring a more precise account of the concrete rights of neighbouring landowners when abstract rights seem to conflict. On the contrary, they set aside all thoughts of the standing legal rights of the parties as individuals, just as a legislature might do when altering a legal regime in the interests of commerce.

The second story is the story of principle. The judges saw these cases as hard cases about the concrete rights of neighbours under changing economic circumstances. They assumed, perhaps without much reflection, that in the case of rights over the use of real property, at least, considerations of consequence played an important part in the definition of these rights. They held that assumption as part of what would be called, if made articulate, their political theory. They would have said, if asked to describe the general situation in background moral terms, that though one has an abstract right to use his own property as he wishes, it is not fair for him to use his property so as to prevent his neighbours from enjoying like rights over their own property; but that, on the other hand, it is not fair for one landowner to expect that others will refrain from useful employment of their own land so as to allow him to indulge his preference for a socially less valuable employment of his own land. They might have supposed, reasonably or unreasonably, that this very rough and abstract description of the moral rights of competing landowners provided the best justification (in the *Hard Cases*[1] sense) of the law as they found it, and then set out to do their best to fashion rules of law governing riparian use that most accurately declared and most effectively protected the concrete rights that flowed from that analysis under governing economic conditions. As these conditions changed, of course, then, given that analysis, concrete rights changed and new rules faithful to the old principles would be required. It does not follow from the fact that these judges held a consequentialist view of the dimension of concrete rights over land use that they held a similarly consequentialist theory about other sorts of rights. They might have felt differently about rights to be protected against physical invasion of one's property or person, for example. It would then be fair, and indeed necessary, to ask why they took a different view about riparian use, or nuisance, or any other matter to which their consequentialist theory extended. But an answer might be found in some view that rights in property are more institutional in their origin than more personal rights, or in some other feature of a more-or-less articulate political theory.

How shall we choose between these two stories? Some critics will wish to say that the two stories are only different ways of saying the same thing, or that it can make no practical difference which we choose as a general description of adjudication. I shall come to that charge soon; but if we assume for the moment that the two stories are different, it may not be a simple matter to decide which is to be preferred as a description of the particular legal decisions in question. I hope it is plain, however, that the appeal to consequences to be found in the opinions is not decisive, or even probative, in favour of the story of policy. It would be probative only if it were implausible to suppose that the judges could hold a consequentialist theory of rights in real property. I hope it is plain, also, that Horwitz's argument, that the rules developed by the judges were in fact the rules best suited to promote the development of a capitalist economy, is consistent with either story. If the judges had reached the same rules, but with no reference to the consequences of allowing or prohibiting different uses, then Horwitz's claims would support what I called, in *Hard Cases*, the anthropological thesis, which holds that members of a community will develop a theory of rights that in fact promotes general prosperity as they understand it. These claims would not contradict the different thesis that the judges took themselves to be enforcing rights in reaching their decisions. They can have no more force against the further thesis that the judges took themselves to be enforcing rights under a theory that made

[1] See above, Chapter 4.

consequences relevant to rights. Horwitz's arguments are intended, indeed, to support what might be called a neo-Marxist version of the anthropological thesis. This version supposes that members of a dominant class will develop a theory of rights that will work to the benefit not of the community as a whole, as more sanguine anthropologists might suppose, but only of their class. If that is so, then it is an important discovery for both history and politics, but it does not argue against the story of principle, though of course it qualifies any evaluative or normative conclusions that might be drawn from that story.

But all this is about considerations that do not count in choosing between our two stories. What considerations do count? We must remember that, though we are choosing between two competitive descriptions of what judges *did* do, the success of one or the other description depends upon matters that, for these judges, were matters of what they *should* do. I do not mean to suppose that these judges (or indeed contemporary judges) have made our distinction between arguments of principle and arguments of policy, and were consciously attempting to make decisions that they would characterize one way or the other in the language of that distinction. On the contrary, though the distinction is certainly not novel in either political or legal philosophy, it has not been a staple of jurisprudence. I mean rather that the best method of choosing between our two characterizations is to ask which fits better with political and moral theories that we can plausibly attribute to those whose practice we are trying to describe.

The story of principle would be implausible, for example, if it is implausible to suppose that the judges held a consequentialist attitude about what one landowner can fairly expect from another. But, as a matter of fact, it is implausible to suppose that they did *not* hold that consequentialist attitude, for it has been part of conventional morality in both Britain and the United States for centuries. People believe that ownership of land carries certain rights, both to determine what shall be done on that land, and to be free from interferences from what is done on neighbouring land; they understand that these two sorts of rights may conflict, and they do not believe that in that case neither of two neighbours has any moral rights at all against the other, or that one sort of right always is sovereign over the other. They believe instead that in such cases one party has what might be called the 'greater' right, by which I understand that one party has a concrete right in the circumstances, and that consequences, not only for the two neighbours, but for society generally, are relevant in deciding who that is. It is true that these consequentialist aspects of what it is reasonable for a landowner to expect are mixed with other, non-consequentialist aspects, like the question of which of the two conflicting uses was prior, or, as in the case of the present controversy about landing rights for Concorde, which is more 'natural' or to be preferred on grounds of political morality that are not consequentialist. Popular theory draws on all these, and other, considerations in judging what fairness requires in such cases, and ordinary men and women disagree about their right mix from case to case, though rarely do they deny any role at all to considerations of consequence. The story of principle supposes only that judges take the same general attitude toward questions of fairness, and appeal to consequences, in ways and with emphases that differ from judge to judge and from period to period, just as these differ from person to person in ordinary life. The social anthropologist may insist that these theories of fairness arise through some communal perception of common need, rather than through the intermediary of any more abstract principles of morality; or, if he prefers the Marxist interpretation, the result of a class perception of its own interest. But these different versions of the anthropological thesis confirm rather than challenge the story of principle.

B. *Counter-examples*

I do not wish to continue the historical question of whether Horwitz's judges decided the riparian cases on principle or policy, though of course I think it was on principle. Instead, I want to use the factual circumstance of these cases as the subject of a tedious exercise. I shall distinguish in some detail the different moral, political, and judicial questions that might be raised about these circumstances. *A* and *B* own neighbouring land; a stream runs through both plots, *A*'s land being upstream of *B*'s. *A* proposes to dam the stream to irrigate his land, or to provide power for his factory, or for some other purpose; but that will make the stream much less useful to *B* for the same or other purposes.

(1) There is first the direct moral issue of fairness. If there is no explicit law prohibiting *A* from damming the stream, does *B* nevertheless have a right (we might call it a 'moral' right) that *A* not interfere with the enjoyment of *B*'s land in this way? If *B* has no such right that *A* not dam the stream, does *B* have a right that *A* make good any loss that *B* suffers because the value of the stream to *B* is diminished? If *B* has no right that *A* not dam the stream, and no right that *A* compensate him for the loss, does he at least have a right that *A* take care to cause no more damage to *B*'s interests than is necessary for *A*'s purposes? Or does *B* have none of these rights, even as a matter of morality, so that *A* is perfectly free, morally as well as legally, to use his land in any way he wishes, leaving *B* to look after himself as best he can? After all, *B* did buy land downstream, and may have paid a lower price on that account.

It is plain that people will differ in their answers to these questions of private morality, and that the different answers will reflect larger or more abstract differences in their morals or submerged ethical theories. It is also plain, as I just said, that those who are willing to think about the issues at all are likely to take into account the consequences for the parties, and even for society as a whole. They may say, for example, that though one has in principle a right to enjoy the resources of one's own property, that right cannot extend so far as to block social gains for the community as a whole, because that would be using private property to hold the community to ransom.

(I speak of what 'many people' would think because I am anxious to distinguish the question whether it is plausible to take the argument someone makes as, for him or her, an argument about rights from the different question whether it is in fact a good argument about rights. As we shall see, the former question is central when we ask whether a particular judicial decision stands as a counter-example to the descriptive aspect of the rights thesis. The latter question is more important when we are concerned to test the normative aspect of the rights thesis (and so are concerned to see what decisions would in fact be right decisions under that thesis). Both questions become important when we consider whether the rights thesis is trivial or (as some would put it) more modest than it might seem on the surface. When I say that many people are likely to give consequences an important place in their theories of certain rights, which speaks to the former question, I neither suggest nor deny that they are right to do so, either in general, or in the case of these particular rights.)

(2) We now come to the different question whether it would be proper for the legislature to adopt a statute either (a) giving downstream owners a legal right to enjoin dams upstream, or a legal right to damages if such a dam is built, or some more complex right like the right that such dams shall be reasonable, all things considered, or (b) providing that downstream owner shall not have any such right, thus repealing any earlier statute or judicial precedent like (a). Suppose a legislator has answered our first set of questions (subsection 1 above) by deciding that B has a moral right to the protection that statute (a) would provide. He has, in that decision, an argument of principle for voting in favour of that statute. He may also think that statute (a) would promote some community goal; indeed, if his grounds for supposing that B has the right are heavily consequentialist, it is probable (though not inevitable) that he will think the statute would promote some common goal. If so, then he has, additionally, an argument of policy in favour of the statute. But the fact that the same consequences figure in that argument as figured in the argument of principle does not mean that the argument of policy is the same argument.

But now suppose that he has answered the first set of questions negatively: he does not believe that *B* has a right to what statute (a) provides.
In that case he has no argument of principle in favour of the statute, but
he may have the argument of policy all the same. If so, then he may
properly vote for the statute, and create a legal right where no moral right
existed, because the argument of policy would be sufficient justification
alone. (I am assuming that though the legislator thinks *A* is morally free
to dam the stream, he does not think that *A* has a political legislative right
to do so; he does not think, that is, that *A* has a political right that no
statute preventing him from doing so be enacted.)

But suppose the statute proposed is statute (b), which denies rather than
affirms a right in *B*, and suppose that our legislator believes there are good
policy grounds for voting for *that* statute. If he has answered the first set
of questions negatively, then he has, in that answer, a negative argument
of principle. Supporters of *B* may claim that since *B* has a right to what
statute (b) denies, it is wrong to vote for statute (b) on grounds of policy
alone. Our legislator deploys his argument of principle, to the effect that
B has no such moral right, and then supports his affirmative vote for the
statute on grounds of policy. If he has answered the first questions
affirmatively, on the other hand, then he has an argument of principle
against statute (b) if he believes that moral rights of that sort furnish
political legislative rights, that is, rights that the legislature support the
moral rights. If he does not believe that (as he well might not), then he
will not suppose that he has an argument of principle against the statute,
and will think it proper to vote for the statute on grounds of policy.

(3) Suppose that the issue raised by *A*'s conduct has not been presented
to the legislature and that there is no statute like (a) or like (b). Suppose
also that there is no clear precedent at law having the effect either of these
statutes would have. Now *B* sues *A* asking either for an injunction, or for
damages, or for some more complex relief. It is a hard case. Suppose the
judge has given an affirmative answer to the issues of fairness described
above – he thinks that *B*, to put it briefly, has a moral right to what he
asks. Also suppose the judge takes such a view of the precedents that the
question raised above – the question of *B*'s moral rights against *A* – will
be decisive of *B*'s legal rights. (The more general arguments of *Hard
Cases* show, I hope, the circumstances in which our judge might think
that the moral question has that decisive impact on the legal question.)
If the judge answers the moral question affirmatively, and thinks that *B*
has, all things considered, a moral right to the same relief as he seeks in
court, then he will think that *B* has a legal right to that as well. He then
has an argument of principle in favour of a decision for *B*, and also an
argument of principle in favour of announcing a new rule favouring those

in the position of B for the future. He may also have an argument of policy available in favour of the same rule for the future. Indeed, if his argument in favour of the moral right is heavily consequentialist, then (like the legislator in the same position) the same consequences will almost inevitably provide an argument of policy. But the two arguments are not the same argument, and only the argument of principle will count substantially in favour of a decision for B in the actual case.

Suppose that he has, however, an argument of policy in favour of the *contrary* rule (b) as a rule for the future. That seems improbable, but possible, particularly if his argument of principle in favour of B's moral right relied heavily on non-consequentialist factors. If the judge announces rule (b) for the future, and applies that rule so as to hold against B in the present case, then his decision is plainly generated by an argument of policy that defeats a competing argument of principle. The decision would stand as a counterexample to the rights thesis. The case would provide no counterexample, however, if the judge announced rule (b) for the future, as a 'prospective only' change in the law, but found for B in the present case. But that is extremely unlikely in a hard case of this sort.

Now suppose the judge decides the questions raised in subsection 1 above negatively – he does not think that B has a moral right to what he seeks in court. He also finds that decision conclusive of the legal right under the analysis of *Hard Cases*: he therefore does not accept that B has a legal right to the relief he seeks. He has a negative argument of principle in favour of a decision for A, and in favour of announcing rule (b) as a rule for the future. If his negative argument of principle relies heavily on consequentialist considerations, he will probably also have an argument of policy available in favour of rule (b) as a rule for the future. But the availability of that argument of policy does not mean that the argument of principle is not enough to justify his decision. The plaintiff asks for the intervention of the state, through the office of the court; it is a sufficient answer to the plaintiff that he has no right to what he seeks. But now suppose that the judge has a policy argument in favour of rule (a) as a rule for the future. Again, that is possible, particularly if his negative argument of principle, against B's claim of a right, did not heavily rely on consequentialist considerations. If he announces rule (a) as a rule for the future, and then applies that rule to the present case so as to allow B his remedy against A, then the decision has been generated by an argument of policy. The case also stands as a counter-example to the rights thesis. (But, again, not so if his choice of rule (a) is 'prospective only'.) The court does not think that any argument of fairness is available to support B's claim that it was wrong for A to have done what A has done, but the court nevertheless uses its authority to give B what he asks from A.

I warned that this account would be tedious, but it has the merit, at least, of isolating those cases that might provide counter examples to the rights thesis. We must search for such counter-examples amongst cases in which the opinion relies on consequentialist arguments of some kind, but we will find them only in a subset of those cases. These will be cases in which either (i) decision is for the plaintiff, but the court does not think that the plaintiff has, even all things considered, a moral right to what he asks and is given, or that a principle describing that right forms part of a better justification of the settled law, or (ii) decision is for the defendant, but the court does not think that the plaintiff has no legal right to what he asks. If, in cases in which the decision is for the plaintiff, the court does accept that the plaintiff has a moral right to what he asks, then it is incredible that the case will provide a counter-example to the rights thesis. It would prove to be a counter-example only if there were reasons why that moral right could not also be taken to be a legal right; but if the background legal material is such as to permit a decision for the plaintiff, then it can hardly be strong enough against the moral right to exclude a legal right of the same tenor. Cases cannot provide counter-examples to the rights thesis, of course, if decision is for the defendant and the court is of the opinion that the plaintiff has no legal right to what it asks. The rights thesis supposes that if, at least is an ordinary private civil action, the plaintiff has no legal right to what it asks, then that is a decisive argument of principle in favour of decision for the defendant.

I concede that it may be difficult to decide whether the court does or does not think that the plaintiff has some kind of a right when the court does not make plain, in its opinion, that it is addressing itself to that question. It is a matter of what is reasonable to attribute to judges, by way of moral positions or assumptions, even though the judges themselves did not use the precise vocabulary, or make the precise distinctions, we must use in making that attribution. This must be a matter of speculation, but, as we shall see, there are certain general principles we might follow in deciding whether any such attribution is plausible or not.

We many now ask how well Greenawalt's putative counter-examples succeed on these tests. He takes, first, a pair of hypothetical negligence cases:

> Defendant *A*, driving carefully, sees a live baby on the road in front of him; he swerves to miss it and unavoidably smashes into plaintiff's parked car. Defendant *B*, also driving carefully, sees a dead rabbit on the road and, since he hates to run over dead animals, swerves and unavoidably smashes into plaintiff's parked car. Defendant *A* is not negligent and Defendant *B* is negligent precisely because the welfare of the live baby made *A*'s act of swerving reasonable while

the welfare of the dead rabbit [!] was not enough to make *B*'s act reasonable.[1]

In *A*'s case, the defendant wins, but it would be unreasonable to attribute to the hypothetical court the view that the plaintiff had even a moral right that a baby be killed in order to avoid damage to the plaintiff's car. So the case cannot be a counter-example. In *B*'s case, the plaintiff wins, but it is unreasonable not to attribute to the hypothetical court the view that people have a right that their valuable property not be injured simply out of squeamishness. So *B*'s case cannot be a counter-example either.

Greenawalt next turns to nuisance cases like those I have already discussed.

A person can act perfectly reasonably by starting in a remote area a business that necessarily involves offensive odours or air pollution. As long as the surrounding population remains small and the damage to each landowner is not very great, no one may have a right to have the business stopped. But if, even for fortuitous and unforeseeable reasons, the area becomes heavily populated, the business can become a nuisance, and each surrounding homeowner, or the municipality, may have a right to abate it, even though no more damage is done to each affected person than was done to those who lived nearby when the population was very small. . . . It would be stretching matters to say that mandatory abatement [in the second case] is simply the application of a principle requiring a decent respect for others.[2]

In the first case, when the affected area was remote, the plaintiff loses, but it seems inappropriate to attribute to the hypothetical court any idea that the plaintiff has a concrete right that the factory owner desist. Each side has an abstract right to use his own land free from interference from outside, and some compromise between these rights is required. The defendant is morally free, all else being equal, to use his land as he sees best. The moral question is whether, under all the circumstances, any one of a very few people, each of whom is less adversely affected than the defendant would be if forced to abate, is entitled that the defendant not use his land to manufacture odours. Our sense that decision for the defendant is right – the sense on which the hypothetical example relies – assumes that we would give that question a negative answer. In the second case, however, the moral issue is quite different. Now the defendant must be urging, against the claim of any particular plaintiff, moral

[1] Greenawalt, *op. cit.* ('Policy' etc), 1012 (exclamation mark added).
[2] *Ibid.*, 1013 (footnote added).

freedom to use his land in a way that causes harm to a great many people. That is, considered just as a moral claim, much less appealing. It is, in fact, an important part of conventional morality that someone who shows 'decent respect for others' must take into account the number of people who will be damaged by what he does as well as the amount of damage that each will suffer. If the same action, for the same benefit to himself, injures a larger number of people, even in the same degree, then he shows less respect for *each* in persisting than if the number injured had been smaller. So even if each plaintiff in the second case had only the same interest to assert that the plaintiff had in the first, the defendant's moral freedom, given a general obligation to treat his neighbours with respect, is much less. It might well seem plausible, under these changed circumstances, to insist that each plaintiff's right to that level of respect yields a concrete right to have the nuisance abated in this case. If we think that the decision in the second case is correct, it is because we feel that it does.

Greenawalt's discussion of the nuisance cases (and his more general discussion of how the interests of third parties might be thought to affect the decision of private law suits) suggests that he fails to notice the difference between an argument of policy and an argument of principle that relies on considerations of consequence. He may have been misled, in this connection, by my failure to develop the points made in the next paragraph, and by my discussion, which he cites, of Hand's negligence test. I said that though Hand, and others who decide negligence cases as he suggested, appeal to consequences, these appeals are methods of compromising competing rights of the parties. And I pointed out, in that connection, that the consequences taken into account were consequences for the two parties, and not (as would be the case if the argument were an argument of policy) consequences for the community as a whole.[1] I contrasted the Hand rule to an imaginary rule which provided that it was negligent for someone not to incur danger in rescuing someone else more important to society than himself. I said that this imaginary rule could be the consequence only of an argument of policy, because it would provide for a plaintiff, and require of a defendant, what would be provided and required by a thoroughgoing utilitarian morality. I should have been more careful here; I should have said that it would be incredible to suppose that some court could adopt the imaginary rule on arguments of principle, because it would be implausible to suppose that any court held the view that people have the moral rights and duties that a simple act utilitarian moral theory might suggest, and incredible to suppose that any court would think that a theory of law containing that view could be an adequate justification, in Hercules' sense, of the law of

---

[1] See above, p. 99.

negligence. If any court did adopt such a rule, therefore, the conclusion would be irresistible that its decision was generated by an argument of policy, and a clear counter-example to the rights thesis would, at last, have been provided.

It might be helpful to state more abstractly how considerations touching the interests of third parties might figure in arguments about rights.[1] Though a negligence case does involve a conflict between two competing rights, these are typically rights that are, for Hohfeld's purposes, of different types. The plaintiff has a claim-right that others act towards him and his property with a certain level of concern and respect; the defendant has a liberty to pursue his own affairs free from an exaggerated concern for the consequences for others: The compromise required is a compromise between the demands of that claim-right and the scope of that liberty. Sometimes the considerations that increase or decrease the force of the claim-right are automatically considerations that decrease or increase the force of the abstract liberty. That is so when the potential damage to the plaintiff is especially serious, for example, or when the cost to the defendant of avoiding the threat is especially great. In such a case, considerations of consequence will be limited to considerations affecting the interests of the parties directly concerned. But sometimes considerations of consequence rising from the interests of other parties will affect either the force of the claim-right or the force of the liberty independently, because arguments of fairness that support these rights make such considerations relevant. The second nuisance case just discussed is one example: the greater number of the people with competing abstract claim-rights who would be adversely affected made it no longer morally plausible for the defendant to claim a concrete liberty-right to pollute. Sometimes the interests of others will be great enough, quite apart from any question of competing rights, to defeat an abstract right. But that will happen only when these interests are very important and the impact very severe. Consider the following case,[2] discussed at length in an Oxford seminar. Plaintiff has been denounced by an anonymous informer to the Society for the Prevention of Cruelty to Children, and now sues the Society for damage to her reputation, asking pretrial for the name of the informer, alleging that this information is necessary to prosecute her case. The court refuses, conceding that plaintiffs generally have a right to the

---

[1] In section 3B. of Chapter 4, I discussed only cases (like Hand's negligence test) that used consequences to the parties to the suit to adjudicate competing rights. I did not mention (though I did not exclude) cases discussed here in which consequences to third parties are, for different reasons, relevant in deciding what the rights of parties are. I did discuss such cases in the Rosenthal Lectures described above in note 2, p. 98, and the present paragraph is drawn from that lecture. See also my discussion of utilitarian theories of rights on p. 95.

[2] See *D. v. National Society for the Prevention of Cruelty to Children* (1977) 1 All E. R. 589.

information they need, but arguing that in this case the effectiveness of
the Society would be reduced if it were known that it might be forced to
reveal the names of anonymous informers. Let us suppose that the
plaintiff has some abstract moral right to disclosure. That means that it
would not be a sufficient justification for a rule forbidding disclosure that
agencies would run more efficiently, and that the community would
therefore be better off on the whole, if agency records could never be
opened to plaintiffs. It may nevertheless be that the plaintiff has no
concrete right to disclosure in this case. It might be successfully argued
that the children, who would be better protected by the Society without
disclosure, have competing rights that are, in the circumstances, more
weighty. Even if that argument fails, however, it may still be argued
that the damage to these children is so great that the plaintiff's abstract
right to disclosure must yield, because, while a right, it is not so important
or powerful a right as to trump an especially strong social disadvantage.
Of course, there is involved in any such argument (whether it makes use
of the idea of competing rights or not) some assumption about the relative
weight of the plaintiff's abstract right to disclosure. If the plaintiff were
the defendant in a criminal prosecution, the argument that she had a
right to disclosure notwithstanding the prospective damage to children
would obviously be much more powerful.

Greenawalt reaches further afield for his remaining counter-examples,
into more specialized legal issues. He makes something, for example, of
one of the New York Court of Appeals' more bizarre essays in the conflict
of laws.[1] A New York resident was killed in an automobile accident in
Maine through the negligence of his brother, who lived there then but
moved to New York before the trial. Should a New York court apply the
Maine law which sharply limits recovery in wrongul death statutes? There
are good arguments that the survivors of a New York resident have a
right to the New York wrongful death limits in a New York court, even
if the accident happened out of state, so long as it is not unfair (and it
would not have been here) to hold the real defendant in interest, a
national insurance company, to that standard. I believe that sound theory
in the conflict of laws would sustain that result, notwithstanding the
dissenting opinion in this case. But the majority, working from New
York's distinctive 'centre of interest' approach, said that one of the
factors it might take into account in deciding which law was the 'proper
law of the tort' was the fact that the defendant had moved to New York
before the trial began. That was the result, I think, of misunderstanding
the point of recent developments in conflicts theory, and it has been
condemned, not only by the dissenting opinion, but by decisions in other

[1] See *Miller v. Miller*, 22 N.Y.2d 12,237 NE.2d 877, 290 N.Y.S.2d 734 (1968),
Discussed in Greenawalt, *op. cit.*, 1014.

jurisdictions.[1] But does it nevertheless make this case a counter-example to the rights thesis?

It does not if the argument that the nominal defendant's change of residence to New York should affect the outcome of the case can be understood as resting on the following theory. 'The choice-of-law question is not a question that asks which rights the parties had vis-a-vis each other at the time of or just after the accident. We might say that the plaintiff had one right under New York law and a different, and much less valuable, right under Maine law. The choice-of-law question is this: which of these different rights furnishes an institutional right against a New York court at the time of the trial, so as to justify a particular decision by that court. That question must be answered (according to this theory) by taking many factors into account, including the residence of the parties at the time of the trial. It counts in favour of the plaintiff's claim, that she has an institutional right that the court enforce the wrongful death claim that New York has provided, that the defendant is a resident of New York at the time the plaintiff argues she has that right.'

In fact something like this theory of the connection between the conflicts question and substantive questions is presupposed by much recent conflicts theory, though few jurisdictions accept the conclusion set out in the last sentence. A judge following the full theory, including the last sentence, is not disobedient to the rights thesis, though he may be mistaken all the same.

What alternative account can be given of the case? It seems ludicrous to suppose that the decision was generated by considerations of *policy*. A New York court could not think that the sums involved in the particular case could make any difference whatsoever to the collective welfare of the state. Normally, when it is proposed that courts make law for the sake of policy, it is the forward-looking effects of the rules they announce that are supposed to have the beneficial effects. But the forward-looking effects of this proposition, that if defendants become residents of New York State after an accident, New York law may be used to render judgments against them, are wholly uncertain and in any case minute. Do the judges think that New York State needs more resident tortfeasors, who will come if New York law is more favourable to them or, as in the present case, if they wish to aid the plaintiff against the real party in interest? Or do they wish to discourage other tortfeasors, who might have been tempted to move to New York, because these will keep away (at least until after the trial) if New York law is unfavourable to them? Or do the judges really think that the collective welfare of New York will be improved, enough to justify the decision, just by the effect of the present decision, quite apart

[1] See *Reich v. Purcell*, 67 Cal.2d 551, 432 P.2d 727, 63 Cal. Rptr. 31 (1967), cited in Greenawalt, 1014, n. 64.

from such forward-looking considerations, because money will be transferred from an insurance company with large New York business to a New York family and the insurance premiums of a new New York family will then be raised? If so, the court would have done better to have adopted the principle I suggested, which would justify recovery for New York families against national insurers in foreign accidents whether or not the nominal defendant actually moved to New York. That would cause more beneficial transfers without increasing population pressures. In fact, Greenawalt's case is an especially poor example for the thesis that courts decide so as to promote policy, though the idea is hardly more plausible, from the standpoint of rationality, in the general run of hard civil law cases.

The final counter-examples Greenawalt cites, in passing, reinforce my guess that he has confused policy arguments with arguments of principle depending on consequence.[1] If the consequences of specific performance of a contract would be pointlessly wasteful either to the defendant or to the community as a whole, then that is a negative argument of principle against the plaintiff's having a right, in fairness, to specific performance, even though the plaintiff does have a right to damages. Common law rules about mootness, or *de minimis non curat lex*, may certainly rely on considerations of consequence, including those I mentioned in *Hard Cases*.[2] These considerations of consequence may make all the difference when the question is whether a background moral right to very minor damages, or to a remedy that is no longer of any practical value, is sufficient to support an institutional right to an expensive hearing and disposition, especially when there are other important calls on the community resources that would be spent.

C. Triviality

I must now face the second branch of the dilemma Greenawalt believes I confront. Perhaps the arguments just given are those he expected I might make in response to his and others' challenges. He predicts that my response will make all too plain what he already suspects, which is that the distinction between principles and policies cannot have the theoretical significance I suppose.

We must, however, distinguish two versions of this claim. The first argues that, at least in practice, there is no difference between an argument of principle, as I have described it, and an argument of policy, because one can always be substituted for the other. That claim might be put this way: the instruction, to a judge, that he must always find an

---

[1] See Greenawalt, 1015.
[2] See above, p. 100.

argument of principle to support his decision in a hard case, and cannot rely on an argument of policy, will make no difference to him, because he will decide in the same way under this instruction as without it. The second version claims that, whether or not this is so, the distinction cannot have the jurisprudential significance I claimed, because my reasons for thinking that normative and jurisprudential puzzles are solved if judges are seen to decide on grounds of principle are spurious.

The first version of the claim of triviality must be distinguished from a different claim, which I do not know whether Greenawalt wishes to press. This is the charge that, once it is understood how many different kinds of arguments can count as arguments of principle, the rights thesis loses its power as a critical tool. If it turns out that all kinds of consequentialist arguments may be arguments of principle rather than arguments of policy, if it turns out that judges have, with rare exceptions, all been making arguments of principle all the time, then it can hardly count as an important piece of normative jurisprudence to say that judges should do just what they would do and have done anyway. I conceded the substance of that 'charge' when I said that the rights thesis was meant to be both descriptive and normative. If I thought that my thesis was a banner for revolution, I would hardly argue that judges characteristically do what it recommends. I was at pains to stress that I meant to offer not a programme of reform, but a better characterization of what we all know judges do, better because it would enable us to see that many familiar problems of political and conceptual jurisprudence are caused not by the facts of adjudication, but by our own misleading ways of describing these facts, as if we had got into conceptual troubles by supposing that M. Jourdain spoke blank verse.[1] If the second version of the triviality claim were sound, then this exercise would have no point. We would be no better off, in understanding the legal process, for choosing a different description of the same practices. But if the second version is false, then the objection that there is no revolutionary force in the rights thesis is simply, as I said, a statement of its success.

It does not follow, however, that there is no critical power in the rights thesis. There are now many judges who say that their job is to legislate in the interstices of law, and that this means behaving just as a legislature would behave, pursuing policy when the opportunity arises. Most who say this are simply saying, in the language of old jurisprudence, that their duties include creating new rules in hard cases, not that they are properly guided by what I mean by arguments of policy when they do so. But there are undoubtedly some who try to practise what they seem to preach, and the rights thesis provides a standard for denying that what they do is right. The chief critical value of the rights thesis, however, is found at a

[1] See above, pp. 90, 123.

different level of criticism. We may allow that judges hold to the rights thesis, and still argue that they make mistakes, either because they rely on poor background moral or political theory, or because they make more pedestrian errors of analysis. The rights thesis guides this criticism by exposing the deep structure of judicial arguments in hard cases, including the principles of rights it contains, and therefore the more general political and moral theories these principles presuppose. It shows that effective criticism must isolate and evaluate these principles and theories and, if necessary, oppose them with theories taken to be subtler or sounder. It encourages a connection between law and political and moral philosophy that must be for the benefit of both.

This is a detour, however, and we must return to the first of the two claims I distinguished. Does it make no difference whether we tell a judge that he must decide only on arguments of principle or tell him that, in hard cases, he may use arguments of policy as well? Plainly, the difference it makes must depend on the judge's own political and moral theory, in particular on the degree to which he thinks that consequentialist arguments are proper and forceful in deciding what rights people have. If the judge holds a strict deontological theory of rights, then the two instructions will have very different effects. Though it is doubtful how far the judge will succeed in finding his deontological principles in the best justification of the existing law, allowing him to take consequences into consideration through arguments of policy would free him from deontological constraints that must at least sometimes prevent those consequences from figuring in an argument of principle he accepts. But, as I said earlier, few people hold a rigidly deontological theory of rights. So most judges will think that, even when when moral and political rights are in question, consequentialist arguments will play a role in defining the dimensions of these rights. They may hold, however, a large variety of different theories about the role that consequentialist considerations may properly play. It might be useful to make at least some crude distinctions amongst these various theories.

(1) The most extreme consequentialist theory of 'rights', I suppose, would be an act-utilitarian theory that holds that everyone has a duty to act, on every occasion, so as to produce the best results, as a utilitarian would define these, and that those who would benefit from such acts from time to time have a 'right' to them.

(2) More plausible but still relatively extreme theories of rights might be constructed from one or another form of rule-utilitarianism. Someone might hold the theory, for example, that everyone has a duty to act in accordance with that rule of conduct which, among all those rules of

conduct that people in like situations might plausibly consider, would produce the best consequences as a rule if everyone in that situation accepted that rule. According to that theory, someone about to build a factory on land near a residential area would have to consider which of the rules about creating nuisance that might plausibly be considered by everyone in his situation would produce the best consequences if everyone did accept it, and act accordingly. Those who would be benefited by performances of that duty would have the corresponding right.

(3) Less demanding theories of rights would follow from other forms of rule utilitarianism. Someone might believe that people have the rights and duties provided by existing rules of social practice, but only if these accepted rules produce better consequences than any other rule that is likely to be accepted would produce, or only if they produce better consequences than would be produced in the absence of any rule whatever.

(4) Someone may reject all forms of utilitarianism and yet accept a prominent place for considerations of consequence in arguments about rights. I have already described such a theory in a general way. Someone may think that people have a right to the concern of others, from which it follows that others may not cause them great injury for relatively small gains to themselves, or may not neglect to save them from great harm if they are in a position to do so with little danger to themselves. That abstract right will make considerations of consequence relevant whenever one person's act or omission is likely to have serious consequences for the welfare of others, but the theory may insist on a variety of distinctions that will make the role of consequences different in different situations. It may provide a higher standard of care or sacrifice when the risk is of damage to persons rather than to property, for example; and it may make certain competing rights, like the right to express one's opinion in politics or to choose one's associates, so important that these fail, in concrete cases, only when the consequences of their exercise would be immediate and grave, while it may make other rights, like the right to conduct the business one wishes on a particular piece of land one owns, so much less important that much less grave consequences might be sufficient to deny the right in particular circumstances.

(5) Someone may hold a special theory about institutional rights, like rights under the social institution of property in land, which is both consequentialist and non-utilitarian. He may take the attitude towards these social institutions that the chess referee took towards chess in *Hard Cases*.[1] He accepts that people have the political rights these institutions

---

[1] See above, pp. 101–5.

provide, not because he believes that the institution works for the general interest, but because reasons of fairness require that settled institutions be administered in accordance with their rules and with the expectations these rules generate – like the rule that no one may physically trespass upon another's grounds without his permission. But he believes that the point of social institutions lies in certain general consequences they are popularly supposed to achieve, and that hard cases presented by a conflict of abstract rights within the institution should be settled, just as a matter of fairness, by taking the impact of that point into account. He might believe that the point of customary rules about how others use their land, for example, is to reduce friction between land owners, and decide hard cases about nuisance, just as the chess referee decides hard cases in chess, with his conception of the institution in mind. Once again, someone holding this variety of consequentialist theory may hold a different and non-consequentialist theory of rights that do not arise from social institutions, and may hold a very different opinion about the point of other social institutions.

This list of sample theories about the rights that citizens have against one another is intended simply to illustrate the different theories that are possible, and the potential complexity of each. We must bear in mind, in considering the first version of the triviality claim, that judges may implicitly hold any of these theories, or any other of a variety of theories I have not described. I must be careful not to make a mistake I am sometimes accused of making. I do not believe that all, or even most, judges have devoted their time to abstract moral philosophy, or that they have settled on explicit theories of rights, some keeping copies of Kant under their robes, where others hide copies of Bentham or Teilhard de Chardin. I suppose only that each has a set of attitudes towards the idea of rights, not necessarily articulate or even consistent, upon which he draws when he must say what duties he has to those before him.

I shall make no assumptions about the relative popularity of different forms of consequentialist theories about rights, though I do think that theories like the last two I described are much more common than the first three. If a judge holds some theory like one of the last two, then he will respond very differently to the instruction that he must decide hard cases on arguments of principle, taking consequences into account when principle so requires, than if he were told to decide the same cases on arguments of policy. Consider a judge, for example, who holds some form of the theory of 'respect' described in subsection 4. He has in mind a scheme for the administration of streams running through land some of which is agricultural and some of which is given to manufacturing; if he were in the legislature he would sponsor that scheme as producing the socially most efficient use of such streams. If he were told to decide riparian owner cases on grounds of policy, choosing the most efficient rules for the future, and deciding the cases before him as if those rules were already in place, then he would design rules that come as close as possible to the scheme he would propose to the legislature. He would simplify, no doubt, because he could not write a complex set of regulations into the ordinary-sized judicial opinion (though there is no reason why his own opinions could not increasingly come to look like statutes, thus breaking down that convention). But the simplifications would be those, so far as possible, that left the cutting edge of the scheme intact. If he were told, as part of his instructions, that he must regard himself as a junior partner to the legislature, and keep his new rules within guidelines already established by the legislature, this qualification would have almost no effect in cases in which the legislature had already left the development of the law to the courts, as in the case of riparian rights. In other cases the qualification would require him to take certain strategies established by the legislature as fixed, but the decision as to how much of his own scheme was therefore ruled out would have nothing to do with any considerations of fairness or rights.

But suppose, on the other hand, that he is told that he must decide riparian cases on grounds of principle, and set his own cherished scheme aside. He must now ask himself, for example, whether the plaintiff farmer's abstract right to his neighbour's concern entitles the farmer to insist that the neighbour not dam the stream to construct a factory that will give needed employment to the community. For reasons I described earlier, our judge will no doubt take into account the importance to the community of those jobs, the expense and consequent inefficiency of adapting the factory to run without the energy provided by the dam, the plaintiff's alternate sources of water for irrigation, as well as non-consequential factors also affecting the issue of respect, like the question of whether the adjoining land was already used for manufacture when the plaintiff set himself up in farming. But there is no reason to think, and considerable reason to doubt, that these factors, properly weighted under the judge's general theory of fairness, would produce just the rules that his policy scheme, modified for considerations of simplicity and consistency, would provide. The policy scheme might have as one of its aims, for example, reduction in the cost of food as against manufactured products. It might choose, as a matter of strategy, to divide the state into riparian areas, permitting a use of streams without regard to the effect on others in one area, but not in others. It might provide, as a different matter of strategy, one regime for the first several years of the programme it launches, which yields to a different regime in later years when gains in the first stage will have been secured, or when circumstances are anticipated otherwise to change. These are all familiar aims or strategies of a legislative programme, but they are aims and strategies that someone holding a theory of rights of the sort described in subsection 4 would think irrelevant to what fairness requires of one neighbour towards another.

So if it is reasonable to assume that a substantial number of judges in any community hold either non-consequentialist theories of rights, or consequentialist theories that are not one or another form of utilitarianism, then the direction to these judges to decide cases on grounds of principle cannot have the same effect that the direction to decide on grounds of policy would have. That would be enough to block the first version of the triviality claim, even if I were then to concede that, for utilitarian judges, the effect of the two instructions would be the same. But of course that is not so either. A utilitarian theory of rights is a theory of rights, and even for a utilitarian the question what people may in fairness demand from one another is different from the question what rules a legislature geared for policy may properly impose upon them. The literature of utilitarianism, which is now rich and subtle, makes that apparent.[1] The rule-utilitarian argues that people have the rights specified either in rules that are already established as social rules if these have utilitarian value, as provided by the theory described in subsection 3, or in rules that might be seen as optimal by isolated individuals making decisions without the power to impose any rules whatever on others. In neither case could a utilitarian judge plausibly think that an individual should compose a rule for his own conduct having the detail or the variety of strategies, still less having the administrative sense of economy, of a decent policy programme. The question an individual should confront when deciding what duties he owes to others, even for a rule-utilitarian, is a different question, and must receive a different answer, from the question of what a legislature should, in the name of utility, require all such individuals to do – if for no other reason because the legislature has powers of publicity and powers of enforcement that no individual can or should command.

So the first version of Greenawalt's triviality claim may safely be disregarded. The second version argues that even if there is a difference between arguments of principle and arguments of policy, I am wrong to find any comfort in the idea that judges characteristically decide hard cases on arguments of principle, because the political and jurisprudential arguments I made in favour of that description of their practice are fallacious. One of Greenawalt's points in this connection, like his alleged counter-examples, challenges the descriptive adequacy of the rights thesis, and I shall consider that point first. His remaining points attack the normative claims of the thesis.

I said that the idea that judges decide hard cases on arguments of

[1] See Lyons, 'Human Rights and the General Welfare', 6 *Phil. & Pub. Aff.* 113 (1977) and articles cited therein.

principle has one jurisprudential merit: it explains, better than any competing description, why precedent is given what I called 'gravitational force' in later decisions. Greenawalt quotes the following from my article:

> The gravitational force of a precedent may be explained by appeal, not to the wisdom of enforcing enactments, but to the fairness of treating like cases alike... [The judge] must limit the gravitational force of earlier decisions to the extension of the arguments of principle necessary to justify those decisions. If an earlier decision were taken to be entirely justified by some argument of policy, it would have no gravitational force.[1]

He says that 'Dworkin's argument in this respect seems so clearly mistaken, one wonders if one fully understands it'.[2]

One may well wonder. Greenawalt, for one, misunderstands it because he overlooks its main analytical device, which is the distinction I made between the enactment force and the gravitational force of precedents. The enactment force of a precedent requires later judges to follow the rules or principles laid down in the earlier case as if these were laid down in statutes. The gravitational force tugs on later cases that are plainly beyond the language of any such rule or principle. Greenawalt says, 'The reasons why courts follow precedents are numerous. In addition to the notion of justice that like cases should be treated alike, some of these, as Llewellyn suggests, are convenience, reliance on accumulated experience, and the usefulness for planning of being able to predict what a court will decide.'[3] These are indeed reasons why precedents are given enactment force. If the precedents were taken to be generated by arguments of policy, there would be an additional and much more important reason, which Greenawalt does not mention: that judicial rules could not improve policy unless later judges were required to follow those rules.

The distinctive fact about common law adjudication, which gives rise to the jurisprudential puzzles I discussed, is that precedents are given gravitational force as well. But gravitational force cannot be explained by the catalogue of reasons Greenawalt takes from Llewellyn. Inertia and convenience are not respected by agonized and controversial arguments about what a chain of precedents requires when properly understood; 'accumulated experience' cannot explain occasions on which novel interpretations of forgotten cases are used to support a decision; and Greenawalt himself argues that precedents whose gravitational force is uncertain or controversial are little help in predicting what a court will do. Plainly

---

[1] See above, p. 113, quoted in Greenawalt, *op. cit.*, 1008.
[2] Greenawalt, 1008.
[3] *Ibid.* (footnote omitted).

Hercules, in seeking some justification for the practice of gravitational force, had to go beneath these chestnuts of lectures on precedent.

So Greenawalt has missed the point of this argument. However, he also wants to challenge a different feature of the argument. I said that if precedents have gravitational force, and if this must be justified on the ground that fairness requires consistency, then it follows that these precedents must be supposed to have been generated by arguments of principle, as the rights thesis stipulates, because, as I said,

> [if] an earlier decision were taken to be entirely justified by some argument of policy, it would have no gravitational force. Its value as a precedent would be limited to its enactment force . . . [because] [t]here can be . . . no general argument of fairness that a government which serves a collective goal in one way on one occasion must serve it that way, or even serve the same goal, whenever a parallel opportunity arises.[1]

Greenawalt disagrees. He offers a brief story about family life to illustrate his claim that (at least sometimes) decisions based on policy generate claims of fairness for parallel decisions later.[2] If there are policy grounds for sending a slightly younger child to bed first, like a desire to avoid the noise of bedtime conversation, then that child will have a claim, in later years, to go to bed later than a still younger child, even if the policy reasons have disappeared because the family has been prosperous and has bought a larger house, for example. I quite agree that the younger child may press that claim, and that it may prove difficult to explain to it the distinction between principle and policy. It may be wiser, for arguments of policy, to yield to its demands instead. It hardly follows that the child's claim is right in moral theory. If the parents had succeeded in explaining the force of new circumstances to the child, who then agreed to withdraw the claim, we should congratulate all around. We should hardly say that the parents had lulled the child into accepting an injustice.

The remainder of Greenawalt's argument here is contained in this proposition: 'A moment's reflection is enough to suggest that when a legislature grants rights to one group of people, even if it does so on policy grounds, other groups that are not justifiably distinguishable have a strong claim of fairness to similar treatment.'[3] Of course that statement, as it stands, is a truism. It begs the question of when other groups *are* 'justifiably' distinguished. I pointed out that groups are justifiably distinguished, when policy is in play, for reasons that would be inappropriate

---

1 See above, p. 113.
2 Greenawalt, 997–8.
3 *Ibid.*, 1009.

if the argument were an argument of principle because they are not reasons made relevant by fairness. These include reasons of convenience or administration or simply that a policy already launched has been sufficiently successful already. I cited legislative subsidies as a clear example, but Greenawalt objects that these are a special case, and that what I say does not apply when the legislature creates rights or adopts rules of 'general application' on grounds of policy. I do not understand what distinction Greenawalt means to take here, and he gives no examples of what he has in mind. Once the legislation is passed, subsidies are matters of right, and the rules providing them are, I would have thought, rules of general (though of course not universal) application. It is just my point, moreover, that decisions to confer benefits on grounds of policy are always subsidies; every time the legislature grants rights to a group, not because that group is in fairness entitled to what it receives, but because creating rights in that group contributes to the general welfare, then the grant is a subsidy to that group. But nothing turns on whether we use the word 'subsidy' in a narrower way. Are the capital gains provisions in the tax code, designed to encourage certain forms of investment against others, cases of subsidy? What about the original proposal of rebates for efficient, low-fuel-consuming automobiles in President Carter's energy saving programme? What about, for that matter, the proposed special tax on inefficient, high-fuel-consuming cars in the same programme? In any case, if that programme was adopted, we should not think that those who bought efficient motor boats, not covered in the legislative scheme, would have an argument of fairness that they should be given rebates as well, nor that manufacturers of efficient boats would be entitled to demand that purchasers of inefficient boats should be made to pay an equivalent tax. It would be a sufficient answer that the energy saving from motor cars was enough to get on with. Suppose Congress sets up special collective bargaining procedures in some industries, with agency review, in order to reduce labour friction or increase productivity. Is that a subsidy to whoever happens to benefit from the special procedures? In any case, we would not say that either the employers or the employees in other industries have a right in fairness to similar opportunities, simply because the same investment of administrative time and money would have produced equivalent gains there.

We must be very careful to avoid confusion here. I do not mean that government by policy may be irrational. I do not mean to deny what I have elsewhere laboured to explain,[1] that regulations serving policy may be improper (and often unconstitutional as well) if they violate independent principles carrying rights against the state. I was careful to say that

---

[1] See above, Chapter 7.

the government has a general duty not to let the burdens of policy-directed programmes fall too heavily on any particular individual or section of the community, even if technical efficiency must be sacrificed to avoid this. I now add that the government must not be allowed to use its power to pursue policy piecemeal in order to discriminate against unpopular or politically weak groups.[1] Each of these points must find room in any comprehensive theory of government, and each raises both theoretical and practical questions of great interest and complexity. But they do not, singly or together, impeach the following proposition: If a legislative decision benefits some particular group, not because that group is thought entitled to the benefit, but because the benefit is a by-product of a scheme thought to advance a particular collective goal, then others have no political right to the same benefit, *even if providing that benefit for them would, in fact, advance that same collective goal even further.* That proposition is the foundation of the argument about the gravitational force of precedents, for the same proposition does not hold when a benefit is conferred on some group because it is thought that members of that group have a right to that benefit. Even if the right is established or limited by consequentialist considerations, it is still a right, and once the principle is stated accurately, everyone falling under the beneficence of the principle has, in fairness, a right to what it provides.

Someone might object to the proposition about policies by pointing out that it does not hold in the case of one collective goal – the general welfare of the community as a whole as this might be defined by one or another form of utilitarianism. A utilitarian might argue that the legislature has a duty to seek the general welfare and therefore that everyone has a right to what he would receive under legislation that is, in fact, productive of the highest general welfare. I am myself reluctant to say that this 'right' is a genuine right, but that is unimportant here, because even if we do, the case of the general welfare is not a genuine exception to the proposition about policies. Someone who appeals to his supposed rights under the general welfare could not add to the force of his argument by citing any earlier statutes passed to secure that general welfare. Everything would turn on the independent and decisive issue whether it would now improve the general welfare to give him what he asks. In any case, this alleged

[1] This and the preceding sentences raise questions about the proper scope of the 'equal protection' clause of the fourteenth amendment to the United States Constitution. How far does that clause prohibit unequal distribution of the benefits or burdens of policy-generated legislation? Is its scope limited to cases of unequal legislation in matters of policy only insofar as this offends an independent political right including the right not to be subject to discrimination as a member of an unpopular group? I meant to raise that question in a brief footnote, above, p. 113 n.1. Greenawalt calls that note 'confused'; I concede that it is at least opaque. It provides no argument against the more conventional view of the equal protection clause, which Greenawalt now reaffirms, but only supposes that the conventional view is unsatisfactory.

exception could not count as an objection to my argument about gravitational force. If someone thinks that judicial decisions are generated by arguments of policy, and that these arguments nevertheless carry gravitational force for future decision, then he must think that the force is exerted by the choice, in the earlier decision, of some collective goal *more specific* than the goal of improving the general welfare, like accident reduction or clean air or reduced unemployment or smoother management-labour relations, even if this more specific goal is taken to be, as normally it would be, instrumental in securing that more general goal. He thinks that a party to a later action appeals to the earlier choice of that more specific goal as an argument that a rule should be fashioned in his case that serves that very same goal and that would (as a by-product) benefit him. So the argument supposes that policies more specific than general utility must themselves have gravitational force.

Greenawalt also wishes to criticize another argument I made. I said that the familiar argument that in a democracy the legislature and not the courts should make the law would be a powerful objection to judicial originality if judge-made law were generated by policy, but is not so powerful against judicial originality in matters of principle. Greenawalt objects that the legislature does not seem to concern itself with some areas of the law at all, so that the courts must perforce make whatever policy decisions are to be made in these areas, and that judges may be just as skilful in making at least some kind of policy decisions as congressmen.[1] As to the first of these points, he rejects a response he imagines I might make, which is that legislatures decide to leave certain areas to courts because legislatures have taken a deliberate decision that these areas are better developed through concern for principle than policy. He says that it is more realistic to suppose that the legislature abstains because of 'some vague sense that the problems are being adequately handled by courts'.[2] No doubt, but that avoids the important question. Perhaps the 'vague sense' arises just because these areas are *in fact* adequately developed through considerations of principle, including consequentialist consideration, so that the legislature is under no pressure to intervene in the name of policy.

Two points encourage this particular explanation of the fact that the so-called 'common-law' areas have been able to develop, to the extent they have, through judge-made rather than statutory law. First, the common-law areas are just those in which Professor Coase's celebrated theorem has most force.[3] Coase pointed out that, if we disregard transaction costs, it will not make any difference to the overall efficiency of

[1] See Greenawalt, 1004.
[2] *Ibid.*, 1005.
[3] See Coase, 'The Problem of Social Cost', 3 *J. L. & Econ.* 1, 19–28 (1960).

resource allocation whether liability in tort or contract falls on one or the other of two private parties to a transaction or an event, though of course it makes a great difference to the parties. Of course, transaction costs are genuine costs, so that the choice of one rule of tort or contract makes a marginal difference to overall economic efficiency, but, as commentators have pointed out, considerations of equity – considerations about which economic role ought in fairness to bear a certain cost – are likely to be more significant.[1] Second, the transactions and events that give rise to common law problems are drawn from relatively familiar sorts of situations, and these are situations exhibiting the familiar conflict between the abstract right of members of a community to a measure of concern from those whose acts affect them, and the abstract liberty of others who wish to pursue their own interests and ambitions. They are therefore situations as to which some degree of moral consensus will have developed, within the community, as to what fairness requires – a consensus that will inevitably make considerations of consequence relevant to that determination. That has two consequences germane here. It will mean that a court will be more likely to reach decisions of principle that will seem satisfactory to the community as a whole – more satisfactory to all groups than the decisions courts can reach when controversial or novel rights are in play. It will also mean that when a common law case does present a problem whose solution will for some reason have important economic consequences in spite of Coase's theorem, like the case of the polluting factory that employs large numbers of workers, then arguments of principle will be at hand that will make those decisive economic consequences relevant.

Greenawalt's second point, that judges can be clever about policy, is simply wide of the mark. There is indeed a popular argument to the effect that judges simply do not have the training or resources available to study complex economic or other instrumental claims, but I think that argument is wrong. I know of no reason to think that the average judge has less talent or time available for such study than the average congressman, or that he could get no more from books than the authors of these books dictate into committee reports that congressmen do not in any case have time to read.

My point was a different one. It is unrealistic to think that individual legislators decide how to vote by measuring the programmes submitted to them against Benthamite conceptions of the general good, deciding on nice calculations how far to pursue one strategy, and when to leave it off in favour of another. The institution of representative democracy is an imperfect machine for pursuing the general welfare; it works, to the degree it does, as a kind of black box, in which various sorts of political

[1] See, e.g., Baker, 'The Ideology of the Economic Analysis of Law', 5 *Phil. & Pub. Aff.* 3 (1975).

pressures compete, so that (if the community is lucky) an invisible hand will produce an approximation of the general good over the long run, or at least a closer approximation than we have reason to think a different institution would produce. The institution may provide an example of what Rawls called procedural justice,[1] and it may be, as this description suggests, that in spite of the efforts of welfare economists and utilitarian party theoreticians, we cannot produce any independent non-institutional definition of the general welfare, but must instead rely on some intuitive idea that the general welfare consists in what a well-designed institution of this sort produces. There are, of course, other arguments in favour of legislation by representative democracy, like the argument that this institution provides popular political participation that is a good for its own sake, or for the communitarian feelings it encourages. But the argument from procedural justice is the argument I had in mind when I said that the theory of democracy provides objections to judges deciding cases on grounds of policy that do not hold when the judge decides on grounds of principle. I did not think that the politician's mail bag gives him technical information, or information about the shape of the social indifference curve, that is unavailable to the judge, but rather that it puts him under weights of political pressure from which the judge is rightly immune.

It now remains to consider Greenawalt's most explicitly normative position. He believes that even if I am right that judges characteristically decide hard cases on arguments of principle, there is in fact no good reason why they should not sometimes decide such cases on arguments of policy.[2] He relies principally on bizarre non-legal hypothetical examples. Normally, hypothetical examples coax out intuitions that can then be tested against theory. But when the examples are fantastic the intuitions they summon are often correspondingly insecure, if indeed, they summon any intuitions at all. Did the tribal council believe that though the moral conventions of the society, properly understood, permitted Barking Dog to kill Crazy Fox, he was not, from the standpoint of genuine morality, morally free to do so?[3] If it did, then it faces a case of conflict between institutional right and moral duty, not a simple conflict between institutional right and social welfare. If, on the other hand, the council thought that, all things considered, Barking Dog was morally as well as institutionally free to do what he did, then my intuition holds that they were wrong to punish him, even by requiring reparations. It would have been an ideal case for the council to adopt a legislative posture, and to announce whatever reforming rules they thought they had the power to impose for the future. Likewise, Greenawalt's case of the first forward pass cries out for

[1] See J. Rawls, *A Theory of Justice* (1971).
[2] See Greenawalt, 1052.
[3] See Greenawalt, 999–1001.

prospective-only legislation.[1] The referee supposes that the team throwing the pass had no right to do so, and that a decision in its favour would violate the legitimate expectations of the other side – legitimate not because the issue was free from doubt, but because (as the referee believes) the team was in fact entitled that passes not be thrown. If (incredibly) no means exist for changing the rules of a commercially important spectator sport except through official lying, this is a defect, but my intuitions do not suggest that the defending team should suffer an injustice in consequence. I suspect that Greenawalt does not see the injustice because he thinks that the moral relevance of an institutional right is exhausted by the notice that right gives, so that when it is doubtful whether the right exists, no injustice occurs in ignoring it even if it does. (That mistake, as we shall see, dominates the second half of Professor Munzer's article.[2])

Late in his éssay, Greenawalt offers some examples of lawsuits in which he thinks that judges may properly ignore legal rights, sometimes in favour of policy, and sometimes in favour of competing moral rights. On the side of policy, he imagines a 'badly drafted' antipollution statute that raises problems, in a civil case, whether a particular practice is covered.[3] He tells us that if a case had been brought just after the statute was enacted the judge would have 'properly' decided that the practice was not covered, but that the judge may 'properly' decide the other way years later, if public opinion has changed but 'all relevant legal materials have remained unaltered'. This is mysterious. If the legal issue turns on the consequences to the community of the practice in question (which would be very likely, as we have seen, if the case were a common law case, and, which is almost certain here, in the case of a statute[4]) then these consequences are part of the 'legal materials'; if the consequences have not changed in the intervening years, it is hard to see why a decision that is 'proper' now was not 'proper' then. It is, of course, understandable that the particular judge in question, and the legal community as a whole, would be more likely to attend to the undesirable consequences if the community had grown indignant over them; but that argues only that the decision is more likely to be the proper one now than then, which is something different. It is also possible that the community would in some way have resisted the proper decision earlier, but is ready to accept it now; but, once again, that is a different issue.

Greenawalt also cites an actual case, *City of El Paso v. Simmons*,[5] in

---

[1] See Greenawalt, 998–9.

[2] See section 3 below.

[3] See Greenawalt, 1048.

[4] Greenawalt argues in his essay that judges must use arguments of policy in interpreting statutes. He seems unaware of my argument to the same effect. See above, p. 107.

[5] 379 U.S. (1965), discussed in Greenawalt, 1049.

which, as he thinks, the Supreme Court 'without doubt' violated political rights guaranteed by the Constitution in the interests of the general welfare, and he notes that Mr. Justice Black, in dissent, agreed with that characterization of the Court's decision. It is, of course, a different question whether the majority of the Court believed that was what it was doing. I think not, and certainly the language of the majority opinion stoutly denies the charge, which, it suggests, would be decisive if it were true. But Greenawalt apparently thinks that even if those in the majority thought that the Constitution guaranteed what Texas took away, they would have been right to stand aside provided they approved of Texas's arguments of policy. I find that extraordinary.

Greenawalt's remaining cases are those in which he thinks it would be right for courts to ignore legal rights in favour of competing moral rights. Such cases, of course, raise very different issues from the so-called policy cases. He uses as examples those pre-Civil War cases about escaped slaves[1] that I discussed in a review of a recent book by Professor Cover.[2] I said that many of those cases (particularly those involving interpretation of the due process clause) were wrongly decided, just as a matter of law, and that the failure of judges who hated slavery to reach correct decisions in favour of escaped slaves could be attributed to a failure of jurisprudence. Greenawalt apparently disagrees, but that is not important in this context, because I do not want to deny that realistic cases can be found that present true conflicts between legal and moral rights, if not in America, then those in despotic countries, Nazi Germany and at present South Africa, to which jurisprudence often turns.

Legal rights, in my view, are institutional rights, and these are genuine rights that provide important and normally very powerful reasons for political decisions. Background moral rights enter, in ways I have tried to describe, into the calculation of what legal rights people have when the standard materials provide uncertain guidance, and some positivists' thesis, that legal rights and moral rights are conceptually distinct, is therefore wrong. But there are of course cases in which the institutional right is clearly settled by established legal materials, like a statute, and clearly conflicts with background moral rights. In these cases the judge seeking to do what is morally right is faced with a familiar sort of conflict: the institutional right provides a genuine reason, the importance of which will vary with the general justice or wickedness of the system as a whole, for a decision one way, but certain considerations of morality present an important reason against it. If the judge decides that the reasons supplied by background moral rights are so strong that he has a moral duty to do

---

[1] See Greenawalt, 1050.

[2] See Dworkin, 'The Law of the Slave Catchers' (review of R. Cover, *Justice Accused*, 1975), *Times Literary Supplement*, 5 Dec. 1975, p. 1437.

what he can to support these rights, then it may be that he must lie, because he cannot be of any help unless he is understood as saying, in his official role, that the legal rights are different from what he believes they are. He could, of course, avoid lying by resigning, which will ordinarily be of very little help, or by staying in office and hoping, against odds, that his appeal based on moral grounds will have the same practical effect as a lie would.

I agree with Professor Hart,[1] however, that it would be unwise to make this lie a matter of jurisprudential theory, by saying that in such a case the legal rights are in fact just what morality requires. We do well enough, in such a case, with the accurate description, which is that legal and moral rights here conflict. There is no need to abandon that description when the case is a hard rather than an easy case. If the institutional legal right does conflict with morality, in spite of the influence that morality must have on the right anwer in a hard case, then jurisprudence must report the conflict accurately, leaving to the judge both the difficult moral decision he must then make and the lie he may be forced to tell.

I am unclear whether Greenawalt means to disagree with any of this, or how far he thinks I have said anything to the contrary. He says that in a case in which legal and moral rights conflict, it would be wrong to suppose that it is the judge's *legal* duty to decide in favour of the legal right.[2] What distinction does he mean to make here? We might want to describe the moral conflict a judge faces in such a case by distinguishing his 'legal' duty, which is to find for legal rights, from his 'moral' or 'overall' or 'final' duty, which may require him to ignore legal rights. This is not the distinction Greenawalt intends, however, because he says the judge may have no legal duty to enforce legal rights. Perhaps he uses 'legal' duty to mean overall or final duty, in which case, though this usage seems likely to mislead, he does not disagree with me. Or perhaps he wants, in this way, to join the party of those who hold that legal and moral duties, properly understood, can never conflict. But then he contradicts his own assumption, that in just these cases they do.

D. Discretion

I shall use this occasion to discuss an argument Greenawalt made, not in the essay I have been discussing, but in another long essay on my work published several years ago.[3] In Chapter 2 I distinguish three senses of 'discretion' and identify a 'strong' sense. Judges have discretion, in that

---

[1] See Hart, 'Positivism and the Separation of Law and Morals', 71 *Harv. L. Rev.* 593 (1958).

[2] See Greenawalt, 1051.

[3] Greenawalt, 'Discretion and Judicial Decision: The Elusive Quest for the Fetters that Bind Judges', 75 *Colum. L. Rev.* 359 (1975).

strong sense, only when no party has a right to a decision. Several Chapters argue that judges typically have no discretion, in that strong sense, in deciding claims of right in ordinary civil cases, no matter how controversial these claims are. Greenawalt's essay suggests a short-cut around the various philosophical arguments I make. He says that if we attend to the 'ordinary discourse' use of 'discretion' or to what it makes 'good sense' to say in certain contexts, then we shall see that the idea that judges typically do not have discretion in a hard case 'is simply incorrect'.

Here are the two crucial passages in Greenawalt's argument. 'In ordinary discourse discretion exists if there is more than one decision that will be considered proper by those to whom the decision maker is responsible, and whatever external standards may be applicable either cannot be discovered by the decision-maker or do not yield clear answers to the question that must be decided. If I am correct about ordinary discourse, there is no good reason to use the term "discretion" differently in describing the the responsibilities of judges in legal cases.' 'When authoritative standards yield no clear answers, when a judge must rely on debateable personal assessments to decide a case, and when more than one result will widely be regarded as a satisfactory fulfilment of his judicial responsibilities then it does not make good sense to say that the judge is under a duty to reach one result rather than another; as far as the law is concerned, he has discretion to decide between them.'

These two statements (which I take to be different ways of saying the same thing) harbour an important ambiguity. Suppose a case in which 'authoritative' or 'external' standards yield 'no clear answer' so that the judge must rely on 'debateable personal assessments'. (I assume that means only that there is, in my vocabulary, a hard case.) A judge will have discretion to decide either way, according to these statements, if more than one decision will each be widely considered 'proper' or 'a satisfactory fulfilment' of judicial responsibilities. The ambiguity lies in the phrases 'proper' and 'a satisfactory fulfilment.' Do these require that two decisions be considered *equally sound*, or only *both respectable*, that is, both decisions that a competent, responsible and sincere judge might well make? Moral practice distinguishes these two ideas. Someone who believes (even passionately) that people who eat meat are violating the rights of animals might concede that he has no argument for this view which must inevitably convince any honest person, and therefore that someone who has reflected on the matter with due attention to his arguments, but remains unconvinced and continues to eat meat, is behaving responsibly though what he does violates the rights of others.

The distinction is especially important in legal criticism. I may think that the Supreme Court reached the wrong decision in (say) the *Rodruiguiz* case, and yet wish to deny that the decision the judges reached was so plainly wrong, or the manner in which they reached it so clearly inappropriate, that it would be fair to say that they behaved irresponsibly. I might say that though the plaintiff class had a legal right to win, in my opinion, the decision against them was nevertheless within the group of decisions that it was proper, in this sense, for the Court to reach. This distinction – and the ability of citizens to make it – is of very great practical importance in securing respect for the law when decisions must be controversial.

So we must choose between two interpretations of Greenawalt's theory about the ordinary use of 'discretion' and what it makes good sense to say. (1) Strong discretion exists if it is widely considered that neither party has a right to win, that is, that either decision is, from the standpoint of the parties' rights, equally correct. (2) Strong discretion exists if it is widely considered that more than one decision could be the outcome of a sincere and responsible effort to make the right decision about the rights of the parties.

Interpretation (2) would be an acceptable account of what I called the first 'weak' sense of discretion. (I said that a judge has discretion in that weak sense 'if his duty is defined by standards that reasonable men can interpret in different ways'.[1] But interpretation (2) is incoherent as an account of the strong sense of discretion. For it licenses someone to say that a judge has discretion though one of the parties has, all things considered, a right to the decision he seeks. Suppose a defender of (2) tries to meet this objection by arguing that (2) is also a correct 'ordinary discourse' account of having a right to a decision. One party has a right to a decision, on this account, only when it is false that either decision would be considered respectable. (Greenawalt suggests this extension when he says that 'In very difficult cases, however, neither litigant is "entitled" to the result he wants'. The quotes around 'entitled' (in the original) suggest that some ordinary language work is in hand.) This only compounds the trouble, because lawyers who want to make the distinction just described, and say that the petitioners in *Rodruiguiz* had, all things considered, a right to win though the decision was certainly not irresponsible, now cannot make that distinction without self-contradiction.

So we must settle for interpretation (1). Discretion exists if most lawyers believe that neither party has a right to win, so that each decision is equally correct. This is not, of course, the same as a third possible interpretation of the original statements: (3) Discretion exists if more than one decision would be considered correct by some group, that is, if each of two decisions has substantial support among lawyers. *That* situation will, I think, typically hold in hard cases. But if anyone proposed (3) as an 'ordinary discourse' account of 'discretion', then he would make inco-

---

[1] See above, p. 69.

herent what each of the lawyers wishes to say in such a case. Each wishes
to say that, in spite of the fact that a large party of lawyers believes the
contrary, one party has a right to win and the judge has no discretion to
decide against that party.

If (1) were the correct account of discretion, then whether I am 'simply
incorrect' (in believing that discretion rarely exists in deciding questions
about legal rights) would depend upon the factual question of whether
lawyers in such cases are often agreed that neither party has a right to
win. I am sure that typically they are not agreed, though I may be wrong.
It does not matter, however, because (1) cannot be a correct account of
discretion. It fails to make the natural distinction between the widespread
belief that a judge has discretion and the *fact* that he does. On the
contrary, it makes the fact consist in the popularity of the belief. But there
are famous difficulties in any theory that makes the existence of some fact
consist in the belief that the fact is so. What is it that someone believes,
on this account, when he believes that judges have discretion? He believes
that others believe that neither party has a right to win. But that means
he believes that each of them believes that others believe that neither
party has a right to win, and so on. Quite apart from these plain logical
difficulties, interpretation (1) runs contrary to ordinary usage. For it is
perfectly sensible for one lawyer to say that each of two decisions is equally
correct, and therefore that the judge has discretion, even when he knows
that no one else agrees (perhaps because they are the victims of bad
theories of adjudication.) But on Greenawalt's thesis (understood as
interpretation (1)) that lawyer must be wrong, and, indeed, speaking
nonsense.

So some repair is necessary. But only one repair will do. We must drop
the reference to what is widely believed, so that the thesis becomes the
thesis that discretion exists if two decisions are (not simply are believed to
be) equally correct because neither party has a right to a decision in the
matter. I grant *that* thesis straightaway. It is just one way of starting what
I take to be the strong sense of discretion. But no one can rely on that
thesis to maintain, without further argument, that it is simply false that
judges have no discretion in hard cases. That claim must be supported,
either by philosophical arguments that show, *a priori*, that neither side
can have a right to win in a hard case, or by legal arguments that show,
case-by-case, from the inside, that the arguments in favour of either side's
right are no stronger than the arguments in favour of the other's. I
discussed the possibility of such arguments in Chapter 13, and in 'No
Right Answer?' So far as I know, Greenawalt has made none.

3. MUNZER AND NO RIGHT ANSWER

A. Is there no right answer?

When reasonable men disagree about some issue of law, and do not agree on a test that would resolve the disagreement if all physical facts and facts about mental states were known, can their disagreement be genuine? Or should we rather say that there is no right answer to the question under dispute? The latter view is popular among academic lawyers, and is presupposed in much modern jurisprudence. It also has its supporters in philosophy, though no philosopher I know thinks the matter is as straightforward as the lawyers seem to think. I wrote an article,[1] and Chapter 13 of this book, trying to show the complexities of the issue, and also to show that no good argument has been made for the no-right-answer thesis in law. In the former I suggested that the lawyers had failed to distinguish two versions of their claim. On the first version, two lawyers debating whether the plaintiff has a right to a decision, or whether, on the other hand, the defendant has a right to win, may both be wrong, because the right answer is that neither party has a right to win. On the second version, neither lawyer is right, but neither is wrong either; what each says is, for some reason, neither true nor false.

I gave, as an example of an enterprise in which the second version of the thesis might be thought sometimes to hold, a literary exercise in which the participants debate about, for example, whether David Copperfield really loved his mother, or whether he had Type-A blood. In Chapter 13 I offered a further distinction, between two different standpoints from which the judgment that some issue has no right answer, in the sense of the second version, might be made. The judgment might be made as an internal judgment which regards the 'no-right-answer' answer as an answer that is competitive with other possible answers, but to be preferred, all things considered, to the others. Suppose a literary critic says that though he believes that David really hated his mother, in spite of the fact that most other critics disagree, he also believes that the question of whether David had Type-A blood has no right answer because nothing in the story bears on it either way. He reaches the no-right-answer decision, in the latter judgment, from within the enterprise, as a participant applying its standards as he understands them. But suppose a philosopher says that no proposition about a fictional character can be either true or false except by virtue of convention or some other form of agreement, and therefore that no statement about which critics disagree, such as the

---

[1] See Dworkin, 'No Right Answer?', in P. Hacker and J. Raz (eds), *Law, Morality and Society: Essays in Honour of H. L. A. Hart*, pp. 58ff., reprinted and expanded in a forthcoming issue of the *New York University Law Review*.

statement that David really hated his mother, can be either true or false. He intends, at least, to take a standpoint external to the enterprise; he does not regard his judgment, that there is no right answer to the question about David's mother, as competitive with the other two possible judgments, and requiring support from the same sorts of arguments as those who make the other judgments try to supply. His point is that the attempt to supply this sort of argument for any proposition about a fictional character is misconceived, for philosophical reasons, because the truth or falsity of such a proposition can consist only in agreement.

My arguments are supposed to show that any sensible version of the no-right-answer thesis for law must be based, not on this external, critical posture, but rather on internal judgments like that the literary critic might make about David. That means that the no-right-answer thesis is a thesis about particular legal issues, which argues that the no-right-answer answer is a better answer than its competitors, on the merits, in particular cases. I gave reasons for thinking that the no-right-answer answer will rarely be the right answer in a developed legal system, though of course my general theory of adjudication makes plain the possibility that it will be the right answer sometimes.

These issues, I should repeat, are extremely complex. I do not mean this summary to be a substitute for the arguments of the essays they summarize, and I am conscious that these essays only scratch the surface of difficult and contested issues in the philosophy of language. I shall have to write more than I have on the subject. But the arguments I made in these essays were intended to show that one argument for the no-right-answer thesis is too simple. No one has yet shown that it follows, from the fact that reasonable people disagree over some proposition, and do not agree on a test that will make some further discovery decisive, that the proposition is for that reason alone neither true nor false. Professor Munzer now replies. He says that I cannot be right, because in the examples I give reasonable people disagree and do not even agree on a test that will make some further discovery decisive.[1]

I confess that I do not know how best to continue the discussion with him. I wish he had taken notice of the distinctions I offered, telling us either which version of the thesis he means to maintain, or why, if that is what he thinks, the distinctions I propose are not helpful. I wish he had taken notice of the arguments I made against his simple claim, that disagreement in principle means no truth value. As matters stand, I can only show how the arguments I have already made are illustrated rather than opposed by Munzer's remarks.

Because Munzer accepts the analogy between law and literary criticism,

---

[1] See Munzer, 'Right Answers, Pre-existing Rights and Fairness', 11 *Ga. L. Rev.* 1055, 1060 (1977).

at least to the degree presupposed by the argument he makes, he might well mean to defend the second version of the no-right-answer thesis, and to defend it from the internal standpoint. He discusses, for example, the question of whether Maggie Verver knew about the new affair between Charlotte and the Prince, and says that

> literary critics may marshall substantial evidence on both sides of the issue. . . . Very likely no right answer exists to these questions or thousands of others that are raised about works of literature. . . . There are, we might say, alternative fictional possible worlds of comparable plausibility in which [the] proposition or its negation holds.[1]

The words 'substantial' and 'comparable' cause trouble here. Does Munzer (who has read the novel and thought about the question) himself think that the evidence is not only substantial on both sides, but of equivalent force, all things considered, so that the two possible worlds he contemplates are not only of 'comparable' but of 'equal' plausibility? I mean by 'equivalent force' and 'equal plausibility' not the same numerical point on some quantitative scale, but only that the cases on both sides are so well balanced that no reason exists for preferring either, which is of course a stronger claim than that both sides are of 'comparable' plausibility. If so, then Munzer disagrees with all the literary critics he cites, each of whom supposes that the case on one side or the other is stronger, though of course they disagree among themselves as to which. He may be right — each reader of the novel will have to make up his mind for himself, and some may agree with Munzer rather than with the party of critics. But if unpopularity is any evidence that a position is wrong, it is Munzer, and not either group of the critics who unite in opposing him, who suffers most from that evidence. (It makes no difference that, as Munzer says, each critic will be relying, not simply on judgments of consistency, but on such controversial criteria of literary criticism as he mentions. Presumably Munzer means to include the choice and application of these criteria when he says that the arguments on both sides are substantial and comparable — an argument that relied on an obviously silly literary theory would not be substantial — and we may still ask whether he thinks that, these considerations taken into account, the arguments on both sides are of equivalent force.)

But suppose Munzer does not think that the arguments are of equivalent force. If he were a literary critic, he would join the party which maintains that Maggie did know, even though he acknowledges that the arguments on the other side are 'substantial'. (If he were the judge in some hard case,

[1] *Ibid.*, 1957.

he would decide that the plaintiff had the better of the argument of principle, even though he cannot dismiss the defendant's case as trivial.) Now he cannot say, from the internal standpoint, that there is no right answer to the question of which side has the better case, because he thinks one side is in fact better. May he now say that he wishes to press not the internal but the external standpoint of criticism? He might say that when arguments are of comparable, though not necessarily equivalent, strength, then as a matter of the theory of truth, or of some other philosophical consideration, the propositions they support cannot be either true or false. But he must then answer some very difficult questions, including these: Can propositions about fictional characters (or propositions of law) ever be true or false? If so, in what can their truth or falsity consist? Is it in the fact of agreement, if that exists, or in the fact that the proposition or its negation logically follows from some more abstract proposition that is agreed? Can either of these theories of truth be squared with the practice of lawyers and literary critics, who do not think, when they make a judgment, that they are reporting or predicting the fact of agreement, directly or indirectly? What can Munzer himself mean when as a participant he says (or in any case believes) that one side or the other has the better argument, even if only narrowly? How can we dissolve the apparent conflict between what he says as a critic and believes as a participant? I do not mean that nothing can be said in answer to these questions; indeed many philosophers believe, I think, that they are less testing than I suppose. But we need to know what answers Munzer would give if we are to proceed to examine his arguments, taking them to be made from the external standpoint.

At the close of his argument for the no-right-answer thesis, Munzer makes what I think is a revealing and important statement. He notices what he calls my concession 'that it is logically possible for some lawsuits not to have uniquely correct results'.[1] If he means that I believe that it is 'logically possible' that in some cases the arguments for each side should be of equivalent power, then he is right, though I should hardly call it a concession. But he then adds this: 'No doubt Dworkin's position [that there are likely to be few such cases] is compatible with the existence of a few disagreements among reasonable lawyers. But the large number of important controversies is strong empirical evidence for the proposition that right answers are often wanting in hard cases.'[2]

His use of the word 'empirical' here supports my assumption that he speaks from the internal rather than the external standpoint. But from the internal standpoint, persistent and heated controversy about propositions of law is hardly strong evidence against 'Dworkin's position'. Munzer

---

[1] *Ibid.*, 1059.
[2] *Ibid.*, 1059–60.

apparently assumes that if two lawyers sincerely disagree, and neither can convince the other, that is evidence for the fact that both are wrong, because neither side can then have even marginally the better case. But Munzer himself would, presumably, have trouble convincing *either* of the two lawyers that *that* lawyer is wrong, and the disagreement between Munzer and him would be persistent and possibly even heated. Does it follow, on Munzer's assumption, that Munzer is wrong in his *third* view as well? That would leave him with exactly nothing at all.[1]

B. *Does it matter?*

There is a reason, however, why Munzer has not explored the question of whether legal questions have right answers with as much care as my article suggests is necessary. He thinks, as he explains in the second half of his essay, that the question has no practical importance. His argument to that effect 'depend[s] . . . on the modest assumption that no practical interest would attach to classifying a right as antecedently existing unless it were in principle possible to establish its pre-existence',[2] and 'establish' means demonstrate in such a way that no reasonable lawyer could resist the demonstration. He concedes, *arguendo*, that in a hard case like the negligence cases I discussed in the last section, the plaintiff may have a legal right to damages for the injury he has suffered, even though reasonable lawyers disagree about whether he does, but that in that case the fact that he does would have no practical importance. This conclusion rests, in turn, on a surprising assumption, which is that the only interest that attaches to saying that a right exists before any decision is actually announced is that if there is a pre-existing legal right, then the defendant may be on notice that he must not infringe it. Since that is the only interest we have in the question whether the plaintiff has a legal right to be compensated, the question loses all interest when the right, if it exists, is so controversial that the defendant may be excused for not knowing the plaintiff had it.

This argument misconceives what an argument about rights is about. It is about rights. If someone has a right to a political decision of any sort, that is in itself a powerful, and normally a decisive reason, in favour of a judicial decision awarding him damages. The connection between someone having a right to a decision and there being a reason in favour of that decision is not contingent but conceptual. No plausible account can be given of what a right is that does not include, as belonging to the concept of a right, the idea that if someone has a right, then it is wrong for others

---

[1] If the criticism is meant externally, based on some philosophical theory about truth, then the large number of indissoluble controversies would not be evidence that 'right answers are often wanting in hard cases', but would be the fact itself.

[2] Munzer, *op. cit.*, 1063.

to treat him otherwise than as specified, at least unless some strong counter-vailing reason for doing so is available. Any other account of what a right is – supposing that whether someone has a right is one question, and whether his having that right requires anyone to treat him differently is another – makes the mistake of reifying rights.

Of course, the question of whether someone has a particular right may be complex, and any answer may be controversial. But the question of what political decision is the right one is not an *independent* question from the question of whether someone has a right to that decision. If the latter question is controversial, then the former question must be, for that very reason, controversial as well; if someone believes the plaintiff in a negligence case has a right to damages, even though others disagree, then he must also believe that a most powerful argument exists for a decision for the plaintiff, even though others will also disagree with that. If he tries to separate these two beliefs, by supposing, even *arguendo*, that the plaintiff has a legal right but that nothing follows about what a court should do, then what he says is not coherent. So much for the claim that no practical interest can attach to the question of whether the plaintiff has a legal right in a hard case. Nothing attaches to that question except practical interest.

How can so able a legal philosopher have gone so wrong here? The answer, at one level, seems clear. He has mistaken the question of notice, which is often a factor in deciding whether a particular judicial decision is fair, with the question of fairness itself. An argument about legal rights, even in a hard case, is an argument about something relevant to fairness; if the court believes that the plaintiff has a right, then it believes, all things considered, including the question of surprise, that a decision against the plaintiff would be, at least *prima facie*, unfair. Of course, the question of rights, and therefore of fairness, may be controversial. But if the court is charged with the decision, the court's decision about what is, all things considered, the fair thing to do must as a practical matter dispose of the case. I spoke to that issue, anticipating Munzer's present argument, in *Hard Cases*, and will not repeat here what I said there. But it might be useful to see how absurd Munzer's argument would seem if pressed in a moral rather than judicial context. Suppose I have damaged your property by my carelessness, and you now say that I had no right to behave as I did, and now have a duty to make good the damage I caused. We discuss the matter, and I now agree that you are right on both counts, but I say that this is of only academic interest, and of no practical importance, because your right and my duty, which I now concede, are controversial, so that I could not be blamed for not recognizing them when I acted. I am confused. What I say may establish that I should not be blamed or thought wicked for behaving as I did. But I must not say that it shows that what I did was not wrong, or that you are not entitled that I bear the loss, because that is just what I have conceded in conceding your arguments.

But that explanation of Munzer's mistake simply raises the same puzzle at a different level. Why should Munzer have mixed up the question of controversiality and the question of fairness in his theory of legal rights when, presumably, he would not make the same mistake about moral rights? The answer lies, I think, in a more general and more popular mistake about what legal rights are. In easy cases legal rights can be deduced, in something close to a syllogistic fashion, from propositions reported in books that are available to the public, and even more readily available to lawyers the public can hire. It is fatally tempting to draw two conclusions. The first is that legal rights provide reasons for judicial decision *because* they come from books, that is, because the propositions that create them give notice of their birth. The second is the further conclusion that in a hard case, if the plaintiff really does have the right he urges, then since that right cannot be deduced from propositions in public books, it must be deducible from propositions written in some *secret* books, available to neither the public nor lawyers nor judges. In that case judges, in purporting to decide hard cases on arguments about legal rights, are simply guessing what they would find in those secret books if only they could get at them. (Professor Brilmayer, who shares this picture with Munzer, applies the principle of indifference, and concludes that judges have only a fifty-fifty chance of guessing right.[1]) This picture has, I think, exercised a great hold on jurisprudence. It lies behind Holmes' famous observation that legal rights must be only the rights that are laid down in actual, terrestrial books because law cannot be a 'brooding omnipresence'. It also lies behind the assumption that non-positivists must believe in something called natural law, which is taken to be the contents of celestial secret books.

If someone thought that rights in hard cases could only be rights because they are written into secret books, it might seem to follow that these secret rules could be relevant in adjudication only by virtue of the notice they provide to guide conduct, which is none. But the secret-book picture is no part of any proper account of why people can have legal rights even though reasonable lawyers disagree that they do. People have such rights by virtue of reasons of fairness of the sort I described in *Hard Cases*. If Munzer concedes that they may have such rights, even *arguendo*, then he cannot deny that the same reasons of fairness argue in favour of enforcing these rights.

But perhaps we should reinterpret Munzer's arguments here, so that they call for reform of our legal system. He might be understood as

[1] See Brilmayer, 'The Institutional and Empirical Basis of the Rights Thesis', 11 *Ga. L. Rev.* 1173, 1198–9 (1977).

proposing a new theory of legal rights, according to which a party simply does not have a legal right unless he is able to demonstrate to the satisfaction of all reasonable lawyers that he does. In that event, hard cases would not be decided, as they now are, after thorough and perhaps agonized attempts to decide whether, all things considered, the plaintiff does have the institutional right he claims. If the plaintiff is unable to make a knock-down case for a right, he has no right, and that is that. It is unclear what process of decision Munzer would substitute, and therefore what we should gain by the change. But it is fairly clear what we should lose.

Under the present system, we aspire that adjudication be a matter of principle. The aspiration cannot be fully realized, because each of us will think that judges sometimes, and perhaps often, make mistaken arguments of principle. But we gain even through the attempt. Citizens are encouraged to suppose that each has rights and duties against other citizens, and against their common government, even though these rights and duties are not all set out in black-letter codes. They are therefore encouraged to frame and test hypotheses about what these rights are, and to treat one another, and demand to be treated by the state, under the beneficial and unifying assumption that justice is always relevant to their claims even when it is unclear what justice requires. The courts participate in this process, by providing an occasional forum for public considerations of these controversial issues of justice, and by providing leadership whose power is rightly qualified by the force of the arguments it can command.

We take a mean view of ourselves if we suppose that this practice is valuable only to the extent that it provides reliable predictions about how official power will be used. Of course, the practice can be, and has been, abused by governments anxious to take the good name of law for tyranny. There are nations in which citizens would be better off if no claim could be made in the name of law that was not drawn from a public book, and there are those, I know, who think that Britain and the United States are among those nations. But even they must concede that something would be lost by the change. The rule of law is a nobler ideal than the rule of legal texts.

4. RICHARDS AND POSITIVISM REVIVED

Professor Richards' essay[1] is not in the main a critique of my views, but an essay of much more general interest about the connections between law and morals. He is anxious, however, to distinguish his views from mine

---

[1] Richards, 'Rules, Policies and Neutral Principles: The Search for Legitimacy in Common Law and Constitutional Adjudication', 11 *Ga. L. Rev.* 1069, 1095–6 (1977).

about that problem. He thinks, as I understand him, that though in practice my work follows the tenets of what he calls 'methodological natural law', there are defects, happily not affecting that practice, in the more conceptual claims I have made. I think that we disagree less, even at the conceptual level, than Richards now supposes, because the disagreements he sees are more verbal than substantial. Such disagreement as we have arises, in my view, because Richards does not sufficiently appreciate the differences between orthodox natural law theory and the different theory of law I have tried to defend. Something like the latter theory, improved and clarified as certainly it needs to be, provides much more substantial support than legal positivism can for just the 'methodological natural law' studies that Richards recommends and does so well.

Richards' criticism is aimed at two points in my general argument. He agrees with me that what I have called principles (using that word, for the moment, comprehensively, so as not to distinguish policies from principles more narrowly defined) play an important role in establishing what the law is on some matter, and that the role of these principles is therefore not limited to arguments about what the law ought to be. But he believes that traditional legal positivism, which insists that what the law is is just a matter of fact, is nevertheless sound. Positivism can admit the role of principles of law, because the question of what principles are indeed principles of any particular legal system is itself a question of fact, and the question of what these principles require in a particular case is just a matter of ordinary professional judgment. Richards' arguments to this effect are captured in these statements:

> Legal principles are, after all, legal; in order to be binding, they must be implicit in past judicial tradition and practice, inferable by the usual methods of legal reasoning by analogy. . .
>
> . . . Legal principles, like legal rules, depend at bottom on an issue of fact, that is, the critical attitudes of judges. . .
>
> . . . Indeed, it is possible that the principles legally binding on a judge may be so morally defective that the unmitigated application of those principles would violate the judge's moral duties. Distinctions of this kind can still be drawn, and the moral question must always be independently raised.

I have discussed, on other occasions, the question of whether the identification of legal principles can be said to be simply a matter of ordinary fact.[1] I said it could not, and I should be interested in knowing why Richards finds my arguments unsatisfactory. Perhaps the difficulty arises from an ambiguity in the first of the three statements collected in

[1] See above, pp. 64–8.

the preceding quotation. If principles are properly to figure in adjudication, he says, then these principles must be 'implicit' in 'past judicial tradition and practice, inferable by the unusual methods'. But what does this mean? If it means, as Richards' reference to 'critical attitudes' suggests, that principles do not count unless there is a tradition of actually citing those principles, he is wrong, because the actual practice of using principles often ignores that stricture. He does not mean, as the word 'inferable' might be thought to suggest, that principles follow deductively from a batch of precedents, so that if two lawyers disagree over whether a particular principle is 'legally binding', one of them must be making a logical mistake. That suggestion is silly, and even sillier if it is then maintained that not only the content of a principle, but its weight as well, are matters for deduction. Richards says that the content is inferable by the 'usual methods of reasoning by analogy'. But that is not helpful because precisely the issue in question is whether the 'usual methods' of reasoning in hard cases, which lawyers call reasoning by analogy, make the issues presented by these cases matters of fact, and that depends on further analysis of what this 'reasoning by analogy' really is.

In *Hard Cases*,[1] I offered an account of what it means to say that a principle is 'embedded in' or 'implicit in' or may be 'inferred by analogy from' a set of earlier decisions. I said that a principle bears that relationship to earlier decisions, or other legal material, if the principle figures in what I called the best justification of that material. That makes it, of course, a matter of judgment, about which lawyers may and will disagree, whether a particular principle is indeed 'inferable' from past material. One justification may be better than another (I also said) in two different dimensions: it may prove a better fit, in the sense that it requires less of the material to be taken to be 'mistakes', or it may prove a morally more compelling justification, because it comes closer to capturing sound political morality. If a theory containing one principle is better on the dimension of fit, but a theory containing a contrary principle is better on the dimension of morality, then the jurisprudential question is raised as to which dimension is more important in determining institutional rights in cases of that sort. One answer to that jurisprudential question (stated in a crude and simple form) would be this: No theory can count as an adequate justification of institutional history unless it provides a good fit with that history; it must not expose more than a low threshold number of decisions, particularly recent decisions, as mistakes; but if two or more theories each provide an adequate fit, on that test, then the theory among these that is morally the strongest provides the best justification, even though it exposes more decisions as mistakes than another. That answer must be expanded,

[1] See above, p. 81.

but it illustrates how a full theory of adjudication might develop, in one direction, from the schematic theory I described.

But no such account of reasoning by analogy, which includes a dimension of morality in the test for principles, can reconcile positivism to principles in the way Richards hopes. Perhaps Richards wishes to join in the view of Professor Sartorius here.[1] Sartorius says that I should have been content with the first of the two dimensions I described, and not added the second, because one theory will almost inevitably provide a better fit with the data simply on the basis of the canons of best explanation used in the sciences, and judges do and should choose that theory. I once thought that this was so myself, but I was persuaded against it by considerations I have described at length.[2] I do not think that there are agreed criteria of superior theoretical explanation even in the case of scientific explanation, and experience shows that in the case of law one account is often preferred to another on reasons that cannot realistically be understood as reducible to the relative number of earlier decisions explained, or the simplicity or elegance of the explanation, or anything of that sort. No one familiar with the run of judicial opinions could suppose that judges choose among theories of justification in the way that legal historians, for example, might choose amongst historical explanations for patterns of decision. If judges did decide cases by citing canons of theory construction, counting the number of precedents explained by competing hypotheses, and contrasting the theoretical elegance of these hypotheses, we might at last have a genuine example of 'mechanical' decision making, a description that has for a long time been supposed to be derogatory in law, though not, as I understand it, in other fields where a moral dimension is lacking, like engineering.

So it is mysterious just how the question of what principles are 'implicit' in past traditions and practices could be an issue of fact according to a positivist's conception of what facts are. Why does Richards insist that this question is just a matter of fact? He tells us in the third, and most revealing, of the sets of statements I quoted. He is rightly anxious to resist the absurd view that the law is always morally sound or (to put the same point in a more revolutionary way) that a morally bad law cannot be the law. He wants to say that a principle that is 'legally binding' on judges may nevertheless be a very nasty principle, so nasty that it may even be the judge's duty to refuse to apply it. I said much the same things a few pages ago. I said that in some cases it might be the judge's duty to lie and falsely to report what the law is, and that description supposes that the law may not be what it should be. Richards apparently thinks that I am somehow forced to the absurd view, because he thinks that legal philosophy has only

1 See Sartorius, 'Social Policy and Judicial Legislation', 8 *Am. Phil. Q.* 151 (1971).
2 See above, pp. 64–8.

two choices here. We must stand with the positivists, who insist that it is always just a question of fact what the law is. Or we must fly with the most extreme of the natural lawyers, who say that there can be no difference between principles of law and principles of morality. But both of these extreme views are wrong. In some cases the answer to the question of what the law requires may depend on (though it is never identical with) the question of what background morality requires, so that it is a mistake to describe the first question as simply a question of fact, in the Humean spirit in which that description is meant. This is so not only in cases in which some legislative source deliberately embeds moral tests in legal rules, but also in cases in which it is controversial what the law requires because no legislative source has said anything decisive at all. It is so not only when legal principles embodying moral concepts are concededly decisive of legal arguments, but also when the question in play is just the question of what principles are to be taken as decisive.

But of course it does not follow from any of this either that the law is always morally right, or that what is morally right is always the law, *even in hard cases.* Consider the plausible view I sketched out just now. It says that no principle can count as a justification of institutional history unless it provides a certain threshold adequacy of fit, though amongst those principles that meet this test of adequacy the morally soundest must be preferred. If that test is applied to a wicked legal system, it may be that no principle we would find acceptable on grounds of morality could pass the threshold test. In that case the general theory must endorse some un-attractive principle as providing the best justification of institutional history, presenting the judge with a legal decision and also, perhaps, a moral problem. Positivism uses a simple distinction between factual and normative issues. If we accept that distinction, then we must say that the question of whether a principle counts in adjudication, and how much, is a normative question. But we must be careful not to think (as some philosophers often seem to think) that there is only one kind of normative question, which is the final question about what to do. The issue of whether a particular principle counts (in deciding what the law is) is in part normative, because it includes a judgment about the soundness of the principle in political morality. It is nevertheless distinct from another normative issue, which is whether that principle, even if it does count, would be the best principle on which to found a legal system if the slate were clean, and also distinct from a third normative issue, which is whether the principle is so unjust that it would be wrong for the judge to enforce any legal right it supplies, and right for him to lie in order to avoid doing so.

I shall mention here two additional matters that are of only peripheral interest. Richards accuses me of this mistake: 'From the fact that legal principles are sometimes moral principles he unwarrantably infers that they always are.'[1] Of course, that particular inference would be a mistake, but I think he means to accuse me of the belief, not the inference. Do I think that legal principles are always moral principles? There is an ambiguity here. The proposition might mean that legal principles are always sound or correct moral principles, and if that is what it means then, as I have just been at pains to repeat, I do not think that. But it might mean that legal principles are always moral principles in form (whether they are sound or unsound, compelling or despicable as moral judgments) rather than, for example, prudential judgments or historical generalizations. That is a more interesting claim, and I do hold it, at least in the following sense. The word 'moral' may cause trouble here, as it often does, but I take the proposition to mean that the principles that figure in legal arguments make claims about the rights and duties of citizens and other legal people, rather than stating, for example, prudential judgments or historical generalizations. As I have just said, I suppose that the process of 'drawing' principles from institutional history is the process of judging justifications of that history, where justification is distinguished from explanation. Even if it is right that all the decisions reached in contract law in Wisconsin for a period of years were such as to benefit the local Republican party, that fact, however important it might be to the historian or sociologist or critic, might not be thought to provide a justification (even a bad justification) for these decisions, and therefore would not require judges to decide future cases under the alleged principle that what is good for Republicans is good for justice. I might add that the fact that legal principles must be moral principles, in the sense just described, bears slightly on the earlier discussion of this section. It might, under certain circumstances, rule out arguments for alleged principles in wicked legal systems.[2] But I should not want to put much reliance on the screening power of the concept of a moral principle. There is no persuasive analysis of that concept that insures that the principle that blacks are less worthy of concern than whites can be rejected as not a principle at all.

I do want to reject, however, the picture of 'existing law' I described earlier, which I think is held by those who are anxious to deny that legal principles are always moral principles. They think that the law of a community is a distinct collection of particular rules and principles (and heaven knows what else) such that it is a sensible question to ask whether, at any given moment, a particular rule or principle belongs to that collection. If a principle does belong to the collection, then it is a legal principle; if it also belongs to the different collection of sound moral principles, then it is a moral principle as well, so that the question may

[1] Richards, *op. cit.*, 1096.
[2] See above, Chapter 10.

then be asked whether these two collections are identical, or overlapping, or extentionally distinct. If someone does hold this view of the matter (it is a cousin, I think, of the secret-book theory I discussed earlier on page 337), then he will think it important for legal philosophers to provide necessary and sufficient conditions for membership of the collection of legal principles, and necessary to answer the question of whether these conditions include or exclude membership in the different collection of sound moral principles. For my part, I do not think that we need in this way to individuate particular principles and assign them to collections, any more than we need to individuate and assign the 'principles' of a particular science. I did not mean, in rejecting the idea that law is a system of rules, to replace that idea with the theory that law is a system of rules and principles. There is no such thing as 'the law' as a collection of discrete propositions, each with its own canonical form. People have legal rights, and principles of political morality figure, in ways I have tried to describe, in deciding what legal rights they have. If we mean, by a 'legal principle', a principle that is in principle eligible for this role, then all the principles of political morality that have currency in the community in question, at least, are legal principles. We sometimes use 'legal principle' in a different way, to refer to those principles that have in fact often been cited by judges, and that therefore find their way into text books and law school lectures. But no one thinks that the only principles that may properly figure in legal arguments are legal principles in that confined sense, that is, those that have been made familiar in this way.

So Richards is wrong in thinking that a positivistic theory of law, like Hart's, can easily be adapted to capture the role that principles play in legal argument, and he is also wrong in thinking that the only alternative to positivism is an extreme natural law theory that denies the difference between legal and moral argument in hard cases. He also disagrees with the rights thesis I have defended, which argues that hard cases should be, and characteristically are, decided on arguments of principle rather than policy. He has in mind, as counter-examples, cases like those Greenawalt cited, and I need not repeat what I said earlier about these cases. Richards also reminds me that courts do consider policy issues when they apply statutes they take to be generated by policy, and I must repeat that I believe I said just that in *Hard Cases*.[1] He adds to these points made by others, however, reference to a different set of cases.[2] These are cases in which the court announces rules of administration, sometimes simple, as in *Mapp*,[3] and sometimes complex, as in *Miranda*,[4] not because the

[1] See above, pp. 107–10.
[2] See Richards, 1098.
[3] *Mapp v. Ohio*, 367 U.S. 643 (1961).
[4] *Miranda v. Arizona*, 384 U.S. 436 (1966).

court supposes that any individuals are entitled to just what they receive under these rules, but for the different reason that these rules provide one scheme, though not the only or even the best scheme, through which other rights of individuals may be protected or secured. Professor Chayes has recently published an article,[1] likely to be very influential, in which cases of that sort are considered more generally and for different purposes; he rightly calls our attention to the role of courts in fashioning and administering complex antitrust decrees, intricate business reorganizations and, most remarkably, school desegregation orders that sometimes bring courts into the day-to-day business of school boards.

The administrative business of courts, which Chayes thinks provides a new style of adjudication, raises a great many problems for jurisprudence and political theory, and, though they touch the rights thesis only obliquely, they are problems that any theory of adjudication must one day confront. For the purpose of this appendix, however, I need only point out two facts about the rights thesis that seem to have been overlooked. First, the thesis does not prohibit courts from deciding criminal or public law cases in favour of an individual and against the state or some department of the state on grounds that do not suppose that the individual has a right to the decision. I said that the rights thesis is asymmetrical in that respect, and I gave the *Mapp* case, which Richards cites, as one of my examples. Second, the thesis does not prohibit what is often called prospective legislation by courts, so long as rules created for the future, not taken to be accurate reports of existing rights, are not applied retrospectively to justify awards or denials in the instant case. Prospective legislation clearly does not offend the consideration of political morality I mentioned as supporting the rights thesis, when the legislation is conceived as necessary to protect individual rights, as in the cases Richards mentions; indeed, in constitutional cases, it might be thought that these considerations require just that. I should like to repeat, however, that much more needs to be said about the energetic administrative role courts now seem to have assumed, and the impact of that practice on the rights thesis.

5. SOPER AND POSITIVISM REDEFINED

A. Positivism less positive

Professor Soper's excellent essay[2] discusses connections between my arguments and various forms of legal positivism. He suggests a form of

[1] Chayes, 'The Role of the Judge in Public Law Legislation', 89 *Harv. L. Rev.* 1281 (1976).
[2] Soper, 'Legal Theory and the Obligation of a Judge: The Hart/Dworkin Dispute', 75 *Mich. L. Rev.* 473 (1977).

positivism that might simply incorporate all of my claims about legal practice, if they are sound, as refinements. Positivism, on this view, insists that propositions of law, if true, are true in virtue of some social practice specifying their truth conditions. But it does not insist that the truth conditions thus specified cannot include moral conditions. Suppose I am right, for example, that judges characteristically decide hard cases by appealing to principles that are themselves justified as figuring in the best justification of settled law, and that this process of justification includes a moral dimension as described in Chapter 4 and in section 4 of this appendix. The entire scheme of decision I describe is then itself a social practice, which identifies as true propositions of law supported by the principles that provide the best justification. Suppose two lawyers or judges disagree about some proposition of law because they disagree about some proposition of political morality. They might both be positivists, on this account of positivism, even though each thinks some proposition of law is true which cannot be proved true by appeal to pedigree, and even though each argues that the truth of his proposition depends upon the truth of some principle of morality. They are both positivists because each acknowledges that morality is made relevant by social practice, namely the social practice that I describe.

Soper points out that Professor Hart himself noticed that some statutes and constitutional provisions, like certain provisions of the American Constitution, 'incorporate morality by reference'. The present proposal simply extends the idea latent in that point, by supposing that the incorporation of morality may take place, not simply in some specific piece of legislation or constitutional provision, but in the more general social practice that defines what counts, in the community in question, as adjudication.

Professor Lyons, in his review of my book,[1] makes a very similar point. He, too, takes the nerve of positivism to be the claim that some social practice lies at the background of every claim of law, even though that practice itself makes morality sometimes – or even always – decisive. I do not, of course, wish to debate with Soper or Lyons about names. I had taken positivism to make two important and related claims that their version of positivism does not make, however, and my quarrel is with these claims, not with a label. The first argues that it is characteristic of a legal system that some more-or-less mechanical test provides necessary and sufficient conditions for the truth of propositions about what the law is, as distinct from propositions about what the law should be. In Chapter 2 I described this as a test of pedigree distinguished from content; I meant that positivism insists that the tests for law should be matters of social

[1] Lyons, 'Principles, Positivism and Legal Theory – Dworkin, *Taking Rights Seriously*', 87 *Yale L. J.* 415 (1977).

history rather than matters of policy or morality that might be inherently controversial. Hart, for example, describes his rule of recognition, not simply as just another obligation-imposing rule, but as a secondary rule stipulating public features whose presence or absence will be decisive in identifying other rules as legal rules. He says that the acceptance of this sort of secondary rule marks the transition from a pre-legal society to a society with law, because the public features made decisive by the secondary rule will cure the defect of uncertainty latent in pre-legal practice. It is, no doubt, compatible with this picture that the secondary rule may itself contain vague terms, or in some other way include some mild degree of indeterminacy. But a secondary rule that simply referred all issues of obligation directly back to standing social practices of obligation would (as Hart makes plain in his discussion of international law) make no change at all in the *status quo*. Such a secondary rule would introduce no further determinacy and could not mark a transition to anything. These objections would apply *a fortiori*, I would have thought, to a secondary rule of the sort Soper contemplates when he imagines a sovereign who commands only: Do what justice requires.

The important question is not, however, whether Hart or any other particular legal philosopher is committed to the thesis that the test for law must make law reasonably demonstrable. That thesis is connected to a more general theory of law – in particular to a picture of law's function. This is the theory that law provides a settled, public and dependable set of standards for private and official conduct, standards whose force cannot be called into question by some individual official's perception of policy or morality. This theory of law's function acknowledges, as it must, that no set of public rules can be complete or completely precise. But it therefore insists on a distinction between occasions on which the law, so conceived, does dictate a decision and occasions on which, in the language of positivists, the judge must exercise his discretion to make new law just because the law is silent. The distinction is vital, on this view of the law's function, because it is important to acknowledge that when reasonable men can disagree about what the law requires, a judicial decision cannot be a neutral decision of the sort promised in the idea of law. It is more honest to concede that the decision is not, in this case, a decision of law at all.

So the thesis that some more or less mechanical test of pedigree identifies law is in this way connected with a political theory about the point or function of law, and with the theory of judicial discretion that is a necessary part of that theory. The theory I defend, on the contrary, supposes the different and more ambitious function for law I described at the end of Section 3 of this appendix. If positivism is relaxed in the way Soper and Lyons suggest it might be, so as to accommodate the description of legal practices I provide, then the case for the orthodox theory about the point of law is correspondingly weakened, and the case for the view I endorse advanced.

The second claim I took positivism to make is also connected with a more general theoretical position that would have to be modified if this claim were abandoned. This second claim is most clearly put in the following way. We may suppose propositions of law to be true or false, accurate or inaccurate, without thereby accepting any ontology beyond an empiricist's ontology. The truth of a proposition of law, when it is true, consists in ordinary historical facts about individual or social behaviour including, perhaps, facts about beliefs and attitudes, but in nothing metaphysically more suspicious. Oliver Wendall Holmes made that claim when he said that law is not a brooding omnipresence in the sky. Positivists need not be reductionist in the *semantic* sense: they need not argue that propositions of law mean the same thing as historical propositions about behaviour of beliefs or attitudes. But it is part of their programme (or so I thought) to be reductionist in the weaker sense captured in the claim that the truth conditions of propositions of law do not include anything but such historical conditions.

This claim is, of course, consistent with the causal thesis, plainly true, that beliefs about justice are often causally responsible for the behaviour that constitutes law. Legislators, for example, often enact law because it seems to them just. The claim is also consistent with the different thesis that *beliefs* about justice may be part of the truth conditions of propositions of law. A positivist may hold a theory of statutory interpretation such that, if a statute provides that a contract is invalid when it is unconscionable, and the vast majority of people thinks that a particular sort of contract is unjust, then that sort of contract is, as a matter of law, invalid. This theory makes beliefs about moral facts, not moral facts themselves, decisive for propositions of law. But for a Soper-Lyons positivist the legal validity of a contract might depend, not on whether a contract is believed to be unjust, but whether it is unjust. That theory *is* inconsistent with the reductionist's claim, because it makes a moral fact itself part of the truth conditions of a proposition of law.

The weak programme of reductionism is not satisfied by showing that propositions of law are sometimes true in virtue of historical facts alone. It must be shown that all the propositions the theory takes to be true are true in virtue of such facts. Soper-Lyons positivism cannot claim this. If a social practice makes morality systematically relevant to legal issues (and Soper and Lyons each concedes, *arguendo*, that our own legal system may well do so), then the truth of propositions of law will systematically depend upon the truth of propositions of morality. The truth of the former will consist, at least partially, in the truth of the latter. So the promised ontological separation of law from morals fails. In order to suppose that there are legal facts within such a system, one must suppose that there are moral facts as well.

This explains why Hart's point, that positive law sometimes uses explicit moral language, is not a pocket into which a general theory of law that makes morality systematically relevant, even in the absence of any explicit incorporation, can be dropped. Hart presumably would extend his discussion of the 'open texture' of legal languages (which he applies to words like 'reasonable') to moral terms that figure in positive law (like the 'cruel and unusual' clause of the American Constitution) as well. He would then say that the word 'cruel' has a settled core of application in the United States (it applies to the bastinado) but a penumbra of uncertainty (reasonable men and women differ whether capital punishment is in itself cruel). When a case (like *Furmson v. Georgia*) falls within the penumbra, then a judge must exercise his own discretion to decide, though his decision thereafter extends the core of the concept for legal purposes.

This analysis of the role of moral language in legal provisions is entirely consistent with the weak reductionist programme I described. It makes the truth of the proposition of law, that the bastinado is unconstitutional, consist in beliefs that it is cruel. But it could not be extended to cover the theory of adjudication I describe. Suppose, however, that my understanding is wrong, and that Hart would reject this analysis of moral language in law. Suppose he would say that whether capital punishment is unconstitutional depends entirely on whether it is, as a matter of moral fact, cruel, and not just on whether it is sufficiently widely believed to be so, or on whether some judge, in the exercise of his discretion, so decides. (We should then wonder why he did not offer a parallel analysis of all 'open texture' language and shrink the role of judicial discretion accordingly.) But if this is a sensible distinction, and if propositions about the constitutionality of punishment can be true, then there must be (to put the point in an old-fashioned way) an objective realm of moral facts. I had thought it was part of Hart's ambition (and of the ambition of positivists generally) to make the objective standing of propositions of law independent of any controversial theory either of meta-ethics or of moral ontology.

Hart would not need to accept an objective realm of facts about cruelty, of course, if he did not insist that propositions about capital punishment can be true in the way in which propositions that do not depend upon the correct understanding of moral language can be true. He might say that, once the Constitution has made the constitutionality of punishment depend upon its cruelty, then all such claims, taken literally, are either false or neither true nor false.[1] But that is a plausible extension of Hart's

[1] See Mackie, *Ethics: Inventing Right and Wrong* (1978), Chap. 1.

general theory (if at all) only on the assumption that the use of moral language is an occasional, rather than a systematic, feature of familiar legal systems. If my account of our own legal practice is right, and Hart sought to embrace that account within his own system in this way, he would end by saying that, for us, hardly any propositions at all are true. In any case the marriage of the two theories, which Soper contemplates, would be dissolved by that last radical claim.

B. Conceptual or descriptive?

Soper raises another interesting issue at the beginning of his essay. He distinguishes conceptual theories of law from descriptive theories. He says that the positivist's theory is conceptual and my theory descriptive, for the following reason. Positivists make a claim that holds good (if they are right) for all legal systems, not simply as a matter of generalization, but as a matter of necessity. I make claims, on the other hand, about a particular legal system only. I argue that the characteristic practice of judges in our own legal system does not fit the positivist's account of what all legal systems must be like. If I am right, then the positivist's claim, which is universal, must be wrong. But it does not follow that my description is therefore true of any legal system but our own. So my position must be descriptive while theirs is conceptual.

I am glad that Soper raised this issue, because I am often asked whether I mean my theory to be conceptual like positivism, or descriptive only. Do I mean to offer a general theory of what law must be like, or only a better account of one particular version of law? I do not, I am afraid, understand the force of the distinction in this context. The positivist's theory of law is surely conceptual in some sense. But in what sense? Does Soper think that the positivist's theory (that propositions of law cannot be true in virtue of morality) is a linguistic theory about the 'standard' or 'ordinary language' use of the word 'legal' or 'law'. On that interpretation, the positivist claims that it follows from the way 'legal' is used that a legal right simply cannot depend on moral facts in the way I argue it can, just as someone else might say that it follows from the way 'sister' is used that a sister cannot be a man. But if I produce an alleged counter-example – if I produce an instance of a legal right that I say is a legal right in virtue of a moral right – then my claim must *also* be a linguistic one. I must claim that the word 'legal' is properly used in such a way as to include this case. My claim is as much linguistic as his, though it may be more guarded. It cannot be 'merely' descriptive – or merely about the facts of the one case cited as a counter-example – the way that a counter-example to an empirical generalization can be. Suppose I claimed to have found a male sister, and thus to have produced a counter-example to the claim that, as a matter of linguistic usage, sisters cannot be men. I do not simply claim to have discovered a new non-linguistic fact which refutes a linguistic theory. Unless I show the linguistic theory to be *linguistically* incorrect, I cannot have found the fact I say I have found. Suppose I found a man whom the speech-community was in the habit (knowing him to be a man) of calling a sister. If I cite him as a counter-example, I do so because I take this linguistic practice to be part of the practice that provides the correct use of 'sister'. That is a point about the correct use of a word, not simply about the facts of an isolated case. If positivism is conceptual because it is linguistic, and if my theory provides even one counter-example, then my theory must be conceptual because linguistic as well.

I put the matter hypothetically, because I do not accept that positivism is a theory about linguistic practice. (I doubt that there is a standard use of the words 'legal' or 'law' to which the positivist can appeal. In any case, he does not rely on dictionary definitions nor statistics of linguistic usage in his arguments.) But in what other sense shall we understand the positivist to be making a conceptual claim rather than simply a descriptive generalization? If the positivist merely said that, in every country or political subdivision he has studied, legal rights are not taken to be established by moral arguments, and that he therefore believes that they are never taken to be established in that way, then his claim would not seem to be conceptual at all. Someone may suggest that positivism is conceptual because it *proposes* that legal concepts should be used in a certain way, for clarity or convenience or for some political motive. But if positivism is simply hortatory in that way, and if my theory does produce a 'counter-example' in our own legal system, then this must be because I have shown that competing and better motives recommend contrary usage of these concepts. If so, then I must be relying on some theory about desirable conceptual divisions of the same sort as the theory on which he relies, though my theory may not be as articulate as his. Once again, if his theory is properly called conceptual because hortatory, so is mine.

I speak hypothetically, again, because I think it misunderstands positivism just as much to say that it is hortatory as to say that it is linguistic. Theories of law are conceptual, but not in either of these ways. Earlier in this book I described a special kind of intellectual activity, which I called defending a particular conception of a concept. I do not pretend to have yet given an adequate or even clear account of that activity, but I hope that the examples I gave will suggest how the activity is different from empirical generalization, linguistic study, and linguistic exhortation. We all – at least all lawyers – share a concept of law and of legal right, and we contest different conceptions of that concept. Positivism defends a particular conception, and I have tried to defend a competing conception. We disagree about what legal rights are in much the same way as philosophers who argue about justice disagree about what justice is. I concentrate on the details of a particular legal system with which I am especially familiar, not simply to show that positivism provides a poor account of that system, but to show that positivism provides a poor conception of the concept of a legal right. My argument is not that positivism is wrong as an account of our legal system though it might be right in its account of other legal systems as, for example, some historian might argue that a particular theory about the causes of war is wrong in its explanation of the War of the Austrian Succession though it might be right about several other wars.

The analogy to arguments about the concept of justice is useful. Suppose someone argues against utilitarian theories of justice by showing that these theories fail to explain why slavery is unjust in some actual or imaginary situation in which slavery in fact maximises utility. He might concede that in other actual or imaginary situations slavery is counter-utilitarian, but his argument is meant to show that even then slavery is not unjust *because* it is counter-utilitarian. He intends to show that utilitarianism is not a satisfactory conception of justice; if that is right, *nothing* is unjust simply in virtue of being counter-utilitarian. My argument has the same ambition. I appeal to complex, modern legal systems to show that since, in these systems, the truth of a proposition about legal rights may consist in some moral fact, the positivist conception of legal rights must be false. I conclude that we must abandon the positivist conception in favour of a different conception of the sort I describe in Chapter 4, and earlier in this appendix. This conception makes the institutional practice and history of each jurisdiction relevant to the truth of propositions about legal rights, though not necessarily decisive. It follows that in some jurisdictions legal rights are sharply at variance with any defensible background political morality. They hold, in spite of this variance, by institutional fiat. This is not, however, because positivism provides a good conception of legal rights for these jurisdictions, but rather because the right conception yields that conclusion there.

In his final paragraphs Soper suggests that my theory would cause more difficulty for positivism, as he understands it, if my theory became more normative, and less a theory about what the facts or our practice really are. But the issue he takes to divide us – what is our legal practice really like? – is not a dispute about facts of the ordinary sort. Positivists and I do not dispute about details of practice that could be settled by looking more carefully to see what is said in books, or by framing more intelligent questionnaires for judges. We may disagree about matters of that sort, but this disagreement is not fundamental. We fundamentally disagree about what our practice comes to, that is, about which philosophical account of the practice is superior. I tried to explain, in the final section of Chapter 4, why disputes among citizens about what the morality of their society really is have that character, and why it would be wrong to see these disputes as simply disputes about popular morality, that is, about statistical functions of the moral beliefs that particular individuals have. If we insist on the contrast, then disputes about what social morality is are normative rather than (merely) factual. The book argues for the same view about disputes among lawyers and judges about about what institutional history really comes to on some issue. The question of what principles are 'embedded' in institutional history is normative rather than (merely) historical. So is the question of what our legal practice, as a whole, really is. The contest between theories of law has the same form as contests between theories of the equal protection clause or theories of negligence, though the former is more general.

6. NICKEL AND MYOPIA

I agree with much of what Professor Nickel, in his thoughtful essay, says about political rights. He discusses, for example, my account, in an essay on Rawls' theory of justice, of what I called a 'constructive' model of coherence in moral theory.[1] I said that that constructive model furnishes a better justification for the use Rawls makes of the idea of reflective equilibrium than does a different model, which I called the 'natural' model, and which many critics have thought is presupposed by Rawls' argument. Nickel believes that I supplied no reasons for thinking that the constructive model offers a good account of private moral reasoning, and I agree. Indeed, I am unclear that any form of coherence theory, whether based on the constructive or natural model, would be adequate for that.

Nickel is dubious about my arguments against the familiar idea that it is proper, in deciding whether important political rights of individuals must yield in particular cases, to balance these individual rights against the 'rights' of the community as a whole. He does not claim that the community has a right, competitive with individuals' rights, just to marginal improvements in the general welfare, however that may be defined. He says that the idea of such a right is 'a mere caricature of the conservative's position'.[2] (I disagree – I think many conservatives have spoken as if the community has just such a right, though of course none thinks that that community right must trump all individual rights always.) He seems to think however, that the idea of some community rights, competitive with individual rights, is necessary in order to 'limit the scope of individual

[1] See above, Chapter 6.
[2] Nickel, 'Dworkin on the Nature and Consequences of Rights', 11 *Ga. L. Rev.* 1115, 1137 (1977).

rights in situations where protecting them is very costly in terms of other values'.[1] But surely we can say all that we should want to say without the idea, which I find confusing, that the community as such has rights. Nickel speaks, for example, of the 'right' of the majority in a fair election to have its candidate installed;[2] but insofar as this is a matter of right, it is a matter of the rights of the individuals who make up the majority. We call this a majority right only to indicate the basis or conditions under which individuals have the right, namely, when they are members of the majority. I conceded, moreover, that even the grand individual rights are not absolute, but will yield to especially powerful considerations of consequence, which I called, too dramatically, 'emergencies'. The argument of principle that establishes the individual right as an abstract right must recognize, in more concrete circumstances, negative arguments of principle from which it may follow, for example, that no one has a right to speak his mind freely when the result would be to cripple the defence capacity of the nation. We may accept or debate that negative argument of principle without supposing that the nation, considered apart from the individuals who make it up, has rights competitive with the rights of those who want to speak.

Nickel is also dubious about my argument that if an individual has a political right that the government not hinder him from doing something by making it a crime to do so, then he has a political right to violate that law.[3] He says that I seem to think that, in such a case, it is not even *relevant* to the question of whether someone has a moral right to do something that it is against the law to do it, and he finds that counter-intuitive and implausible. I was careful, in the essay in question, to distinguish the question of what someone had a political right to do, in the strong sense there defined, from the question of what was the right thing to do, and I was careful to point out that the illegality of an act is certainly relevant to the latter question.[4] But does the government have any more justification for enforcing a law that violates someone's fundamental political rights than it has for enacting the law in the first place? I thought not, and still think not, though perhaps some qualification should be made to the way I put the point. I can imagine circumstances in which, by virtue of the fact that a law had been passed, grave damage would be done – an emergency would arise – if an unjust law were not enforced, an emergency that would not have arisen if the law had never been passed. Nickel would be right in insisting that in such a case the change made by the law would certainly be morally relevant, and possibly

[1] *Ibid.*
[2] *Ibid.*
[3] *Ibid.*, 1140.
[4] See above, Chapter 7.

even decisive, against the concrete right to break the law in those circumstances. That was not the situation I had in mind, of course, and it is unreasonable to suppose that that situation will arise in the United States in the foreseeable future. I had in mind the popular argument that some damage is always done when a law is not enforced in a democracy. Damage of that limited character cannot provide an argument against the political right to break a law if that law is illegitimate because it violates a fundamental political right.

Nickel's principal objection to my theory of rights is very different from these problems he rightly raises. He is worried by what he takes to be my belief that the only argument available in favour of any political right at all is the argument that such a right is necessary in order to protect what I have called the fundamental right to equal concern and respect. 'Dworkin's myopia here derives, I suspect, from completely equating the issue of human rights with the issue of political equality.'[1] We should set aside two issues he raises. He doubts that a theory about the rights individuals have against fellow citizens, as distinct from political rights, can be shown to follow from the right to equal concern and respect. I have never said it could, though plainly the right of any individual to be treated with 'certain' respect, which I have discussed earlier in this essay, is a related right. Second, he is doubtful that even all the political rights I would want myself to recognize can be defended through the distinction I made between personal and external preferences. Once again, I agree. In a recent essay I have tried to show how the fundamental right to equal concern and respect can be shown to yield economic rights, for example, and the argument there makes no use of this distinction.[2]

Nickel's more fundamental and important criticism is that suggested by his statement about my myopia. He worries that my theory of rights is too closely tied to rights we feel should be rights against the majority in a democracy, and wholly ignores rights that we intuitively feel should be rights against any form of government, like the right, for example, not to be tortured. Surely a government could not be said to respect fundamental human rights if it tortured everyone, and tortured them equally. Even if it only tortures some, moreover, our objection is not an objection against discrimination; we do not believe the situation would be improved by torturing more.

It does not seem to me so clear, however, that our belief that people have a right not to be tortured even for good purposes is not derivative, in the end, from some conception of equality. But before I try to defend that judgment, let me repeat, if only to make the record clearer, that I have

---

[1] Nickel, 1129.
[2] See Dworkin, 'Liberalism', in S. Hampshire (ed.), *Public and Private Morality* (1978).

never claimed that the arguments I have made in favour of certain political rights are the only arguments that can succeed in favour of any. I was careful to deny that claim in the Introduction and Chapter 12 of this book:

> I put the matter this vaguely because there is no reason to assume, in advance, that only one kind of reason would support that moral position. It might be that a just society would recognize a variety of individual rights, some grounded on very different sorts of moral considerations from others. In what remains of this chapter I shall try to describe only one possible ground for rights. It does not follow that men and women in civil society have only the rights that the argument I shall make would support; but it does follow that they have at least these rights, and that is important enough.[1]
>
> It might be wise to repeat here what I say [in the chapter Nickel discusses], which is that neither the rights there described, nor the method used to argue for these rights, is meant to be exclusive of other rights or of other methods of argument. The general theory of rights allows that there may be different sorts of arguments, each sufficient to establish some reason why a collective goal that normally provides a justification for a political decision does not justify a particular disadvantage to some individual.
>
> The book nevertheless suggests one favoured form of argument for political rights, which is the derivation of particular rights from the abstract right to concern and respect taken to be fundamental and axiomatic.[2]

That abstract right does require that officials and those who control officials not discriminate amongst citizens in a way that denies equal concern or respect to one group in favour of another. That is a very abstract requirement, and in the recent essay I mentioned I have tried to show what, on different conceptions of respect, the abstract principle requires in more concrete circumstances. In a democracy, this non-discriminatory aspect of the fundamental requirement will be very important. But of course the principle of equal concern and respect requires that officials and those who control them treat citizens with the same concern and respect as they show themselves, and in totalitarian states that aspect of the principle will be more important still. It might be said that in that case the reference to equality in the principle is unnecessary or even confusing; it would be better to say that officials must treat all citizens with respect and concern, or as autonomous human beings, which would rule out torture. Perhaps, but the idea of equality is meant to suggest

[1] See above, p. 272.
[2] See above, pp. xiv–xv.

content for the ideas of respect and autonomy: those in power are meant to treat others as they treat themselves, not in the sense of supplying for them only the same goods and opportunities they take themselves, so that a masochistic tyrant could justly torture everyone along with himself, but in the more fundamental sense of attempting, so far as it is possible, to see the situation of each person defined through the ambitions and values of that person, just as he must see his own situation defined through his own ambitions and values in order to have that grasp of himself as an entity that is necessary to self-consciousness and therefore to self-identity.[1] I cannot now improve on that possibly confusing statement of the sense in which I think that the idea of equality has power beyond the range it is normally thought to have, though of course I must do so if I wish to extend my claims for the fundamental principle beyond those made in the introduction from which I have just quoted. I want now only to say that it may not be absurd to find ideas of equality even behind our belief that torture is wrong.

This is an appropriate place to mention a misinterpretation Nickel does not make but which others have. They say that the arguments I make in Chapters 9 and 12, using the distinction between personal and external preferences, constitutes a general endorsement of utilitarianism cleansed of external preferences, so that I am committed to support any political decision dictated by every utilitarian argument that does not rely on such preferences. I find no support for that position in my text, nor do I hold it. My arguments are arguments against an unrestricted utilitarianism, not in favour of a restricted one. I argue that a utilitarian argument cannot be a good argument if it relies on external preferences;[2] but it does not follow that a utilitarian argument is a good argument just because it does not. I do believe that trade-off arguments including utilitarian arguments have an important place in political theory, not because total pleasure is a good in itself, but because and only insofar as they are arguments in the service of equality; and utilitarian arguments, as I point out in 'Liberalism',[3] may be inegalitarian for reasons quite independent of external preferences.

I have also been interpreted – even less plausibly – as arguing that external preferences are in themselves bad, and that people should strive not to have them and should vote ignoring the ones they do have. I have never used the distinction between personal and external preferences to

---

[1] See also Williams, 'The Idea of Equality', in P. Laslett and W. Runciman (eds), *Philosophy, Politics and Society* (1962), reprinted in B. Williams, *Problems of the Self* (1973).

[2] Since Chapter 12 was written I have discovered that something like my distinction between external and personal preferences is necessary, in economics, to avoid what has come to be called 'Sen's paradox'. See Sen, 'Liberty, Unanimity and Rights', 43 *Economica* 217 (1976) and literature there discussed.

[3] In S. Hampshire (ed.), *Public and Private Morality* (1978).

describe how people should act or vote. Nothing could be further from what I suppose than the idea that people should act only in their own interests and never in the interests of children, lovers, friends or humanity, or that their votes should not represent their ideals of justice or other political ideals as well as their selfish interests. The distinction is a distinction between preferences, and it is made in the context of a discussion of preference utilitarianism. I argue only against counting external preferences, whether malevolent or altruistic, good or bad, in some utilitarian justification for a political decision. People will inevitably have, and in their personal lives act upon, external preferences of a variety of sorts. Good people will have good external preferences and bad people will have bad ones. They will vote their external preferences; they will vote for legislators, for example, who share their own theories of political justice. How else should they decide for whom to vote? But when these legislators are elected, they are subject to constraints about how far preference utilitarianism provides a justification for their decisions; that is, how far the fact that a majority prefers a particular state of affairs (as distinct from the justice of what the majority wants) counts as an argument for a political decision to promote it. The fact that a majority personally prefers a sports stadium to an opera house might count as an argument in favour of the stadium. The fact that the majority thinks that homosexuality is immoral or that cruelty to children is wrong should not, in my view, count as an argument for anything, although, of course, the different fact that cruelty harms children does count very much.

Is this distinction implausible? Consider two societies, in each of which a few cripples are unable to support themselves. In the first the majority is indifferent to the cripples' fate, while in the second the majority holds external altruistic preferences that the cripples' misery be relieved. I argue that the justification for helping the cripples by political action, all else being equal, is no stronger in the second society than in the first, though of course it is much more likely that the second will take that action. I need hardly add, I hope, that the principle of justice in which the second majority believes does furnish a good reason for a political decision. But since it is the soundness of the principle that furnishes the reason, not the fact of its popularity, the reason is equally strong in the two societies.

I might mention, finally, an unrelated objection raised by Nickel to my description, in *Hard Cases*,[1] of how judges do and should decide cases. I said that Hercules, who has superhuman skills and therefore works very quickly, could develop in advance an entire political theory, in very rich detail, with which he could then confront particular hard cases. I did not mean to suggest that more ordinary judges in fact do the same thing, though carrying the work only so far as full use of their more limited skill

[1] See above, p. 81.

and time permits them.[1] I meant rather that they do very little bits of the same job, as and when the occasion requires, so that they produce not some general theory, but at best only pockets of a general theory, or, as is no doubt often the case, pockets of different theories. In doing even this, they rely not on formal training in philosophy, but on intuitive ideas of what a more general scheme would justify, made more articulate by such experience of defending their intuitions against actual and hypothetical cases as their practice has provided. As I said, in the parallel case of a philosophically sophisticated chess referee, '[t]his is, of course, only a fanciful reconstruction of a calculation that will never take place; any official's sense of the game will have developed over a career, and he will employ rather than expose that sense in judgments'. I repeat this now because others, in addition to Nickel, have objected to my description on the ground that judicial opinions do not read like essays in political philosophy. Some of them do, and I wish that more did, but I should not want to stake the plausibility of the rights thesis, as a model for understanding what lies behind a judicial decision, on the number of opinions in which the model is evident on the surface.

7. MACKIE AND PLAYING FAST AND LOOSE

John Mackie's main comments about my theory of adjudication[2] are political, but before he states his political reservations he notices what seem to him to be at least problems for my views. Some of these have been raised by others, and have already been taken up in this appendix, but one problem is raised by Mackie alone. In Chapter 13 of this book I allow that in certain cases (which I suppose must be very rare in complex legal systems) the argument for one side may be equally as good as the argument for the other. I call such cases 'ties'. Mackie argues that my claim that ties must be rare is based on what he calls too simple a 'metric'. It assumes an ordinary balance between two weights exactly counterpoised, so that if the slightest additional weight were added to either side the balance would be destroyed and the scales would tip. But, Mackie argues, cases that have no right answer may be cases in which one cannot choose between two sides, not because they are in this sense exactly in balance, but because the cases are incommensurate. In print he offers an example of facial likeness, but the point can be put more forcefully, as Mackie has done in conversation, directly about hard cases. Let us imagine a case that seems to provide a tie in the sense I described. We believe that

---

[1] See Nickel, 1135.
[2] J. L. Mackie, 'The Third Theory of Law', *Phil. and Pub. Aff.*, vol. 7, n.1 (1977) p. 3.

two theories of law, which yield contrary decisions, offer exactly as good a justification of the preceding statutes and precedents. But now suppose we find one old, unimportant and dim precedent that is justified on one theory but not the other. If the two theories were in exact equipoise, the newly discovered precedent, however dim, must be decisive. But in fact the newly discovered precedent may not affect our conviction that there is nothing to chose between the theories. We may well be reluctant to say that the discovery of such a case could make all that difference. If so, Mackie argues, then the original stalemate was not a tie of exact equipoise, but a case of incommensurability, and my arguments that exact ties must be rare do not show that incommensurabilities must be rare.

Mackie's argument assumes, however, an account of the way in which theories justify institutional history that is in two ways different from the account I recommend. First, he assumes that a justification of a body of material automatically becomes better, as a justification, when it justifies a greater percentage – even a very marginally greater percentage – of that material. I see no reason why that should be so. When two theories compete along what I have called the dimension of fit, the contest is not to see how many distinct bits of institutional history each explains. (Indeed, we have no principle of individualization of bits of history of the sort such a contest would require. How many bits of history are there in a complex statute? Does a complex case, with many parties, or a group action, count as more bits than a simpler case?) The contest along that dimension supposes a metric that is less precise and more a matter of characterization. Each of two theories may fit 'reasonably' but not very well the 'great bulk' of precedents, and yet one be preferred to the other because it can more plausibly be seen as explaining the 'trend' of recent decisions. In that case, the justification for neither is improved simply by the discovery of one or two older cases explained by one but not the other. Secondly, the conception of justification I described does not provide that any improvement along the dimension of fit is automatically an improvement in overall justification. It provides for a threshold of fit that must be met by any theory that is ultimately to qualify, but argues that if two theories each pass that threshold, the choice between the two will be governed by political morality. (In a recent expansion of *No Right Answer?*[1] I conceded that my thesis, that ties will be rare, presupposes a conception of morality other than some conception according to which different moral theories are frequently incommensurate).

Mackie's main objection is, as I say, a political objection. He notices that in a short book-review I said that in certain of the pre-Civil War slavery cases (I had in mind principally the due process cases) the better legal argument justified a decision against the slave catchers and in favour

[1] Forthcoming in the *New York University Law Review*.

of the alleged slaves, though the judges reached the opposite decision. Mackie constructs a legal argument, meant to follow the form of argument I recommend, that would justify the decision the judges reached, and remarks that reasonable judges of good will might just as easily have accepted his argument as mine. He does not mean (I think) that each of the two arguments is in fact of equal weight. No doubt he thinks that his argument is in fact better than mine, on the particular cases in question. But his point is simply that it is not certain that the judges who had to decide these questions would have found my argument better, so that readers should not think that the method of adjudication I recommend would necessarily provide more attractive decisions even in the United States or Britain.

I am reluctant to agree even to this more limited claim. The judges who decided these cases were, as citizens, politically committed: they were anti-slavery on grounds of principle. They therefore had views about the rights of individuals, and in particular about the rights of blacks as people, that I think would have made my argument preferable to them, as a legal argument, had they recognized the proper role of such principles in legal argument. My historical claim assumes a legal position that I share with Professor Cover (the author of the book I reviewed) but which Mackie contests: it assumes that the due process slavery cases were hard cases, not decided in advance by the plain meaning of constitutional provisions and statutes. But of course if the judges thought that the matter was foreclosed by such positive law, then they would not have entertained the arguments Mackie constructed for them either.

This is simply quibbling about particular historical cases, however, and does not touch Mackie's more general point. This is that my theory of adjudication gives judges more political power than positivism does, and that we should recommend my theory only if (or when) we are satisfied that we want judges rather than legislators or other officials to have that power. Is this correct? Mackie anticipates that I will make the following reply: 'Positivism gives judges as much political power as my theory does. Positivism also recognizes the distinction between easy cases, in which the law is settled and the judge is duty bound to decide as the law dictates, and hard cases in which the judge is free to exercise a legislative discretion. My theory only recommends that judges make political decisions in hard cases, and positivism also recommends this, because the exercise of a legislation discretion is the exercise of political power'. Mackie responds, in advance, that my reply fails because my theory designates more cases as hard cases – allows more room to challenge what is taken to be settled law – than positivism does. His argument here consists only in citing my view that the due process slavery cases were not governed by settled law. But that is a bad argument. Mackie himself says, on this point, only that 'it is far from clear that (the pertinent) provisions offend against due process'. That is not to say that it is clear that they do not. But suppose that he is in this case a better American constitutional lawyer than Cover is or I am, and that he is right. It follows only that we have made a mistake in our analysis of the law, not that my theory of adjudication in some way legitimises that mistake. Nor does legal history suggest that lawyers who call themselves positivists – like, for example, Holmes – are especially reluctant to find unsettled what others thought clearly established.

It is in fact a difficult question whether my theory allows more 'settled' law to be challenged. Much depends upon details of doctrine and practice in particular jurisdictions – for example whether these allow over-ruling of undesirable precedents. But Mackie might have made a stronger argument than he did. He might have said that positivism allows a judge to be more deferential to other institutions when he makes 'new law' in hard cases, and perhaps even encourages him to do so. Since positivism argues that no party has a right to any particular decision in a hard case, a positivist judge may accept a general responsibility to reach the decision that he thinks the legislature would have reached, either in deference to some theory of democracy or in the interests of smooth government. (I suggested, in the book review, that the pre-Civil War judges may have been influenced by a sense of that responsibility.) My theory of adjudication, on the other hand, insists that parties have legal rights in hard cases, and a judge who accepts a duty to try to identify these rights cannot be moved, against his theory of what these rights are, by any competing consideration of democracy or efficient government. So Mackie may be right, for this reason, in supposing that the political convictions of judges matter more under my theory.

But there are two countervailing considerations. First, it is a notorious complaint against both British and American judges that they smuggle political convictions into decisions under cover of pretending to discover what the legislature 'really' intended or 'would have done if aware of the problem'.[1] Some critics charge that this is deliberate; others that it is unconscious. Indeed, in many cases in which apparently deferential judges appeal to legislative intention, or to counterfactuals about what the legislature would have done, it is silly to suppose that they succeed in finding the right answer to these questions because there are no right answers to find.

These charges of hypocrisy or self-deception provide a useful check to Mackie's own charge that my theory plays fast and loose with the law. (I am indebted to him for explaining to me what the latter charge really means. I had thought the allusion was to women who were, perfectly consistently, both fast and loose at the same time.) He thinks that my

---

[1] See, e.g., Griffith, *The Politics of the Judiciary* (1977).

theory will increase deception, because judges will pretend that they are finding determinate solutions to legal issues when they are really legislating their personal convictions. This accusation, of course, begs the question of whether the theoretical background to my recommendations is sound. If it is, then judges *are* doing their best to find the rights of the parties, and there is no deception. But even if my theoretical claims are indefensible, the fraud, if there is any, seems to be in the other court. Hercules makes plain, in his opinions, the influence of political morality on his decisions. Positivists who appeal to legislative intention or counter-factuals often hide the influence of their convictions behind a screen decorated by nonsense.

The second countervailing fact is more complex in its implications. Positivism argues that judges, in the exercise of their discretion to make new law in hard cases, are free to make new law in the name of policy as well as principle. My theory includes the rights thesis, which argues that since the duty of judges, even in hard cases, is to identify the rights of the parties, judges in such cases should appeal to arguments of principle and not arguments of policy. Section 2 of this appendix discusses the issue whether the rights thesis makes much difference in practice. I argue that it will always make some difference, and that the degree of the difference will depend upon the area of the law in question – in particular whether the judge holds a consequentialist theory of the rights that make up that area. This issue is relevant now, because the risks to individual freedom are far greater, I think, when judges are invited to make new law on judgments of policy (like the judgment that a certain sort of conduct is damaging to the public welfare, or that penalties should be increased so as to provide greater deterrence) than when judges are asked to protect the moral and political rights citizens of their community have. The risk, in the former case, is that judges will erode individual liberty to a degree greater than that which the ordinary political process, with its checks and inertias, could do unaided. The risk, in the latter case, is largely negative: that judges will be conservative and will make less use of their power than they might by refusing to recognize individual rights that the political process has not already established in positive law. These are generalizations, and neither holds true inevitably or absolutely. It is not difficult to imagine cases in which judges can do great harm, even in civil cases, by enforcing a false conception of the rights of property. But the rights thesis poses a practical question that Mackie should at least add to his list of political questions made relevant by my theory. Suppose it is true that judges applying the rights thesis are unlikely substantially to limit individual freedom, beyond what the legislature has done, when their political convictions are conservative, but will increase personal freedom when their convictions are liberal. Then liberals at least will find that thesis a better bet than Mackie's ancient con game.

8. RAZ AND THE BANALITY OF RIGHTS

Dr Raz raises a great many issues in his highly compressed essay.[1] Several of these have already been discussed in this appendix;[2] but the issue to which he devotes most attention has not, and his discussion reveals an important misunderstanding that others might share. I argue that claims of political right must be understood functionally, as claims to trump some background collective justification that is normally decisive. The political force of claims of right therefore depends upon the general structure of the political community in which they are made. It depends, in particular, on which type of collectivist justification is taken as a general background justification in that political community, either explicitly, in the shared political morality of that community, so far as this exists, or implicitly, in the design of its principal legislative institutions.

In contemporary United States and Britain some appeal to the general welfare, understood as an appeal to a utilitarian maximization of preferences, provides a general justification for political decisions, and the structure of legislatures and parliaments is designed to determine and serve the general welfare. So a claim of political right is a claim to a trump over the general welfare for the account of a particular individual. When someone claims a right of free speech, for example, he claims that it would be wrong for the state to prohibit him from speaking on some matter even if the general welfare would be improved by preventing him from speaking. The hypothetical nature of the claim is important. We emphasize the special injustice of torture, for example, when we speak of a right against torture, because we claim that torture would be wrong even if it were in the general interest. But it is appropriate to speak of a right not to be tortured

---

[1] Raz, 'Professor Dworkin's Theory of Rights', XXVI *Political Studies* 123 (1978).

[2] With respect to his discussion of external and personal preferences, for example, see pp. 357–8 above. Much of the review discusses legal as distinct from political theory. Raz argues that the rights thesis is 'devoid of content'. But he bases this charge on his erroneous interpretation of my account of rights, discussed in the text below, and also on the assumption, discussed at length in section 2 of this appendix, that if rights sometimes turn on consequences, then all arguments of consequence are arguments about rights. His discussion of what he calls my 'conservative thesis' (a description I enjoy as an antidote to the widespread assumption, reflected in Mackie's criticism, that my legal theory is radical) ignores the distinction I make between legal rights and background moral rights with which legal rights may conflict, and the impact of that distinction on the question of what a judge, in an immoral legal system, should do at the end of the day (see pp. 326–7 above). With respect to his discussion of what he calls my argument from fairness (see pp. 320–2 above). He describes my claim, that the truth conditions of propositions of law sometimes include conditions of morality, as a 'natural law thesis'. But he misstates various arguments I have made for that claim (see Chapters 2, 4 and 13, and sections 3, 4 and 5 of this appendix) and defends his contrary claim only with a reference to his earlier article, with no discussion of my reply to that article in Chapter 3, and with a flat statement of an especially simple version of legal positivism.

even when torture would serve only private or illegitimate interests. Torture in this latter case is wrong *a fortiori*.

I give special place to claims of right as claims of a trump over a general utilitarian justification, in the explicitly political chapters of this book, because I am discussing political decisions in communities in which the general collective justification is utilitarian. I do not mean that individuals have rights only in such a community. Suppose a political community in which the general background justification consists in some appeal to the glory or improved military position of the state, or in the triumph of some class or the absolute wealth of the nation, in each case as a goal valued for its own sake. In such a society the practical force of claims of right would consist in the claim that some decision that disadvantages an individual is wrong even if it improves these political goals. The arguments of Chapter 12 show, however, that even the content of rights may vary with background justification, or with the structure of political institutions designed to enforce different background justifications. For rights that exclude external preferences from the political process may be necessary in a political community whose legislative structure presupposes a utilitarian background justification, and whose members have systematic prejudices, that would not be necessary elsewhere. The claim that members of some minority have particular rights in such a society (like the right to an integrated education, possibly) will appeal to features not necessarily present elsewhere. But many rights are universal, because arguments are available in favour of these rights against any collective justification in any circumstances reasonably likely to be found in political society. It is these that might plausibly be called human rights.

Raz points out that the idea of rights as trumps may be used in such a way as to inflate the number of rights grotesquely, and so make the appeal to a right banal. That is certainly possible – we might stipulate that someone will be said to have a right if his disadvantage provides a reason stronger than *some* other reason of *any* sort that might exist arguing for that disadvantage. Most rights (on this account) would be of no practical importance whatsoever. We should then need a new concept of rights as trumps over important collective justifications, which is what I propose in the first instance. No one has a political right (on my account) unless the reasons for giving him what he asks are stronger than some collective justification that normally provides a full political justification for a decision.[1] Someone's strong preference for pistachio ice cream is, indeed, a reason for society's producing pistachio, and it is a stronger reason than others that can be found or invented for not producing it – like some one else's mild preference for vanilla. But it is pointless to speak of a right to have pistachio (or a more general right to have strong preferences served) unless

[1] See, e.g., pp. 92, 269 above.

we mean that that preference provides a reason for producing pistachio even if the *collective* preferences of the community would be better served by producing vanilla. I say 'pointless' rather than 'wrong' because I do not claim (as I was careful to say) that my account of rights captures ordinary language exactly or completely. My account is in that sense a stipulation. (It is certainly not, as Raz sometimes suggests a theory of rights might be, an empirical discovery.) But it is a stipulation (or so I think) that isolates a distinctively important idea in political theory, which is the idea of an individual trump over decisions justified collectively. It is also a stipulation that captures the idea of individual rights used in American constitutional practice.

I should add here (though this simply repeats what is explicit in the book) that the theory of rights I offer does not deny that some rights are more important than others. No alleged right is a right (on my account) unless it overrides at least a marginal case of a general collective justification; but one right is more important than another if some especially dramatic or urgent collective justification, above that threshold, will defeat the latter but not the former.

Raz's misunderstanding causes confusion in his discussion of what he calls 'rights to welfare'. He says that I deny that people can have rights to welfare, and that this is contrary to what many people think. But he lumps together, under the category of claims to welfare, very different kinds of claims. It does follow from the account of rights I suggest that it is silly to say, in a society whose general background justification is utilitarian, that someone has a right to just the level of welfare that that general background justification recommends. It is silly because this putative right functions only to confirm, and not to trump, the collective justification. It claims nothing more than the collective justification, unaided by any idea of individual rights, would supply. But suppose that the claim of a right to the welfare that utilitarianism recommends is made against the background of some other collective justification, like the justification of military power or national glory for its own sake. Now the claim is too strong to count as a claim of right of the sort the theory contemplates. It argues that the background collective justification in place should be annihilated and replaced with utilitarianism, not simply that it must yield on particular occasions to rights as trumps. For once the idea is recognized, that it is wrong to deny individuals whatever welfare the utilitarian justification would recommend, no room is left for the challenged goals of military power or national glory for their own sakes. Someone who claims such a right is therefore not using the idea of a right in the way I recommend, and (as Bentham insisted) he might make his point more simply by avoiding the idea of rights altogether.

When Raz speaks of 'rights to welfare', however, he has in mind not simply the alleged right to whatever level of welfare a utilitarian background justification would demand. He has in mind also a claim that some person (or group) has a right to a particular minimum level of welfare; or to not less welfare than some specified fraction of the welfare of the best-off person (or group); or, possibly, to exactly as much welfare as any other person (or group) has. But these popular claims are very different from the claim that a person or group has a right to the welfare demanded by some overall collective justification. The claim that someone has a right to a minimum level of welfare, for example, can easily be understood as the claim that it is wrong for government to maintain an economic system under which certain individuals or families or groups fall below minimum welfare even if that economic system produces higher average utility (greater overall collective welfare) than any other system. That kind of claim is not excluded by the account of rights I propose. On the contrary it is, I think, a virtue of that account that it makes plain that it is precisely the competition between minimum levels of welfare and overall collective welfare that is at stake when this sort of 'right' to welfare is debated.

Raz believes that there is an important change between the political theory presupposed in the earlier chapters of this book and that suggested in Chapter 12. The earlier chapters suppose the account of rights I have just now been defending, in which rights act as trumps over some background justification that appeals to the collective welfare. In Chapter 12 this antagonism between particular rights and the collective welfare disappears, he says, because both particular rights and the collective welfare are seen to be the consequences of a very general right, which I call the right of all members of a political community to be treated as equals. But there is no inconsistency here.

Particular political rights can only be understood functionally, as I have just said, by attending to the role of these rights in the political process. This role supposes, in our political community, an antagonism between appeals to rights and appeals to the general welfare. But that description raises the following important question. Does this antagonism at the level of political argument reflect a deep antagonism at a more fundamental level? Do particular rights reflect some deep political ideal, like the idea of individual dignity or autonomy, and collective welfare *another* and competing ideal, like the idea that pleasure is a good in itself? If so, the political theory (or at least the political theory that would be necessary to justify institutions, like our own, that appeal to both rights and the collective welfare) is pluralistic at a fundamental level. Or, on the other hand, is the surface antagonism between rights and collective welfare the product of a political theory that is unified at a deeper level? Chapter 12, and parts of both the Introduction and this appendix, support the latter hypothesis, and it is further supported in a later essay, *Liberalism*, to which I have

already referred. I suggest that particular political rights, *and* the idea of
the collective welfare, *and* the idea that these function as antagonists at
the level of political debate, are all consequences of the fundamental ideal
of a political community as a community of equals. I did speak of a 'right'
to be treated as an equal, with equal concern and respect, but I pointed
out that this is 'a right so fundamental that it is not captured by the
general characterization of rights as trumps over collective goals, except as
a limiting case, because it is the source both of the general authority of
collective goals and of the special limitations on their authority that justify
more particular rights'.[1] Raz's comments suggest, however, that it was misleading to speak of the idea of treatment as an equal as a 'right' at all.

Raz has something to say about the content of the idea of treatment as
an equal, whether it is described as a right or not. He says, following
Professor Benn,[2] that this idea does not really appeal to equality at all. (I
mentioned and commented on that suggestion earlier.[3]) He also says that
the idea is empty, because it is consistent with many different patterns of
distribution. But this is a mistake, in two ways. First, even as an abstract
statement, the proposition that a government must treat those over whom
it claims authority with equal concern and respect is not empty because it
excludes political positions that were once dominant and are still, in
certain circles, popular. Second, the inference on which Raz's accusation
is based – that if two different conceptions of an abstract concept can each
be maintained with some plausibility, then the abstract concept recommends neither of these – misunderstands the role of abstract concepts in
political theory and debate. In *Liberalism* I argue that the most popular
political positions can be understood, and the important distinctions
among them recognized, when it is seen that each stands for a different
conception of the abstract requirement of equality. It is true that these
different conceptions are in competition, because they recommend, among
other things, different schemes of economic distribution. But it hardly
follows that one conception cannot be, as a conception, superior to the
others.

[1] See above, p. xv.
[2] See Benn, 'Egalitarianism and the Equal Consideration of Interests', in Pennock
and Chapman (eds), *Nomos IX: Equality* (1967) pp. 66–7.
[3] See above, p. 356–7.

Index